HONG KONG'S WAR CRIMES TRIALS

# Hong Kong's War Crimes Trials

Edited by

SUZANNAH LINTON

OXFORD
UNIVERSITY PRESS

OXFORD
UNIVERSITY PRESS

Great Clarendon Street, Oxford, OX2 6DP,
United Kingdom

Oxford University Press is a department of the University of Oxford.
It furthers the University's objective of excellence in research, scholarship,
and education by publishing worldwide. Oxford is a registered trade mark of
Oxford University Press in the UK and in certain other countries



First Edition published in 2013



Published in the United States of America by Oxford University Press
198 Madison Avenue, New York, NY 10016, United States of America

British Library Cataloguing in Publication Data
Data available

Library of Congress Control Number: 2013937974

ISBN 978–0–19–964328–8

# *Foreword*

Hon Justice Liu Daqun
Judge of the Appeals Chamber of the International Criminal Tribunals for the Former Yugoslavia and Rwanda

When we contemplate the war crimes trials that took place after the Second World War, no doubt Nuremberg stands out. Digging only a bit deeper, we might recall the International Military Tribunal for the Far East (known widely as the Tokyo Trial) and the trials in the domestic courts of the Western nations. But only the most knowledgeable and committed of scholars and historians would mention the trials in the Allies' Occupied Area in Asia after the surrender of the Japanese Imperialist Army. Because archival materials have been buried and researchers have remained focused on more prominent post-war developments, the facts of those trials—in China, Singapore, Malaysia, the Philippines, Indonesia, Taiwan (China), and Hong Kong—have remained hidden.

Until now, that is. Thanks to the brilliant research and tireless efforts of Professor Suzannah Linton, as well as the learned interventions of this volume's contributors, Oxford University Press presents 'Hong Kong's War Crimes Trial'. The compilation fills an important gap in the conversation about the war crimes trials that occurred in the years following World War II.

The Japanese invasion of Hong Kong began on 8 December 1941, less than eight hours after the air attack on Pearl Harbor. It ended just 17 days later, on 25 December 1941, with the surrender of the British army, and three years and eight months of occupation ensued. In the time that the Imperial Japanese administration ruled Hong Kong, the Japanese army committed hideous crimes against Prisoners of War ('POWs'), medical personnel, and civilians. It murdered and tortured, raped, and plundered. It subjected the citizens of occupied Hong Kong to inhumane treatment and arbitrary detention, and it forcibly displaced thousands.

The Japanese army's crimes were numerous and indiscriminate. The most notorious crimes, committed against medical personnel and the wounded and sick, came just before the British surrendered: Japanese soldiers entered St Stephen's College, which was being used as a hospital, and they shot two volunteer doctors when entry was refused. They then burst into the wards and slaughtered 170 recuperating soldiers and several members of the staff. The hospital's nurses were brutally raped and slaughtered. No less egregious were the atrocities committed at Hong Kong Red Cross Hospital, which housed hundreds of injured British soldiers. There, the Japanese army cut the eyes, ears, noses, tongues, and limbs off dozens of victims, and 70 soldiers were killed while they were convalescing in bed. These actions were subsequently found to violate the 1864 Geneva Red Cross Agreement (the seeds of what would become the International Red Cross Convention) regarding the treatment of POWs.

All of this we know. But as Professor Yuma Totani reports in these pages, the crimes committed in occupied Hong Kong were not confined to this sort of isolated incident. The Japanese administration held 7,000 British soldiers as POWs in camps in Hong Kong, such as at Sham Shui Po, and in Taiwan, China. What is more, thousands of civilians were incarcerated, among them Hong Kong Governor Mark Young. Sickness, malnourishment, famine, inhumane treatment, and even torture were pervasive. Professor Totani provides a unique and important analysis of the legal cases that arose out of those horrifying events.

But the Japanese soldiers did not simply detain POWs and local citizens. Professor Linton's chapter shows how they also terrorized the local population by murdering, raping, and looting, among other crimes. The *Kempeitai* treated the native population as something less than human; they routinely performed executions at King's Park in Kowloon without any pretence, using local citizens for shooting and bayonet practice and even beheading some. Moreover, as many as ten thousand women were raped in the first few days of the occupation. Perhaps twice that number, including women and children, were killed, and thousands more starved to death. Many parts of Hong Kong were ransacked and burned, food became scarce, and disease flourished. Conditions deteriorated to the point that the administration had to pursue a policy of repatriation, through which it deported the unemployed and the sick to Mainland China, discussed in detail in Professor Linton's chapter. Many of the residents who were not deported actually chose to leave, such was the quality of life on the island, only to find that famine and disease were no less common on the mainland. This combination of voluntary and forced emigration caused the population of Hong Kong to dwindle from 1.6 million in 1941 to just 600,000 in 1945.

After the unconditional surrender of Japan, control of Hong Kong fell to the Allied Land Forces of South-East Asia (ALFSEA). For thousands of years, it had been common and accepted practice in Asia for victors in war to retaliate against their opponents, often by summarily executing war criminals upon their capture. In contrast, it has long been a tenet of International Law that nations have 'territorial jurisdiction'—that is, every state has the authority to set up special courts to try war criminals for crimes committed on its own territory. After Japan's surrender, only one of those principles could prevail.

What happened next changed the course of history. Beginning in January 1946, the British military courts put the Japanese war crimes suspects on trial. The mere existence of the Hong Kong trials was an important triumph for international justice and represented a critical development for East Asian relations. But the principles espoused by those courts were no less crucial; for starters, only those whose criminal conduct was proved beyond a reasonable doubt were punished.

That important principle in place, all that remained was to determine the law that the courts would apply. That question was answered on 18 June 1945 with the promulgation of the Royal Warrant and its annexed Regulations. Significantly, the law that the Hong Kong tribunals would apply was not an arbitrary exercise of power on the part of the victorious nations, but rather an expression of the principles of International Law prevailing when the courts were created. This adherence to the concept of legality is itself an important contribution to International Law.

Several sources of law were available to the Hong Kong tribunals: Japan had ratified the 1907 Convention (IV) Respecting the Laws and Customs of War on Land, and, where treaty law was inadequate, customary international law could serve as a source of substantive criminal law. In other words, it was established that pre-existing international law bound the defendants at the time they committed the acts charged. Moreover, because the crimes in question took place in Hong Kong, a British colony, domestic British substantive criminal law was also applicable. As for procedure, the Royal Warrant defined the rules as those applicable to British Field General Courts Martial, and the rules of evidence were set forth in separate regulations. From all of these sources, the tribunals would draw their rules.

Those rules were numerous and detailed. As Professor Alexander Zahar points out in his comprehensive research on the subject in these pages, the accused had a number of due process rights before the Hong Kong courts. For example, during the proceedings, the accused was always provided with an interpreter free of charge and had the right to obtain the counsel of his choice. Most of the accused had Japanese lawyers with British officers acting as advisors. In addition, although Defence Counsel often had to operate with limited resources, they were provided with a charge sheet, an abstract of the evidence to be presented, and copies of any exhibits. The accused had the right to present their own witnesses and documents, to examine all documents submitted by the prosecution, and to address motions applications and other requests to the Court. Although the convicted had no right of appeal, they did have the right to invoke review proceedings before the Commander of Land Forces of Hong Kong. On review, the Commander could reverse and acquit, uphold a conviction, or adjust verdicts and sentences. In sum, the accused's rights to a fair trial and due process of law were guaranteed.

At the same time, Professor Bing Bing Jia suggests that the Allies would not allow the crimes of the Japanese occupation to go unpunished. Jia points out, for example, that the most common plea during Hong Kong Trial, the defence of 'superior orders' was rarely credited. In other words, the accused were not permitted to argue that they 'did what they were told'. Professor Jia observes that under the-then applicable customary law, superior orders may constitute a defence if the recipient did not believe it to be unlawful, either after his own assessment or without making such assessment due to the urgency of the situation in which the order was issued to him, provided that the order was not obviously/manifestly illegal, or should not have been so in his view as a reasonable person. In considering whether to allow a claim, the courts upheld the illegality prerequisite, as well as the knowledge on the part of the recipient of superior orders. Moreover, new modes of liability were invoked to punish war criminals who otherwise may have evaded liability. According to Professor Nina Jørgensen's research, for example, joint criminal enterprise, 'the chili pepper of modes of liability' today, can be traced back to the Hong Kong trials, albeit in the form of a mode long recognized in English common law.

In the end, Professor Zahar notes, the British military courts in Hong Kong tried 123 Japanese and Taiwanese suspects, of whom 86 were sentenced to a term of imprisonment, 14 were acquitted, and 21 were put to death. In light of the comprehensive due process rights accorded the accused, as well as the ultimate outcomes of the Hong Kong trials, the signal to the world was clear: on the one hand, mass atrocities would no longer go unpunished, but on the other hand, law and order would prevail—a simple fact that took on enormous importance in light of millennia of practice in East Asia. In short, the Allies had shown the world that the international order should be based on reason and justice instead of military might and political power.

Nearly 70 years have now passed since the Japanese war criminals were put on trial in Hong Kong. Most of the participants in those trials have passed away, and no doubt there is a risk that the memory of the Japanese Imperial Army's atrocities, as well as of the Hong Kong trials, will be lost to obscurity. If the lack of awareness today is any guide, future generations will likely be entirely unaware that the trials—not to mention the underlying events—occurred at all.

That risk is heightened by the attitude of the modern Japanese government. Unfortunately, instead of learning from history to avoid repeating the mistakes of the past, the Japanese authorities have denied that those crimes occurred. Leaders publicly proclaim that the events described here in this book were fabricated—despite so many eyewitness accounts described in this volume and elsewhere—and allies of the ruling class have rewritten history in the country's history textbooks. Perhaps worse, senior government leaders regularly pay homage to the war criminals: since 1985, Japanese Prime Ministers have made an annual, official visit to the Yasukuni shrine, a religious location honouring the more than two million people who died in the service of the Empire. The enshrined include 12 convicted Class A war criminals and two defendants who died during the Tokyo Trial, as well as two Governors of Hong Kong who served during the Japanese occupation and were convicted by the Chinese Nanking War Crimes Military Tribunal. Those visits have prompted many to allege that the country's official stance is one of defiance, rather than conciliation, and that has a predictable and lasting impact on diplomatic relations between Japan and many of its East Asian neighbours.

It is crucial that we understand the past if we are to address today's challenges. We have a complete record of the war crimes proceedings that took place in Europe following World War II, and historians and international lawyers alike have examined and re-examined the evidence used to convict Nazi leaders for the genocide of the Jews. This evidence is comprehensive, and it is detailed. For instance, we have records of meetings, conversations, orders, and killings, including a full account of the atrocities committed at the extermination camps. That evidence was recounted by eye witnesses during court proceedings, tested by the prosecution and defence, and admitted into evidence by judges following a standardized and well-thought-out process. As a result their conclusions are defensible and, in most cases, undeniable.

In Asia, by contrast—and especially in China—as a result of the nature of the crimes committed and the post-conflict instability that reigned, similar crimes are not well documented. Most of the documents from Asia's post-World War II war crimes trials still sit in piles in the deepest of archives, untouched and unutilized. In his chapter, Professor Roger S Clark comments on this disparity in order to place the Hong Kong trials in perspective alongside the contemporary trials about which we know so much more. As Professor Clark notes, the events that took place in the occupied parts of Asia during and after World War II can provide some insight into the roles and best practices of modern tribunals, such as the International Criminal Court.

Viewed more broadly, Professor Linton's entire volume is a remarkable contribution to our understanding of the military and legal atmosphere in Asia at the end of the War. Perhaps the most precious piece of history Professor Linton presents, though, is her interview with Major Murray Incell Ormsby, who was a panel member (that is, a Judge) and then a Prosecutor at War Crimes Court No 7 in Hong Kong. Major Ormsby was involved in 27 of the 46 trials that were held in Hong Kong, and he provides a compelling firsthand account. Like the rest of the research presented here, the precision and consistency of Major Ormsby's recollections are a precious asset as we begin—some would say six decades too late—to study the prosecution of the Japanese atrocities committed in Hong Kong during World War II.

In a characteristic moment of clarity, Major Ormsby declared, 'I feel that we pioneers of the War Crimes trials, we started it and we finished it and we should have got some kind of recognition.' Let this volume serve as the first step towards recognizing those contributions to the development of international justice and International Criminal Law, but let it not be the last.

# *Foreword*

Mr Kevin Zervos, SC
Director of Public Prosecutions, Hong Kong, China

*Hong Kong's War Crimes Trials* provides a rare and important insight into the evolution and development of international criminal justice.

In the aftermath of the cruelty and horror of war, comes a time for reckoning. In the past, that reckoning would be dispensed by the victor, which invariably would be one-sided and arbitrary. As to whether justice was served, if at all, depended on the magnanimity, or otherwise, of the victor.

The war crimes trials of the Second World War were a major turning point in bringing to account the perpetrators of atrocities, committed in the course of the hostilities and ensuring that this was done through the proper process of the law. Whilst we have come a long way since then, the seeds were sown for the development of international humanitarian and criminal law for which we and future generations will benefit. The underlying principle that emerged and continues to gain force is that bringing someone to account requires justice to be dispensed in a just and fair manner. The distinguished English jurist Tom Bingham observed that in the aftermath of war '... scrupulous observance of the rule of law may be seen to serve the common interest of mankind'. So it was with the war crimes trials of Hong Kong.

On 8 December 1941, the Japanese attacked Hong Kong, a day after they had attacked Pearl Harbor. The British forces surrendered on Christmas Day and the Japanese commenced a brutal occupation that lasted nearly four years. The atrocities inflicted on the Allied forces and the people of Hong Kong were horrific and long lasting. It had been variously declared throughout the Second World War that the perpetrators would be brought to justice and in its aftermath, war crimes trials were convened at Nuremberg, Tokyo, and various other places, including Hong Kong.

The war crimes trials of Hong Kong were conducted by the British military authorities over a period of three years. In all, there were 46 trials with 123 defendants. At the end of the trial process, 108 were convicted and 14 were acquitted. The sentences imposed on the guilty varied but 24 were sentenced to death with three reduced after review. As in the trials in the British areas of occupied Europe, the courts in Hong Kong operated under the authority of a Royal Warrant. It was thus by royal fiat of the Crown that their jurisdiction, powers, and procedures were based on traditional courts-martial.

Despite the inhumanity of war, there has been a growing realization that international conflicts were to be conducted subject to basic humanitarian principles. Over time, international treaties were adopted that provided formal statements of the laws of war and war crimes. This was seen with the Hague

Conventions of 1899 and 1907, the four Geneva Conventions which were adopted and expanded from 1864 to 1949 with two Additional Protocols in 1977, and the Genocide Convention of 1948.

The London Charter of the International Military Tribunal of 8 August 1945 provided the principles on which war crimes trials were to be conducted. This in turn, through the momentous developments of the 1990s, was to inform the principles leading in part to the Rome Statute of the International Criminal Court on 1 July 2002.

Professor Suzannah Linton has, through her comprehensive research and fine scholarship, put together an excellent compendium of articles that take us back to the war crimes trials of Hong Kong. In Professor Linton's interview of Major Murray Incell Ormsby, we are given a first hand account of what confronted the people with the responsibility of conducting the trials. It reveals an instinctive focus on fairness and due process and a deep appreciation of the importance of the task at hand.

This book provides a rich tapestry of information about the conduct of war crimes trials both generally and specifically in relation to those conducted in Hong Kong. Professor Linton and Professor Alexander Zahar, in their well-researched and detailed expositions of the British Military Courts, both explain the trial practice and procedure. The process was carefully crafted to ensure a full and proper presentation of the case against an accused which followed a procedure that aimed to be fair and consistent. The convictions and sentences after trial were reviewed by Judge Advocates who would decide whether or not to endorse them. Professor Zahar highlights certain disadvantages faced by the accused, such as, single legal representation for multiple accused, a Japanese legal representative who was generally unfamiliar with English laws, and the adducing of testimony without oral examination. He questions the notion of justice, by stressing that victor's justice can be selective and biased.

Professor Yuma Totani provides case studies of the trials in relation to the treatment of Prisoners of War, who suffered horrifically, and issues as to individual and collective responsibility for the crimes alleged. This issue is further explored by Professor Nina Jørgensen, who considers in the context of the Hong Kong trials and beyond whether 'concerned in a crime' is to be equated with 'joint criminal enterprise': this notion is subjected to critical analysis.

It comes as no surprise that a key issue that arose in the trials was the plea of superior orders; either as a defence, or as a mitigating factor, or both. The tracing of the plea of superior orders by Professor Bing Bing Jia provides an invaluable insight and analysis that brings into sharp focus the issue in the current context. The plea as a defence was resisted by the British Military Courts, but the controversy surrounding it remains to this day, notwithstanding the recognition of it under Article 33 of the Rome Statute.

Professor Roger Clark completes this amazing journey in time by noting the importance of learning from the past and putting it in the context of the evolutionary development of international criminal justice.

Professor Linton should be congratulated, not only for preserving a significant moment in the development of international criminal justice, but also for providing a comprehensive exposition of the principles and issues that are likely to arise in war crimes trials.

As we get closer and closer to forging a truly global order with the development of a universal set of standards and obligations, our paramount consideration must be our commitment to justice and fairness at all times, no matter who the accused may be and no matter what the nature of the crime.

In order 'to serve the common interest of mankind' it is imperative that we call upon persons to account for crimes committed in the course of war but that we do so with strict adherence to a just law and fair process. We must never drop our standards and engage in the conduct we seek to condemn. The war crimes trials of Hong Kong allow us to understand the difficulties that confronted those charged with the responsibility for ensuring that justice was done and how they displayed a sensitivity and understanding that provided a solid foundation for the future. It will undoubtedly be viewed that they planted the seeds for the development of modern international criminal justice.

# *Acknowledgements*

This project is built on the support of many people, over several years.

Thanks must first go to Paul Harris, Hong Kong Senior Counsel, a former student of mine at the University of Hong Kong. Through supervising Paul's LLM dissertation on Colonel Noma Kennosuke, I learned about the Hong Kong trials for the first time. Then, the Hong Kong Research Grants Council saw the potential of my proposed research into Hong Kong's legal history, and awarded me a generous grant to enable me to bring this project to life. I thank the UK National Archives for allowing me to copy their files and use them on the database, and for the wonderful facilities for researchers at Kew. My fantastic team at the University of Hong Kong was instrumental in helping set up the Hong Kong War Crimes Trials Database, which we have all relied on in this book. I thank, in particular, Ernest Ng, Dixon Tse, Janet Man, Dave Low, and David Palmer. Ernest and Dave have continued to provide me with assistance during this stage of the project.

I am deeply grateful to all the contributors to this volume for their painstaking work, which has led to wonderful and important contributions. I am touched by the warm and generous support of Hon Justice Liu Daqun and Kevin Zervos, Senior Counsel in their forewords. Hon Justice Liu has been an enormous support to me from the moment he learned of the work that I was doing. My friends from the ICRC in Beijing have been very supportive too. The late Antonio Cassese, who inspired so many of us in so many ways *inter alia* through his trailblazing work on the Tokyo trials, was very encouraging of my efforts. At Oxford University Press, Anthony Hinton has been very supportive throughout, and I thank the editorial team. Thanks to Sinan Ali, Guo Cai, Damian Etone, Mairwen Owen, and Marie Parker, who have helped me with the preparation of the manuscript, and with some research. Thomas Arwel Bullock was a great assistance with the transcription of my interviews with Major Murray Ormsby. I thank Lord Anglesey and the National Trust for allowing me to access original copies of early editions of the *British Manual of Military Law* from his personal collection at Plas Newydd, Anglesey.

I owe thanks of a different nature to the late Murray Incell Ormsby and his wonderful wife, Chris, for so generously letting me into their lives. Thanks also to Donal Lowry, who brought us together. I thank Luba Estes for her constant support since we met on the internet when she shared the story of her life, and that of her father as a prisoner of war in Hong Kong. I thank the many other friends that I have made through this project, and those others who have telephoned, come to see me, or written to me over the years from so many different countries, to encourage me in my work. I think in particular of Lawrence Tsui, Stephen Tsui, Dennis Ching, Michael Liu, Song Jie, Tony Banham, John Lowe, and Judy Buntrock-Lewis.

Thank you also to those others who I should thank but have failed to do so. Please forgive my absentmindedness.

Suzannah Linton
1 August 2013

# *Contents*


*Table of Cases and Legal Materials* xix
*List of Contributors* xxix

1. Introduction 1
   *Suzannah Linton*
2. Trial Procedure at the British Military Courts, Hong Kong, 1946–1948 13
   *Alexander Zahar*
3. The Prisoner of War Camp Trials 71
   *Yuma Totani*
4. War Crimes 95
   *Suzannah Linton*
5. On Being 'Concerned' in a Crime: Embryonic Joint Criminal Enterprise? 137
   *Nina H B Jørgensen*
6. The Plea of Superior Orders in the Hong Kong Trials 169
   *Bing Bing Jia*
7. Concluding Thoughts 199
   *Roger S Clark*

*Appendix: Major Murray Ormsby: War Crimes Judge and Prosecutor 1919–2012* 215
Suzannah Linton

*Bibliography* 247
*Index of Names* 253
*General Index* 257

# *Table of Cases and Legal Materials*

## TRIALS AT THE HONG KONG MILITARY COURTS


Trial of Choichi Sato (HKWCT Collection, File No WO235/1027). . . . . . . . . . . . 147 nn. 59–60

Trial of Lt Gen Eiichi Kinoshita and Sgt Bunzo Yoshida (HKWCT Collection, File No WO235/1116). . . . . . . . . . . . . . . . . . . . . . . . . . . . 27, 30 n. 118, 49, 53, 67, 68 nn. 398–9, 149, 150 nn. 71–6, 154, 156, 160

Trial of Sgt Hanada Zenji and three others (HKWCT Collection, File No WO235/895). . . . . . . . . . . . . . . . . . . . . . . . . 27, 33 n. 143, 34 n. 146, 49, 52, 53 n. 288, 61 n. 356, 138 n. 3, 148 n. 66

Trial of Maj Hirao Yoshio (HKWCT Collection, File No WO235/1098) . . . . . . . . . . . . .21 n. 51, 27, 44 n. 241, 45 n. 242, 49, 53, 63 nn. 367–8, 118, 120, 122 n. 151, 183, 184 nn. 83–6

Trial of Sgt Maj Honda Isamu (HKWCT Collection, File No WO235/1045). . . . . . . . .27, 50, 52

Trial of Sgt Maj Kamada Yasushi (HKWCT Collection, File No WO235/1057). . . . . . . . . . . . . . . . . . . . . . . . . . . . . 27, 38, 39 n. 190, 50, 51 n. 284, 53

Trial of Inouye Kanao (HKWCT Collection, File No WO235/927). . . . . . . . . . .21, 21 nn. 45–7, 27, 46 n. 258, 49, 52, 146 n. 56, 146 n. 57, 147 n. 58, 187 nn. 109–114

Trial of Sgt Maj Ito Junichi (No 1) (HKWCT Collection, File No WO235/914) . . . . . . .23 n. 62, 27, 52, 57 nn. 317–18, 125 n. 164, 183 nn. 79–82, 213 n. 66

Trial of Sgt Maj Ito Junichi (No 2) (HKWCT Collection, File No WO235/1048) . . . . . . . 27, 50, 52, 57 n. 318, 63 nn. 369–70, 125 n. 164, 213 n. 67

Trial of Lt Gen Ito Takeo (HKWCT Collection, File No W0235/1107). . . . . . . . . . . . 27, 50, 53, 97 n. 6, 99 nn. 22–3, 106 n. 56, 128 n. 184, 133 n. 215, 215

Trial of Sgt Kaname Kawamoto (HKWCT Collection, File No WO235/921) . . . . . . . . . .21 n. 52, 27, 34 n. 152, 46 n. 257, 49, 52, 61–2 nn. 356 –7, 146 nn. 54–5

Trial of Lt Col Kanazawa Asao (HKWCT Collection, File No WO235/1093). . . . . . . . . 6, 27, 50, 53, 61 n. 350, 64 nn. 373–5, 66 n. 393, 109, 113 nn. 96–98, 114 n. 99, 115, 118, 120, 124 n. 160, 125 nn. 167–9, 133, 186 nn. 102–5, 208

Trial of Lt Kishi Yasuo and fourteen others (HKWCT Collection, File No WO235/993) . . . . . . . . . . . . . . . . . . 6, 23 n. 62, 26 n. 86, 27, 29 n. 98, 33 n.142, 33 nn. 144–5, 36 n. 161, 48 n. 271, 49, 52, 55 n. 306, 56, 57 n. 313, 66 n. 391, 67 n. 396, 67 n. 396, 97 nn. 10–11, 118 n. 125, 124 n. 158, 128 nn. 185–8, 129 nn. 191–3, 129–30 nn. 194–9, 131 nn. 201–8, 132 nn. 209–13, 133 n. 214, 134, 138, 147 nn. 61–3, 148 nn. 64–5, 156, 160, 191 n. 142, 192 nn. 143–9

Trial of Sgt Maj Kuwaki Kiyomori and Sgt Nakajima Tokuzo (HKWCT Collection, File No WO235/1106) . . . . . . . . . . . . . . . . . . . . . . .27, 50, 53, 59 nn. 334–335

Trial of Sgt Kuwano Nobuyuki (HKWCT Collection, File No WO235/1078) . . . . . . . . . . 27, 50, 53, 59 n. 337

Trial of Kyoda Shigeru (HKWCT Collection, File No WO235/1114) . . . . . 13 n. 4, 25, 26 n. 83, 26, 27, 33 n. 139, 38 nn. 183–4, 40, 43 nn. 226–7, 46 n. 256, 50, 51 nn. 281–2, 52, 55 n. 301, 55 n. 306, 56 n. 310, 56 n. 312, 59 n. 36, 60 n. 338, 61 n. 350, 69 n. 408, 193 nn. 155–7

Trial of Sgt Matsuda Kenichi (HKWCT Collection, File No WO235/846). . . . . 27, 33, 40 n. 201, 49, 52, 60 nn. 339–340, 66 n. 392, 106 n. 59, 127 nn. 180–3
Trial of Sgt Maj Matsunobu Shigeru (HKWCT Collection, File No WO235/894) . . . 21 n. 51, 27, 34 n. 152, 36 n. 152, 36 n. 172, 38 n. 184, 43 n. 223, 45 n. 244, 50, 52, 54 n. 296, 60 n. 343, 60 n. 343, 61 n. 356
Trial of Sgt Miyasue Suekichi (HKWCT Collection, File No WO235/915) . . . . . . . . . . . . 27, 50, 52, 60 n. 344
Trial of Col Nakano Junichi and two others (HKWCT Collection, File No WO235/1044). . . . . . . . . . . . . . . . . . . . . . . . . . . . . . 27, 43 n. 231, 44 nn. 232–3, 49, 52, 72 n. 4, 73 n. 6, 82, 85 nn. 60–4, 86 n. 65, 87 n. 73, 88 n. 80, 88 n. 82, 89, 99 n. 18
Trial of R Adm Naomasa Sakonju and Capt Haruo Mayazumi (HKWCT Collection, File No WO235/1089). . . . . . . . . . . . . . . . . . . . . . . . . 25 n. 80, 27, 46 n. 259, 48 n. 270, 50, 53, 54, 59 nn. 32–3, 155 n. 96, 188 nn. 115–20, 189 nn. 121–4, 208
Trial of Niimori Genichiro (HKWCT Collection, File No WO235/892) . . . . . . 27, 50, 51 n. 283, 52, 61 n. 356, 126 nn. 170–1, 154 nn. 92–5, 156, 193 n. 158, 194 nn. 159–64, 222, 225, 239
Trial of Col Noma Kennosuke (HKWCT Collection, File No WO235/999). . . . . . . . . xv, 6, 8–9, 10 n. 22, 26 n. 87, 27, 29 n. 99, 47 n. 264, 50, 52, 55 n. 306, 61 n. 356, 66, 105 n. 52, 106 n. 58, 107 n. 61, 107 n. 63, 108 nn. 66–7, 109 nn. 75–7, 110 nn. 78–82, 111 nn. 83–7, 112 n. 88, 112 n. 90, 112 nn. 92–3, 113 nn. 94–5, 114, 115, 118 n. 126, 119 nn. 130–1, 120 n. 132, 120 n. 136, 120 n. 138, 121 nn. 139–41, 122 , 123 nn. 152–6, 124 n. 157, 124 n. 159, 124 nn. 162–3, 125 nn. 164–5, 125 n. 166, 126 n. 172, 133, 149 nn. 67–8, 152, 156, 184, 186, 208, 215, 220, 225, 230, 239
Trial of Sgt Maj Ogasawara Maruji and Sgt Kawai Hisao (HKWCT Collection, File No WO235/1011). . . . . . . . . . . . . . . . . . . . . . . . . . . 27, 49, 52, 55 nn. 305–6, 189 nn. 125–9, 190 nn. 130–5
Trial of Lt Obata Chikuro and seven others (HKWCT Collection, File No WO235/1073). . . . . . . . . . . . . . . . . . . . . . . . . . . . . . . . . . . . . . . . . . 27, 49, 53
Trial of Lt Oita Yoshijiro and Lt Ashida Tsumoru (HKWCT Collection, File No WO235/1036). . . . . . . . . . . . . . . . . . . . . . . . . . . . . . . . . . . . . . . . . . . . . . . 27, 49, 52
Trial of WO Omura Kyoshi (HKWCT Collection, File No WO235/893) . . . . . . . . . 16 n. 19, 27, 37 nn. 175–6, 39 n. 192, 41 n. 210, 42 n. 219, 45 n. 243, 49, 52, 61 n. 356, 63 n. 365, 118 n. 125, 135
Trial of WO Omura Kyoshi and four others (HKWCT Collection, File No WO235/1112). . . . . . . . . . . . . . . . . 27, 37 nn. 175–6, 39 n. 195, 45 n. 243, 49, 51 n. 280, 53, 63 n. 365, 119 n. 128, 120 n. 137, 121 nn. 143–5, 122 nn. 146–50, 125 nn. 165–6, 135
Trial of Sgt Ozawa Tomukuchi (HKWCT Collection, File No WO235/1038) . . . . . . . . 27, 50, 52
Trial of Col Sazawa Hideo and two others (HKWCT Collection, File No WO235/1029). . . . . . . . . . . . . . . . . . . . . . . . . . . . . . . 27, 36 n. 173, 49, 52, 73 n. 6, 82
Trial of Capt Shibata Shigeo and Sgt Maj Oba Takao (HKWCT Collection, File No WO235/1007). . . . . . . . . . . . . . . . . . 22 n. 53, 27, 49, 52, 151 nn. 77–80, 156, 160
Trial of Maj Gen Shoji Toshishige (HKWCT Collection, File No WO235/1015) . . . . . . . . . . . 27, 39 n. 194, 50, 52, 99 n. 20, 99, 106 n. 55, 241
Trial of Lt Suzuki Nebuo and three others (HKWCT Collection, File No WO235/954). . . . . . . . . . . . . . . . . . . . . . . . . . . 27, 49, 52, 182 nn. 72–4, 183 nn. 75–8
Trial of Lt Tamaki Koji and two others (HKWCT Collection, File No WO235/982). . . . . . . . . . . . . . . . . . . . . . . . . . . . . . . . . . . . . . . . . . . . 27, 43 n. 230, 49, 52
Trial of Col Tamura Teiichi and two others (HKWCT Collection, File No WO235/1021). . . . . . . . . . . . . . . 25 n. 82, 27, 32 n. 135, 48 nn. 272–3, 49, 52, 55 n. 300, 61 n. 354, 63 n. 366, 106 n. 57, 155 nn. 97–8, 156, 158, 184 nn. 87–91, 185 nn. 92–4, 208

Trial of Maj Gen Tanaka Ryosaburo (HKWCT Collection, File No WO235/1030). . . . . . . . . . . . . . . . 27, 37 n. 177, 38 nn. 187–8, 52, 56 n. 311, 97 nn. 7–8, 99 n. 21, 104 n. 42, 106 n. 54, 215, 232, 241

Trial of Sgt Tashiro Toranosuke and two others (HKWCT Collection, File No WO235/905). . . . . . . . . . . . . . . . . . . .27, 39 n. 193, 44 n. 225, 49, 52, 56 n. 307, 62 n. 356

Trial of Toda Mitsugu and eight others (HKWCT Collection, File WO235/1028). . . . . . . . . . . . . . . . . . . .20 nn. 41–3, 21 n. 44, 27, 32 n. 134, 44, 49, 52, 66, 74 n. 7, 82, 83 nn. 50–1, 84 nn. 52–7, 90 nn. 88–90, 91 nn. 91– 6, 92 nn. 97–100, 93, 99 nn. 18–19, 153, 154 nn. 90–1, 156

Trial of Col Tokunaga Isao and four others (HKWCT Collection, File No W0235/1012) (Parts 1, 2, 3). . . . . . . . . . .9, 27, 36 n. 174, 49, 52, 55 n. 302, 56 n. 308, 61, 64 nn. 376–7, 73 nn. 5–6, 74, 75 nn. 11–13, 76 nn. 15–20, 77 nn. 21–3, 78 nn. 24–8, 79 nn. 25–33, 80 nn. 34–7, 81 nn. 38–44, 82, 89, 93, 98 nn. 12–13, 98 n. 16, 104 n. 43, 152 nn. 81–3, 156, 160, 185 nn. 95–100, 186 n. 101, 204, 205, 208, 223, 225

Trial of Sgt Tsubota Kanji (HKWCT Collection, File No WO235/1037). . . . . . . . . . . .27, 50, 52

Trial of Maj Uete Taichi and six others (HKWCT Collection, File No WO235/1105). . . . . . . . . . . . . 27, 49, 53, 61, 73 n. 6, 82, 88 n. 80, 88 n. 82, 89 nn. 83–5, 90 nn. 86–7, 106 n. 52, 192 n. 150, 193 nn. 151–4, 208

Trial of Capt Ushiyama Yukio and three others (HKWCT Collection, File No WO235/1041). . . . . . . . . . . . . . 27, 38 n. 189, 47 n. 265, 49, 53, 149 nn. 69–70, 150, 156

Trial of WO Yabuki Rikie and two others (HKWCT Collection, File No 235/937) . . . . . . . . . . . . . . . . . . . . . . . . . . . . . . . 27, 43, 46, 49, 52, 54 n. 292, 54 n. 296

Trial of Sgt Maj Yamada Kiichiro and Sgt Awa Isao (HKWCT Collection, File WO235/887). . . . . . . . . . . . . . . 27, 34 n. 152, 46 n. 254, 49, 52, 60 nn. 341–2, 61 n. 352, 119 nn. 128–9, 125 n. 166, 126 nn. 172–8, 127 n. 179, 182 nn. 68–70

Trial of Sgt Maj Yokohata Toshiro (HKWCT Collection, File No WO235/1117). . . . . . . . . . . . . . . 21 n. 51, 27, 31 n. 125, 43 nn. 228–9, 44 nn. 234–5, 50, 53, 56 n. 309, 58 nn. 319–23, 194 nn. 165–166, 195 nn. 167–70

Trial of Capt Yoshimi Taneyoshi and six others (HKWCT Collection, File No WO235/1099). . . . . . . . . . . . . . . . 25 n. 77, 27, 49, 53, 190 nn. 136–7, 191 nn. 138–9

## JUDGMENTS FROM WORLD WAR I TRIALS

Llandovery Castle, Annual Digest of Public International Law Cases (1923-1924) Vol 2 436 . . . . . . . . . . . . . . . . . . . . . . . . . . . . . . . . . . . . . . . .107 n. 4, 173 n. 18

## JUDGMENTS FROM WORLD WAR II TRIALS

**Judgment of the International Military Tribunal (Nuremberg)**

Judgment of the Nuremberg International Military Tribunal 1946 (1947) 41 AJIL 172. . . . . . . .30, 101 n. 27, 103 n. 37, 170 n. 7, 177 n. 43, 177 n. 45, 178 nn. 52–4, 179 n. 55, 186 n. 107, 195, 196, 197

**Judgment of the International Military Tribunal (Tokyo)**

Hirota and Others (Judgment 12 November 1948) (1948) 15 Annual Digest of Public International Law Cases 1948 (Butterworth and Co 1953) . . . . . . . . . . . . . . . . . . . 179 n. 56

International Military Tribunal (Tokyo), Judgment, in Röling B V A and Rüter C F (eds), The Tokyo Judgment: The International Military Tribunal for the Far East (IMTFE), 29 April 1946–2 November 1948 (APA–University Press, 1977) . . . . . . . . . . . . . . . . . 10 n. 20, 95 n. 1, 103 nn. 36–7, 104 nn. 44–5, 105 n. 48, 200 n. 5, 207 n. 47

**Judgments of the Military Tribunal, Nanking**

The Judgment of the Chinese Military Tribunal at Nanking, dated '22 July in the 36th year of the Chinese Republic (1947)', in File WO325/135, UK National Archives (Trial of Lt Gen Rensuke Isogai) . . . . . . . . . . . . 6, 114, 115 nn. 105–8, 118, 119 n. 127, 134
Judgment of the Military Tribunal, Nanking, regarding Takashi Sakai, 27 August 1946, in File WO311/563, UK National Archives . . . . . . . . . . . . . 99 n. 24, 108 n. 70, 114 n. 104, 133 n. 215, 133 n. 217
Judgment of War Criminal Takashi Sakai, 27 August 1946, original (reserved) judgment, National Archives Administration, Taiwan, China . . . . . . . . 99 n. 24, 108 n. 70, 114 n. 104, 133 n. 215, 133 n. 217

**Judgements reported by the United Nations War Crimes Crimes Commission (Law Reports of Trials of War Criminals)**

Trial of Josef Alstötter and others (Justice trial), United Nations War Crimes Commission, Law Reports of Trials of War Criminals, Vol VI (His Majesty's Stationery Office 1949) 1 . . . . . . . . . . . . . . . . . . . . . . . . . . . . . . 160 n. 112, 130 n. 200, 160 n. 112
Trial of Kapitenleutnant Heinz Eck and four others (The Peleus trial), United Nations War Crimes Commission, Law Reports of Trials of War Criminals Vol I (His Majesty's Stationery Office 1947) 19 . . . . . . 106 n. 53, 172 n. 14, 173 n. 17, 202 n. 23
Trial of Karl Adam Golkel and thirteen others, United Nations War Crimes Commission, Law Reports of Trials of War Criminals, Vol V (His Majesty's Stationery Office 1948) 45 . . . . . . . . . . . . . . . . . . . . . . . . . . . . . . . . . . . . . 157 nn. 101–2, 158 n. 103
Trial of Eric Heyer and six others (Essen Lynching case), United Nations War Crimes Commission, published in Law Reports of Trials of War Criminals, Vol 1 (His Majesty's Stationery Office 1949) 88 . . . . . . . . . . . . 2 n. 7, 140 n. 40, 159 nn. 109–10, 160 n. 111, 162, 165
Trial of Erich Killinger and four others, United Nations War Crimes Commission, Law Reports of Trials of War Criminals, Vol III (His Majesty's Stationery Office 1948) 67 . . . . . . . . . . . . . . . . . . . . . . . . . . . . . . . 160 nn. 113–15, 161 nn. 116–17, 163
Trial of Werner Rohde and eight others, United Nations War Crimes Commission, Law Reports of the Trials of War Criminals, Vol. I (His Majesty's Stationery Office 1948) 54 . . . . . . . . . . . . . . . . . . . . . . . . . . . . . . . . . . . 130 n. 200, 159 n. 108, 163
Trial of Otto Sandrock and three others (Almelo case), United Nations War Crimes Commission, Law Reports of the Trials of War Criminals, Vol I (His Majesty's Stationery Office 1947) 35 . . . . . . . . . . . . . . . . . . . . . . . . . . . . . . . . 130 n. 200, 139 n. 12
Trial of Franz Schonfeld and nine others, United Nations War Crimes Commission, Law Reports of Trials of War Criminals, Vol XI (His Majesty's Stationery Office 1949) 64 . . . . . . . . . . . . . . . . . . . . . . 139 n. 12, 140, 158 nn. 104–6, 162 nn. 121–3
Trial of Martin Gottfried Weiss and others (Dachau Concentration Camp case), United Nations War Crimes Commission, Law Reports of Trials of War Criminals, Vol XI (His Majesty's Stationery Office 1949) 5 . . . . . . . . . . . . . . . 140 n. 13
Trial of Max Wielen et al. (the Stalag Luft III trial), United Nations War Crimes Commission, Law Reports of Trials of War Criminals Vol XI (His Majesty's Stationery Office 1949) 31 . . . . . . . . . . . . . . . . . . . . . . . . . 156 n. 99, 158, 159 n. 107, 163, 177 n. 42

**Trials of War Criminals Before the Nuremberg Military Tribunals Under Control Council Law No 10**


US v Karl Brandt et al (Medical case) (1947) Trials of War Criminals Before the Nuremberg Military Tribunals Under Control Council Law No 10 (United States Government Printing Office 1947) vol II 227 . . . . . . . . . . 180 n. 66, 227

US v Alfried Felix Alwyn Krupp von Bohlen und Halbach (The Krupp case), Trials of War Criminals Before the Nuremberg Military Tribunal under Control Council Law No. 10, Vol IX (United States Government Printing Office 1950) 1327. . . . .114 n. 100, 114 n. 102, 118 n. 123

US v von Leeb (High Command case), Trials of War Criminals Before the Nuremberg Military Tribunal under Control Council Law No. 10, Vol IX (United States Government Printing Office 1950) 462. . . . . . . . . . 114 n. 101, 114 n. 103

In re List (Hostages trial) 15 Annual Digest of Public International Law Cases 1948 (Butterworth and Co 1953) 632 . . . . . . . . . . 170 n. 5

US v Otto Ohlendorf et al. (Einsatzgruppen case), Trials of War Criminals Before the Nuremberg Military Tribunals under Control Council Law No. 10, Vol IV (United States Government Printing Office 1951) 480 . . . . . . . . . . 140 n. 12, 179 n. 60, 187 n. 108, 191 nn. 140–1


**Misc. post World War II judgments**


Trial of Feurstein and others (Ponzano case), 24 August 1948, (2007) 5 JICJ 238 . . . . . .140 n. 12, 157 n. 100, 162, 165 n. 137

Trial of Gustav Alfred Jepsen and others, Judgment of 24 August 1946, (2007) 5 JICJ 228. . . . . . . . . . 139 n. 12

Trial of Hoelzer and others, Vol. I, 341, 347, 349 (RCAF Binder 181.009 (D2474) . . . . 139 n. 12

Trial of V Adm Hara Teizo and eight others (Andaman Islands case) (UK National Archives, File No WO235/839) . . . . . . . . . . 115 nn. 109–13, 116 nn. 114–19, 117 nn. 120–1

PPI v Shigenori Kuroda – Rationale, 6-7, in 'Shigenori Kuroda – Public Trial, Vol 14' (Box 1702), Records of the General Headquarters Supreme Commander for the Allied Powers (SCAP), Records of the SCAP Legal Section, Prosecution Division—'Entry 1323: Philippines v Various Japanese War Criminals Case Files 1947-1949.' This record is part of RG 331 (Records of the Allied Operational and Occupation Headquarters, World War II), National Archives and Records Administration (NARA), College Park, MD, USA. The entire record of the Kuroda Trial is contained in Boxes 1699-1702/ Entry 1323/ RG 331 . . . . . . . . . . 71

In re Yamashita, 327 US 1 66 S.Ct. 340, 90 L.Ed 499 (1946) . . . . . . . .3 n. 11, 4, 153, 207 n. 46


## LEGAL COMMENTARIES (LAW REPORTS)


United Nations War Crimes Commission, Law Reports of Trials of War Criminals, Vol IV (His Majesty's Stationery Office 1948). . . . . . . . . . 191 n. 40

United Nations War Crimes Commission, Law Reports of Trials of War Criminals, Vol. XV (His Majesty's Stationery Office 1949) . . . . . . . . . . 1 n. 6, 169 n. 1, 172 n. 13, 173 n. 15, 179 n. 57, 180 n. 63, 180 n. 65, 182 n. 71, 191 n. 141


## TRIALS BEFORE CONTEMPORARY INTERNATIONAL COURTS AND TRIBUNALS

**International Criminal Tribunal for the former Yugoslavia**


Prosecutor v Milutinović, Šainović and Ojdanić, Case No. IT-99-37-AR72, Decision on Dragoljub Ojdanić's Motion Challenging Jurisdiction – Joint Criminal Enterprise, 21 May 2003 . . . . . . . . . . 140 n. 15, 141 n. 20

Prosecutor v Stakić, Case No. IT-97-24-A, Judgment (Appeals Chamber), 22 March 2006 . . . . . . . . 164 n. 133, 165
Prosecutor v Dŭsko Tadić, Case No. IT-94-1-A, Appeal Judgment, 15 July 1999 . . . . . . . . 6, 137, 138 n. 4, 139 nn. 7–12, 140 nn. 13–14, 141, 142, 143, 159, 162, 163 n. 127, 164 n. 134, 165 n. 140, 166
Prosecutor v Dŭsko Tadić, Case No. IT-94-1-T bisR117, Sentencing Judgment, 11 November 1999 . . . . . . . . 139 n. 5
Prosecutor v Dŭsko Tadić, Case No. IT-94-1-A and IT-94-1-Abis, Judgment in Sentencing Appeal, 26 January 2000 . . . . . . . . 139 n. 6

**International Criminal Tribunal for Rwanda**

Rwamakuba v The Prosecutor, Case No. ICTR-98-44-AR72.4, Decision on Interlocutory Appeal Regarding Application of Joint Criminal Enterprise to the Crime of Genocide, 22 October 2004 . . . . . . . . 140 n. 16, 141

**Extraordinary Chambers in the Courts of Cambodia**

Criminal Case File No. 002/19-09-2007-ECCC/OCIJ, Co-Prosecutors' Supplementary Observations on Joint Criminal Enterprise, 31 December 2008. . . . . . . . 163 n. 125
Charged Persons Ieng Thirith, Ieng Sary and Khieu Samphan, Case File No. PP 002/19-0902007-ECCC/OCIJ (PTC38), Public Decision on the Appeals Against the Co-Investigative Judges Order on Joint Criminal Enterprise (JCE), 20 May 2010 . . . . . . . . 137 n. 2, 141 nn. 19–25, 145 n. 51, 163 n. 128, 165 n. 135, 165 n. 141, 167 n. 147
Ieng Sary, Criminal Case File No. 002/19-09-2007-ECCC/OCIJ, Co-Prosecutors' Response to Ieng Sary's Motion on Joint Criminal Enterprise, 11 August 2008 . . . . . . . . 141 nn. 17–18
Nuon Chea, Ieng Sary, Ieng Thirith and Khieu Samphan, Case File No. 002/19-09-2007-ECCC/TC, Co-Prosecutors' Request for the Trial Chamber to Consider JCE III as an Alternative Mode of Liability, 17 June 2011 . . . . . . . . 141 n. 18
Nuon Chea, Ieng Sary, Ieng Thirth, Khieu Samphan, Case File No. 002/19-09-2007/ECCC/TC, Decision on the Applicability of Joint Criminal Enterprise, 12 September 2011 . . . . 142 n. 27
Kaing Guek Eav alias Duch, Case File No. 001/18-07-2007/ECCC/TC, Judgment, 26 July 2010 . . . . . . . . 141 n. 26

**International Criminal Court**

The Prosecutor v Ngudjolo Chui, ICC-01/04/12, Concurring Opinion of Judge Van den Wyngaert, 18 December 2012 . . . . . . . . 209 n. 54, 209 n. 54
The Prosecutor v Germain Katanga and Mathieu Ngudjolo Chui, ICC-01/04-01/07, Decision on the Confirmation of the Charges, 30 September 2008 . . . . . . . . 164 n. 134, 165 n. 136
The Prosecutor v Thomas Lubanga Dyilo, Case No. ICC-01/04-01/06, Decision on the Confirmation of the Charges, 29 January 2007 . . . . . . . . 164 nn. 129–32
The Prosecutor v Thomas Lubanga Dyilo, ICC-01/04-01/06, Judgment pursuant to Article 74 of the Statute, 14 March 2012. . . . . . 164 n. 129, 205 n. 33, 209 n. 54, 210 n. 54
Prosecutor v Thomas Lubanga Dyilo, ICC-01/04-01/06, Separate Opinion of Judge Adrian Fulford, 14 March 2012 . . . . . . . . 209 n. 54

**Special Tribunal for Lebanon**

Case No STL-11-01/I, Interlocutory Decision on the Applicable Law: Terrorism, Conspiracy, Homicide, Perpetration, Cumulative Charging, 16 February 2011. . . . . . . . 142 n. 28, 166 nn. 143–4

## DOMESTIC TRIALS


Calder v Halket (1840) III Moore PC 28, 13 ER 12; [1835-42] All ER 306 . . . . . . . . . . 143 n. 35
Hyde v Cogan (1781) 2 Douglas 699, 99 ER 445 . . . . . . . . . . . . . . . . . . . . . . . . . . . 143 n. 34
Macklin, Murphy and Others (1838) 2 Lew CC 225, 168 ER 1136. . . . . . . . . . . . . . . . 144 n. 43
Pinkerton v US (1946) 328 U.S. 640 . . . . . . . . . . . . . . . . . . . . . . . . . . . . . . . . . . . 206 n. 39
R v Blake, R v O'Connor (1978) 68 Cr App Rep, CA 1. . . . . . . . . . . . . . . . . . . . . . . . 144 n. 42
R v Pillay [1922] All ER 437 . . . . . . . . . . . . . . . . . . . . . . . . . . . . . . . . . . . . . . . . 143 n. 35
R v Powell; R v English [1997] 4 All ER 545 . . . . . . . . . . . . . . . . . . . . . . . . . 166 nn. 145–6
R v Hughes (1985) 81 Cr App Rep, CA 344. . . . . . . . . . . . . . . . . . . . . . . . . . . . . . . 144 n. 41
The King v John Borthwick and sixteen others (1779) 1 Douglas 207, 99 Eng Rep 136 . . . . . . . . . . . . . . . . . . . . . . . . . . . . . . . . . . . . . . . . . . 144 n. 45, 159
The Queen v Dudley and Stephens (1884) 14 QBD 273. . . . . . . . . . . . . . . . . . . . . . . . 211 n. 61
The Queen v Serva, Majavel et al (1845) 1 Denison 104, 169 ER 169 . . . . . . . . . . . . . . 143 n. 37
Woolmington v DPP [1935] AC 462 . . . . . . . . . . . . . . . . . . . . . . . . . . . . . . . . . . . . 207 n. 42


## DOMESTIC LEGISLATION


Constitution of the Republic of Ireland, at <http://www.constitution.ie/reports/ConstitutionofIreland.pdf> . . . . . . . . . . . . . . . . . . . . . . . . . . . . . . . . . . . . . . . . . . 143 n. 39
Allied Land Forces South East Asia (4 May 1946), War Crimes Instruction No. 1, 2nd Edition. Allied Land Forces South East Asia, in File WO32/12197, UK National Archives, as amended by Amendment No 1 of 12 June 1946, Amendment No 2 of 27 June 1946, Amendment No 3 of 16 July 1946, Amendment No 4 of 21 November 1946, Amendment No 5 of 4 December 1946, Amendment No 6 of 22 January 1947, Amendment No 7 of 14 March 1947 and Amendment No 8 of 26 March 1947 . . . . . . . . . . . . . 3 nn. 9–10, 15 n. 14, 16, 20 n. 39, 21 nn. 48–9, 22 n. 54, 23 n. 63, 25 n. 79, 25 n. 81, 26 nn. 91–2, 28 nn. 93–4, 30 nn. 116–17, 32 nn. 130–1, 33 n. 140, 34 nn. 148–51, 34 nn. 153–4, 35 n. 156, 35 nn. 158–9, 35 nn. 161–2, 35 nn. 164–5, 36 n. 170, 40 nn. 199–200, 40 n. 203, 41 nn. 205–7, 44n. 240, 46 nn. 250–3, 48 n. 269, 51 nn. 278–9, 53 n. 285, 53 n. 289, 54 nn. 294–6, 54 nn. 298–9, 60 nn. 347–9, 96 n. 4, 101 nn. 31, 102 n. 32, 124 n. 161, 135 n. 219, 145 n. 49, 201 nn. 15–16, 202, 204 n. 30, 244
Army Act (1939), Rules of Procedure, 1926, reproduced in Manual of Military Law 1929 (Edition Reprinted December 1939), including amendments up to 31 December 1928. . . . . . . . . . 14 nn. 10–11, 15, 16, 17 nn. 21–5, 18 n. 26, 18 nn. 28–32, 22 nn. 59–60, 23 n. 65, 24 nn. 73–4, 25 n. 75, 28 n. 97, 29 n. 112, 30 n. 120, 31 n. 120, 31 nn. 123–4, 32 n. 126, 36 n. 166, 38 n. 180, 38 n. 185, 39 n. 191, 39 nn. 196–7, 40 n. 198, 41 nn. 208–9, 41 nn. 211–12, 42, 44, 45 n. 247, 47 n. 267, 50 n. 274, 51 n. 277, 53 nn. 285–7, 53 n. 289, 57 n. 315, 58, 59 n. 329, 62 n. 360, 62 n. 363, 65 n. 389, 200 n. 8
Great Britain War Office (1945), Royal Warrant 0160/2498, 18 June 1945, promulgated by the War Office, Army Order 81 of 1945 AO 81/1945 . . . . . . vi, vii, xi, 7, 13 n. 1, 14 n. 9, 20, 22, 23, 30, 65, 68, 97 n. 11, 100 n. 25, 105, 135, 145 n. 49, 171 n. 8, 172, 173, 176, 177, 181, 195, 200 n. 3, 200 n. 6, 200 n. 8, 201, 202 n. 19, 204 n. 29, 204 n. 32, 205, 206, 207, 208, 209, 211 n. 61

Great Britain War Office (1945), Regulations for the Trial of War Criminals Attached to Royal Warrant 0160/2498, 18 June 1945, Promulgated by the War Office, Army Order 81 of 1945 AO 81/1945. . . . . . . . 14 n. 9, 14 n. 11, 15, 16, 22 n. 61, 23 n. 68, 24 nn. 72–3, 25 n. 76, 25 n. 78, 26 nn. 84–5, 30 n. 115, 35 n. 161, 35 n. 163, 38 n. 181, 41 n. 213, 42 nn. 214–18, 42 n. 221, 46 n. 249, 46 n. 252, 48 n. 268, 57 n. 316, 58, 59 n. 330–1, 60 n. 346, 60 nn. 348–9, 62 n. 364, 100 n. 25, 145 n. 49, 172 n. 9, 172 n. 11, 200 n. 3

UK Misuse of Drugs Act 1971 . . . . . . . . . . . . . . . . . . . . . . . . . . . . . . . . . . . . . . . . 144 n. 40

## INTERNATIONAL LEGAL MATERIALS

Charter of the International Military Tribunal (Nuremberg)

Charter of the International Military Tribunal, attached to the Agreement by the US, France, UK and USSR for the Prosecution and Punishment of the Major War Criminals of the European Axis, 8 August 1945 in Friedman L (ed), The Law of War: A Documentary History, Vol 1 (Random House 1972) . . . . . . . . . . . . . . 177 nn. 46–7, 178

Charter of the International Military Tribunal (Nuremberg Charter/IMT Nuremberg Charter), annexed to Agreement by the Government of the United States of America, the Provisional Government of the French Republic, the Government of the United Kingdom of Great Britain and Northern Ireland and the Government of the Union of Soviet Socialist Republics for the Prosecution and Punishment of the Major War Criminals of the European Axis; Judgment of the International Military Tribunal for the Trial of German Major War Criminals, (1946) Cmd 6964 . . . . . . . . . . . . . . xii, 22 n. 55, 103 n. 37, 112, 113, 145 n. 51, 170 n. 7, 177 n. 43, 177 nn. 45–6, 178 n. 49, 179, 195, 197, 200 n. 4, 200 n. 6, 201 n. 10, 205, 206 n. 36, 210, 212

Charter of the International Military Tribunal for the Far East, TIAS No. 1589 at 3, 4 Bevans 20, 19 January 1946, amended 26 April 1946 . . . . . . . . . . . . . . . 178 n. 48, 200 n. 5

Control Council Law No 10, Punishment of Persons Guilty of War Crimes, Crimes against Peace and against Humanity, 3 Official Gazette Control Council for Germany 50-55 (1946), 20 December 1945. . . . . 145 n. 51, 163 n. 125, 177 n. 47, 179, 180 n. 64, 191, 197

Convention for the Amelioration of the Condition of the Wounded in Armies in the Field, opened for signature 22 Aug 1864, 129 Consol TS 361 (entered into force 21 June 1865) . . . . . . . . . . . . . . . . . . . . . . . . . . . . . . . . . . . . . . . . . v, xii, 97 n. 9

Convention for the Amelioration of the Condition of the Wounded and Sick in Armies in the Field, opened for signature 6 July 1906, 202 CTS 144 (entered into force 9 August 1907) . . . . . . . . . . . . . . . . . . . . . . . . . . . . . . . . . . . . . 97 n. 9, 102 n. 33

Convention for the Amelioration of the Condition of the Wounded and Sick in Armies in the Field, opened for signature 27 Jul 1929, 118 UNTS 303 (entered into force 19 Jun 1931) . . . . . . . . . . . . . . . . . . . . . . . . . . . . . . 97 n. 9, 103 nn. 39–40, 106 n. 56

Geneva Convention relative to the Treatment of Prisoners of War with Annex, opened for signature 27 July 1929, 118 LNTS 343 (entered into force 19 June 1931). . . . . . . . v, 96 n. 5, 98 n. 15, 103 n. 38, 104, 105, 106 n. 56

Hague Convention (IV) respecting the Laws and Customs of War on Land and its Annex: Regulations concerning the Laws and Customs of War on Land, opened for signature 18 October 1907, (1910) UKTS 9 (entered into force 26 January 1910) . . . . . . . . . . 97 n. 8, 97 n. 11, 98 n. 14, 103 nn. 34–7, 103 n. 3, 115, 117, 118 n. 124, 129, 177 n. 14, 199 n. 2, 200 n. 2

Protocol Additional to the Geneva Conventions of 12 August 1949, and relating to the Protection of Victims of International Armed Conflicts, opened for signature 8 June 1977, 1125 UNTS 3 (entered into force 7 December 1978) . . . 129 n. 190, 207 n. 45

Rome Statute of the International Criminal Court, UN Doc A/CONF.183/9 (as corrected by the procés-verbaux of 10 November 1998, 12 July 1999, 30 November 1999, 8 May 2000, 17 January 2001, and 16 January 2002), (1998) 2187 UNTS 3 . . . . . . . . . . . . . .xii, 7, 169 n. 2, 195, 196 n. 171, 197 nn. 177–84, 198, 199 n. 1, 201 nn. 13–14, 202 n. 18, 203, 204 n. 29, 206, 207 n. 47, 208 nn. 49–50, 209 n. 52, 209 n. 54, 210 n. 55, 211, 212

Rules of Procedure and Evidence, adopted by the Assembly of State Parties, First Session, New York, 3-10 September 2002, Official Records ICC-ASP/1/3 . . . . . 197 n. 183, 209 n. 53

Statute of the International Criminal Tribunal for Rwanda, adopted by Security Council Res 955 (1994) . . . . . . . . . . . . . . . . . . . . . . . . . . . . . . . . . . . . . . . . . . . 201 n. 12

Statute of the International Criminal Tribunal for Former Yugoslavia, adopted by Security Council Res 827 (1993). . . . . . . . . . . . . . . . . . . . . . . . . . . . . . . . . . . . . . . . 201 n. 11

Treaty of Nanking, Nanking, 29 August 1842, Peace Treaty between the Queen of Great Britain and the Emperor of China, Ratifications Exchanged at Hong Kong, 26 June 1843 . . . . . . . . . . . . . . . . . . . . . . . . . . . . . . . . . . . . . . . . . . . . . 107 n. 65

## UNITED NATIONS AND CONFERENCE MATERIALS

CDDH/405/Rev1, Report of Committee I, 21 May 1977, Official Records of The Diplomatic Conference On The Reaffirmation And Development of International Humanitarian Law Applicable In Armed Conflicts Geneva (1974-1977) Vol. X (Federal Political Department Bern, 1978) 181 . . . . . . . . . . . . . . . . . . . . . . . . . . . . . . . . . . . . . . . 195 n. 171

CDDH/SR.45, 30 May 1977, Official Records of the Diplomatic Conference on the Reaffirmation and Development of International Humanitarian Law applicable in Armed Conflicts, Geneva (1974-1977) Vol VI (Federal Political Department Bern, 1978) 307. . . . . . . . . . . . . . . . . . . . . . . . . . . . . . . . . . . . . . . . . . . . 195 n. 171

Declaration of Basic Principles of Justice for Victims of Crime and Abuse of Power, 29 November 1985, United Nations General Assembly Resolution 40/34 (1985) . . . . . 208 n. 48

Formulation of the Nürnberg Principles, UN Doc A/RES/488 (V), 12 December 1950. . . . . . . . . . . . . . . . . . . . . . . . . . . . . . . . . . . . . . . . . . . . . 178 n. 51

Office of the Prosecutor, International Criminal Court, Report on Prosecutorial Strategy, September 2006 <http://www.icc-cpi.int/>. . . . . . . . . . . . . . . . . . . . . . . . . . . . . . . 211 n. 62

Report of the International Law Commission, covering the work of its Second Session, Yearbook of the International Law Commission 1950, Vol II, UN Doc A/1316, 363 . . . . . . . . . . . . . . . . . . . . . . . . . . . . . . . . . . . . . . . . 178 n. 49

UN Doc A/CONF.183/C.1/WGGP/L.2, 16 June 1998 . . . . . . . . . . . . . . . . . . . . . . 196 n. 173

# *List of Contributors*

**Professor Roger S Clark** is Board of Governors Professor at Rutgers School of Law, Camden, USA, and a prolific author. He served as a member of the United Nations Committee on Crime Prevention and Control between 1987 and 1990. He has been a visiting or adjunct professor at numerous institutions, including the University of Iowa, the University of Pennsylvania, the University of Miami, the University of Graz in Austria, the University of the South Pacific (Fiji), and his alma mater, Victoria University of Wellington, in New Zealand. Professor Clark serves on the editorial boards of various publications, including *Criminal Law Forum*, the *Human Rights Review*, and the *International Lawyer*. He has been the general editor of the *Procedural Aspects of International Law* monographs since 2004. He is a board member of several international non-governmental organizations. In 1995 and 1996, he represented Samoa in arguing the illegality of nuclear weapons before the International Court of Justice. Since 1995, he has represented Samoa in negotiations to create the International Criminal Court and to get the Court running successfully. He was very active in the Court's Special Working Group on the Crime of Aggression.

**Hon Justice Liu Daqun** is a Judge of the Appeals Chamber of the International Criminal Tribunals for the former Yugoslavia (ICTY) and Rwanda, having been appointed a Judge of the ICTY in 2000. He is also a Judge of the International Residual Mechanism for Criminal Tribunals. Judge Liu regularly lectures and teaches around the world, and annually judges the ICRC's International Humanitarian Law moots in China. Before joining the ICTY, Judge Liu was China's Ambassador to Jamaica and also Permanent Representative of the People's Republic of China to the International Seabed Authority. From 1984 to 1993, Judge Liu was Director of the Private International Law Division, the Law of the Sea Division, and the Treaty and Law Department of the Foreign Ministry. From 1993 to 1998, Judge Liu was the Deputy Director General and Legal Adviser, Treaty and Law Department at the Ministry of Foreign Affairs. Judge Liu was also Professor of International Law at the China University of Law and Political Science. Judge Liu served several times as a member of the Chinese delegation to legal forums and negotiations. In 1998, he was Deputy Head and Chief Negotiator of the Chinese delegation to the Rome Conference on the establishment of the International Criminal Court.

**Professor Bing Bing Jia** is Professor of Law at Tsinghua University, China. From 1996 to 2004, he served in various capacities within the Chambers of the United Nations International Criminal Tribunals for the former Yugoslavia and Rwanda. He is, *inter alia*, a member of the editorial boards of the *International Review of the Red Cross*, *Chinese Journal of International Law*, and the *Journal of International Criminal Justice*. He received the Chinese Society of International Law Outstanding Research Award 2004–2009 ('Space Technology'), has been invited by the Hague Academy of International Law to give a special course in Public International Law in the summer of 2016, and was conferred the Friedrich Wilhelm Bessel Research Award by the Humboldt Foundation, Germany in 2010.

**Dr Nina H B Jørgensen** has been Associate Professor at the Faculty of Law of the Chinese University of Hong Kong since 2010. She previously worked for eight years in different capacities (prosecution, judges' chambers, defence) at the Special Court for Sierra Leone in Freetown and The Hague, the Extraordinary Chambers in the Courts of Cambodia in

Phnom Penh, and the International Criminal Tribunals for the Former Yugoslavia and Rwanda in The Hague and Arusha respectively. She has also worked for the OSCE Office for Democratic Institutions and Human Rights in Warsaw as the legal adviser for tolerance and non-discrimination. Prior to these assignments, she was a post-doctoral research fellow in international criminal law at the University of Leiden after obtaining her DPhil (1998) from the University of Oxford. She has a current practising certificate as a barrister and is a door tenant at Argent Chambers in London.

**Professor Suzannah Linton**, a UK solicitor, is Chair of International Law at Bangor University Law School in the UK. She is also the founding Director of the Bangor Centre for International Law. Her project on Hong Kong's War Crimes Trials, culminating in this book, was funded by the Hong Kong Research Grants Council when she was Associate Professor at the University of Hong Kong. Her recent publications include *International Criminal Procedure: Principles and Rules*, co-edited with Göran Sluiter, Håkan Friman, Sergey Vasiliev, and Salvatore Zappalà, and 'Rediscovering the War Crimes trials in Hong Kong, 1946–1948' in the *Melbourne Journal of International Law* Vol 13(2). Professor Linton has wide field experience and has worked at international courts and tribunals, and international organizations, including at the International Criminal Tribunal for the former Yugoslavia, the Special Panels for Serious Crimes in East Timor, and the UN Office of the High Commissioner for Human Rights in Cambodia.

**Dr Yuma Totani** is Associate Professor of History at the University of Hawaii and the author of *The Tokyo War Crimes Trial: The Pursuit of Justice in the Wake of World War II* (Cambridge, MA: Harvard University Asia Center, 2008). Its Japanese expanded edition, *Tōkyō saiban: dai niji taisen go no hō to seigi no tsuikyū* (Tokyo: Misuzu shobō, 2008), is translated and edited by the author.

**Dr Alexander Zahar** is Senior Lecturer at Macquarie Law School, Macquarie University, Sydney, Australia. He joined the United Nations in 2000 as a lawyer, first at the ICTR, and from 2003 to 2007 at the ICTY. Dr Zahar's research interests are split between international criminal law and climate change law. His most recent books are *The Legacy of the International Criminal Tribunal for the Former Yugoslavia* (Oxford University Press, 2011), edited with B Swart and G Sluiter, and *Australian Climate Law in Global Context* (Cambridge University Press, 2012), co-authored with J Peel and L Godden.

**Mr Kevin P Zervos, Senior Counsel**, is Director of Public Prosecutions with the Hong Kong Department of Justice. Mr Zervos has conducted the full ambit of trials and appeals in all fields of law. Mr Zervos is a specialist in human rights and in the prosecution of white collar crime. In 1984, he worked in Australia with the Special Prosecutor's Office responsible for the investigation and prosecution of large scale revenue frauds. From 1985, he was Senior Assistant Director of the office of the Commonwealth Director of Public Prosecutions at the Melbourne and Sydney Offices where he was in charge of the Major Fraud Section. From 1989 to 1992, he was General Counsel to the Independent Commission Against Corruption in New South Wales. From 1992 to date, he has worked as counsel with the Hong Kong Department of Justice, initially attached to the Commercial Crime Unit where he mainly prosecuted white collar crime cases, then as head of Appeals specializing in Human Rights and later as Chief of Staff. In May 2003, Mr Zervos was appointed Senior Counsel in Hong Kong. In 2009, he completed a Masters of Laws (Human Rights) at the University of Hong Kong.

# 1

# Introduction

*Suzannah Linton*

This book is an endeavour to excavate the war crimes proceedings that took place in Hong Kong from 28 March 1946 to 20 December 1948,[1] when four British military courts adjudicated violations of the laws or usages of war from across the British colonial territories of Hong Kong, Kowloon, and the New Territories, and also from China (the mainland and Taiwan), Japan, and from the High Seas. These trials were part of the larger project of war crimes prosecutions that the leaders of the Allied nations had promised well before the War ended, and took place as part of the British programme of prosecutions through military courts.[2]

Records show that in July 1946, of the 10,000 Japanese captured in Hong Kong after the surrender, 239 were held as suspected war criminals.[3] Some were repatriated, and others were sent from other parts of Asia to Hong Kong, leaving 123 men to stand trial.[4] In total, there were 46 trials of Japanese and Taiwanese from military and civilian backgrounds. Forty-four of the judgments were confirmed against 108 individuals, with 14 acquittals and 21 executions.[5]

In line with the prevailing practice for British military trials of that time, the Hong Kong trials produced verdicts only, that is, there were no reasoned decisions.[6] This clearly creates significant obstacles for legal research. However, as I believe will be clear from the chapters in this book, the contributors have, with great caution

[1] The abuse and massacre of civilians at Lantau Island's Silver Mine Bay was the subject matter of the first trial, commencing on 28 March 1946; the last judgment, in the matter of detainee abuses in Shanghai, was delivered on 20 December 1948.

[2] For more on the background to the trials, see S Linton, 'Rediscovering the War Crimes Trials in Hong Kong, 1946–48', (2012) 13(1) MJIL 284 ('Linton, "Rediscovering the War Crimes Trials in Hong Kong, 1946–48"').

[3] *Hong Kong Annual Report* 1946 72.

[4] For example, in late 1946, 58 Japanese and Taiwanese were sent for trial for war crimes in Taiwan (China) in relation to Prisoners of War and ten Japanese were sent from Japan to stand trial in relation to crimes committed in Shanghai against British nationals. During 1947, 55 Japanese were located in China and brought to Hong Kong, and 92 detained Japanese were repatriated: *Hong Kong Annual Report* 1946 72, *Hong Kong Annual Report* 1947 94.

[5] For more statistical information about the Hong Kong war crimes trials, see <http://hkwctc.lib.hku.hk/exhibits/show/hkwctc/hkwct>.

[6] See however United Nations War Crimes Commission, *Law Reports of Trials of War Criminals* vol XV (HMSO 1949) 20, discussing a number of exceptions to the normal practice of non-reasoned decisions.

and skill, nevertheless managed to extract some very interesting and important legal issues. This has been possible because of the expertise of the contributors, and also because of the method of conducting direct research into the case files, using the primary materials contained in them, backed up with secondary materials such as expert commentaries, journal articles, and leading texts, and also comparison with cases from other courts and tribunals. We have also been able to gain priceless insights thanks to interviews with the late Major Murray Incell Ormsby, a former Judge and Prosecutor at the Hong Kong trials. All the case files contain, *inter alia*, complete official transcripts of proceedings, documentary evidence such as Japanese legislation, and sworn affidavits and statements. We clearly had far more material to rely on than the reporter of the *Essen Lynching Case* for the United Nations War Crimes Commission, who lamented that

> the considerations as to the facts and as to the law which guided the Court cannot, therefore, be quoted from the transcript in so many words. It is only possible to attempt by inference to derive them from the verdict and from the sentences imposed, having regard to arguments brought forward by Counsel.[7]

In addition, most of the Hong Kong cases also have both the opening and closing submissions from Prosecution and Defence, and almost all contain reviews of the proceedings by Judge Advocates. These reviews, in the form of reports to the Commander of Land Forces Hong Kong as the Confirming Officer, are certainly important for understanding the cases. The quality of the reports was admittedly patchy, but all were in the form of advice to the Confirming Officer on the conduct of the case, the evidence and arguments, and made recommendations on whether or not to confirm the decisions of the court. In all of these documents, we have the next best thing to reasoned judgments, and through the hands of expert researchers, fascinating and important analysis is presented in this collection. I agree with the United Nations War Crimes Commission, when it observed that the decisions of British military courts are 'declaratory of the state of the law and illustrative of actual State practice'.[8] The Hong Kong cases, carefully dissected by the contributors, do provide us with the *usus* and *opinio juris* going towards the identification of what was already customary law, and that can also go towards the establishment of new rules.

While they will not shake the foundations of modern international criminal justice, the Hong Kong war crimes trials have clearly provided us with much to write about. Anyone reading about these war crimes cases will surely wonder why they fell into oblivion. 'Minor' may have been the categorization of such cases, but the crimes were far from insignificant. The post-World War II prosecutions distinguished 'major' alleged war criminals from the rest. The International Military Tribunal at Nuremberg, and more relevant to us, its sister at Tokyo, tried the so-called 'A class' suspects, meaning leaders, organizers and instigators, with the

[7] *Erich Heyer and six others*, United Nations War Crimes Commission, *Law Reports of Trials of War Criminals*, vol 1 (HMSO 1947) ('*Law Reports of Trials of War Criminals*, vol I') 91.

[8] *Law Reports of Trials of War Criminals*, vol I (n 7) 110.

focus on Crimes against Peace. Those persons charged with war crimes alone were categorized as 'B Class', and those charged with Crimes against Humanity alone were categorized as 'C Class'. These Hong Kong trials were 'minor' war crimes cases, although the term 'Class B' was not used. The British military courts within the jurisdiction of Allied Land Forces South-East Asia ('ALFSEA') were to concentrate on 'minor' war criminals, meaning persons alleged to have committed war crimes on a relatively small scale, such as killing without justification, torture, other forms of ill-treatment causing the infliction of bodily harm, and withholding sufficient food, water, or medical care.[9] ALFSEA issued an Instruction providing that major war criminals were those responsible for 'organized brutalities and the design and execution of plans for acts of aggression'—they were not for the British military courts run out of Singapore, but were to be tried by the international tribunal in Tokyo.[10]

For the hundreds of thousands affected by these events, the B and C trials were hardly insignificant, so why the amnesia about them? This is a different issue from the War itself, and Japanese conduct in the Asia Pacific region, which has not been forgotten. The tribunal at Tokyo and the *Yamashita* trial[11] are held out as if they are all that was done in the Asia Pacific region. The minor war crimes trials are almost always ignored, even in contemporary scholarly works and judgments. In Hong Kong, generations of students, passing through the corridors of its eminent law schools, have not been taught that there were historic war crimes trials in Hong Kong. The uncovering of these cases, and the project from which this book sprung, generated extensive media and public interest in Hong Kong.[12] Whether new and original research in Hong Kong has actually been inspired remains to be seen. But, the forgetting of the minor war crimes trials appears to cut across jurisdictions where there were such trials, from China where the documents are still kept under lock and key more than half a century on, to today's Southeast Asian nations,

[9] Allied Land Forces South-East Asia, War Crimes Instruction No 1 (2nd edn) in File No WO 32/12197, UK National Archives [not part of the HKWCT Collection] ('ALFSEA Instruction'), art 3–4.

[10] ALFSEA Instruction (n 9) art 2. See also Peter Vine, 'Experiences as a War Crimes Prosecutor in Hong Kong' (1995) 35 *Journal of the Hong Kong Branch of the Royal Asiatic Society* 205, 206.

[11] *In re Yamashita*, 327 US 1 (1946).

[12] See, for example, Simpson Cheung, 'Sad tale of unsung hero's war death uncovered', *South China Morning Post*, 13 September 2010; Wong Yat Hei, 'Lessons from Our Darkest Era', Young Post, *South China Morning Post*, 14 October 2010; and Chinese language coverage in the *Ming Pao Daily*, 13 September 2010, <http://life.mingpao.com/cfm/dailynews3b.cfm?File=20100913/nalgo/goh1.txt> 港大推日戰犯資料庫 記述淪陷史無名英雄 (Hong Kong University Established a Database on Japanese Criminals of World War II, illuminating the history and nameless heroes during the occupied periods) (author not stated); *China News*, 13 September 2010, <http://www.chinanews.com/ga/2010/09-13/2528249.shtml> 港 大推二战日本战犯数据库 档案揭日军酷刑 (Hong Kong University Established a Database on Japanese Felons/Criminals of World War II, Revealing the Crucial Torture Used by Japanese Armies), by Xiang Ji (editor); *Sina News*, 13 September 2010, <http://news.sina.com.hk/news/3/1/1/1852154/1.html> 港大推日戰犯資料庫 (Hong Kong University Established a Database on Japanese Felons of World War II), by Mansi Lu; *South China Morning Post*, 13 September 2010, <http://chinaoutlook.scmp.com/zh-cn/article.php?ArticleID=1000014072&OtherID=1000014073&Section=topstory> 袪遗忘的二战英雄事迹重见天日 (Uncovering the forgotten story of a hero in World War II) (author not stated). I continue to receive regular email enquiries from all over the world, seeking information about family members, and also from academics.

Singapore, Malaysia, Burma, the Philippines, and Indonesia (formerly the Dutch East Indies). For the latter nations, it is possible that in the post-colonial years, the trials reeked of Empire's revenge. The use of the trials to boost British prestige after her humiliation at the hands of Japan has certainly been documented.[13] The Hong Kong cases do demonstrate an effort to prosecute crimes committed against local Chinese and not just British or Commonwealth nationals. It was not by accident that the very first case involved a massacre of local Chinese.[14]

The 46 cases that lie at the heart of this study were only declassified in 1978. This is certainly one reason for the lack of academic study of the trials. Another obvious possibility for these cases falling into oblivion within the legal community may be because there were no reasoned judgments. There is no denying that their absence does limit the extent of their contribution to the legal world, and render much of the legal analysis of the 'reading between the lines' variety. There is something else that may lie behind the lack of interest in the lesser trials in the Asia Pacific region. It may well be rooted in the widely perceived inadequacies of the Tokyo trial, in Japan and outside it, possibly rendering all the Asia Pacific trials suspect. The *Yamashita* trial was exceptional, but that was probably because it was an American case and drew in the Supreme Court; on the other hand, that trial has also been severely criticized. For example, Prévost raises the issue of racism against the Japanese.[15] One may observe the rigorousness of the Anglo-Saxon Prisoner of War ('POW') camp survivor movement that remembers the horrors of the experiences of Allied prisoners in Asia, and wonder if the forgetting of the Asian victims may support Prévost's claims of racism, which were of course preceded by the famously stinging criticisms of the Indian Judge on the Tokyo tribunal, Judge Radhabinod Pal.

It has been suggested that the lack of academic interest in the hundreds of post-War trials held in Asia, of which the Hong Kong trials were part, was because the realpolitik of the post-War age rendered focus on issues of 'justice' irrelevant for the majority.[16] It would, to the present author, be more appropriate to say that most people moved on, the world moved on, especially in Asia where independence struggles soon erupted and new nations were born. Narayanan's argument does not, however, explain the voluminous research and writing conducted into the 'justice' or otherwise of the Nuremberg trials, and the flurry of activity that would follow domestic, primarily European, trials such as *Eichmann*, *Barbie*, *Touvier*, *Dachau* etc and the steady work carried out by pioneering lawyers over the decades after Nuremberg.[17] This is not to suggest that many people outside a small group of historians and specialized lawyers, mainly working in the USA and Europe, were

[13] Linton, 'Rediscovering the War Crimes Trials in Hong Kong, 1946–48' pp 291–3 (n 2).

[14] See n 1.

[15] For arguments about racism, see Ann Marie Prévost, 'Race and War Crimes: The 1945 War Crimes Trial of General Tomoyuki Yamashita', (1992) 14(3) HRQ 303.

[16] A Narayanan, 'Japanese Atrocities and British Minor War Crimes Trials after World War II in the East' (2006) 33 *Jebat (Mal J Hist Pol St S)* 10 ('Narayanan, "Japanese Atrocities and British Minor War Crimes Trials after World War II in the East"').

[17] The elder statesmen of modern international criminal law, such as Professors Otto Triffterer, Theodor Meron, the late Antonio Cassese, and M Cherif Bassiouni, have been researching and writing in the area long before it became popular.

interested in such matters, for it is true that war crimes were not a matter of much global interest until they became fashionable in the 1990s with the advent of the ad hoc tribunals. But still, it is certainly remarkable that until now, there has been so little home-grown interest in these trials in the Asia Pacific region, or international interest in them.

In any event, international criminal law is now more than merely fashionable, it is a permanent fixture on the international community's agenda and a vital tool in the effort to ensure international peace and security. In the Asia Pacific region, a new generation has recently been inspired to research the war crimes trials that were held all those years ago.[18] All of us involved in this book hope that our work makes an important contribution to the genre, recalling what Lord Wright of Durley wrote in his foreword to the very first volume of the United Nations War Crimes Commission's *Law Reports of Trials of War Criminals*:

> I cannot sufficiently emphasise what I regard as the great importance of these reports from the point of view of the future development of International Law as applied to war crimes. Several hundred cases of war crimes have already been tried in courts of the different members of the United Nations; these reports will show, for the practitioner or the student, the particular problems which have arisen and how in practice they have been dealt with and also show to the historian of the laws of war the practice of courts in applying those laws to particular cases. These reports are of the highest value and will prevent what would otherwise happen, namely the want of a correct record of the most significant cases which have been tried. It is with a view to illustrating as far as possible important points of law and procedure that these volumes of these cases and those to be contained in the succeeding volumes have been selected and reported. It is by studying them that the precise record can be secured and an appreciation formed of the problems to be solved and the methods adopted in solving them.[19]

## Introducing the Chapters

Dr Alexander Zahar's study of 'Trial Procedure at the British Military Courts, Hong Kong, 1946–1948' cuts through to the heart of the war crimes process in Hong Kong. His challenging chapter uses three benchmarks of assessment: the degree of departure from the normally applicable court-martial procedure current at the time; the degree to which the stated principles governing the trials were

[18] The revival of international justice, with the advent of the ad hoc tribunals and the International Criminal Court, has sparked recent academic interest in this area. Obviously, this book is part of the rediscovering of legal history in the Asia Pacific. Other examples include *Australia's Post World War II War Crimes Trials: A Systematic and Comprehensive Law Reports Series* (Martinus Nijhoff, forthcoming), Narayanan, 'Japanese Atrocities and British Minor War Crimes Trials after World War II in the East' (n 16), and Cheah Wui Leng, 'Post-WWII British Hell-ship Trials in Singapore: Omissions and the Attribution of Responsibility' (2010) JICJ 1035. In the Philippines, the Ortigas Foundation's library has gathered a complete set of the records of the Japanese war crimes trials and original newspapers, magazines, and photographs from the war years. The War Crimes Research Centre at the University of California, Berkeley, has for some years been working to gather trial documents from the Asian trials.

[19] Foreword by Lord Wright of Durley, *Law Reports of Trials of War Criminals*, vol I (n 7) x.

complied with in practice by the courts and the authorities associated with them; and the aftermath of the trials, and in particular, the way that the military-court system was wound up. Dr Zahar's thesis is that the proceedings were designed to be summary, and that in fact they were summary, offering a standard that was not just highly problematic by the identified benchmarks, but also much lower than that which applied to British servicemen at the time. His conclusion provides us with much to reflect upon.

Professor Yuma Totani, in her chapter on 'The Prisoner of War Camp Trials', places the Hong Kong trials in a wider historic context. In her search for the correct allocation of responsibility for the widespread maltreatment of captured Allied personnel detained by the Japanese military, she dissects five war crimes trials, drawing in the highest ranking officers of the Japanese POW camps in Hong Kong and Taiwan, China and the important case of the civilian staff of the Japan Mining Company at Kinkaseki, Taiwan (China). Professor Totani finds that the records of the Hong Kong trials point to the War Ministry as the centre of the planning process, their policies having been executed in collaboration with a wide range of supporting agencies in the colonial governments, military administration in the occupied territories, and in the corporate world of wartime Japan. She also reveals the critical role that individuals played, and the symbiotic relationship between the individual and the system.

Professor Linton's chapter on 'War Crimes' begins with an overview of the different categories of war crimes that were tried. She examines the notion of 'the laws and usages of war' that lay behind the concept of war crimes in these proceedings. Professor Linton then moves to focus on the trials for war crimes committed against civilians in occupied territory, where the cases provide more material for substantive assessment. She untangles the trials of the two *Kempeitai* chiefs in relation to the involuntary displacement of approximately one million persons from Hong Kong to occupied China, and attempts to understand the resulting judgments in *Noma* and *Kanazawa* through comparison with the contemporaneous Chinese trials of *Sakai* and *Isogai* (also raising the same involuntary displacement), and the *Andaman Islands* case from Singapore. She also reveals the standardized, widespread, and systematic nature of *Kempeitai* abuse of civilians, sometimes leading to death, and ascertains the central challenge of proving causation in many of these cases. Professor Linton also unearths the numerous cases of civilian resistance to the Japanese occupation, an unsettled matter in international law. Through *Kishi et al* and other cases, she engages with the issue of what the Japanese occupying forces, in the Second World War, could or could not do, in relation to civilians allegedly involved in 'anti-Japanese' activity or resistance, as opposed to giving their obedience.

Professor Nina Jørgensen engages with the question of whether the mode of 'being concerned in crime', as used in the Hong Kong trials, was an embryonic form of that controversial doctrine that has been haunting International Criminal Law since the *Tadić* Appeals Chamber decision in 1999, 'joint criminal enterprise' (JCE). She begins with the roots of the concept, delving into historic cases in the English common law, and moving to the British World War cases (excavating, *inter alia*, the handling of Regulation 8(ii) of the Regulations annexed to the Royal

Warrant of 1945), and into contemporary times. Shining a light into the Hong Kong case materials in the absence of judgments, Professor Jørgensen is able to identify the conceptual approaches underpinning the use and understanding of 'being concerned in crime'. She places that in the wider context by contrasting the Hong Kong trials with other Royal Warrant cases. She finally brings us back to the contemporary debate about policy considerations in international criminal law, JCE, and whether 'being concerned in crime' fits into that notion.

In his chapter on Superior Orders, Professor Bing Bing Jia delves into the practice of the Hong Kong military tribunals in this area. He identifies that the plea, in its pure form, was not successful as a defence, but it could have a marked effect of mitigation if accompanied by compulsion, as well as form a separate defence of duress. Professor Jia tracks the fate of the plea of superior orders in the Hong Kong trials through several points of reference: (1) when raised as a defence with and without duress, (2) when raised in conjunction with other factors present at the time of the commission of the crime, (3) when raised by civilian officials, and (4) when raised as a mitigating factor. He concludes that the decisions were consistent in this regard, suggesting that the judges had a fairly clear conception of the law of superior orders in international law prohibiting it as a defence. Professor Jia fixes the Hong Kong trials along the evolving trajectory of the law of superior orders, and brings us back to the present with discussion of the position in Article 33 of the Rome Statute of the International Criminal Court.

Professor Roger Clark rounds up the collection with a reflection that juxtaposes the preceding chapters on the Hong Kong trials with the International Military Tribunal trials in Nuremberg and Tokyo, and makes some modern comparisons, based especially on the contents of the Rome Statute of the International Criminal Court and the early decisions of that court. For all the progress we have made since those days, he also notes how today's International Criminal Court judges are being left with the same amount of direction in their constituent instrument—next to nothing—on how to manage sentencing. Professor Clark observes how 22 of the 108 accused convicted in the Hong Kong trials were ultimately subjected to the death penalty. When compared with the 11 death sentences issued in Nuremberg and the seven in Tokyo where the highest level of criminals were tried, he points out that this suggests that 'something harsh was going on here'.

Professor Suzannah Linton's interview of the late Major Murray Incell Ormsby was conducted in 2011, a year and a half before he passed away on 6 December 2012. Ninety-three-year-old Major Ormsby appeared until recently to have been the last surviving British official participating in the trials. However, in May 2013, Professor Linton discovered that former Defence Counsel, Lieutenant D C J Banfield, is still alive. Through his lengthy interview, Major Ormsby provided an extraordinarily precise insight into a world now long gone, and an exceptional account of a young man's remarkable experience as a Judge and Prosecutor of the Hong Kong war crimes process. The interview is presented here in extracted form; the complete transcript can be viewed at the website of the Hong Kong War Crimes Trials Database, at <http://hkwctc.lib.hku.hk/exhibits/show/hkwctc/accountsoftrials/oral>.

Unfortunately, we were not able to include the chapter on Command Responsibility.

## Research and Methodology

Some explanation is necessary in order that the reader may understand how the research was conducted. First of all, this book would not have been possible without the Hong Kong Research Grants Council's award to me, in June 2008, of a generous grant to conduct research on Hong Kong's War Crimes Trials [Project No HKU 748208H, Year 2008/2009]. This support enabled me to identify, purchase copies of, and study the case files of war crimes trials held in Hong Kong in the period 1946–1948. These files are held in original form at the UK National Archives in Kew. With the assistance of my researchers and the staff of the University of Hong Kong Libraries, I was able to create a database to house digital copies of the files within the Hong Kong's War Crimes Trials Database, at <http://hkwctc.lib.hku.hk/exhibits/show/hkwctc/about>. It is this collection that we have all relied upon in our work, which we refer to as the 'HKWCT Collection'.

These Hong Kong cases come from the UK National Archives' WO 235 collection. They are recorded as being part of the files of the Judge Advocate General relating to persons tried before British military courts after World War II for war crimes in Europe and the Far East. The HKWCT Collection maintains the specific file numbers, and the names as used in the original files in the National Archives (the names followed Japanese style, meaning the surname comes first, and then the given name).

In our referencing system, we have sought to provide as much information as possible, to facilitate the work of others who may wish to retrace our steps.

1. The HKWCT Collection retains the original numbers allocated to the files (WO235/xyz), and we have maintained this. When we have used cases from the collection, we have referred to them using the following formulation:

   *Trial of [rank followed by full name]* (HKWCT Collection, File No WO 235/xyz).

A concrete example of a first reference to a case file would be:

*Trial of Col Noma Kennosuke* (HKWCT Collection, File No WO235/999) ('*Trial of Col Noma Kennosuke*').

2. An example of a later reference to this case file would be

   *Trial of Col Noma Kennosuke* (n zzz).

3. Every page of a Hong Kong case cited has a slide number, which records the number of the scan. This is only visible on the digitized copies in the HKWCT Collection, and is obviously not on the originals in the UK National Archives. They will assist those who are able to access the HKWCT Collection online.
4. Oral testimony was recorded by way of transcript. The following citation format is used for oral testimony:

Testimony of Prosecution Witness John Doe, *Trial of Colonel Noma Kennosuke* (n zzz), transcript bbb, slide ccc.

5. Documents are identified according to type or name as listed in the file, for example,

   Prosecution Closing Submission, *Trial of Colonel Noma Kennosuke* (n zzz), exhibit aaa, bbb [page number of the submission], slide ccc.

   Affidavit of Jane Doe, *Trial of Colonel Noma Kennosuke* (n zzz), exhibit aaa, bbb [page number of the affidavit], slide ccc.

   Judge Advocate's Report, 21 April 1947, *Trial of Colonel Noma Kennosuke* (n zzz), aaa [page number of the report], slide bbb.

   Charge Sheet, *Trial of Colonel Noma Kennosuke* (n zzz), slide aaa.

6. The careful reader may note that documents of the same class sometimes bear different names. This is because we have maintained the original wording, which was not always consistent. For example, a document may sometimes be identified as 'Prosecution Opening Statement', sometimes 'Opening Statement of the Prosecution' or just 'Opening Statement'. Since this is what the different creators called their documents, we have respected that in our referencing system.
7. The careful reader may also note that sometimes the opening and closing statements are listed as exhibits and sometimes as transcripts. This is because in the early cases, the opening and closing statements were included in the transcripts, while in later cases they were read out but submitted as exhibits.
8. Some documents that were presented at the trials were in Japanese. All chapter contributors have relied on the English-language records unless indicated otherwise, since all verdicts and sentences of the UK Hong Kong courts were rendered on the basis of the English version.
9. One of the cases, the *Trial of Colonel Tokunaga Isao and four others* (HKWCT Collection, File No WO 235/1012) was particularly large, and comprised three files. This explains why the reference to the case may be to File 1, File 2, or File 3.

## Commonly Used Terms

We have not considered it necessary to have a table of commonly used terms, as we have endeavoured to explain certain terms as they arise in the particular chapters. For example, Professor Yuma Totani explains the meaning of the terms '*hanchō*' and '*kantoku*' in her chapter on the Prisoner of War Camp Trials. Professor Alexander Zahar explains the function of the Judge Advocate in his chapter on Trial Proceedings. Professor Nina Jørgensen explains the meaning of 'concerned in' as she explores whether we can find the roots of the modern concept of 'joint criminal enterprise' in this.

The many references to the Japanese Army do not need elaboration. On the other hand, a term that regularly appears across this book is '*Kempeitai*', and it is appropriate to explain this here. According to the judgment of the International Military Tribunal at Tokyo, the *Kempeitai* or Military Police were 'administered by the War Ministry. A *Kempeitai* training school was maintained and operated by the War Ministry in Japan. It is a reasonable inference that the conduct of the *Kempeitai* and the camp guards reflected the policy of the War Ministry.'[20]

In the areas of Japanese occupation, the *Kempeitai*, sometimes referred to as Gendarmerie, operated as a tool for controlling the civilian population, and engaged in counter espionage activities.[21] They worked with locally recruited civilian police called '*kensa*'. Colonel Noma Kennosuke, the first and longest serving *Kempeitai* Commander in Hong Kong, explained to the Court that the

> duties of the gendarmes were to carry out the military police functions while assisting the Armed Forces in carrying out their war operations. To explain about this in more detail: In order to make it easier for the Army to carry out military operations, the gendarmes would also carry out with their police force the maintenance of peace and will also try to secure military advantage. To secure the general military interests means the following: maintenance of military secrets, arrests of spies, prevention of enemy propaganda and sabotage, gathering of information necessary for the maintenance of public peace and order and decensoring of means of communications such as mail and speeches, suppression of hostile residents and punishment of misconduct and offences.[22]

## Names

Finally, some clarification on individual and place names is called for. As noted earlier, we have followed the Hong Kong military courts in their use of romanized Japanese names of individuals (surname first, personal name second). However, the reader should beware that documents from other sources did sometimes use the personal name first and surname last, so there may be occasions where the order is reversed (an example is Lieutenant General Sakai Takashi, who is referred to in some documents as 'Takashi Sakai'). With Chinese names, we also follow the format used by the courts (ie surname first unless a westernized name was used). All the names were romanized by the courts, and we have adhered to that

[20] *IMT Tokyo Judgment*, in B V A Röling and C F Rüter (eds), *The Tokyo Judgment: The International Military Tribunal for the Far East (IMTFE) 29 April 1946–2 November 1948* (APA–University Press Amsterdam 1977) 406.

[21] There are few scholarly English language studies of the *Kempeitai* in circulation. One of the oldest books on Japanese atrocities in World War II is that of Lord Russell of Liverpool, who had a chapter on the *Kempeitai* in his *Knights of Bushido: The Shocking History of Japanese War Atrocities* (Dutton 1958) 274–82. For more recent books, see Richard Deacon, *Kempei Tai: The Japanese Secret Service Then and Now* (Tuttle Publishing 1998); Mark Felton, *Japan's Gestapo: Murder, Mayhem and Torture in Wartime Asia* (Pen & Sword Military 2012).

[22] Testimony of Col Noma Kennosuke, *Trial of Col Noma Kennosuke* (HKWCT Collection, File No WO235/999), transcript 321, slide 328. His testimony also contains many details about the operations and functioning of the *Kempeitai* in Hong Kong.

practice. Generally, we have also sought to preserve the integrity of the original place names. For example, today's Nanjing was then referred to as 'Nanking'. But, there were sometimes inconsistencies, for example, with Hong Kong sometimes referred to as 'Hongkong' although mostly 'Hong Kong'. The island that is today known as 'Taiwan, China' was called 'Formosa' during the time of Japanese control. It is a term that has fallen out of use, and we therefore have endeavoured to refer to the island as 'Taiwan, China' or 'Taiwan (China)'. However, in all cases, where we refer to quotes, we have preserved the originals. Thus, for example, original citations to 'Formosa' are maintained.

# 2

# Trial Procedure at the British Military Courts, Hong Kong, 1946–1948

*Alexander Zahar*

## 1. Introduction

The British military courts were established in both Europe and the Far East under the authority of a Royal Warrant issued on 18 June 1945 ('Royal Warrant').[1] The first of the courts began to hear evidence in January 1946, and the last verdict was handed down in December 1948.[2] Many of the trials were completed prior to the delivery of the judgment of the Nuremberg International Military Tribunal ('IMT Nuremberg') in October 1946—and almost all had concluded by the time that the International Military Tribunal for the Far East ('IMTFE') handed down its own judgment in November 1948.[3] There is some evidence that the British military courts took into account the legal findings of the IMT Nuremberg.[4] On the whole, however, they were a domestic (British) affair that adapted and simplified court-martial procedure to facilitate expedited trials and to deliver what the UK government at the time presumably saw as justice for crimes committed by its enemies during the War. Nevertheless, the government was quickly to lose its enthusiasm for the trials, as discussed in section 5.2.

According to Pritchard's calculations, 678 German war criminals were convicted by British military courts. Of this number, 160 were executed and the remainder sentenced to terms of imprisonment.[5] In Southeast Asia, 12 standing British

[1] Royal Warrant 0160/2498, 18 June 1945, promulgated by the War Office, Army Order 81 of 1945 ('Royal Warrant'). For the history, constitutional basis, and proper context of application of the Royal Warrant, see A P V Rogers, 'War Crimes Trials under the Royal Warrant: British Practice 1945–1949', (1990) 39 ICLQ 780 ('Rogers, "War Crimes Trials under the Royal Warrant"') 788–9, 795–6.

[2] R John Pritchard, 'The Historical Experience of British War Crimes Courts in the Far East' (1978) 6 *Int Rels* 311 ('Pritchard, "The Historical Experience of British War Crimes Courts in the Far East"') 316.

[3] Pritchard, 'The Historical Experience of British War Crimes Courts in the Far East' (n 2) 316.

[4] The clearest example comes from the second day of the trial of Kyoda Shigeru, where proceedings were delayed in an attempt to obtain a copy of the judgment of the IMT Nuremberg, which had just been released. The Court hoped to find guidance in it on a matter of law. See *Trial of Kyoda Shigeru* (HKWCT Collection, File No WO235/1114) ('*Trial of Kyoda Shigeru*'), slide 26.

[5] R John Pritchard, 'British Postwar War Crimes Courts: The Gift of Clemency Following British War Crimes Trials in the Far East, 1946–1948 (1996) 7(1) CLF 15 ('Pritchard, "British Postwar War Crimes Courts: The Gift of Clemency"') 16, fn 1.

military courts held approximately 305 war crimes trials in more than 20 locations in the region.[6] Pritchard estimates that the Asia cases, of which more than half involved two or more joined accused, amounted to 930 individual prosecutions of 890 Japanese defendants (40 of whom stood trial more than once).[7] A total of 533 of the 930 prosecutions of Japanese accused ended in convictions carrying terms of imprisonment; and 287 were sentenced to death, of whom 220 were eventually executed.[8]

In Hong Kong, which is the focus of this chapter, the British military courts tried 123 accused, resulting in 21 being shot or hanged, 86 sent to prison, and 14 set free (see Table 2.2).

## 1.1 Sources

The mandate and direct source of law for British military courts, including those in post-War Hong Kong, was the aforementioned Royal Warrant of 18 June 1945. The body of the Warrant is only a few lines long. It makes 'provision for the trial and punishment of violations of the laws and usages of war committed during any war' in which the King had been engaged since 2 September 1939.

To the Royal Warrant were annexed the Regulations for the Trial of War Criminals ('Regulations for the Trial of War Criminals').[9] These provided that the rules of procedure that applied to courts-martial under the Army Act (1926)[10] ('Army Act 1926') would also apply to the military courts to the extent amended by those Regulations. Within this framework, the new military courts were to operate as if they were field general courts-martial.[11] The model was really just a point of departure because, as discussed later, it became heavily modified.

[6] Pritchard, 'British Postwar War Crimes Courts: The Gift of Clemency' (n 5) 15. Little scholarship exists on the British military courts in Southeast Asia; see Pritchard, 'The Historical Experience of British War Crimes Courts in the Far East' (n 2); Rogers, 'War Crimes Trials under the Royal Warrant' (n 1); Pritchard, 'British Postwar War Crimes Courts: The Gift of Clemency' (n 5); and S Linton, 'Rediscovering the War Crimes Trials in Hong Kong, 1946–48 (2012) 13(1) MJIL 284 ('Linton, "Rediscovering the War Crimes Trials in Hong Kong, 1946–48"'). On the background decisions leading to the Southeast Asia trials, see Linton, 'Rediscovering the War Crimes Trials in Hong Kong, 1946–48', 288–91.

[7] Pritchard, 'British Postwar War Crimes Courts: The Gift of Clemency' (n 5) 15–16. These calculations have fluctuated over time. See Pritchard, 'The Historical Experience of British War Crimes Courts in the Far East' (n 2) 321, for Pritchard's early numbers. Bloxham's estimates are different again: 'just over a thousand Axis nationals and collaborators were tried by British military courts'; Donald Bloxham, 'British War Crimes Trial Policy in Germany, 1945–1957: Implementation and Collapse' (2003) 42(1) *J Brit Studies* 91 ('Bloxham, "British War Crimes Trial Policy in Germany, 1945–1957"') 108.

[8] Pritchard, 'British Postwar War Crimes Courts: The Gift of Clemency' (n 5) 16.

[9] Great Britain War Office, Regulations for the Trial of War Criminals Attached to Royal Warrant 0160/2498, 18 June 1945, Promulgated by the War Office, Army Order 81 of 1945 ('Regulations for the Trial of War Criminals').

[10] Army Act, Rules of Procedure, 1926, reproduced in *Manual of Military Law 1929* (Edition Reprinted December 1939), including amendments up to 31 December 1928, S.R.O. 989/1926 ('Army Act, Rules of Procedure (1939)').

[11] Regulations for the Trial of War Criminals (n 9) art 3 ('the provisions of the Army Act and the Rules of Procedure made pursuant thereto so far as they relate to Field General Courts-Martial and to

The general procedure of the Army Act 1926 for courts-martial, as well as the special provisions for field general courts-martial, were detailed in the British *Manual of Military Law 1929 (as amended)*.[12] The evidence rules applicable to courts-martial (and therefore also to the new military courts, unless provided otherwise) were to comply as much as possible with the procedural law and traditions that had been developed in the civil courts of England.[13] To further complicate matters, in Southeast Asia, the rules of procedure of the Army Act 1926, as qualified by the Regulations for the Trial of War Criminals, were further qualified, but also elaborated with a view to practical implementation, by an 'Instruction' issued by the Allied Land Forces, South-East Asia ('ALFSEA') Command ('ALFSEA Instruction').[14]

To those involved in the trials, the substantive law must have been even more difficult to pin down than the applicable procedure.[15] The difficulty was to be expected, considering that trials for 'violations of the laws and usages of war' in international law had rarely been conducted before. In the sphere of conventional international law, Japan had ratified the 1907 Convention (IV) Respecting the Laws and Customs of War on Land (with annexed Regulations),[16] but not the 1929 Convention Relative to the Treatment of Prisoners of War.[17] Most of the Hong Kong cases would deal with prisoner of war ('POW') mistreatment, so Japan's non-ratification of the 1929 Convention created a serious lacuna in the applicable conventional law. Other cases would deal with incidents on the High Seas, to which the 1907 Convention, as indicated by its title, did not extend.

An especially tough legal problem was the derivation from the conventional international law of the time of individual criminal responsibility for the so-called 'violations'—an intricate task, at a time when a breach of international law, unless it were a case of piracy, was synonymous with state responsibility.

The alternative to treaty law was to look to customary international law as a source of both the substantive criminal law and individual criminal responsibility. The difficulty in deriving usable law from custom—ie, a legal rule so specific as to

any matters preliminary or incidental thereto or consequential thereon shall apply so far as applicable to Military Courts under these Regulations and any matters preliminary or incidental thereto or consequential thereon in like manner as if the Military Courts were Field General Courts-Martial and the accused were persons subject to military law charged with having committed offences on active service').

[12] Great Britain War Office, *Manual of Military Law 1929* (7th edn, Great Britain War Office 1929) (Reprinted December 1939) (HMSO, 1940) 43–68. The 7th edition underwent amendments in 1936 (the replacement of ch XIV) and in 1944 (an amendment to para 443 of ch XIV). This chapter employs the short reference '*Manual of Military Law 1929 (as amended)*'.

[13] *Manual of Military Law 1929 (as amended)*, 70.

[14] Allied Land Forces South-East Asia, *War Crimes Instruction No 1, 2nd Edition* (4 May 1946), File No WO 32/12197, UK National Archives ('ALFSEA Instruction').

[15] See also the other chapters in this book dealing with the substantive law.

[16] Signed at The Hague, 18 October 1907. Germany, the United Kingdom, and the United States all ratified the Convention on 27 November 1909; Japan ratified on 13 December 1911.

[17] Signed at Geneva, 27 July 1929. Japan signed on that date, but never ratified. The United Kingdom ratified the Convention on 23 June 1931, the United States on 16 January 1932, and Germany on 21 February 1934.

facilitate the criminal prosecution of an individual—is an order higher than deriving law from available treaties. The content of legal custom for war crime prosecutions was remarkably imprecise in 1946, when there existed nothing like today's mass of international case law and the general state approval of it. In the immediate post-War period, elaborate and rather moralizing arguments had to be mustered to demonstrate any judicial consensus on the rules of customary international law applying to war criminals—as the judgment of the IMT Nuremberg illustrates.[18]

In the resulting uncertainty, the prosecutors at British military courts often cited ordinary UK criminal law to elucidate the applicable substantive law, even though the court was supposedly trying the accused under international law.[19] Linton has observed that 'what was actually used in these courts is probably correctly described as a hybrid of international and domestic law'.[20] Besides being a hybrid, it was ad hoc—a made-up law (if 'law' is the right term for it). Because the military court judges did not allow motions dealing with such questions of legality and did not themselves attempt to elucidate the law, the underlying uncertainty about the applicable law rarely surfaced in the military court proceedings.

The sources of procedural and substantive law for the British military courts were therefore multiple, indistinct, and, one may presume, difficult to make sense of in their combined effect, especially in a court system where, as we shall see, legal expertise was rare, the process was abbreviated, and the Defence was straight-jacketed.

## 1.2 The model trial procedure under the Army Act 1926

The Regulations for the Trial of War Criminals and the ALFSEA Instruction together combined to make the trial procedure of British military courts in the ALFSEA Command different from standard UK court-martial procedure. How fundamental was the difference? Methodologically, it makes sense to start with this question, to reduce the risk of anachronism. If the standard court-martial is to be our main reference point for understanding the post-War military courts, and those in Hong Kong in particular, an understanding of the elements of the model procedure for courts-martial is necessary. The outline in Box 2.1 will be supplemented later in the chapter with more detail to facilitate the contrast.

The Army Act 1926 created three types of court-martial: district, general, and field general. The difference between the first two types went mainly to subject-matter jurisdiction (serious charges like murder could not go before a district court-martial), whereas the difference between the general and field general courts-martial

[18] Pritchard comments, rather inaccurately, that '[a]lthough the Courts sometimes considered infractions of customary as well as conventional law, invariably the Japanese cases were judged according to standards which had been established or declared in international treaties to which the majority of civilized states subscribed'; Pritchard, 'The Historical Experience of British War Crimes Courts in the Far East' (n 2) 315–16.

[19] For example, *Trial of WO Omura Kyoshi* (HKWCT Collection, File No WO235/893) ('*Trial of WO Omura Kyoshi*'), slides 73–4.

[20] Linton, 'Rediscovering the War Crimes Trials in Hong Kong, 1946–48' (n 6) 300.

**Box 2.1**

Basic steps in British court-martial procedure (c. 1946). The procedure served as the model for British military courts. The main difference, at the level of abstraction shown here, was that the Judge Advocate (step 6) was removed from the military court trial process and given instead a much-attenuated role in connection with confirmation (step 9). Other differences between the two systems become apparent at the next level of detail, which is developed throughout the rest of the chapter.

1. *Case documentation presented to judges.* On the court-martial assembling, the President of the judicial panel was to be given the charge-sheet and the summary (or abstract) of the evidence.[21] (The summary was prepared during the investigation phase and presented to the Convening Officer for onward distribution to the trial participants. The role of the Convening Officer is examined later in the chapter.)
2. *Opening Address.* The Prosecutor could make an Opening Address (or had to, if so instructed by the court). The address was to state the substance of the charge against the accused and the nature and general effect of the evidence which the Prosecutor proposed to adduce in support of the charge.[22]
3. *Prosecution evidence.* The evidence for the Prosecution was to be taken next. Prosecution evidence was to be limited to what was relevant to the facts alleged in the statement of particulars in the charge, and no evidence was to be allowed that would not have been admissible according to the rules of the civil courts in England.[23]
4. *Defence evidence.* The accused was then to be asked whether he wished to give evidence as a witness himself, and whether he intended to call any other witnesses to the facts of the case.[24] In the Hong Kong context, where no accused appeared without representation, the two relevant domestic sub-procedures at this point were:
    (a) *If the accused wished to give evidence himself and call witnesses of fact*: Counsel for the accused could make an Opening Address. The accused was then to give his evidence and call his witnesses, including, if he so wished, character witnesses. After the evidence of all the witnesses was taken, Counsel for the accused could make a Closing Address, to which the Prosecutor had a right of reply.[25]
    (b) *If the accused did not wish to give evidence himself but intended to call witnesses of fact*: The accused could make a statement giving his account of the subject of the charge. The statement could be made orally or in writing, but the accused was not to be sworn and no question was to be put to him by the court or

(*Continued*)

[21] Army Act, Rules of Procedure (1939) (n 10) art 22(A).
[22] Army Act, Rules of Procedure (1939) (n 10) art 39(B).
[23] Army Act, Rules of Procedure (1939) (n 10) arts 39(C) and 73(A).
[24] Army Act, Rules of Procedure (1939) (n 10) art 40(B). For simplicity, but also for accuracy, the masculine pronoun is used throughout the chapter.
[25] Army Act, Rules of Procedure (1939) (n 10) art 41(A).

**Box 2.1** *Continued*

anyone else. If the accused made no such statement, his Counsel could make an Opening Address. The accused was then to call his witnesses, including any character witnesses. After the evidence of all the witnesses was taken, Counsel for the accused could make a Closing Address, to which the Prosecutor had a right of reply.[26]

5. *Questioning by Court.* After completion of re-examination of a witness by the Prosecution, the President, Judge Advocate (if one had been appointed), and, with the permission of the President, any judicial member, could question a witness before he or she withdrew.[27]
6. *Summing up by Judge Advocate.* The Judge Advocate (who was normally appointed in legally or factually complex cases) was to sum up in open court the whole case for the court, unless the Judge Advocate and the court were both of the view that a summing up was unnecessary.[28]
7. *Deliberation.* The court was to deliberate on its finding in private. The opinion of every member of the court as to the finding was to be given orally on each charge separately. The opinions of the members of the court were to be taken in succession, beginning with the junior in rank.[29]
8. *Sentence.* Wherever possible, the court, before deliberating on the sentence, was to take evidence of the character, age, service, rank, and any 'recognised acts of gallantry or distinguished conduct' of the accused. The court was to award one sentence in respect of all the offences of which the accused was found guilty.[30]
9. *Confirmation.* Proceedings, except those leading to acquittal, were to be transmitted as soon as possible to the Confirming Officer for confirmation. The Confirming Officer could direct the re-assembly of the court for the revision of the finding or sentence, in which case he had to state the reasons for revision. A finding of acquittal did not require confirmation.[31]
10. *Promulgation.* The charge, finding, and sentence, and any recommendation as to mercy, together with the confirmation or non-confirmation of the proceedings, were to be promulgated in such a manner as the Confirming Officer directed.[32] Promulgation involved certain record-keeping formalities, but its essence was to conclusively inform the accused of the outcome of the trial.

was one of operational context—in particular the existence of, and proximity of the proceedings to, armed conflict. A field general court-martial was a wartime field court equipped to dispense necessary justice in the context of hostilities. It could be

[26] Army Act, Rules of Procedure (1939) (n 10) art 41(B).
[27] *Manual of Military Law 1929 (as amended)* (n 12) 55.
[28] Army Act, Rules of Procedure (1939) (n 10) art 42(A).
[29] Army Act, Rules of Procedure (1939) (n 10) arts 43 and 69(C).
[30] Army Act, Rules of Procedure (1939) (n 10) arts 46(A) and 48.
[31] Army Act, Rules of Procedure (1939) (n 10) arts 50, 51(A), and 51(B).
[32] Army Act, Rules of Procedure (1939) (n 10) art 53.

convened without a convening warrant, by any officer commanding a detachment of troops 'abroad', by the commanding officer of any corps on active service, or by any officer in immediate command of a body of forces on active service.[33]

No explanation of the choice to designate the British military courts as field general courts-martial was supplied by the UK government, although we may surmise (see later in the chapter) that the procedural economy of a field general court-martial was a major consideration.[34]

## 1.3 Approach in this chapter

Rules of procedure are best understood in the context of their application in practice. One reason for this is that, as we know from general experience, formal rules are not always strictly followed, not even by courts. There is no rule that fits every situation. Equity considerations, time pressures, discretions, oversights, errors, and so forth, can cause a court to depart from formal rules, or make up its own rules. Deviation and innovation will be considered lawful or unlawful depending on the legal and cultural context. Only actual court practice, as found in court records or participant commentary on court practice, can tell us if, and to what extent, formal rules were followed.

For the record of court practice, this chapter, like much of this book, draws on the Hong Kong military courts' archive of transcripts, exhibits, submissions, and associated formal documents. For participant commentary, it draws on the text of a 2011 interview of Professor Linton with Major Murray Ormsby, a military court Judge and later Prosecutor in several of the Hong Kong trials.[35] I have also drawn on a short published account by Peter Vine, another Hong Kong Prosecutor.[36]

A larger methodological issue concerns the criteria that might be applied to assess British military court practice in Hong Kong in the period 1946–48. What could be the basis of an evaluation of a court process carried out in extraordinary circumstances more than 60 years before our time and which ran for less than three years? One basis of assessment, as I have indicated, is the degree of departure from the normally applicable British court-martial procedure current at the time. Similarities and differences would provide a basis for reflection on how the trials of Japanese were viewed by the British according to their own standards of military justice. Another basis of assessment is the degree to which the stated principles governing the trials (their desired aims and objectives) were complied with in practice by the courts and by the authorities associated with them. Thirdly, we

[33] *Manual of Military Law 1929 (as amended)* (n 12) 67.

[34] Answers may yet come to light from the unexplored areas of the UK national archives.

[35] Suzannah Linton, Record of Two Interviews with Major Murray I. Ormsby, on 21 July 2011 and 4 August 2011 ('Linton, "Record of Two Interviews with Major Murray I. Ormsby"'), available in full at <http://hkwctc.lib.hku.hk/exhibits/show/hkwctc/accountsoftrials/oral>, and published in extracted form in this collection. I have relied on the full version.

[36] Peter Vine, 'Experiences as a War Crimes Prosecutor in Hong Kong' (1995) 35 *Journal of the Hong Kong Branch of the Royal Asiatic Society* 205 ('Vine, "Experiences as a War Crimes Prosecutor in Hong Kong"').

could look to the aftermath of the trials, and in particular to the manner in which the military court system was wound up. In section 5.2 I discuss how the legacy of the trials had, already by 1949, become a political liability for Britain. Within a few years, all convicts had been freed. A fourth plausible basis of assessment is to consider the ways in which contemporaries of the trials themselves evaluated them; unfortunately, I have not been able to locate any material in this category.[37]

## 2. British Military Court Structure

### 2.1 Jurisdiction

The Royal Warrant defined a 'war crime' as a violation of the laws and usages of war committed during any war since 2 September 1939. According to Rogers, the definition was wide enough to cover alleged perpetrators who were military personnel as well as civilians 'and the nationals of occupied countries and neutral countries who were in the employ of the enemy'.[38] In the ALFSEA Instruction, issued in the wake of the Royal Warrant, the personal jurisdiction of the military courts was narrowed: they were to have jurisdiction over members of the Japanese armed forces, as well as over civilians of Japanese nationality who were attached to those forces or were in the service of the occupying power.[39]

The reach of the personal jurisdiction is illustrated in the *Toda et al* case. All the accused were civilians in the service of the Japanese army.[40] They worked at the Kinkaseki Nippon Mining Company. In his petition following his conviction, Toda, who had been the mine's general manager,[41] argued that he was never attached to the Japanese army and had never served as a civilian attached to that army. He claimed that the army had taken a unilateral decision to make the POWs work in the mine, absolving him of any responsibility for their welfare.[42] The Judge Advocate reviewing the trial was of the view that the petition should be dismissed.[43] As was often the case with such reviews, the Judge Advocate gave no reasons for disagreeing with individual points in the petition. The Court's decision, including

[37] Pritchard finds a 'lack of publicity given to the Japanese trials in the British press'; this, he claims, contributed to the 'remarkable freedom of action enjoyed by the British Minor War Crimes Courts'; Pritchard, 'The Historical Experience of British War Crimes Courts in the Far East' (n 2) 315.

[38] Rogers, 'War Crimes Trials under the Royal Warrant' (n 1) 796–7. Rogers writes that '[a]lthough, in theory, British nationals could have been tried under the Royal Warrant, they were in practice dealt with in the ordinary courts': at 797.

[39] ALFSEA Instruction (n 14) art 38. On the military courts' personal jurisdiction, see also Pritchard, 'The Historical Experience of British War Crimes Courts in the Far East' (n 2) 317–18; see moreover at 319–20, where Pritchard questions the conflation of Japanese servicemen and civilians (in particular the conflation of war crimes and civil offences) for the purposes of jurisdiction.

[40] For a discussion of the case, see Linton, 'Rediscovering the War Crimes Trials in Hong Kong, 1946–48' (n 6) 328–31.

[41] *Trial of Toda Mitsugu and eight others* (HKWCT Collection, File WO235/1028) ('*Trial of Toda Mitsugu and 8 others*'), slide 117.

[42] *Trial of Toda Mitsugu and eight others* (n 41) slides 117–21.

[43] *Trial of Toda Mitsugu and eight others* (n 41) slide 5. The procedures for reviewing, petitioning, and so on, are discussed later in the chapter.

the implicit assertion of jurisdiction over Toda, was upheld by the Convening Officer.[44]

Another accused, Inouye, was a civilian born in British Columbia. In his petition against conviction he challenged the jurisdiction of the military court, arguing that it was never intended that British subjects should be tried by such courts, and that since the completion of the trial he had obtained documentary evidence to prove his Canadian nationality.[45] The Judge Advocate wrote in his advice to the Convening Officer that there was no doubt that Inouye was a Canadian subject. 'Such being the case he is not amenable to the jurisdiction of a War Crimes Court and his trial was invalid.'[46] He advised that should the Confirming Officer agree and refuse to confirm the proceedings, the effect would be that Inouye could be deemed not to have been tried at all. He could accordingly be tried by the civil authorities in Hong Kong or sent to Canada to stand trial there.[47]

According to the ALFSEA Instruction, the British military courts were to concentrate on 'minor' war criminals. These were persons alleged to have committed war crimes on a relatively small scale. A 'minor' war crime, in the ALFSEA Instruction's definition, included killing without justification, commission of torture and other forms of ill-treatment causing the infliction of bodily harm, and withholding sufficient food, water, or medical care.[48] 'Major' war criminals were those responsible for 'organized brutalities and the design and execution of plans for acts of aggression'. They were to be tried by the international tribunals.[49]

The majority of the cases that came before the British military courts concerned the torture, beating, or execution of small numbers of victims in isolated incidents.[50] Torture linked with interrogation was very commonly charged. Indeed, in the narrative of the Hong Kong courtrooms, Japanese torture had settled into standard types. As alleged against the *Kempeitai*, in particular, the main types were water torture, electric torture, throwing the victim through the air blindfolded, beatings, and burning.[51] Of one prisoner, it was said that he had been subjected to 'the usual tortures'; they included savage beatings and water torture.[52] The use of

[44] *Trial of Toda Mitsugu and eight others* (n 41) slide 10.

[45] *Trial of Inouye Kanao* (HKWCT Collection, File No WO235/927) ('*Trial of Inouye Kanao*'), slide 9.

[46] *Trial of Inouye Kanao* (n 45) slide 5.

[47] *Trial of Inouye Kanao* (n 45) slide 5. For more on the temporal jurisdiction of the Hong Kong courts, see Linton, 'Rediscovering the War Crimes Trials in Hong Kong, 1946–48' (n 6) 305–7.

[48] ALFSEA Instruction (n 14) arts 3–4.

[49] ALFSEA Instruction (n 14) art 2. See also Vine, 'Experiences as a War Crimes Prosecutor in Hong Kong' (n 36) 205–6.

[50] Pritchard, 'The Historical Experience of British War Crimes Courts in the Far East' (n 2) 313.

[51] *Trial of Maj Hirao Yoshio* (HKWCT Collection, File No WO235/1098) ('*Trial of Maj Hirao Yoshio*'), slide 5. See also *Trial of Sgt Maj Matsunobu Shigeru* (HKWCT Collection, File No WO235/894) ('*Trial of Sgt Maj Matsunobu Shigeru*'), slide 5 ('The ill-treatment described included beatings, suspension by thumbs or wrists and water torture'); *Trial of Sgt Maj Yokohata Toshiro* (HKWCT Collection, File No WO235/1117) ('*Trial of Sgt Maj Yokohata Toshiro*'), slides 4–5 (water torture and electrical torture).

[52] *Trial of Sgt Kawamoto Kaname* (HKWCT Collection, File No WO235/921) ('*Trial of Sgt Kawamoto Kaname*'), slide 6.

Alsatian dogs to attack and bite prisoners was also, on the evidence, amongst the usual tortures.[53]

In addition to conventional war crimes, the ALFSEA zone military courts were to have jurisdiction over 'crimes against the laws of humanity'. These were defined in the ALFSEA Instruction as 'crimes and atrocities committed by Japanese or satellite enemy nationals against civilians of whatever nationality during the continuance of hostilities'.[54] In the Instruction's terminology, this class of crime was also to be regarded as a class of 'war crimes' even though (as with the 'crimes against humanity' referred to in the Charter of the IMT Nuremberg[55]) it was a novel category of crime that had no basis in treaty law.[56] No mandate was mentioned for this additional jurisdiction, which is surprising considering that it represents a departure from the very mandate of the Royal Warrant itself. Vine, the Hong Kong Prosecutor, recalled, cryptically, that '[t]he range of offences to be tried as war crimes was never precisely defined, but broadly concerned "offences against humanity"'.[57] In practice, no crime against humanity was charged by the British Prosecutors in Hong Kong.[58]

Under rules applying to a normal court-martial trying a British subject, the accused was able to raise a jurisdictional objection to a charge in an indictment on the ground that it did not disclose an offence under the Army Act 1926.[59] While the Regulations for the Trial of War Criminals took away many other rights, they did not infringe on this one. It was, however, a minor technical right, good for challenging an erroneously formulated charge-sheet but no good for litigation going beyond such formalities. It was not utilized by any of the Hong Kong accused.

Considering that the subject-matter jurisdiction of the British military courts was much more nebulous than that of a regular court-martial, the Japanese defendants could have developed a variety of jurisdictional objections, had they been free to raise them. However, the normal right of a British accused before a court-martial to offer a plea to the court's general jurisdiction and give evidence in support of it ('The accused, before pleading to a charge, may offer a special plea to the general jurisdiction of the court'[60]) was annulled by the Regulations for the Trial of War Criminals.[61] Evidently this was done to avoid bogging down the

[53] For example, *Trial of Capt Shibata Shigeo and Sgt Maj Oba Takao* (HKWCT Collection, File No WO235/1007), slide 4.

[54] ALFSEA Instruction (n 14) art 5.

[55] IMT Nuremberg Charter, art 6(c), 82 UNTS 279 (8 August 1945).

[56] See, eg, M M deGuzman, 'The Road from Rome: The Developing Law of Crimes against Humanity' (2000) 22(2) HRQ 335. Pritchard is thus not right to say that the British military courts were 'restricted to the trial of *conventional war crimes* committed by Japanese since the outbreak of the Anglo-German war in September 1939'; Pritchard, 'The Historical Experience of British War Crimes Courts in the Far East' (n 2) 315 (emphasis added).

[57] Vine, 'Experiences as a War Crimes Prosecutor in Hong Kong' (n 36) 206.

[58] Linton, 'Rediscovering the War Crimes Trials in Hong Kong, 1946–48' (n 6) 307.

[59] Army Act, Rules of Procedure (1939) (n 10) art 32.

[60] Army Act, Rules of Procedure (1939), art 34(A); and *Manual of Military Law 1929 (as amended)* (n 12) 53.

[61] Regulations for the Trial of War Criminals (n 9) art 6 ('The accused shall not be entitled to . . . offer any special plea to the jurisdiction of the Court').

courts in preliminary motions about their legality and the applicable law. The curtailment of that jurisdictional plea in the legally blurred context of national trials for international crimes was one important factor contributing to the swiftness of the Hong Kong proceedings (see Table 2.3).

While an accused before a British military court was not allowed motions on general jurisdiction, the Prosecutor still had to prove that he fell within the court's personal jurisdiction and that the alleged crime was committed within the court's temporal jurisdiction. Thus there was some room for litigation of jurisdictional issues. In *Ito Junichi (No 1)*, the Prosecutor addressed the matter of jurisdiction in his Closing Address. He said that, even though the crimes charged were alleged to have taken place on 17 August 1945, which post-dated Japan's surrender,

> No question arises as to the Court's jurisdiction to hear a case describing events after the surrender because the Royal Warrants [sic] have provided for Courts to be set up to try suspects for offences committed in any war in which Great Britain finds herself engaged in since September 1939; and the surrender, though a cessation of hostilities, does not mean legally an end of the War.[62]

## 2.2 Court constitution

Four British military courts were established in Hong Kong.[63] They dealt with cases from Hong Kong itself, Kowloon, and the New Territories, as well as China (Taiwan, and Waichow, and Shanghai on the mainland), occupied Japan, and the High Seas.[64]

In the original UK system, the officer convening a court-martial (Convening Officer) was to appoint the military officers to form the court.[65] In the case of the courts in the ALFSEA Command, the Commander of Land Forces, Hong Kong, was deemed to be the Convening Officer.

Being equivalent to a field general court-martial, a British military court needed three members to constitute a judicial panel.[66] In having three members, it was the size of a district court-martial, even though hierarchically it was equivalent to a general court-martial, which required five.[67] While the Regulations provided that a military court was to consist of 'at least' two officers in addition to the President,[68]

[62] *Trial of Sgt Maj Ito Junichi (No 1)* (HKWCT Collection, File No WO235/914) ('*Trial of Sgt Maj Ito Junichi (No 1)*'), slide 30. See also the Prosecutor's Final Address in *Trial of Lt Kishi Yasuo and fourteen others* (HKWCT Collection, File WO235/993) ('*Trial of Lt Kishi Yasuo and fourteen others*'), slide 541 ('the final surrender did not take place until September 2 on board the battleship Missouri').

[63] Linton, 'Record of Two Interviews with Major Murray I. Ormsby' (n 35) 1. See also ALFSEA Instruction (n 14) art 27.

[64] Linton, 'Rediscovering the War Crimes Trials in Hong Kong, 1946–48' (n 6) 285.

[65] Army Act, Rules of Procedure (1939) (n 10) art 17(D).

[66] *Manual of Military Law 1929 (as amended)* (n 12) 68 ('A field general court-martial has the same power as a general court-martial, provided that the court is composed of at least three officers').

[67] A general court-martial's members were moreover to be more senior than district court-martial appointees, and with longer service experience. *Manual of Military Law 1929 (as amended)* 45–6. A district court-martial could not award a sentence higher than two years' imprisonment; at 44.

[68] Regulations for the Trial of War Criminals (n 9) art 5.

suggesting that a three-member panel was merely the lower threshold and that more members could be appointed, there was never, in fact, a Hong Kong panel with more than three judges on it.

As we have noted, a field general court-martial was a kind of pared-down general court-martial reserved for the context of military exigency. Subject to the preservation of basic requirements of justice, the speed of its operation could be adjusted to fit the exigency: 'a large number of rules which are applicable to district or general courts-martial should be applied to a field general court-martial so far as is practicable'.[69] In 1946, with the War over, there was no military exigency in the ALFSEA zone, let alone in Hong Kong itself.[70] In circumstances of relative peace, a British serviceman charged with a crime carrying the death penalty would be tried by a five-member panel. The fact that the three-member field general court-martial model was chosen for the Japanese accused before the British military courts could indicate that at the time the decision was taken to establish those courts, the British were still concerned about the stability of the military situation. More likely, though, it is a measure of the justice that the system was intended to dispense to Japanese accused in Hong Kong and to Axis accused elsewhere: it was to be a summary justice, facilitated by many time-saving devices, foremost among which was the smaller panel of judges empowered to impose the death penalty on former enemy servicemen and nationals.[71]

The accused before the British military courts were not entitled to object to the person appointed as President or to any member of the court.[72] This was another right of the Defence under the original, domestic, model that was not carried over to the military courts.[73]

The Army Act 1926 provided that in the case of a general court-martial, four at least of the members were not to be below the rank of captain,[74] and that in no case should an officer under the rank of captain be a member of a court-martial for the

[69] *Manual of Military Law 1929 (as amended)* (n 12) 68.

[70] British troops had retaken Hong Kong on 30 August 1945: F S V Donnison, *British Military Administration in the Far East, 1943–46* (HMSO 1956) 152. By the beginning of the next year, '[t]he situation in the Far East was . . . relatively placid': Pritchard, 'The Historical Experience of British War Crimes Courts in the Far East' (n 2) 315.

[71] Linton quotes UK Foreign Secretary Ernest Bevin's statement from 29 September 1945 that 'our reputation in Germany and the Far East is certainly dependent to a great extent upon the expedition and efficiency with which these trials are carried through': Linton, 'Rediscovering the War Crimes Trials in Hong Kong, 1946–48' (n 6) 293.

[72] Regulations for the Trial of War Criminals (n 9) art 6.

[73] See Army Act, Rules of Procedure (1939) (n 10) art 25(A) ('The order convening the court shall be read in the hearing of the accused and the court shall ascertain that it is constituted of officers to whom the accused makes no reasonable objection'). This was further detailed in the section of the rules setting out the field general court-martial procedure ('The names of the president and members of the court will be read over in the hearing of the accused persons, and they will be asked if any of them objects to be tried by any of those officers. If any accused person objects to an officer, and any member of the court thinks the objection reasonable, steps will be taken to try the accused before a court composed of officers against whom he has no reasonable objection'; art 110), a provision specifically annulled through the Regulations for the Trial of War Criminals (n 9) art 3.

[74] Army Act, Rules of Procedure (1939) (n 10) art 21(A).

trial of a field officer.[75] The Regulations were less directive, providing that if the accused was an officer, the Convening Officer was to 'try' to appoint to the panel as many officers as possible of equal or superior relative rank to the accused.[76] At the Hong Kong trials, all the Presidents held the rank of Lieutenant Colonel; there was always at least one panel member at the rank of major; and the lowest-ranked member was a captain (unless a second major had been appointed), except in one case where the third member was a plain lieutenant.[77]

There is no evidence that any effort was made at the Hong Kong military courts to try accused persons more senior in relative rank to Lieutenant Colonel by one or more judges of equal or superior rank. This impacted on the fortunes of the Japanese accused not simply at the level of relevant judicial expertise (both factual and legal) but also on the point of military honour: a lowly ranked tribunal would have been experienced by senior Japanese officers as a humiliation.

The Regulations provided that if the accused belonged to Japan's Navy or Air Force, the Convening Officer was to appoint at least one Navy officer or Air Force officer, as the case may be, as a member of the court, if feasible.[78] The same rule was reiterated in the ALFSEA Instruction.[79] It was clearly intended to improve the combined understanding among panel members of wartime conditions and service traditions. It did have an effect on the constitution of one Hong Kong panel. In *Sakonju and Mayazumi*, the first-named accused was a Rear Admiral in the Japanese Navy. The Convening Officer responded semi-appropriately by appointing a Lieutenant Commander of the Royal Navy as a court member.[80] (In this case, the service rule was complied with but not the rank rule.)

Where a *victim* of an alleged war crime was a member of the Royal Navy or Royal Air Force, the Convening Officer was *obliged* to invite the senior local Royal Navy or Royal Air Force officer onto the court as a member.[81] The rule was not always observed in practice. In the *Hockley* case (*Col. Tamura Teichi et al*), where the victim was a Royal Navy pilot, all three panel members were from the Army.[82] It is possible that an invitation to the Navy was extended, and declined, but we have no evidence either way. In the *Kyoda* case (also known as the *Lisbon Maru* case), the accused was a Captain in Japan's merchant fleet who was pressed into the service of the Japanese Army. He was charged with a war crime committed against British POWs while on the High Seas. A Lieutenant Commander of the Royal Navy was

[75] Army Act, Rules of Procedure (1939) (n 10) art 21(B).

[76] Regulations for the Trial of War Criminals (n 9) art 5.

[77] *Trial of Capt Yoshimi Taneyoshi and six others* (HKWCT Collection, File No WO235/1099), slide 3.

[78] Regulations for the Trial of War Criminals (n 9) art 5.

[79] ALFSEA Instruction (n 14) art 43(e)–(f).

[80] *Trial of R Adm Sakonju Naomasa and Capt Mayazumi Haruo* (HKWCT Collection, File No WO235/1089) ('*Trial of R Adm Sakonju Naomasa and Capt Mayazumi Haruo*'), slide 25.

[81] ALFSEA Instruction (n 14) art 43(e)–(f).

[82] *Trial of Col Tamura Teichi and two others* (HKWCT Collection, File No WO235/1021) ('*Trial of Col Tamura Teichi and two others*'), slide 71.

appointed as one of the judges.[83] It is not clear whether this was in response to Kyoda's status, or to the status of one or more of the POW victims. More likely, it was in simple recognition of the Royal Navy's interest in this case.

The sittings of military courts were to be open to the public.[84] The court could, on the grounds of 'national interest', the interests of justice, or 'for the effective prosecution of war crimes generally, or otherwise', prohibit the publication of any evidence given or any statement made in the course of the proceedings, or direct that the public was to be excluded during any part of the proceedings, except during the announcement of the finding or sentence.[85] Ormsby recalled that although proceedings were indeed open, it was rare to have anyone in the audience. The exception was in notorious cases like *Kishi et al*[86] and *Noma*[87] which generated interest leading to increased attendance.[88] In *Kyoda*, too, the proceedings opened before a crowded courtroom; on the last day of trial, the room was crowded again.[89] According to Vine, 'the Hong Kong Commodore sent out a signal that all Naval Officers not on sea duty were to attend the opening of the [*Kyoda*] trial in No. 1 uniform with medals and swords'.[90] One wonders whether such an overt and spectacular level of interest might not have been meant to intimidate the accused—and perhaps even the judges.

## 2.3 Judges' legal qualifications and duties

The President of a British military court was to be legally qualified unless a legal qualification was deemed 'unnecessary'. by the Convening Officer.[91] In the military courts for the Far East, the President was to be seconded from the staff of ALFSEA's Department of the Judge Advocate General ('DJAG') in Singapore.[92]

As seen in Table 2.1, most of the Hong Kong court Presidents were lawyers. However, the President with the third-heaviest case load, Lieutenant Colonel Wait, was not legally qualified. There is no information on why in this particular case the Convening Officer considered the appointment of a qualified lawyer to the position of President unnecessary. Another point to note is that not all Presiding Judges were actually taken from DJAG. President Ball and President Warwick, in addition to President Wait, were from other divisions.

83 *Trial of Kyoda Shigeru* (n 4) slide 6.

84 Regulations for the Trial of War Criminals (n 9) art 8(v).

85 Regulations for the Trial of War Criminals (n 9) art 8(v).

86 *Trial of Lt Kishi Yasuo and fourteen others* (n 62).

87 *Trial of Col Noma Kennosuke* (HKWCT Collection, File No WO235/999) ('*Trial of Col Noma Kennosuke*').

88 Linton, 'Record of Two Interviews with Major Murray I. Ormsby' (n 35) 11, 18.

89 Vine, 'Experiences as a War Crimes Prosecutor in Hong Kong' (n 36) 207; and Tony Banham, *The Sinking of the Lisbon Maru: Britain's Forgotten Wartime Tragedy* (Hong Kong University Press 2006) ('Banham, *The Sinking of the Lisbon Maru: Britain's Forgotten Wartime Tragedy*') 243.

90 Vine, 'Experiences as a War Crimes Prosecutor in Hong Kong' (n 36) 207.

91 ALFSEA Instruction (n 14) art 26.

92 ALFSEA Instruction (n 14) art 26(a).

**Table 2.1** Presiding Judges, their qualifications, and case loads at the British military courts in Hong Kong.

| Rank and name | Qualification* | Home unit | Cases presided over |
|---|---|---|---|
| Lt Col. R C Laming | Barrister | DJAG India | *Ito Junichi (No 1)*<br>*Kamada Yasushi*<br>*Kuwaki Kiyomori and Nakajima Tokuzo*<br>*Kyoda Shigeru*<br>*Obata Chikuro and seven others*<br>*Ogasawara Haruji and Kawai Hisao*<br>*Oita Yoshijiro and Ashida Tsumoru*<br>*Sakonju Naomasa and Mayazumi Haruo*<br>*Shibata Shigeo and Oba Takao*<br>*Shoji Toshishige*<br>*Tamura Teiichi and two others*<br>*Tanaka Ryosaburo*<br>*Tashiro Toranosuke and two others*<br>*Toda Mitsugu and eight others*<br>*Tokunaga Isao and four others*<br>*Tsubota Kanji*<br>*Uete Taichi and seven others* |
| Lt Col. J C Stewart | Solicitor | DJAG India | *Hanada Zenji and three others*<br>*Inouye Kanao*<br>*Kawamoto Kaname*<br>*Kishi Yasuo and fourteen others*<br>*Matsuda Kenichi*<br>*Matsunobu Shigeru*<br>*Miyasue Suekichi*<br>*Niimori Genichiro*<br>*Omura Kyoshi*<br>*Yabuki Rikie and two others*<br>*Yamada Kiichiro and Awa Isao* |
| Lt Col. N G Wait | Not legally qualified | Intelligence Corps | *Hirao Yoshio*<br>*Kanazawa Asao*<br>*Kuwano Nobuyuki*<br>*Nakano Junichi and two others*<br>*Ozawa Tomukichi*<br>*Sato Choichi*<br>*Sazawa Hideo and two others*<br>*Ushiyama Yukio and three others*<br>*Yoshimi Taneyoshi and six others* |
| Lt Col. C F Ball | Barrister | DJAG India | *Honda Isamu*<br>*Ito Junichi (No 2)*<br>*Noma Kennosuke*<br>*Suzuki Nobue and three others*<br>*Tamaki Koji and two others* |
| Lt Col. P Warwick | Barrister | Royal Army Service Corps | *Ito Takeo*<br>*Omura Kyoshi and four others* |
| Lt Col. S R Kerr | *[Not stated]* | General List | *Yokohata Toshiro* |
| Lt Col. L A Massie | Solicitor | *[Not stated]* | *Kinoshita Eiichi and Yoshida Bunzo* |

* The information on the judges' legal qualifications (or lack thereof) is from the 'Order convening the Court' in each case.

There was provision in the ALFSEA Instruction for the appointment of a 'legal member' to the panel of judges.[93] A legal member, if appointed, would have powers additional to those of ordinary members. In particular, he would be entitled to put any questions he thought proper to witnesses without having to seek the President's permission; and the other judges would be obliged to consult him before any decision was taken on a point of law or procedure.[94] As it happened, no legal member was appointed to the Hong Kong courts.

The question thus arises whether some Hong Kong trials (at least those under Lieutenant Colonel Wait) were conducted wholly by persons without a legal qualification. This appears to have been the case. The panel members below the President had no training in the law, as far as it is possible to tell. Like the ordinary members of courts-martial, ordinary members of British military courts were not expected to be legally qualified. Moreover, the judges in Hong Kong had no personal legal advisors to help them with the law.[95] More importantly, no Judge Advocate was ever appointed to a Hong Kong panel (see further later in the chapter). We may conclude from these facts that in several of the Hong Kong cases, legal knowledge or advice on substance or procedure was meagre or non-existent.[96]

This situation risked a fundamental departure from the courts' objectives. Among the duties of a British court-martial President was to ensure that justice was administered and that the accused had a fair trial. The accused was not to suffer any disadvantage 'in consequence of his position as a person under trial or of his ignorance, or of his incapacity to examine or cross-examine witnesses or to make his own evidence clear or intelligible'.[97] These challenging duties of the Presiding Judge were carried over undiminished to the British military courts. In this new context, they were rendered even more challenging by the courts' limitations on jurisdictional motions, the absence of a Judge Advocate, abbreviated procedures including a heavy reliance of affidavit evidence (see later), and the practice of assigning one Counsel to multiple accused (Table 2.2). The linguistic obstacles confronting Japanese defendants also implied a need for a court sensitive to fair-trial rights. It is hard to see how a legal qualification, at least for the President of the Court, could have been considered unnecessary in such circumstances.

At the level of the ordinary panel member there appears to have been a great diversity of military experience, but the idea of a war crime was in fact a novelty. It was not as firmly rooted in the officer corps as it is today. Major Ormsby's experience illustrates the point. He was the ordinary member of the Hong Kong panels about whom we have a relative wealth of background information. As a Judge, he served mostly under the presidency of Lieutenant Colonel Stewart,

[93] ALFSEA Instruction (n 14) art 43(g).

[94] ALFSEA Instruction (n 14) art 43(g).

[95] Linton, 'Record of Two Interviews with Major Murray I. Ormsby' (n 35) 10, 15. Nor, for that matter, did the prosecuting staff: at 21–2, 40. Ormsby went from being a Judge (without legal qualifications) to being a Prosecutor. When he needed legal advice, he asked one of his fellow Prosecutors: at 23.

[96] Linton, 'Record of Two Interviews with Major Murray I. Ormsby' (n 35) 40.

[97] Army Act, Rules of Procedure (1939) (n 10) art 59(B).

including in important cases such as *Kishi*[98] and *Noma*.[99] He had no prior court-martial experience.[100] 'I wasn't qualified, legally qualified, to do it',[101] 'I was a simple soldier'.[102] At the Sandhurst Royal Military Academy, where he trained as an officer, war crimes was not a topic he could recall studying.[103] His first court-related assignment, under the direction of the DJAG in Singapore, was as a Defence Advisory Officer on procedure. In this role he came to know for the first time about war crimes and the fundamentals of criminal proceedings. Looking back on the experience, he wondered: 'How was I to know the court martial procedure?'[104] '[I had] no training. I used to sit in the War Crimes court in Singapore where they noticed me.'[105] He learned through experience[106] and by putting '2 and 2 together'.[107]

Ormsby did not remain a lowly Defence Advisory Officer for long. He was recruited to a judicial position in the Hong Kong military courts following a chance encounter in a Singapore bar with Lieutenant Colonel Stewart. Already appointed to a presidency position, Stewart was on the lookout for ordinary members to complete his panel.[108] The offer delighted Ormsby, as it 'would have been a pleasure from [the alternative of] soldiering in the sticks somewhere'.[109] As a Major, he would be the panel's senior member, one level under the President.[110] According to Ormsby, his progression from soldier with no legal experience to a judicial position in the trials of Japanese for war crimes was not atypical. The local force was, as he put it, '[a] reservoir . . . of learning lawyers or would-be lawyers or trained lawyers who could be inveigled to join the War Crimes court'.[111]

## 2.4 The Judge Advocate

Under the rules of procedure of the Army Act 1926, a Judge Advocate was necessary for every general court-martial. The appointment of a Judge Advocate was optional only at the district court-martial, which as we have noted was limited to lesser offences.[112] The importance of a Judge Advocate to trials with higher potential consequences for the accused is indicated by the fact that the omission to

98 *Trial of Lt Kishi Yasuo and fourteen others* (n 62).
99 *Trial of Col Noma Kennosuke* (n 87).
100 Linton, 'Record of Two Interviews with Major Murray I. Ormsby' (n 35) 2–8.
101 Linton, 'Record of Two Interviews with Major Murray I. Ormsby' (n 35) 17.
102 Linton, 'Record of Two Interviews with Major Murray I. Ormsby' (n 35) 26.
103 Linton, 'Record of Two Interviews with Major Murray I. Ormsby' (n 35) 41. As late as 1966, the laws of war were not being taught at British military academies: G I A D Draper, 'The Place of the Laws of War in Military Instruction' (1966) 111 (643) *RUSI Journal* 189, 193–4.
104 Linton, 'Record of Two Interviews with Major Murray I. Ormsby' (n 35) 7.
105 Linton, 'Record of Two Interviews with Major Murray I. Ormsby' (n 35) 8.
106 Linton, 'Record of Two Interviews with Major Murray I. Ormsby' (n 35) 20; 'I just picked up knowledge really and I thought I could do it', Ormsby said about the time leading up to his appointment as Prosecutor (see later).
107 Linton, 'Record of Two Interviews with Major Murray I. Ormsby' (n 35) 21.
108 Linton, 'Record of Two Interviews with Major Murray I. Ormsby' (n 35) 7.
109 Linton, 'Record of Two Interviews with Major Murray I. Ormsby' (n 35) 8.
110 Linton, 'Record of Two Interviews with Major Murray I. Ormsby' (n 35) 8.
111 Linton, 'Record of Two Interviews with Major Murray I. Ormsby' (n 35) 8.
112 Army Act, Rules of Procedure (1939) (n 10) art 101(A).

appoint a Judge Advocate at a general court-martial was sufficient to invalidate the entire proceedings.[113]

In the case of a field general court-martial, in view of the implicit circumstances of military exigency, the Convening Officer was not obliged to appoint a Judge Advocate.[114] The Regulations attached to the Royal Warrant provided that if no Judge Advocate were appointed to a military court, 'the Convening Officer should appoint at least one officer having one of the [recognized] legal qualifications . . . as President or as a member of the Court, unless, in his opinion . . . no such officer is necessary'.[115] The same arrangement is reflected in the ALFSEA Instruction, which provided that if a 'legal member' were not appointed to the court, his duties were to be carried out by a Judge Advocate, 'if appointed'.[116] In other words, both the Regulations and the ALFSEA Instruction made the appointment of a legally qualified officer to a military court whether as a legal member or as Judge Advocate advisable but optional. If a Judge Advocate were appointed, he was to be nominated by the ALFSEA zone's DJAG and appointed in the convening order.[117]

As already noted, Judges Advocate were not appointed to any of the Hong Kong trials. We know that a Singapore-based DJAG officer did once attend a Hong Kong trial as an observer—that is, as an ordinary member of the audience.[118] But even this was the exception. So what role did Judges Advocate finally play in the Hong Kong trials? The brief answer is that they had a hands-off role, consistent with the expedited track on which these trials were run. Based in Singapore, the Judges Advocate limited themselves to file reviews of the Hong Kong trials.[119]

Under the original, domestic, court-martial model, the presence of a Judge Advocate compensated for the fact that even a general court-martial (having the power to try serious offences and impose the death penalty on the accused) could be made up of officers without any legal qualification. The Judge Advocate was responsible for informing the court of any informality or irregularity in the proceedings;[120] he was to provide court-martial members with a summing-up of the facts if they were difficult or complicated; he was to issue 'special legal directions' where they were required; and he was to be present during deliberations on the court's finding.[121] In deciding questions of law, a court-martial was expected to be guided by the advice of the Judge Advocate.[122] The integrity of the court-

[113] *Manual of Military Law 1929 (as amended)* (n 12) 50.
[114] *Manual of Military Law 1929 (as amended)* (n 12) 68.
[115] Regulations for the Trial of War Criminals (n 9) art 5.
[116] ALFSEA Instruction (n 14) art 43(g).
[117] ALFSEA Instruction (n 14) art 43(c).
[118] See *Trial of Lt Gen Kinoshita Eiichi and Sgt Yoshida Bunzo* (HKWCT Collection, File No WO235/1116) ('*Trial of Lt Gen Kinoshita Eiichi and Sgt Yoshida Bunzo*'), slide 15 ('Having carefully considered these Proceedings and attended the trial on two days [out of a total of 15 trial days], I am of the opinion that the case was well conducted').
[119] Linton, 'Rediscovering the War Crimes Trials in Hong Kong, 1946–48' (n 6) 310.
[120] Army Act, Rules of Procedure (1939) (n 10) art 103.
[121] *Manual of Military Law 1929 (as amended)* (n 12) 57.
[122] *Manual of Military Law 1929 (as amended)* (n 12) 69.

martial system, which did not provide for appeal to a higher court, depended among other things on the presence of Judges Advocate in complex cases.

Importantly from the Defence perspective in the domestic model, the court-martialled accused stood directly to benefit from the appointment of a Judge Advocate. As provided for in the Army Act 1926, he was entitled to the Judge Advocate's opinion on any question of law or procedure, and while the Prosecutor could also benefit from such advice, the Judge Advocate 'will be careful to maintain an entirely impartial position'.[123] Equally with the President, the Judge Advocate had the duty to ensure that the accused did not suffer any disadvantage. For that purpose, he could, for example, advise the court that witnesses should be called or recalled 'for the purpose of being questioned by [the accused] on any matters which appear to be necessary or desirable for the purpose of eliciting the truth'.[124]

At the Hong Kong trials, the Judge Advocate's role was essentially limited to provision of a summary of the completed trial proceedings for the benefit of the Convening Officer, together with advice to the same person on the confirmation or non-confirmation of the verdict and sentence. The near complete physical absence of the Judge Advocate from the Hong Kong military courts could be attributed to postwar personnel shortages and the appointment of appropriately qualified Presidents (in most cases)—but more fundamentally, it seems to me, it is explained by the intent to effect summary proceedings. From the Defence point of view, an impartial (in principle) source of legal advice had been denied to the Japanese accused in a victor/vanquished context which was in any case weighted against the accused.

On the positive side, and in the absence of a court of appeal in the system of military courts, the Judge Advocate did take on certain review-like functions. These will be discussed shortly, in connection with the Defence petitioning system.

Besides reviewing individual cases, in advising the Convening Officer, the Judge Advocate occasionally commented on matters of uniformity of practice. After several trials had been held at the Hong Kong courts, a defendant was in a position to complain that the punishment he had received was higher than that in a comparable decided case. The Judge Advocate on one such occasion wrote in his advice to the Convening Officer that while 'it is correct to mitigate punishments so that they are uniform', the Convening Officer was under no obligation to reduce a later sentence (15 years' imprisonment) to bring it into line with an earlier sentence (12 years' imprisonment), arising from similar circumstances, if the earlier sentence appeared to him to be too light—for if he were to do so, the result would be *two* sentences that did not 'fit the crime'.[125]

[123] Army Act, Rules of Procedure (1939) (n 10) art 103.
[124] Army Act, Rules of Procedure (1939) (n 10) art 103.
[125] *Trial of Sgt Maj Yokohata Toshiro* (n 51) slide 6.

## 2.5 Duties of the Prosecutor

Under the Army Act 1926, the Prosecutor's duty was to assist the court-martial in the administration of justice, to conduct himself impartially, to present the whole case before the court, and not to suppress any evidence in favour of the accused.[126]

In the ALFSEA context, the Prosecutor had little to do with case preparation. The war crime investigation units (see next section) were responsible for building up cases against suspects by collecting documentary evidence and contacting witnesses. The Prosecutor was to work from a summary of the evidence and from a file of the underlying material prepared by the investigation unit.[127] He was given only about a day to familiarize himself with a case before the trial began.[128] He would meet the witnesses for the first time when they came to court.[129] These practices are of course further indicators of the summary character of the Hong Kong trials. They limited the Prosecutor's knowledge of the case as well as that of the Defence.

According to the ALFSEA Instruction, the Prosecutor was to be legally qualified and have the rank of 'Major Legal'.[130] Like the President of a military court, the Prosecutor was to be taken from the staff of ALFSEA's DJAG.[131] We know from Major Ormsby's case that a Prosecutor could also be recruited from the ranks of a judicial panel—another de facto departure from official design. Ormsby came to want 'more action' than sitting on a war crimes bench, so he became a Prosecutor.[132] He was appointed Prosecutor without any formal process—although not quite as accidentally and casually as he was appointed to the position of military court Judge—and despite the fact that he was not legally qualified as was required in the case of a Prosecutor.[133]

As Prosecutor, Ormsby worked on cases including *Toda et al*[134] and *Tamura et al.*[135] (Altogether, he was in 27 of the 46 Hong Kong trials as either Judge or Prosecutor.[136]) The switch from Judge to Prosecutor in the same court is questionable by our standards, as it affects the appearance of judicial impartiality, but there is no record of a contemporary objection to the arrangement.

Peter Vine was another Prosecutor at the Hong Kong courts. A 24-year-old major in the Royal Marines, he studied law from textbooks while on layover in Singapore in early 1946.[137] The Law Society of England posted him the examin-

126 Army Act, Rules of Procedure (1939) (n 10) art 60(A).
127 Linton, 'Record of Two Interviews with Major Murray I. Ormsby' (n 35) 22.
128 Linton, 'Record of Two Interviews with Major Murray I. Ormsby' (n 35) 22–3.
129 Linton, 'Record of Two Interviews with Major Murray I. Ormsby' (n 35) 16.
130 ALFSEA Instruction (n 14) art 26.
131 ALFSEA Instruction (n 14) art 26(a).
132 Linton, 'Record of Two Interviews with Major Murray I. Ormsby' (n 35) 17.
133 Linton, 'Record of Two Interviews with Major Murray I. Ormsby' (n 35) 20.
134 *Trial of Toda Mitsugu and eight others* (n 41) slide 11.
135 *Trial of Col Tamura Teichi and two others* (n 82) slide 73.
136 Linton, 'Record of Two Interviews with Major Murray I. Ormsby' (n 35) 1.
137 Vine, 'Experiences as a War Crimes Prosecutor in Hong Kong' (n 36) 205.

ation papers for solicitors, and he sat the examination aboard his ship.[138] He was at least technically qualified. In June 1946 he was appointed to the military courts and started work on his first case, *Kyoda*.[139]

The sourcing of key Hong Kong court staff (judges and Prosecutors) from ALFSEA's DJAG may have had the effect of diminishing objectivity and perhaps also the appearance of impartiality. Certainly, the fact that the Convening Officer was to appoint the President and the Prosecutor, as well as the Judge Advocate,[140] from the staff of the same office would raise concerns by today's standards. While not all such appointments were from DJAG, most of them were. Some of the judges had been themselves POWs and had been tortured by the Japanese. Ormsby expressed 'surprise' that they were made judges in the military courts.[141] The Defence Advisory Officers and the British Defence Counsel were also DJAG secondments. The military courts allowed for the appointment of native Japanese as Defence Counsel, but there was no independent Defence bar from which to draw in those cases where a Japanese Counsel was not available or not chosen by the accused. Thus, various kinds of conflict became part of the implementation of the British military court system.

A rather colourful Prosecutor was one Captain J F Reilly. He went from Prosecutor in two of the earliest cases[142] to Defending Officer in a third,[143] after which his name does not appear again in the court record, possibly because his combativeness as an advocate was getting out of hand. The Judge Advocate reviewing the *Kishi et al* case noted that Reilly, who had been the Prosecutor in that case, had been withdrawn from further prosecutions (no reason was given).[144] In fact, right after *Kishi*, Reilly had been assigned to *Matsuda*, as Prosecutor, and then as Defending Officer in *Hanada et al*.

Reilly is responsible for the first recorded statement of prosecutorial integrity at the Hong Kong trials:

> It is not the primary function of the Prosecution to come into this Court in Hong Kong, in a spiteful and vindictive spirit, determined that come what may, by hook or by crook, a terrible revenge will be wreacked upon these unfortunate Japanese who stand before you today accused of this dastardly crime. That is not the British way of justice . . . This is no sham trial, but a serious trial.[145]

Exactly 2.5 months after making this statement, Reilly, who had meanwhile switched to the Defence, appears to have changed his mind about the Prosecutor's ways: 'For reasons best known to himself, the Prosecutor has continuously referred

[138] Vine, 'Experiences as a War Crimes Prosecutor in Hong Kong' (n 36) 205.

[139] *Trial of Kyoda Shigeru* (n 4) slide 11.

[140] ALFSEA Instruction (n 14) art 43(c).

[141] Linton, 'Record of Two Interviews with Major Murray I. Ormsby' (n 35) 40.

[142] *Trial of Lt Kishi Yasuo and fourteen others* (n 62) slide 12.

[143] *Trial of Sgt Hanada Zenji and three others* (HKWCT Collection, File No WO235/895) ('*Trial of Sgt Hanada Zenji and three others*'), slide 10.

[144] *Trial of Lt Kishi Yasuo and fourteen others* (n 62) slide 7.

[145] *Trial of Lt Kishi Yasuo and fourteen others* (n 62) slide 603.

to miasma. [. . . M]iasma is that which settles on the surface of a pond and stinks, putrid matter. That is exactly what the Prosecution's case is. It stinks.'[146]

## 2.6 Investigations

A War Crimes Registry was created within ALFSEA to receive, register, and collate information about war crimes.[147] From this information, registry staff were to compile initial cases against suspect staffs of POW camps, as well as suspect individuals, and forward the cases to the War Crimes Legal Section ('Legal Section') at ALFSEA Command.[148]

On the basis of the registry information, the Legal Section was to decide whether there was a *prima facie* case against an alleged war criminal or group of them. Where such a case was established, the Legal Section, through the services of the ALFSEA Convening Officer, was to obtain further evidence, as required, including affidavits from witnesses.[149] These statements were to be sworn before an investigating officer.[150] Where there was difficulty in establishing identity, a photograph of the accused was to be shown to the witness, who was to be asked to recognize it. The fact of recognition was then to be included in the statement.[151] Identification parades—a less leading method—were also used.[152] The investigation report was to be completed by an officer with legal qualifications or experience in criminal investigations.[153]

Certain wartime enemy staffs were to be presumed guilty by the ALFSEA Legal Section, and their members treated to 'automatic arrest', until such time as further investigation confirmed their status as suspects or absolved them. 'All Kempei Tai' fell into the category of presumed guilt along with the staffs of Japanese POW camps.[154] According to Pritchard, Britain had more than 708,000 Japanese surrendered personnel in custody at the end of the War; they had to be processed and guarded in POW camps until arrangements could be made to return them to Japan.[155]

[146] *Trial of Sgt Hanada Zenji and three others* (n 143) slide 229. The Judge Advocate said that these remarks were 'immoderate and verg[ing] on contempt of Court': at 7.

[147] On the background to the establishment of the war crimes office in Singapore, see Linton, 'Rediscovering the War Crimes Trials in Hong Kong, 1946–48' (n 6) 290.

[148] ALFSEA Instruction (n 14) art 9.

[149] ALFSEA Instruction (n 14) art 10(a), 19(c).

[150] ALFSEA Instruction (n 14) Appendix B, cl 2(a).

[151] ALFSEA Instruction (n 14) Appendix B, cl 2(d).

[152] For example, *Trial of Sgt Maj Matsunobu Shigeru* (n 51) slide 5 ('all these witnesses [= 9] had picked out the accused at identification parades'). In *Yamada and Awa*, the Defence argued that because two witnesses had failed to identify Yamada in identification parades and had identified him only in the dock, their identification evidence should be discredited: *Trial of Sgt Maj Yamada Kiichiro and Sgt Awa Isao* (HKWCT Collection, File No WO235/887) ('*Trial of Sgt Maj Yamada Kiichiro and Sgt Awa Isao*'), slide 10. See also *Trial of Sgt Kawamoto Kaname* (n 52) slide 66.

[153] ALFSEA Instruction (n 14) Appendix B, cl 1.

[154] ALFSEA Instruction (n 14) art 15.

[155] Pritchard, 'British Postwar War Crimes Courts: The Gift of Clemency' (n 5) 20.

The screening of Japanese POWs was to be carried out by special teams. The teams were instructed to separate enemy personnel into those 'surrendered' (to be returned to Japan at the earliest opportunity) and those likely to be put on trial.[156] A subset of the former group would also serve as insider and expert witnesses in the trials. Dozens of Japanese servicemen were prevailed upon to give testimony for the Prosecution.[157]

The commanders of the formations directly under ALFSEA Command were made responsible for the apprehension and detention of suspected war criminals and for assisting with the investigation of war crimes in their areas.[158] Altogether 18 investigation teams, each with a staff of about 15, were established in ALFSEA's zone. Two of the teams were assigned to Hong Kong itself.[159] Linton writes that, as of July 1946, of the 10,000 Japanese captured in Hong Kong after the surrender, 239 were held as suspected war criminals; other suspects were sent to Hong Kong from across Asia, including from occupied Japan.[160]

Once a case had been investigated and was ready for trial, the Legal Section was to transmit to the Convening Officer the draft charge-sheet, an abstract of the evidence, and the file of underlying material.[161] The Convening Officer was to have copies made of all these items for distribution to the Prosecutor, and, as appropriate, to the accused, and, in due course, to the Presiding Judge.[162] The commanding officer of the unit having charge of the accused[163] was to send an officer to formally charge him. After charging, the officer was to request the accused to state in writing his intentions with regard to his defence.[164]

War crimes suspects not formally charged were to be segregated from other persons in military detention. Once charged they were to be placed in solitary confinement and remain in solitary confinement until the completion of their trial.[165] Although the Hong Kong trials were relatively brief once they got started, the waiting time for the accused could run into months. By today's standards, solitary confinement is an extreme measure, regarded primarily as a form of punishment. It tends to have a distressing effect on the defendant and degrade the conduct of his defence. There is no explanation in the court archive of the decision to impose solitary confinement on the Japanese accused in the ALFSEA zone. We may presume that it was a measure against collusion. Whether it was enforced in every case and whether it constituted a departure from accepted practice at the time are questions that I have not been able to determine.

156 ALFSEA Instruction (n 14) art 15(f)–(g).
157 Vine, 'Experiences as a War Crimes Prosecutor in Hong Kong' (n 36) 208.
158 ALFSEA Instruction (n 14) art 11, 19(a).
159 ALFSEA Instruction (n 14) arts 22–3.
160 Linton, 'Rediscovering the War Crimes Trials in Hong Kong, 1946–48' (n 6) 297, 305.
161 ALFSEA Instruction (n 14) art 41. The commanding officer was therefore not required himself to prepare the abstract or summary of evidence, as stated in the Regulations for the Trial of War Criminals (n 9) art 4.
162 ALFSEA Instruction (n 14) art 41.
163 Regulations for the Trial of War Criminals (n 9) art 4.
164 ALFSEA Instruction (n 14) art 45.
165 ALFSEA Instruction (n 14) art 18.

## 3. Proof

### 3.1 Witness evidence

Questioning in chief, cross-examination, and re-examination of witnesses was allowed in the military courts as much as in the British domestic courts-martial.[166] Leading or suggestive questions in chief were not allowed.[167] The two systems had this elementary adversarial architecture in common, but diverged in important respects.

In the regular court-martial setting, it was the duty of the court to see that the rules of evidence were strictly adhered to. Evidence was required to be: relevant to the issue; the best evidence that could be obtained; not impermissible hearsay; except in the case of experts, not a mere expression of opinion;[168] and if the evidence were in the form of a document, the document was to be of a kind that was legally admissible.[169] These same rules were allowed to carry over to military courts without regulatory obstruction, as such, but in practice, as I discuss in the next section, the common-law barriers to the admission of evidence were much reduced in the Hong Kong trials.

The intention revealed in the ALFSEA Instruction was that witness evidence was to be presented orally, if possible: 'The Convening Officer will ensure the personal attendance of as many witnesses as possible required by the prosecution or defence.'[170] In certain Hong Kong cases, a good proportion of the witnesses did in fact testify orally.[171] In a subset of these cases, the Prosecutor arranged matters in a way such that the evidence was led primarily through the live testimony of the key eyewitnesses. In *Matsunobu*, for example, of the nine civilian victims mentioned in the charge, seven were called as witnesses and testified to having suffered various forms of ill-treatment by the accused in the course of interrogations.[172]

More commonly, though, the evidence consisted of a mix of witnesses on the stand and investigator-produced witness statements (declarations, affidavits) by persons who were not called to testify.[173] For example, in *Tokunaga*, a trial lasting more than 50 days, evidence consisted of witnesses on the stand, written statements by persons not called, and exhibits consisting largely of POW records.[174]

166 *Manual of Military Law 1929 (as amended)* (n 12) 55; Army Act, Rules of Procedure (1939) (n 10) art 84(A).

167 *Manual of Military Law 1929 (as amended)* (n 12) 55.

168 The general rule was that the opinion or belief of a witness is not evidence. A witness was to speak only to the particular facts which he or she had seen, heard, or otherwise observed (*Manual of Military Law 1929 (as amended)* (n 12) 88).

169 *Manual of Military Law 1929 (as amended)* (n 12) 98.

170 ALFSEA Instruction (n 14) art 54.

171 For example, *Trial of Lt Kishi Yasuo and fourteen others* (n 62) slide 7.

172 *Trial of Sgt Maj Matsunobu Shigeru* (n 51) slide 5.

173 For example, *Trial of Col Sazawa Hideo and two others* (HKWCT Collection, File No WO235/1029), slide 4.

174 *Trial of Col Tokunaga Isao and four others* (HKWCT Collection, File No WO235/1012) ('*Trial of Col Tokunaga Isao and four others* (Part One)'), slide 13.

The presence of written statements in the evidence mix set the military courts distinctly apart from the courts-martial, as I discuss in more detail in the next section. Suffice to note here that the use of witnesses' previous statements gave rise to a variety of difficulties. The Prosecutor's practice—rare, but still remarkable—of putting a statement in evidence when the author of the statement was in court and able to testify drew criticism (albeit long after the fact) by the Judge Advocate, who pointed out that the practice meant that the Defence was not being given the opportunity to cross-examine the witness even though cross-examination in such a case was perfectly feasible.[175] In another instance, the Judge Advocate reviewing the case for the Convening Officer expressed disagreement with a Presiding Judge who had allowed the Prosecutor to put a previous statement to his own witness. The Judge Advocate said that it was tantamount to the Prosecutor cross-examining his witness and also refreshing the witness's memory.[176] In *Tanaka*, the Presiding Judge acknowledged that the Regulations allowed both sides 'considerable latitude in producing evidence, which in normal Courts will be regarded as hear-say [sic], and it is for the Court to estimate the value, if any, of such evidence'.[177]

In the *Sato* case, the Judge Advocate determined in his report that the Prosecutor had misled the Court in a manner prejudicial to the accused. The matter arose in relation to the cross-examination of witnesses as to evidence they had given in other proceedings. The Defence Counsel had attempted to question the witnesses as to that evidence, 'as he was perfectly entitled to do'. The Prosecutor then 'improperly pressed' the Defence Counsel to indicate the discrepancy that supposedly existed between the two. The Prosecutor argued that the statements made in the other trial should have been produced in court before the relevant questions were put in cross-examination. The Court had come down on the side of the Prosecutor. The Judge Advocate observed that this was 'nonsense': the 'proceedings of an earlier trial are not themselves admissible in evidence though they may be used to refresh the memory of the witness'. He cautioned that the Defence should have been allowed freely to question the witnesses on their previous statements.[178] Yet the opportunity had been lost to the accused, who was convicted. *Sato* was presided over by the legally unqualified Lieutenant Colonel Wait. Had the Judge Advocate been present at the trial, as demanded in domestic cases, the error might have been avoided.

Such examples underscore the fact that the use of prior witness statements in a common law setting is a complex area of evidence law which, if mishandled, could result in prejudice to the accused. The challenge of fairly handling witness statements makes the case as well as any other procedural issue for the presence of legal expertise in the courtroom.

Continuing with our review of the judicial control of the evidence, judicial members of the Hong Kong panels were entitled to question witnesses after re-

175 *Trial of WO Omura Kyoshi* (n 19) slide 6.

176 *Trial of WO Omura Kyoshi* (n 19) slide 6.

177 *Trial of Maj Gen Tanaka Ryosaburo* (HKWCT Collection, File No WO235/1030) ('*Trial of Maj Gen Tanaka Ryosaburo*'), slide 225.

178 *Trial of Sato Choichi* (HKWCT Collection, File No WO235/1027) ('*Trial of Sato Choichi*'), slide 5.

examination had been completed. They were to put their questions through the President. Ormsby said that, in his experience, questioning by ordinary members rarely happened.[179] The Court was entitled to take 'judicial notice' of all matters of notoriety, including all matters within their general military knowledge,[180] such as 'the laws and usages of war'.[181] It was said to be improper of the parties to the proceedings to draw the attention of a witness to facts, whether stated by that witness or another, and then to ask for the witness's opinion as to their accordance with military usage, because the court was the only proper Judge of that.[182] However, while this was true of domestic courts-martial, in the military courts the judges were largely ignorant of the military law of their former enemies. Several witnesses were called to give evidence on Japan's service regulations. In one case, the Prosecutor called a Japanese naval officer, Minoru Yokota, to explain Japan's regulations on the respective responsibilities of the ship's captain and the commanding officer of troops on board a ship.[183] Experts were also used for other purposes. In *Matsunobu*, in order to prove the seriousness of the treatment inflicted on the victims in the case, which allegedly included beating and water torture, the Prosecutor relied on the expert evidence of a doctor.[184]

A field general court-martial 'may, if necessary, view any place'.[185] Court-martial judges under the original system could refine their knowledge of matters relating to a case by visiting crime-site locations. The purpose of a 'view' was to help them to understand the evidence.[186] This power carried over to the military courts. The Hong Kong panels undertook several views. On 28 April 1947, a panel conducted a site visit at Repulse Bay. Besides the judges, present were the Prosecutor, the accused, the Defence Counsel, the Defence Advisory Officer, interpreters, and a shorthand writer.[187] The accused was subjected to questioning by the judges in the course of the view.[188] In another case, the group that assembled for a view of the Hong Kong central police station was considerably larger, with four accused and two witnesses present.[189] In the *Kamada* case, at the close of the Defence case, the Court visited both the central police station and the former *Kempeitai* station at Stanley Prison. The judges examined cells and rooms and conducted tests to ascertain whether the witnesses could have seen or heard what they had testified

[179] Linton, 'Record of Two Interviews with Major Murray I. Ormsby' (n 35) 12.
[180] Army Act, Rules of Procedure (1939) (n 10) art 74.
[181] Regulations for the Trial of War Criminals (n 9) art 8(iii).
[182] *Manual of Military Law 1929 (as amended)* (n 12) 89.
[183] *Trial of Kyoda Shigeru* (n 4) slides 19–30.
[184] Trial of *Sgt Maj Matsunobu Shigeru* (n 51) slides 32–4.
[185] Army Act, Rules of Procedure (1939) (n 10) art 119(D).
[186] *Manual of Military Law 1929 (as amended)* (n 12) 69.
[187] *Trial of Maj Gen Tanaka Ryosaburo* (n 177) slide 174. For background on this case, see Charles G Roland, 'Massacre and Rape in Hong Kong: Two Case Studies Involving Medical Personnel and Patients' (1997) 32(1) *JCH* 43.
[188] *Trial of Maj Gen Tanaka Ryosaburo* (n 177) slides 175–7.
[189] *Trial of Capt Ushiyama Yukio and three others* (HKWCT Collection, File No WO235/1041) ('*Trial of Capt Ushiyama Yukio and three others*'), slides 206–19.

to. The witnesses called to the view were asked to point out locations they had referred to in their in-court testimony.[190]

Under the rules of the Army Act 1926, the Prosecutor was not bound to call all the witnesses whose evidence was in the summary of evidence given to the accused. Nevertheless, the Prosecutor was normally expected to call all those Prosecution witnesses listed in the evidence summary whom 'the accused desires to be called, in order that the accused may, if he thinks fit, cross-examine them'.[191] At the Hong Kong trials, there was occasional concern expressed that key witnesses were not being called because their evidence could be more simply introduced in affidavit form. In one case, the Judge Advocate commented in his report to the Convening Officer that he would have liked to see the Prosecutor give a detailed explanation of his failure to call a particular witness.[192] This was not necessarily out of concern for Defence interests, as is clear from another case, where the Judge Advocate wrote:

> To my mind it is most unfortunate that no evidence was forthcoming from any of the P.O.W. Doctors or the medical orderlies, who must have been in continual contact with the accused; their testimony, if available, would undoubtedly have strengthened the Prosecution case [and] might possibly have resulted in the award of deservedly severe sentences.[193]

The Defence retained the entitlement to respond to the Prosecution's evidence with a submission of 'no case to answer', without calling any witnesses. In one case, the Defence contended that there was no proof that the relevant Japanese infantry unit had had anything to do with certain alleged crimes. The submission was accepted and the accused was acquitted of this charge.[194] Another successful no-case submission was made in the *Omura et al* case by the accused Kawai.[195]

## 3.2 Calling witnesses for the Defence

The rules of the Army Act 1926 applicable to field general courts-martial provided, simply, that '[t]he Accused will be asked what he has to say in his defence, and shall be allowed to make his defence'.[196] As elaborated in the more general parts of the Act, the accused was to be informed that, on his giving the names of any witnesses whom he wished to call to testify in his defence, reasonable steps would be taken to secure their attendance.[197] The Convening Officer or, after assembly of the court, the Court President, was to give orders to facilitate the attendance of witnesses

[190] *Trial of Sgt Maj Kamada Yasushi* (HKWCT Collection, File No WO235/1057) ('*Trial of Sgt Maj Kamada Yasushi*'), slide 8.

[191] Army Act, Rules of Procedure (1939) (n 10) art 75.

[192] *Trial of WO Omura Kyoshi* (n 19) slide 6.

[193] *Trial of Sgt Tashiro Toranosuke and two others* (HKWCT Collection, File No WO235/905) ('*Trial of Sgt Tashiro Toranosuke and two others*'), slide 10.

[194] *Trial of Maj Gen Shoji Toshishige* (HKWCT Collection, File No WO235/1015), slide 3.

[195] *Trial of WO Omura Kyoshi and four others* (HKWCT Collection, File No WO 235/1112) ('*Trial of WO Omura Kyoshi and four others*'), slides 268–9.

[196] Army Act, Rules of Procedure (1939) (n 10) art 116.

[197] Army Act, Rules of Procedure (1939) (n 10) art 15(A).

whom the accused wished to call and whose attendance could 'reasonably be procured'. The accused could be required to undertake to defray the cost of a witness's attendance.[198]

In transitioning this domestic procedure to the military courts, the ALFSEA Instruction provided that the accused was entitled to call any witness whom he may 'reasonably desire' to call. Where the Convening Officer considered such attendance 'unnecessary', the accused in theory could still call that witness if he was prepared to cover the costs of transportation and upkeep,[199] although the de facto indigence of the detained Japanese servicemen rendered this option unlikely. Given the time pressures on each trial, where the summoning of a Defence witness from a 'distant place' could risk postponement of the start of the trial, the Convening Officer was to require the accused to give reasons why the attendance of such a witness was necessary; and, if not satisfied with the reasons, he was to turn down the request, irrespective of any funds available to cover transportation costs.[200]

This arrangement led to several complaints, such as the following one from the Closing Address on behalf of the accused Matsuda:

> The prisoner had desired to call witnesses . . . who were the men closely connected with this case—his own O.C., the medical officer who operated on the deceased [who had been wounded in the course of alleged ill-treatment by the accused] and others. He was not able to do so. . . . It was due to the fact that the General Officer Commanding considered that in view of the great trouble and expense . . . the evidence available was not sufficiently material.[201]

By contrast, in the high-profile case of *Kyoda*, the accused was permitted to call a number of witnesses from Japan.[202]

These restrictions on Defence witnesses did not apply, formally, to the Prosecutor, although undoubtedly the Prosecutor was also working under pressure to get through the cases quickly and dispense with 'unnecessary' witnesses. Still, by the then standards of British court-martial procedure it was certainly a regression in fairness that the Japanese accused were under heavier restrictions than the Prosecutor in the calling of witnesses. A summary defence is rarely possible in factually complex cases, and the British domestic system would not have imposed such tight limits on its own nationals in capital cases.

The limitations on the calling of Defence witnesses caution us that other provisions of the ALFSEA Instruction that were worded generously ('reasonable time must be allowed to the accused for the preparation of his defence'[203]) must be interpreted in the context of a justice that was intended to be summary.

198 Army Act, Rules of Procedure (1939) (n 10) art 78(A).
199 ALFSEA Instruction (n 14) art 51.
200 ALFSEA Instruction (n 14) art 52.
201 *Trial of Sgt Matsuda Kenichi* (HKWCT Collection, File No WO235/846) ('*Trial of Sgt Matsuda Kenichi*'), slide 90.
202 Vine, 'Experiences as a War Crimes Prosecutor in Hong Kong' (n 36) 208.
203 ALFSEA Instruction (n 14) art 52.

The ALFSEA Instruction made provision for a British Defence Advisory Officer. He was to be a liaison link between the Defence Counsel (who in most cases was Japanese[204]), the Convening Officer, and other sections of the court.[205] The Advisory Officer's first duty was to contact the Defence Counsel and arrange for him to interview the accused in jail. He was also to arrange interviews with possible witnesses required by the Defence.[206] Subject to the restrictions discussed, he was responsible for the production in court of the desired witnesses.[207]

Regular court-martial procedure required that, at the close of the evidence for the Prosecution, the accused was to be told by the court that he could give evidence as a witness, but that, if he were to give evidence, he would expose himself to cross-examination.[208] There was also a rule that the decision of the accused not to give evidence was not to be made the subject of any comment by the Prosecutor.[209] These rules applied in principle unaltered to the British military courts. Sometimes, in the Hong Kong trials, the accused was the sole Defence witness.[210]

## 3.3 Hearsay and written witness statements

Under the original court-martial procedure, strict conditions applied to the taking and use of an out-of-court statement by a material witness. It was to be taken on oath if the accused so demanded.[211] For it to be used as evidence in the trial, the following conditions applied: the witness must have died or become insane or fallen so ill as not to be able to appear in court; he or she must have been deposed before a magistrate in the presence of the accused; the accused must have had a full opportunity to cross-examine the witness at the deposition; and the deposition statement must bear the signature of the magistrate before whom it was taken as well as the signature of the deponent.[212]

The Regulations for the Trial of War Criminals considerably relaxed the home-grown rules.[213] British military courts could receive as evidence 'of the facts therein stated any depositions or any record of any military Court of Inquiry or any

204 See Table 2.2.

205 ALFSEA Instruction (n 14) art 49(1)(b).

206 ALFSEA Instruction (n 14) art 49(1)(a).

207 ALFSEA Instruction (n 14) art 49(1)(c).

208 Army Act, Rules of Procedure (1939) (n 10) art 40(A).

209 Army Act, Rules of Procedure (1939) (n 10) art 80(B).

210 For example, *Trial of WO Omura Kyoshi* (n 19) slide 5.

211 Army Act, Rules of Procedure (1939) (n 10) art 3(B).

212 *Manual of Military Law 1929 (as amended)* (n 12) 87. In the context of a domestic court-martial, if the attendance of any witness could not in the opinion of the officer taking the summary statement be readily procured, on grounds which may include 'the expense and loss of time involved', 'a written statement of his evidence purporting to be signed by him may be read to the accused and included in the summary of evidence, provided that, if such person can be compelled to attend, the accused may demand that he shall attend for cross-examination'; Army Act, Rules of Procedure (1939) (n 10) art 4(G).

213 The acceptability of hearsay evidence at the British war crimes courts as contrasted with courts-martial is discussed in Rogers, 'War Crimes Trials under the Royal Warrant: British Practice 1945–1949' (n 1) 789–90, and Pritchard, 'The Historical Experience of British War Crimes Courts in the Far East' (n 2) 315 and fn 10.

summary of any examination made by any officer detailed for the purpose by any military authority'.[214] The accused was to have no right to demand witness depositions to be taken on oath or subject to cross-examination.[215] In cases of death, insanity, or inability to attend to give evidence, as well as in cases where in the opinion of the court the witness could not attend without undue delay, 'the Court may receive secondary evidence of statements made by or attributable to such witness'.[216] Further, any document purporting to have been signed or issued officially by any member of any Allied or enemy force or by any official or agency of any Allied or other government was to be admissible as evidence for the truth of its contents.[217] Even more broadly, 'the Court may receive as evidence of the facts therein stated any diary, letter or other document appearing to contain information relating to the charge'.[218] The lifting of restrictions on hearsay was complete.

As noted in section 3.1, the Hong Kong courts used a mix of written witness statements and viva voce testimony as evidence. There was no rule requiring that more weight be assigned to the latter than the former.[219] In fact, the affidavits were allowed to have as incriminating an effect as anything said by a witness present in court and subject to cross-examination. Charges and whole cases were sometimes proven through written testimonials alone (see later).

This open admission system for documents and, more generally, hearsay evidence, had the effect of extinguishing any nascent Defence 'right' to cross-examination derivable from the Army Act 1926.[220] The Act's strict admissibility criterion which was placed at the front of the process of proof (promoting orality and disallowing the admission of hearsay evidence, with very narrow exceptions) was transformed in the case of military courts into an esoteric weighing exercise at the back of the process: 'It shall be the duty of the Court to Judge of the weight to be attached to any evidence given in pursuance of this Regulation.'[221] The transformed model's effect was to facilitate expedited proceedings by severely restricting adversarial testing of evidence.[222]

214 Regulations for the Trial of War Criminals (n 9) art 8(i)(d).

215 Regulations for the Trial of War Criminals (n 9) art 4.

216 Regulations for the Trial of War Criminals (n 9) art 8(i)(a).

217 Regulations for the Trial of War Criminals (n 9) art 8(i)(b).

218 Regulations for the Trial of War Criminals (n 9) art 8(i)(e). And again: 'At any hearing before a Military Court convened under these regulations the Court may take into consideration any oral statement or any document appearing on the face of it to be authentic, provided the statement or document appears to the Court to be of assistance in proving or disproving the charge notwithstanding that such statement or document would not be admissible as evidence in proceedings before a Field General Court-Martial'; art 8(i).

219 For example, *Trial of WO Omura Kyoshi* (n 19) slide 5.

220 Pritchard thus misses the point when he writes that, at the British military courts, 'access to documentation and rules of evidence concerning the admissibility of hearsay evidence for its probative value remained precisely the same for the Defence and for the Prosecution'; Pritchard, 'The Historical Experience of British War Crimes Courts in the Far East' (n 2) 321. The right to confront one's accuser, nascent though it may have been at the time, was a right only the Defence possessed.

221 Regulations for the Trial of War Criminals (n 9) art 8(i).

222 Vine claims that '[t]ribunals did not attach much weight to affidavit evidence since cross-examination was not feasible': Vine, 'Experiences as a War Crimes Prosecutor in Hong Kong' (n 36) 206. Yet we may wonder how Vine, who was a Prosecutor not a Judge, could have known this.

The compromised model led to protest and confusion. In *Matsunobu*, the Japanese Defence Counsel pleaded that the admitted statement of a Prosecution witness who did not testify in court because he could not be located should not be given any weight. He also asked for the hearsay evidence of two witnesses to be ignored.[223] In the absence of reasons, we do not know if the plea was heeded, but the accused was convicted and sentenced to eight years' imprisonment. Another Japanese Defence Counsel appeared confused by the basic distinction in English law between admitted evidence and weight. In his Closing Address, he twice asked for certain hearsay evidence not to be 'admitted', whereas by this point it had no doubt already been admitted and only the question of weight remained to be decided.[224] If this Counsel truly had not grasped that the evidence of non-testifying witnesses was being admitted throughout the course of the Prosecutor's case, his defence of the accused was proceeding on a very weak footing indeed.

*Tashiro et al* is an example of a case built largely upon affidavit evidence, with only two witnesses testifying in court.[225] In *Kyoda*, the function of the first Prosecution witness was to read into the record two unsworn statement summaries and to present a 'report' that Kyoda himself was said to have written shortly after the major incident which that case concerned.[226] The Prosecutor (Major Vine) then called a series of investigators to the stand to read into the record the affidavits of several of the surviving victims.[227] In the *Yokohata* case, the Prosecutor called no viva voce witnesses to testify about what had happened at the main crime site (the Bridge House in Shanghai). The only two witnesses called testified on secondary issues. The case was supported by numerous depositions, sworn and unsworn, by persons claiming to have been ill-treated by the accused.[228] Counsel for the accused complained that the situation meant that he had not had an opportunity to cross-examine,[229] but the Court's findings were confirmed anyway. In *Tamaki et al*, the Judge Advocate noted the submission in the Defence petition that because of the preponderance of affidavit evidence, the Defence could not cross-examine. He recommended that the complaint be dismissed, giving no reasons.[230]

In *Nakano et al*, the Prosecutor called four witnesses to support two of the charges. With regard to the other four charges, affidavits by high-ranking officers were produced and read in court, without cross-examination.[231] Counsel for Nakano complained that the affidavit evidence 'cannot be held to have the same

Ormsby, who was better placed to know than Vine, did not in any way suggest a lesser role for affidavits when discussing the heavy use made of them at the military courts.

223 *Trial of Sgt Maj Matsunobu Shigeru* (n 51) slide 76.

224 *Trial of WO Yabuki Rikie and two others* (HKWCT Collection, File No WO235/937) ('*Trial of WO Yabuki Rikie and two others*'), slide 81.

225 *Sgt Tashiro Toranosuke and two others* (n 193) slide 9.

226 *Trial of Kyoda Shigeru* (n 4) slides 12–14.

227 *Trial of Kyoda Shigeru* (n 4) slides 15ff.

228 *Trial of Sgt Maj Yokohata Toshiro* (n 51) slide 4.

229 *Trial of Sgt Maj Yokohata Toshiro* (n 51) slide 255.

230 *Trial of Lt Tamaki Koji and two others* (HKWCT Collection, File No WO235/982), slide 4.

231 *Trial of Col Nakano Junichi and two others* (HKWCT Collection, File No WO235/1044), slide 6.

weight as evidence spoken in the court'.[232] The submission was dismissed. The Judge Advocate wrote that it appeared to him that the affidavits in question were substantially true because many of the deponents corroborated one another. 'Even allowing for some exaggeration on the part of the deponents there was ample evidence to support the charges.'[233] This of course is a simplistic view of evidence and evidence-testing, which understates—disingenuously for a lawyer—the power of cross-examination to qualify or extinguish allegations that might seem unshakeable on paper. The Judge Advocate had in effect been placed in the unenviable position of having to rationalize a process that was incompatible with the principles upheld in the Army Act 1926.

In *Yokohata*, the Prosecutor used a single investigator, Major Kyte, to serially read into evidence the statements of all Prosecution witnesses. After each reading the Defence requested cross-examination, and each time the request was denied.[234] The Prosecutor sought, and received, the Court's indulgence of this practice:

> I should like to put it on record that the Prosecution evidence which I have produced to the Court has been entirely written evidence. It has not been possible for me to bring witnesses down from Shanghai due largely to the deteriorating political situation in Shanghai . . . [T]he Court will appreciate that I do not wish to apply for an adjournment for the purpose of bringing live witnesses from such a distant place.[235]

Ormsby, in his 2011 interview, recalled that much of the evidence in the Hong Kong cases was in written form.[236] He mentioned *Toda* as an example of a case built entirely upon affidavits.[237] 'It was new to us. We'd never had to rely on affidavits as Prosecutors, it was the first time ever, I think.'[238] Ormsby acknowledged the problem this created for the Defence, which could not cross-examine witnesses. But he seemed not particularly troubled by it: 'you know, we had to carry on'.[239]

Despite the routine use of written statements as sources of evidence, the ALFSEA Instruction did seek to maintain one aspect of the distinction between direct and indirect evidence. It provided that a witness statement should be recorded in such a way as to make clear whether the witness is speaking of matters 'which he [saw] or heard himself, or of matters of which he has been told'.[240] This gave the Defence an actual platform to complain about the admission of hearsay evidence. In *Hirao*, where the accused was tried for being 'concerned in' the inhumane treatment by his subordinate staff of Chinese and other civilians in *Kempeitai* custody resulting in deaths and suffering,[241] the Defence did not challenge the claim that torture was practised at the *Kempeitai* stations, but contested the admissibility and reliability of

232 *Trial of Col Nakano Junichi and two others* (n 231) slide 451.
233 *Trial of Col Nakano Junichi and two others* (n 231) slide 7.
234 *Trial of Sgt Maj Yokohata Toshiro* (n 51) slides 14–18.
235 *Trial of Sgt Maj Yokohata Toshiro* (n 51) slide 19.
236 Linton, 'Record of Two Interviews with Major Murray I. Ormsby' (n 35) 12, 36.
237 Linton, 'Record of Two Interviews with Major Murray I. Ormsby' (n 35) 36–7.
238 Linton, 'Record of Two Interviews with Major Murray I. Ormsby' (n 35) 36.
239 Linton, 'Record of Two Interviews with Major Murray I. Ormsby' (n 35) 36.
240 ALFSEA Instruction (n 14) Appendix B, cl 5.
241 *Trial of Maj Hirao Yoshio* (n 51) slide 5.

witness testimonies and argued that a large number of witness allegations were hearsay.[242] In *Omura et al*, the Defence complained that 'all evidence' relied on by the Prosecutor was hearsay, as none of the witnesses was an eyewitness to the deaths that allegedly took place.[243] In another case, the Judge Advocate conceded that there was 'considerable hearsay evidence that [a victim] had been water-tortured and severely beaten by the accused'.[244] Nonetheless, the findings of guilt in all of these cases were confirmed without revision.

The conviction of a person for a serious crime on the basis of affidavits alone is problematic enough in an ordinary municipal jurisdiction where the prospect of prosecution for false testimony looms over the deponent. But in the context of the British military-court proceedings, punishment for perjury in a sworn statement was a very unlikely prospect. Even today's relatively powerful and well-resourced ad hoc international tribunals have failed to project any serious threat of prosecution for deliberate falsehood in sworn statements.[245]

## 4. Defence Concerns

Matters of concern to the accused have been touched upon in earlier pages. This part groups the remaining matters, including such vital questions as the accused's legal representation and the preparation time and resources allowed to the Defence.

### 4.1 Representation

Under the Army Act 1926, the Defence and Prosecution were meant to be equal in legal qualifications. If the accused did not intend to be represented by Counsel but Counsel had been obtained on behalf of the Prosecutor, 'the Convening Officer must take steps to inform the accused . . . so that the accused may himself obtain Counsel for his defence, if he so desires'.[246] An alternative to representation by Counsel was representation by a military officer. The officer, who normally had no legal qualifications, was called a 'Defending Officer' (not the same as the Defence Advisory Officer).[247] A Defending Officer had the same functions, rights, and duties as Counsel.[248]

242 *Trial of Maj Hirao Yoshio* (n 51) slides 379–86.

243 *Trial of WO Omura Kyoshi and four others* (n 195) slide 423.

244 *Trial of Sgt Maj Matsunobu Shigeru* (n 51) slide 5.

245 See A Zahar, 'The Problem of False Testimony at the International Criminal Tribunal for Rwanda', in André Klip and Göran Sluiter (eds), *Annotated Leading Cases of International Criminal Tribunals, Vol. 25: International Criminal Tribunal for Rwanda, 2006–2007* (Intersentia 2010) 509–22.

246 *Manual of Military Law 1929 (as amended)* (n 12) 49.

247 Army Act, Rules of Procedure (1939) (n 10) art 87(A); see also art 87(B) ('It shall be the duty of the Convening Officer to ascertain whether an accused person not otherwise represented desires to have a defending officer assigned to represent him').

248 *Manual of Military Law 1929 (as amended)* (n 12) 49.

For the British military courts, the Regulations for the Trial of War Criminals provided that Counsel was to appear on behalf of the Prosecutor and the accused 'in like manner as if the Military Court were a General Court-Martial'[249]—thus transferring across the equality provisions described in the previous paragraph. The ALFSEA Instruction elicited a preference for Defence representation that was legally qualified.[250] Where the Prosecutor was legally qualified and a Defending Officer was appointed, the Defending Officer was also to be legally qualified.[251] As already noted, Japanese Counsel were allowed: '[A]ny person qualified to appear before the Courts of the Country of the accused . . . shall be deemed to be properly qualified as Counsel for the Defence.'[252]

Altogether, the Japanese accused at Hong Kong had four choices of representation: a Japanese Counsel; a British Defending Officer; a civilian lawyer (who 'may be nominated by the British Military Authorities' and whose costs the accused would have to cover); and self-representation.[253] The latter two options were never chosen by the Hong Kong accused. A Defending Officer was appointed in six of the 44 cases (Table 2.2). Not all of them were legally qualified.[254]

In one case, *Kaname*, the Defending Officer, Lieutenant Haggan, made a most superficial job of defending his client, if the length of the Closing Address—a mere 17 lines of text—is anything to go by. (This was too quick even by the standards of the British military courts. A typical length for a defence Closing Address was 9 minutes of reading time, with 19 minutes for the Prosecution.[255] In a few cases, the Closing Addresses were up to three or four times as long.[256]) Kaname was convicted and received a death sentence.[257] In another case, Haggan, in the course of the trial and in his Closing Address, completely overlooked the fact that his client, Inouye, had a claim to having Canadian nationality, which would have defeated the Court's assertion of jurisdiction over him.[258]

The Japanese Defence Counsel all seem to have put in a decent effort at defending, although in the multi-accused cases they must have felt overwhelmed, and in several instances they appeared confused about the law. Some were remarkably well qualified: Sakonju, a Rear Admiral, was defended by a former Judge of the Japanese Naval Military Court.[259]

Ormsby said in his interview that the Japanese Defence Counsel were 'ignorant' of the applicable law[260] and not familiar with the English adversarial system, such

[249] Regulations for the Trial of War Criminals (n 9) art 7.

[250] ALFSEA Instruction (n 14) art 46 (The Convening Officer 'will thereupon appoint a suitable officer, if possible with legal qualifications').

[251] ALFSEA Instruction (n 14) art 46.

[252] Regulations for the Trial of War Criminals (n 9) art 7; see also ALFSEA Instruction (n 14) art 26(c) and 46.

[253] ALFSEA Instruction (n 14) art 46 and Appendix J.

[254] See, eg, *Trial of Sgt Maj Yamada Kiichiro and Sgt Awa Isao* (n 152) slide 8.

[255] *Trial of WO Yabuki Rikie and two others* (n 224) slides 82, 85.

[256] See, eg, *Trial of Kyoda Shigeru* (n 4) slides 463–98.

[257] *Trial of Sgt Kawamoto Kaname* (n 52) slide 67.

[258] *Trial of Inouye Kanao* (n 45) slides 13–14.

[259] *Trial of R Adm Sakonju Naomasa and Capt Mayazumi Haruo* (n 80) slide 30.

[260] Linton, 'Record of Two Interviews with Major Murray I. Ormsby' (n 35) 22.

as the entitlement to make a 'no case to answer' motion for early dismissal of a charge.[261] They were 'too polite' in dealings with the Prosecutor and therefore not as effective as the British Defending Officers assigned to some of the Japanese accused.[262] Even so, Ormsby recalled, 'they [the accused] insisted on having their own lawyers'.[263] The great majority, as we have seen, were granted their request for Japanese Counsel. We know of one case where the accused requested to be assigned an English Counsel in addition to his Japanese Counsel, but the Court was not prepared to wait for the chosen English Counsel to become available, so the accused went to trial represented by his Japanese Counsel only.[264] A request by an accused in another case to have his Japanese Counsel replaced, which was made almost at the end of the trial, was not allowed because it would have made no practical difference, the Court said, except for introducing delay. It appears that the accused, Ushiyama, was frustrated that his Counsel was not asking him the questions that he really wished to answer while testifying in his own defence.[265]

The evidence, however, does not unequivocally support Ormsby's view that the British Defending Officers were more effective than the Japanese Defence Counsel. Their collective result (four death sentences, 15 sentences of imprisonment, and five acquittals) does demonstrate a higher-than-average rate of acquittal, but the set is too small for the difference between the respective performances to be significant.

## 4.2 Concurrent representation of multiple accused

There was no rule in the Army Act 1926 stating or implying that each accused in a joint trial was to have his own Counsel. In Hong Kong in half the cases a sole lawyer was assigned to the Defence of two or more accused joined in a case (Table 2.2).

Looking back on this practice, Ormsby at first did not see an issue with it, although when an example of a conflict of interest was presented to him, he grasped what was wrong. However, he still did not think it important.[266] Even acknowledging the fact that Ormsby had no legal qualifications, it is a surprising reaction from someone at the centre of the Hong Kong trials.

The Army Act 1926 did provide a basis for severing a joint trial where an accused had a need to obtain the evidence of a co-accused:

> Any number of accused persons may be charged jointly and tried together for an offence alleged to have been committed by them collectively... and any accused person may claim... to be tried separately... [T]he convening authority or court, if satisfied that the evidence [of another co-accused] will be material [to the accused's defence], and if the nature of the charge admits of it, shall allow the claim.[267]

[261] Linton, 'Record of Two Interviews with Major Murray I. Ormsby' (n 35) 20–1, 23.
[262] Linton, 'Record of Two Interviews with Major Murray I. Ormsby' (n 35) 13–14.
[263] Linton, 'Record of Two Interviews with Major Murray I. Ormsby' (n 35) 20, 29.
[264] *Trial of Col Noma Kennosuke* (n 87) slides 8–9.
[265] *Trial of Capt Ushiyama Yukio and three others* (n 190) slides 247–8.
[266] Linton, 'Record of Two Interviews with Major Murray I. Ormsby' (n 35) 30.
[267] Army Act, Rules of Procedure (1939) (n 10) art 16.

A severance motion could have been an avenue for a Japanese defendant to secure one-on-one legal representation, but the Regulations for the Trial of War Criminals effectively pre-empted any thought of applying for severance, thus laying the foundation for large, multiple-accused trials:

> Where there is evidence that a war crime has been the result of concerted action upon the part of a unit or group of men, then evidence given upon any charge relating to that crime against any member of such unit or group may be received as prima facie evidence of the responsibility of each member... In any such case all or any members of any such unit or group may be charged and tried jointly in respect of any such war crime and *no application by any of them to be tried separately shall be allowed* by the Court.[268]

The rule, combined with the other measures contributing to a summary form of proceedings at British military courts, as well as (no doubt) personnel shortages,[269] assured the proliferation of joint trials. In these trials, the Defence, riven by conflict, fragmented into incompatible defence strategies which a single Defence Counsel was expected to juggle (or ignore). The typical situation was that of a subordinate officer shifting blame to his superior in the line of command, while the superior, joined in the trial, concurrently alleged that the subordinate had acted on his own initiative. This occurred, for example, in *Sakonju and Mayazumi*, where each of the accused, exceptionally, had his own Counsel.[270]

In *Kishi et al* (one Counsel for all 15 accused), Lieutenant Kishi's defence was that he had orders from his immediate superior to defend against attack and use weapons to that end and had acted in accordance with those orders following attacks on his garrison. By contrast, his 14 subordinates who had been joined with him in the trial raised a combination of defences: alibis, superior orders, mistaken identity, and outright denial of involvement, contradicting, in much of this, their immediate superior, Kishi.[271] This happened again in the *Hockley* case (*Tamura et al*), where two of the accused, Tamura and Fujino, conceded that the execution of Hockley was carried out in the manner pleaded in the charge-sheet, but argued that they were acting on orders from the third accused, Hirano, and that the orders from him left no doubt in their mind that the prisoner had to be killed. Hirano denied that he gave such orders or that he even suggested such a thing. He contended that his instructions were misconstrued.[272] A single Counsel represented all three.[273]

While defendants must to some extent live with such problems where the reasons for joinder outweigh any resulting prejudice to the accused, it cannot be fair—by any standard of justice—to expect one and the same lawyer to put forth contradictory and mutually defeating defences.

268 Regulations for the Trial of War Criminals (n 9) art 8(i) (emphasis added).

269 The Instruction acknowledged the shortage of legally qualified personnel: ALFSEA Instruction (n 14) art 46.

270 *Trial of R Adm Sakonju Naomasa and Capt Mayazumi Haruo* (n 80) slide 11.

271 *Trial of Lt Kishi Yasuo and fourteen others* (n 62) slides 736–54.

272 *Trial of Col. Tamura Teichi and two others* (n 82) slide 7.

273 *Trial of Col. Tamura Teichi and two others* (n 82) slide 7.

**Table 2.2** British military court trials in Hong Kong, 1946–1948, showing the number of legal representatives assigned to the Defence against the number of accused in the case. 'D.O.' stands for 'Defending Officer'. An asterisk (*) indicates Japanese Defence Counsel. The case of *Inouye Kanao*, which was transferred to the Supreme Court of Hong Kong because the accused turned out to be a Canadian national, has not been included. In 20 of the 44 cases the Defence Counsel/accused ratio was 1:1 and in two cases it was 2:1. In the remaining cases (50 per cent of the total) the accused were represented by a single legally qualified person in pluralities of two or more. Perhaps counter-intuitively, the accused in the combined 1:1 and 2:1 group (shown shaded in the bottom half of the table) were more likely than those in the 1:2+ group to be given the death penalty (35% versus 14%) and less likely to be acquitted (4% versus 13%). Given the small data-set and the multiplicity of factors involved, these differences are probably not statistically significant.

| | | Final outcome | | |
|---|---|---|---|---|
| Case | Lawyers/D.O.s per accused | Put to death | Imprisoned | Acquitted |
| *Kishi Yasuo and fourteen others* | 1: 15 | 2 | 10 | 3 |
| *Toda Mitsugu and eight others* | *1: 9 | | 8 | 1 |
| *Obata Chikuro and seven others* | *1: 8 | 1 | 6 | 1 |
| *Uete Taichi and seven others* | *1: 8 | 3 | 4 | 1 |
| *Yoshimi Taneyoshi and six others* | *1: 7 | | 7 | |
| *Omura Kyoshi and four others* | *1: 5 | 1 | 3 | 1 |
| *Tokunaga Isao and four others* | *1: 5 | 2 | 3 | |
| *Hanada Zenji and three others* | 1: 4 | | 3 | 1 |
| *Suzuki Nobue and three others* | *1: 4 | | 4 | |
| *Ushiyama Yukio and three others* | *1: 4 | 1 | 2 | 1 |
| *Nakano Junichi and two others* | *1: 3 | | 3 | |
| *Sazawa Hideo and two others* | *1: 3 | | 3 | |
| *Tamaki Koji and two others* | *1: 3 | | 3 | |
| *Tamura Teiichi and two others* | *1: 3 | 2 | 1 | |
| *Tashiro Toranosuke and two others* | *1: 3 | | 3 | |
| *Yabuki Rikie and two others* | *1: 3 | | 3 | |
| *Yamada Kiichiro and Awa Isao* | 1: 2 | 1 | | 1 |
| *Kinoshita Eiichi and Yoshida Bunzo* | *1: 2 | | 2 | |
| *Kuwaki Kiyomori and Nakajima Tokuzo* | *1: 2 | 1 | 1 | |
| *Ogasawara Haruji and Kawai Hisao* | *1: 2 | | 1 | 1 |
| *Oita Yoshijiro and Ashida Tsumoru* | *1: 2 | | 1 | 1 |
| *Shibata Shigeo and Oba Takao* | *1: 2 | | 1 | 1 |
| *Kawamoto Kaname* | 1: 1 | 1 | | |
| *Matsuda Kenichi* | 1: 1 | | 1 | |
| *Omura Kyoshi* | 1: 1 | | 1 | |
| *Hirao Yoshio* | *1: 1 | 1 | | |

(*Continued*)

**Table 2.2** *Continued*

| Case | Lawyers/D.O.s per accused | Final outcome | | |
|---|---|---|---|---|
| | | Put to death | Imprisoned | Acquitted |
| *Honda Isamu* | *1: 1 | | 1 | |
| *Ito Junichi (No 2)* | *1: 1 | 1 | | |
| *Ito Takeo* | *1: 1 | | 1 | |
| *Kamada Yasushi* | *1: 1 | 1 | | |
| *Kanazawa Asao* | *1: 1 | 1 | | |
| *Kuwano Nobuyuki* | *1: 1 | | 1 | |
| *Matsunobu Shigeru* | *1: 1 | | 1 | |
| *Miyasue Suekichi* | *1: 1 | 1 | | |
| *Noma Kennosuke* | *1: 1 | 1 | | |
| *Ozawa Tomukichi* | *1: 1 | | 1 | |
| *Sato Choichi* | *1: 1 | | 1 | |
| *Shoji Toshishige* | *1: 1 | | | 1 |
| *Tanaka Ryosaburo* | *1: 1 | | 1 | |
| *Tsubota Kanji* | *1: 1 | | 1 | |
| *Yokohata Toshiro* | *1: 1 | | 1 | |
| *Sakonju Naomasa and Mayazumi Haruo* | *2: 2 | 1 | 1 | |
| *Kyoda Shigeru* | *2: 1 | | 1 | |
| *Niimori Genichiro* | *2: 1 | | 1 | |
| *Total (122)* | | *22* | *86* | *14* |

## 4.3 Defence preparation and resources

According to the Army Act 1926, an accused 'shall be afforded proper opportunity of preparing his defence' and allowed 'free communication with his witnesses, and with any friend, defending officer or legal adviser with whom he may wish to consult'.[274] The domestic court-martial was obliged to inquire of the accused at the arraignment whether he wished to apply for an adjournment on the ground that he had had insufficient opportunity to prepare his defence.[275]

This set of rights was qualified in the case of a field general court-martial, which was subject to 'exceptional rules' whereby the procedure was or could be 'of a more summary character than that of an ordinary court-martial'.[276] However, any

[274] Army Act, Rules of Procedure (1939) (n 10) art 14(A); also *Manual of Military Law 1929 (as amended)* (n 12) 48.

[275] *Manual of Military Law 1929 (as amended)* (n 12) 55.

[276] *Manual of Military Law 1929 (as amended)* (n 12) 68.

restriction on Defence rights, and by implication any effort to make the trial more summary in form, would have to be justified by the prevailing circumstances. The fundamental test for attenuation, as I have indicated, was 'military exigency'.[277] A field general court-martial was to uphold as much of the procedural sophistication of a general court-martial as the circumstances permitted.

The ALFSEA Instruction removed the responsiveness to circumstances inherent in the original Army Act scheme, declaring that all the trials were to be of a 'summary nature' and justice was to be administered 'promptly and efficiently'.[278] The Instruction did make provision for a minimum Defence preparation time of *one week*: that is, the time elapsed between the initial meeting of the accused with his Defence representative and the start of the trial was not to be less than one week.[279] The trials themselves averaged two weeks, or five days per accused (Table 2.3).

In *Omura et al*, the Defence Counsel was given two additional days to prepare his case. The Presiding Judge (Warwick) assured him that 'the Court does not wish you to feel that you have been hampered in any way by lack of time or facilities bearing on your defence, and it also appreciates the fact that you only have one interpreter who is working all day in Court'.[280]

When papers vital to the Defence in *Kyoda* had to be obtained from Japan, the Court adjourned for about ten days to facilitate the request. The President (Laming) said: 'every latitude and every assistance must be given to the defence in order that they may place their defence in the very best way possible'.[281] Later, the parties were given a six-day adjournment to prepare their Closing Addresses.[282]

In *Niimori*, the Court was less generous. At the close of the Defence case, the Japanese Defence Counsel asked for five days, including the intervening weekend, to prepare his Closing Address and have it translated. The Presiding Judge (Stewart) said: 'You should be well able to prepare your speech in one day. . . . It is completely unreasonable to suggest any longer.'[283]

In *Kamada* (Laming again) the accused petitioned that he had been given just 12 days to prepare for trial. He sought a retrial with more time allocated to him to bring forward evidence in his defence. The Judge Advocate observed that, at the start of the trial, the accused, upon being asked in the pro forma manner required whether he needed an adjournment for further preparation, had confirmed that he was willing to proceed without one; moreover, in the course of the proceedings he had made no request for additional witnesses. The Judge Advocate advised that the complaint be dismissed.[284]

[277] Army Act, *Rules of Procedure* (1939) (n 10) art 114(C).
[278] ALFSEA Instruction (n 14) art 40.
[279] ALFSEA Instruction (n 14) art 49(1)(b).
[280] *Trial of WO Omura Kyoshi and four others* (n 195) slide 270.
[281] *Trial of Kyoda Shigeru* (n 4) slide 252.
[282] *Trial of Kyoda* Shigeru (n 4) slide 423.
[283] *Trial of Niimori Genichiro* (HKWCT Collection, File No WO 235/892) ('*Trial of Niimori Genichiro*'), slides 296–7.
[284] *Trial of Sgt Maj Kamada Yasushi* (n 190) slide 8.

**Table 2.3** Duration of Hong Kong trials. The 44 cases consumed a total of 595 court days, or an average of 13.5 days per case and 5 days per accused. The most rapid of the trials (*Ito Junichi No 2*) was completed in two days, while the lengthiest (*Tokunaga et al*) ran for 53 days. Not shown in the table are two non-confirmed trials, namely the initial trial of Ito Junichi and the case of *Inouye Kanao* (transferred to the Hong Kong civil authorities).

| Case | Trial period | Trial days | Confirmation |
|---|---|---|---|
| | *1946* | | |
| *Kishi Yasuo and fourteen others* | 28 March–25 April | 22 | 25 April |
| *Matsuda Kenichi* | 10–14 May | 4 | 8 July |
| *Hanada Zenji and three others* | 30 May–11 June | 9 | 3 July |
| *Omura Kyoshi* | 2–4 July | 3 | 1 August |
| *Kawamoto Kaname* | 9–10 July | 2 | 18 November |
| *Yamada Kiichiro and Awa Isao* | 17–22 July | 5 | 23 September |
| *Matsunobu Shigeru* | 25 July–1 August | 5 | 23 August |
| *Yabuki Rikie and two others* | 2–9 August | 5 | 4 December |
| *Miyasue Suekichi* | 13–19 August | 5 | 8 November |
| *Niimori Genichiro* | 28 August–1 October | 18 | 17 October |
| *Tashiro Toranosuke and two others* | 2–14 October | 9 | 31 October |
| *Tokunaga Isao and four others* | 17 October–14 February | 53 | 25 June 1947 |
| *Kyoda Shigeru* | 23 October–29 November | 24 | 18 February 1947 |
| *Suzuki Nobue and three others* | 21 November–2 December | 7 | 8 February 1947 |
| *Ito Junichi (No 2)* | 7–9 December | 2 | 15 September 1947 |
| *Honda Isamu* | 18–21 December | 4 | 23 September 1947 |
| *Noma Kennosuke* | 28 December–24 February | 25 | 14 May 1947 |
| | *1947* | | |
| *Tamaki Koji and two others* | 20 January–7 February | 13 | 12 April |
| *Shibata Shigeo and Oba Takao* | 10 February–7 March | 17 | 3 June |
| *Shoji Toshishige* | 10–17 March | 6 | *[Acquitted]* |
| *Ogasawara Haruji and Kawai Hisao* | 20–31 March | 8 | 3 June |
| *Sato Choichi* | 1 April–5 May | 14 | 30 July |
| *Tanaka Ryosaburo* | 8 April–22 May | 16 | 30 July |
| *Nakano Junichi and two others* | 10 April–28 July | 13 | 21 October |
| *Toda Mitsugu and eight others* | 7–28 May | 16 | 8 August |
| *Sazawa Hideo and two others* | 21 May–9 June | 14 | 14 August |
| *Tamura Teiichi and two others* | 30 May–13 June | 10 | 5 September |
| *Tsubota Kanji* | 17–27 June | 7 | 27 August |
| *Ozawa Tomukichi* | 25–28 June | 3 | 5 September |
| *Oita Yoshijiro and Ashida Tsumoru* | 2–8 July | 4 | 27 August |

| | | | |
|---|---|---|---|
| *Ushiyama Yukio and three others* | 7 July–12 August | 17 | 9 October |
| *Kamada Yasushi* | 11–30 July | 8 | 3 October |
| *Obata Chikuro and seven others* | 5 August–17 September | 29 | 21 November |
| *Kuwano Nobuyuki* | 20 August–1 September | 6 | 5 November |
| *Hirao Yoshio* | 4 September–14 November | 19 | 13 February 1948 |
| *Sakonju Naomasa and Mayazumi Haruo* | 19 September–29 October | 28 | 13 January 1948 |
| *Kanazawa Asao* | 26 September–30 October | 23 | 6 February 1948 |
| *Kuwaki Kiyomori and Nakajima Tokuzo* | 1 November–17 December | 23 | 24 February 1948 |
| *Uete Taichi and seven others* | 13 November–16 January | 35 | 24 March 1948 |
| *Yoshimi Taneyoshi and six others* | 17 November–11 December | 15 | 13 February 1948 |
| | *1948* | | |
| *Ito Takeo* | 19 January–6 February | 12 | 14 April |
| *Omura Kyoshi and four others* | 24 February–31 March | 19 | 21 June |
| *Kinoshita Eiichi and Yoshida Bunzo* | 25 October–24 November | 15 | 2 December |
| *Yokohata Toshiro* | 9–20 December | 3 | 7 February 1949 |
| *Average trial days per case* | | *13.5* | |
| *Average trial days per accused* | | *5* | |

As mentioned earlier, each accused before a British military court was to receive a charge-sheet, an abstract of the evidence, and copies of any exhibits.[285] The Army Act 1926 required that each charge be so explicit as to enable the accused readily to understand what he had to answer.[286] The particulars of the charge were to state 'such circumstances respecting the alleged offence as will enable the accused to know every act, neglect, or omission which it is intended to be proved against him as constituting the offence'.[287] In one case, *Hanada*, the Defence launched a challenge against the vagueness of the charge. After a short adjournment to deliberate, the Court announced that it found the charge to be 'sufficiently specific'.[288]

The accused was to be provided with an interpreter free of charge. The interpreter was to enable the accused—and, if appointed, his Japanese Counsel—to understand the charges, the rules of procedure, and generally 'to enable him to prepare his defence'.[289] Some accused understood English, but most, it seems, did

285 ALFSEA Instruction (n 14) arts 41, 45; see also Army Act, Rules of Procedure (1939) (n 10) art 14(B).

286 Army Act, Rules of Procedure (1939) (n 10) art 23(A)(ii).

287 Army Act, Rules of Procedure (1939) (n 10) art 13(D).

288 *Trial of Sgt Hanada Zenji and three others* (n 143) slides 10–12.

289 ALFSEA Instruction (n 14) art 50.

not have a working knowledge of the language.[290] Pritchard writes that 'translation between Japanese and English appears to have been rough but adequate . . . very few challenges to translation may be found'.[291] However, in *Yabuki et al*, the Defence Counsel complained about the linguistic disadvantage of the accused: 'there is the problem of translating everything [the accused] say into English. During this translation lots of the meanings, in the finer sense of the word are lost.'[292] In the trial of Sakonju and Mayazumi, during the examination in chief of the accused, the interpretation was so bad as to be unintelligible.[293]

Among the resources for the Defence we should count the British Defence Advisory Officer who was supplied to every case in the ALFSEA-zone trials. 'He will generally assist the defence in every way which is practicable and desirable.'[294] The Advisory Officer was required to remain in court throughout the trial and be prepared to advise the Defence Counsel on military law and procedure.[295] His tasks included reading out the Closing Address on behalf of the Japanese Counsel.[296]

How useful to the Defence were these Advisory Officers? Ormsby maintained in his interview with Professor Linton that the guidance that the Japanese Defence Counsel received from their Advisory Officers was 'tokenistic' and superficial because they were not legally experienced (Ormsby, having started out as one, spoke from experience) and did not know about court procedure.[297] Yet even in the case of a knowledgeable Defence Advisory Officer, it could not be said that he was expected to fully dedicate himself to the interests of the Defence. He was, in reality, a watchful liaison for the court administration rather than a loyal servant of the Defence. He was obliged to be present at all interviews between the accused and his Counsel 'in the interests of security'.[298] In the case of a death sentence, he had several duties, including that of identifying the condemned person on the day of his execution and completing the death certificate.[299]

## 4.4 Plea of superior orders

The plea of superior orders (dealt with extensively by Bing Bing Jia elsewhere in this book) was by far the most common defence plea at the Hong Kong trials. Because of the lack of reasoned judgments, we know little about the actual judicial position on the plea. On the whole, confusion and inconsistency seem to have reigned. While the availability and form of this defence is a matter of substantive law, and thus generally outside the scope of this chapter, I include discussion of it here

[290] Vine, 'Experiences as a War Crimes Prosecutor in Hong Kong' (n 36) 207.

[291] Pritchard, 'The Historical Experience of British War Crimes Courts in the Far East' (n 2) 322.

[292] *Trial of WO Yabuki Rikie and two others* (n 224) slide 80.

[293] *Trial of R Adm Sakonju Naomasa and Capt Mayazumi Haruo* (n 80) slide 247.

[294] ALFSEA Instruction (n 14) art 49(1)(c).

[295] ALFSEA Instruction (n 14) art 49(1)(c).

[296] ALFSEA Instruction (n 14) art 49(1)(d). See, for example, *Trial of Sgt Maj Matsunobu Shigeru* (n 51) slide 74; *Trial of WO Yabuki Rikie and two others* (n 224) slide 80.

[297] Linton, 'Record of Two Interviews with Major Murray I. Ormsby' (n 35) 13–14, 22.

[298] ALFSEA Instruction (n 14) art 49(1)(a).

[299] ALFSEA Instruction (n 14) art 49(2).

because it relates to the point I have been developing about the uncertainty in the applicable law and the consequent difficulty this caused the Defence in developing its strategy. The British had tried to side-line the plea, or at best to render it ambiguous, and this was yet another way in which the Japanese Defence was put on the back foot. We may therefore briefly examine the topic from the perspective of procedural fairness.

The plea of superior orders usually involves conceding a central element of the Prosecution's case. For example, in the *Hockley* case, two of the accused went ahead and admitted involvement in the execution of Hockley, precisely as averred by the Prosecution. Both then pleaded that they had been acting on orders of the third accused.[300] Pleading superior orders is therefore a risky defence strategy where there is doubt about whether the trial court recognizes the plea as a complete defence, or even as a factor leading to mitigation of punishment.

What, then, was the law that was applied by the Hong Kong courts? In one case, a Judge Advocate said that 'obedience is not a valid defence where the order is obviously unlawful';[301] in another, the same Judge Advocate wrote: 'The defence of superior orders . . . could only influence the court in mitigation of sentence.'[302] These two statements articulate the UK government's 'revised' position on the plea. The revision had occurred in the course of the years 1936 to 1944. The traditional position accepted the plea as a complete defence; as revised, the plea was considered a motivational matter which, like duress, was relevant only to the severity of the penalty imposed.[303] The lack of explicit reasoning among the British military court judges makes it difficult to know how they themselves regarded the defence. According to Pritchard, they were ambivalent: 'quite a number of Courts took under consideration lengthy defences which hinged upon the claim . . . Other Courts gave the matter short shrift.'[304]

At Hong Kong, many of the accused pleaded 'not guilty' and went to trial with superior orders as their main defence strategy.[305] From the files it often seems as if the Japanese Defence Counsel did not know or had not advised their clients about the uncertain status to which the defence had been reduced in British military law. For this or another reason which is difficult for us now to grasp, the accused would sometimes freely admit to committing the acts with which they were charged.[306] Here is one Japanese Defence Counsel pursuing the defence of superior orders all

[300] *Trial of Col Tamura Teichi and two others* (n 82) slide 7.

[301] *Trial of Kyoda Shigeru* (n 4) slide 10.

[302] *Trial of Col Tokunaga Isao and four others* (Part One) (n 174) slide 14.

[303] See discussion in Linton, 'Rediscovering the War Crimes Trials in Hong Kong, 1946–48' (n 6) 311–15.

[304] Pritchard, 'The Historical Experience of British War Crimes Courts in the Far East' (n 2) 324–5.

[305] See, eg, *Trial of Sgt Maj Ogasawara Haruji and Sgt Kawai Hisao* (HKWCT Collection, File No WO235/1011), slide 5.

[306] For example, *Trial of Sgt Maj Ogasawara Haruji and Sgt Kawai Hisao*, slide 5; *Trial of R Adm Sakonju Naomasa and Capt Mayazumi Haruo* (n 80) slide 11; *Trial of Kyoda Shigeru* (n 4) slides 9–10; *Trial of Col Noma Kennosuke* (n 87) slide 5 ('During the trial he admitted that he had ordered the execution without trial of certain civilians at the command of the Chief of Staff'); *Trial of Lt Kishi Yasuo and fourteen others* (n 62) slides 5–6.

the way through to his Closing Address: 'the 3rd accused was under the orders of a superior officer and thus cannot be charged guilty of the crime.'[307] What could explain such absolutism by the Japanese Counsel?

It is tempting to pinpoint poor legal advice as the main culprit behind this practice of blinkered adherence to the traditional version of the superior orders defence, but in defence of the Japanese Counsel themselves one could say that the substantive law applied by the military courts should have been international law, in which case the British national position on the law of superior orders was no more determinative of its status or content than the Japanese national position, which still upheld the traditional formulation of the defence. In fact, Japan's own position was reiterated over and over again before the judges, possibly to make the point that even if Britain had changed its position on the effect of superior orders as a defence, Japanese law and international law on the plea remained unchanged.

Several Japanese servicemen (witnesses for the Prosecution as well as the Defence) reiterated for the Hong Kong judges that under Japanese military law, orders had to be obeyed in all circumstances. Major Ando Tadashi, a Japanese officer called as a Prosecution witness in the *Tokunaga et al* case to provide expert evidence on the structure and operations of the Japanese Army, testified to the fact that orders in that Army had to be obeyed: 'if the order comes from the direct superior the subordinate should obey that order because the superior officer knows about the legality of the order.' He affirmed that any order given by an officer to any subordinate had to be obeyed at once and without question.[308] In pleading mitigation on behalf of the defendant Yokohata, his Counsel said: 'Japanese military training emphasises one thing above all others. That is, that when an order, legal or illegal, is given by a superior officer, the order will be implicitly obeyed.'[309] The Defence Counsel in *Kyoda* quoted from Japan's armed-service regulations: 'Military discipline lies in obedience, therefore it is necessary to . . . make all servicemen . . . abide by the orders of their superiors. The above should be cultivated as their second nature.'[310] Necessarily, the Counsel implied, a subordinate was absolved of all wrong. The accused Major General Tanaka testified that Japanese troops were trained to obey orders, and that if a soldier disobeyed an order, he would be charged with mutiny under Japan's Army Penal Code.[311] A subordinate's assessment that an order was unlawful or immoral did not make it lawful to disobey the order under Japanese law.[312] On this view, it was *always* unlawful to disobey.

In *Kishi et al*, the Defence Counsel quoted from an edition of *Oppenheim's International Law*, which stated the traditional international law position, that a subordinate may not be punished for a violation of the laws of war ordered by his

[307] *Sgt Tashiro Toranosuke and two others* (n 193) slide 217.

[308] *Trial of Col Tokunaga Isao and four others* (Part One) (n 174) slide 449.

[309] *Trial of Sgt Maj Yokohata Toshiro* (n 51) slide 150.

[310] *Trial of Kyoda Shigeru* (n 4) slides 467–8.

[311] *Trial of Maj Gen Tanaka Ryosaburo* (n 177) slide 182.

[312] See, eg, Prosecution Witness Kaname Araki in *Trial of Kyoda Shigeru* (n 4) slides 72, 76–7, who maintained that even if the subordinate were *morally* right, he would still be tried for disobedience in Japan.

commander. The Prosecutor counter-quoted from a later edition of the work, which now had come under Hersch Lauterpacht's reformist influence and claimed that obedience to superior orders did not confer immunity from punishment. The Prosecutor went on to describe the recent change as a 'somersault in International Law'.[313] The idea that customary international law could 'somersault' forward absent some major event, such as a diplomatic conference, is as implausible to our ears as it must have seemed to the Japanese Counsel: custom changes slowly, and we cannot say that it has changed until there is broad-based agreement that it has. In any case, it would have been difficult to make a convincing case at the time that the Japanese were bound by a rule of customary international law disqualifying superior orders as a complete defence to war crimes. But the British had the upper hand in Hong Kong. The law was not open to debate.

## 4.5 Guilty plea

A British court-martial operating under the Army Act 1926 was prohibited from accepting a guilty plea in a case where the accused was liable, if convicted, to receive the death penalty.[314] Were such a plea to be offered, a plea of 'not guilty' was to be recorded.[315] In the military courts, by contrast, where most charges carried the death penalty, the Regulations for the Trial of War Criminals removed the prohibition against the plea of guilty to a capital charge,[316] no doubt in order to speed up the processing of the case load.

In *Ito Junichi (No 1)*, the Judge Advocate noted 'grave' irregularities with the guilty-plea procedure and recommended a re-trial. The Court had taken evidence to enable it to determine the sentence, but had gone too far, turning the process into 'a trial of the averments in the charge sheet'.[317] The Court should have sought the information it needed in the evidence summary or the witness statements; instead, it allowed examination and cross-examination of Prosecution witnesses, following which the accused himself gave evidence on oath and was cross-examined, despite the fact that on a plea of guilty he could do no more than make a statement in mitigation. Then, at the conclusion of the process, the Court decided after all to alter the plea to one of 'not guilty'. Having done so, it should have re-heard the evidence from the beginning, in accordance with the procedure for a not-guilty plea. But it did not. It adjourned to directly consider the finding and sentence. The Judge Advocate advised the Confirming Officer to 'withhold confirmation . . . You will probably consider that the interests of justice demand that the accused be re-tried before an entirely fresh court.'[318]

313 *Trial of Lt Kishi Yasuo and fourteen others* (n 62) slide 547.
314 *Manual of Military Law 1929 (as amended)* (n 12) 54.
315 Army Act, Rules of Procedure (1939) (n 10) art 35(D).
316 Regulations for the Trial of War Criminals (n 9) art 3.
317 *Trial of Sgt Maj Ito Junichi (No 1)* (n 62) slide 4.
318 *Trial of Sgt Maj Ito Junichi (No 1)*, slide 4. The accused was later retried on the basis of a not-guilty plea and was convicted: *Trial of Sgt Maj Ito Junichi (No 2)* (HKWCT Collection, File No WO235/1048) ('*Trial of Sgt Maj Ito Junichi (No 2)*').

In *Yokohata*, the accused pleaded guilty. The Court heard a witness, Major Kyte, who at the time was the officer commanding the British Minor War Crimes Liaison Section in Tokyo.[319] He appeared as a Defence character witness and said of the accused that it was 'the first time that I ever interrogated a Japanese kempei who was honest, frank and apparently regretted his actions'.[320] The Court at this point reversed the guilty plea and proceeded to a trial on the facts. It gave no reason for doing so.[321] In his petition against the conviction and 15-year prison sentence, the accused stated that the Court had

> changed my plea to one of not guilty with the result that a number of affidavits on behalf of the prosecution, and which being affidavits, I had no chance of cross-examining, were produced to the court. I consider that the Court in this case had no grounds on which to alter my plea, and that I was prejudiced by such an alteration.[322]

Yokohata's petition was dismissed and the result confirmed.[323]

## 4.6 Verdict, sentencing, mitigation

Under the Army Act 1926, a court-martial was accorded an absolute discretion as to the sentence. It could impose the maximum punishment allowable for the offence—or any lesser punishment.[324] A guideline, particular to the military context, was that the proper amount of punishment was 'the least amount by which discipline can efficiently be maintained'.[325] Another guideline was that a habitual offender deserved a far more severe punishment than an infrequent offender; and that a first offender was always, if possible, to be treated leniently.[326]

When punishing enemy nationals for war crimes, the application of these principles (which were left unaltered by the Regulations for the Trial of War Criminals) must have seemed problematic or inapposite. A war crime is an offence in international law. There was at the time no maximum (or minimum) sentence for war crimes in international law. Possibly the judges awarded sentences that were analogous, somehow, to those of domestic court-martial practice. But even this assumption is problematical because—if Ormsby is any guide—most panel members had no prior experience of courts-martial.

Because the judges recorded no reasons, we know little about how they went about sentencing the Japanese accused. Pritchard has argued that British military courts lacked consistency in meting out sentences for similar offences.[327] He attributes it to the varying impact that mitigating circumstances had on the

319 *Trial of Sgt Maj Yokohata Toshiro* (n 51) slide 4.
320 *Trial of Sgt Maj Yokohata Toshiro* (n 51) slide 12.
321 *Trial of Sgt Maj Yokohata Toshiro* (n 51) slide 12.
322 *Trial of Sgt Maj Yokohata Toshiro* (n 51) slide 7.
323 *Trial of Sgt Maj Yokohata Toshiro* (n 51) slide 15.
324 *Manual of Military Law 1929 (as amended)* (n 12) 60.
325 *Manual of Military Law 1929 (as amended)* (n 12) 60.
326 *Manual of Military Law 1929 (as amended)* (n 12) 61.
327 Pritchard, 'The Historical Experience of British War Crimes Courts in the Far East' (n 2) 322.

sentence. However, many more factors were probably at work, including inexperience and lack of appellate level (or other) guidance on sentencing.

Under the Army Act 1926, a death sentence was not to be passed without the concurrence of at least two-thirds of the members of a general court-martial (which as we have noted had at least five members).[328] In the case of a field general court-martial (minimum of three members), unanimity was required.[329] The latter rule was modified slightly by the British military court Regulations.[330] They provided that unanimity was required for a death sentence that was passed *by a panel of three*—but not where more than three judges had been appointed to the panel.[331] The unanimity rule for field general courts-martial was intended to make it more difficult to impose the death penalty in the context of the attenuated processes of that model. In the end, the amendment effected by the Regulations for the Trial of War Criminals made no difference to the Hong Kong trials, as the panels there were always made up of just three judges.

In *Sakonju and Mayazumi*, the Judge Advocate noted that the trial documentation failed to make clear whether or not the imposed death sentence on Sakonju had been passed unanimously. He advised the Convening Officer to contact the President of the Court to obtain confirmation that the unanimity requirement had been complied with.[332] Confirmation was duly obtained.[333]

Military Court verdicts were summarily pronounced without elaboration.[334] Sentences followed after submissions on mitigation. No attempt was made to justify them.[335] In *Kyoda*, the exact law to be applied in the case was a critical issue, so much so that the Court adjourned to consult the judgment of the IMT Nuremberg; but no indication was given in the verdict about the law that was finally applied.[336] 'It is not entirely clear why the Court acquitted the accused on the 1st charge . . . presumably they considered the witnesses unreliable on these points.'[337] The Judge Advocate making this comment sounds a little exasperated.

This having been said, there was no rule in the Army Act 1926 requiring reasons to be given for verdicts or punishments. At the same time, deliberations by the Hong Kong judges were remarkably brief. The Court normally delivered its

328 *Manual of Military Law 1929 (as amended)* (n 12) 62.

329 Army Act, Rules of Procedure (1939) (n 10) art 118(A) ('The court, if consisting of three or more officers, may award any sentence which a general court-martial can award; but if the court pass a sentence of death, the whole court must concur').

330 Regulations for the Trial of War Criminals (n 9) art 3.

331 Regulations for the Trial of War Criminals (n 9) art 9.

332 *Trial of R Adm Sakonju Naomasa and Capt Mayazumi Haruo* (n 80) slide 11.

333 *Trial of R Adm Sakonju Naomasa and Capt Mayazumi Haruo* (n 80) slide 9.

334 For example, *Trial of Sgt Maj Kiyomori Kuwaki and Sgt Tokuzo Nakajima* (HKWCT Collection, File No WO235/1106), slide 411.

335 *Trial of Sgt Maj Kiyomori Kuwaki and Sgt Tokuzo Nakajima* (n 334) slide 415.

336 *Trial of Kyoda Shigeru* (n 4) slide 427. Banham writes about the *Kyoda* case: 'Judgement had been made. But had justice been done?'; Banham, *The Sinking of the Lisbon Maru: Britain's Forgotten Wartime Tragedy* (n 89) 244. He is alluding to the seemingly lenient sentence of seven years' imprisonment in a case where 828 POWs had died. We do not know which of several potential mitigatory factors played a role.

337 *Trial of Kuwano Nobuyuki* (HKWCT Collection, File No WO235/1078), slide 5.

judgment on the very same day—at most, in a larger case, on the day after the end of the trial.[338] In *Matsuda*, deliberation on the verdict lasted about five minutes.[339] The sentence (eight years' imprisonment) took even less time than this to decide.[340] In *Yamada and Awa*, the deliberation on guilt (which included the acquittal of Awa) lasted less than 20 minutes.[341] Less than five minutes later the judges had decided that Yamada was to be put to death by hanging.[342] In *Matsunobu*, it was 20 minutes to decide the verdict and six minutes for the sentence.[343] In *Miyasue* it was ten and seven minutes respectively (death by hanging).[344]

A finding of guilt and the corresponding sentence were to be announced in open court by the President, who was to point out to the accused that both the finding and the sentence were subject to confirmation. There could be no valid conviction or penalty without confirmation.[345] A finding of acquittal did not require confirmation, nor could it be revised in any way.[346]

Prison sentences were to be served in the civilian prisons in Hong Kong.[347]

## 4.7 Petition, confirmation, commutation

According to the Regulations for the Trial of War Criminals, the accused could, within 14 days of the conclusion of the trial proceedings, submit a petition to the Confirming Officer (same person as the Convening Officer) against the finding or sentence, provided that he gave notice within 48 hours of the trial's conclusion of his intention to do so.[348] The petition, together with the complete record of the proceedings was sent, first, to a Judge Advocate in ALFSEA's DJAG office in Singapore. The Judge Advocate prepared an advisory report for the Confirming Officer, which he then forwarded to him with the trial record attached.[349]

A petition was generally submitted only by the convicted person, although in Hong Kong petitions were also occasionally sent in by relatives and other supporters of the accused. Petitioning was the only procedure approximating what we would call an appeal for a person convicted by a British military court.

But it was not much of an appeal. The petition was written in the first person and signed by the accused, without acknowledgment of assistance—although most petitions were clearly prepared with some assistance of Counsel. Petitions did little more than reiterate the accused's view of what the evidence showed, as if the process

338 *Trial of Kyoda Shigeru* (n 4) slides 425–7.
339 *Trial of Sgt Matsuda Kenichi* (n 201) slide 91.
340 *Trial of Sgt Matsuda Kenichi* (n 201) slide 92.
341 *Trial of Sgt Maj Yamada Kiichiro and Sgt Awa Isao* (n 152) slide 126.
342 *Trial of Sgt Maj Yamada Kiichiro and Sgt Awa Isao* (n 152) slides 127–8.
343 *Trial of Sgt Maj Matsunobu Shigeru* (n 51) slides 81–2.
344 *Trial of Sgt Miyasue Suekichi* (HKWCT Collection, File No WO235/915), slides 92–3.
345 *Manual of Military Law 1929 (as amended)* (n 12) 62.
346 Regulations for the Trial of War Criminals (n 9) art 8(iii). This was in accordance with the practice of courts-martial; see *Manual of Military Law 1929 (as amended)* (n 12) 59.
347 ALFSEA Instruction (n 14) art 32.
348 Regulations for the Trial of War Criminals (n 9) art 10; see also ALFSEA Instruction (n 14) art 57.
349 Regulations for the Trial of War Criminals (n 9) art 10.

were a second opportunity for a Closing Address. (Both the judges[350] and the accused[351] commonly referred to the petitions as 'appeals'. We should not be misled by this term. They were pleas for sympathy and reconsideration.) Questions of law or procedure were rarely raised.[352] The Judge Advocate, in his advice to the Confirming Officer, normally summarized the petition only to advise its dismissal.[353] The petition was not otherwise considered by a legally qualified person. It is doubtful that the Confirming Officer read any of the petitions unless the Judge Advocate indicated a problem with the trial. In the absence of a major problem, the Confirming Officer simply confirmed the result.

Uncertainty about the basis of judicial decisions at the British military courts surely is a reason for the neglect of this body of case law. It could have little precedential value. More importantly from the point of view of the accused in these trials, the unavailability of explicit judicial reasoning made petitioning against conviction and penalty difficult to argue in a rational and legally convincing way. Without the benefit of the Court's analysis of the facts and law, the Judge Advocate advising on confirmation must have felt that he generally had little choice but to advise that the petitions should be dismissed.

In *Tamura et al* an unusually large number of petitions were filed by third parties. There were petitions from the father, father-in-law, and mother-in-law of the accused Hirano; from a witness in the trial (his affidavit had been put in as an exhibit); and from inmate friends of Hirano at Stanley Prison where he had been incarcerated pending trial. The friends wrote that Hirano was a sincere Christian, fully aware of the Japanese Army's rules and regulations, and that they could not believe that such a man was implicated in a murder case. All petitions were dismissed.[354] In *Sato*, a supporting petition was filed by Dr Percy Selwyn-Clarke, the Hong Kong Director of Medical Services, who himself had been a POW at Stanley Prison, to the effect that Sato did much to alleviate the position of POWs passing through the Hong Kong hospital.[355]

No petitions whatsoever were filed in seven cases, involving a total of 12 accused.[356] In one of these cases, the Judge Advocate noted that there had been a delay in the confirmation process because the authorities were awaiting a petition which never arrived. He affirmed that the Defence had been informed of its right to petition. Even though a death penalty had been pronounced, the Judge Advocate

350 For example, *Trial of Kyoda Shigeru* (n 4) slide 428; *Trial of Lt Col Kanazawa Asao* (HKWCT Collection, File No WO235/1093) ('*Trial of Lt Col Kanazawa Asao*'), slide 468.

351 For example, *Trial of Col Tokunaga Isao and four others* (n 174) slides 21, 25.

352 See, eg, Yamada's petition: *Trial of Sgt Maj Yamada Kiichiro and Sgt Awa Isao* (n 152) slides 9–11.

353 For example, *Trial of Maj Uete Taichi and seven others* (HKWCT Collection, File No WO235/1105), slide 14.

354 *Trial of Col. Tamura Teichi and two others* (n 82) slide 8.

355 *Trial of Sato Choichi* (n 178) slide 5.

356 See *Trial of Niimori Genichiro* (n 283); *Trial of WO Omura Kyoshi* (n 19); *Trial of Sgt Maj Matsunobu Shigeru* (n 51); *Trial of Sgt Hanada Zenji and three others* (n 143); *Sgt Tashiro Toranosuke and two others* (n 193); *Trial of Sgt Kawamoto Kaname* (n 52) (a death-penalty case); and *Trial of Col Noma Kennosuke* (n 87).

was of the view that 'it is unnecessary to pursue the matter any further'.[357] This is an indication, of course, of the authorities' low regard for petitions. Yet from a present point of view, the failure of 12 accused (10 per cent of the total) to petition is difficult to understand. However ineffectual the petitioning system seems both procedurally and in its overall effects, it was the last chance of mercy offered by the military courts within the framework of the trial procedure. A convicted person, properly advised, should have petitioned no matter what. The fact that many did not suggests that they were not fully aware of their legal rights or were not encouraged to exercise them—in both cases, a failure of legal advice and ultimately a failure of the judicial system.

In the original court-martial setting, the Confirming Officer did not have the power to alter or amend the court-martial's finding of guilt on a charge. He could only confirm the result or refuse confirmation.[358] In the case of a refusal, he had the power to direct the court to reassemble for the purpose of revising the finding.[359] Absent such a revision request, a refusal to confirm operated to annul the trial.[360] Annulment meant that the accused, having not been convicted, could legally be tried again.[361]

In relation to the punishment of the convicted person, in the domestic application of the Army Act 1926, the Confirming Officer had more direct powers. He could mitigate a punishment to a lesser amount of the same punishment; remit the sentence; commute the punishment to a different form of punishment lower in the Act's 'scale of punishments'; or direct the court-martial to reassemble for the purpose of revising the sentence.[362] Where revision was directed, the Confirming Officer could not recommend an increase in the sentence, and the court was not permitted to take further evidence in the case, or itself increase the sentence.[363]

In the case of the British military courts, the Regulations for the Trial of War Criminals reiterated some of the powers of the Confirming Officer just described;[364] the balance of the powers applied *mutatis mutandis*.

If the thinking of the Hong Kong judges is revealed to us from the transcripts only indirectly, the Confirming Officer's thinking remains completely inaccessible. It is another reason not to imagine petitioning as a kind of low-grade appeal. Nothing of legal interest came from the pen of the Confirming Officer, nor, in fairness, could it have. The laconic condition at either end of the military court process makes the Judge Advocate's reports, in the middle, positively stand out for the value of their legal commentary.

Certainly, the Judge Advocate was limited in how deeply he could go into the issues given the anaemic material before him. With few exceptions, he sought to

[357] *Trial of Sgt Kawamoto Kaname* (n 52) slide 5.
[358] *Manual of Military Law 1929 (as amended)* (n 12) 64.
[359] *Manual of Military Law 1929 (as amended)* (n 12) 63.
[360] Army Act, Rules of Procedure (1939) (n 10) art 120(A).
[361] *Manual of Military Law 1929 (as amended)* (n 12) 64.
[362] *Manual of Military Law 1929 (as amended)* (n 12) 64.
[363] Army Act, Rules of Procedure (1939) (n 10) art 120(G).
[364] Regulations for the Trial of War Criminals (n 9) art 12.

assure the Confirming Officer of the propriety of the trial, typically in a comment of this sort: 'The evidence of the five witnesses ... appears to establish beyond reasonable doubt that the deaths [of three civilians] were directly attributable to the ill-treatment and tortures to which they were subjected by this accused.' In a subsequent comment on the same case, he went further: 'There appears to be no reason to disbelieve these witnesses, or to doubt the guilt of the accused. In the circumstances, the death sentence appears to be the only suitable one the Court could pass.'[365] And in a different case: 'Reviewing the evidence against Hirano as a whole I think that the Court were justified in believing that when he issued instructions to the unit he intended that Hockley should be killed.'[366]

The Confirming Officer as a rule accepted the Judge Advocate's (generally) positive assessment of a panel's findings and sentence, but in cases where the Judge Advocate suggested that the result was too harsh and might be in need of revision, the advice was in several cases ignored. In *Hirao*, the Judge Advocate advised the Confirming Officer to commute the death sentence to a less severe penalty:

> The only evidence as to the accused's knowledge of killings was that of [Prosecution witness Joseph Venpin]. This witness worked for the Japanese at the material times and must therefore be regarded to some extent as an accomplice. Moreover he is obviously a pretty despicable character and although the court were entitled to accept his evidence I am bound to say that I do not think much reliance should be placed on it in the absence of any corroboration on this important point.[367]

The advice was not taken and Hirao was hanged.[368] In the *Ito Junichi (No 2)* case, a Judge Advocate wrote to the Confirming Officer late in 1947 pointing out that there had been a long delay in the confirmation process because of the loss of documents on board an aircraft that had gone missing. He suggested commutation of the death penalty on humanitarian grounds.[369] There was no commutation and Ito was hanged.[370] The Confirming Officer, as usual, did not explain his decision.

In Ormsby's account, the independence of the confirmation process was compromised when the Confirming Officer would call upon him, when he was a Prosecutor, for assistance 'to sort it all out'.[371] He recalled the Confirming Officer saying to him words to the effect: 'I've got all this stuff back from the [Judge Advocate in] Singapore, come on give me your opinion.' It was, Ormsby conceded, a 'very

365 *Trial of WO Omura Kyoshi and four others* (n 195) slide 33.
366 *Trial of Col Tamura Teichi and two others* (n 82) slide 8.
367 *Trial of Maj Hirao Yoshio* (n 51) slide 6.
368 *Trial of Maj Hirao Yoshio* (n 51) slide 3.
369 *Trial of Sgt Maj Ito Junichi (No 2)* (n 318) slide 6.
370 *Trial of Sgt Maj Ito Junichi (No 2)* (n 318) slide 5.
371 Linton, 'Record of Two Interviews with Major Murray I. Ormsby' (n 35) 15.

unofficial' procedure.[372] It perhaps explains why adjustments favouring the convicted person were rarely made.

In a few cases, though, the Judge Advocate did succeed in having a moderating influence on the final outcome. In *Kanazawa*, the accused had been the Commissioner of Police and the Chief of the Gendarmerie in Hong Kong. He was sentenced to death by hanging. In summarizing the evidence adduced in support of the first charge, the Judge Advocate noted that there was, in his professional view, just enough evidence for the Court to have been able to infer that the accused could not have been ignorant of what was going on—and therefore for the Court to conclude that the accused was 'concerned in' the ill-treatment of the persons in custody.[373] However, the Judge Advocate strongly advised against confirmation of the *second* charge, which concerned the death of a Chinese person during deportation. There was nothing inherently illegal, wrote the Judge Advocate, in the deportation of 'undesirable residents' from Hong Kong; moreover, the accused Kanazawa had taken reasonable measures to ensure that the deportations were carried out humanely. He advised the Confirming Officer that, should he be inclined to leave the second charge unconfirmed, he should also consider commuting the imposed death sentence, which would now rest only on the first charge.[374] The Confirming Officer followed the Judge Advocate's advice on non-confirmation of the second charge but not on commutation of the sentence—a win that must have been cold comfort to Kanazawa.[375]

The Judge Advocate proved more influential in the case of *Tokunaga et al*, where he recommended commuting the death sentence of one of the accused, Saito. Although Saito was 'undoubtedly guilty of criminal and callous neglect in the highest degree', his offences were offences of omission rather than commission.[376] The Confirming Officer commuted Saito's sentence to 20 years' imprisonment.[377]

Pritchard writes that under the British military court system there was nothing automatic about the confirmation of a sentence: 'more than 17 per cent of all Japanese convicted war criminals sentenced by British Military Courts . . . had their sentences reduced or were released failing confirmation of sentence.'[378] In Hong Kong, where the process seems to have been compromised by an improper association between Prosecutor and Confirming Officer—but perhaps for other reasons as well that the case files do not disclose—the percentage of favourable interventions was much lower.

[372] Linton, 'Record of Two Interviews with Major Murray I. Ormsby' (n 35) 15.
[373] *Trial of Lt Col Kanazawa Asao* (n 350) slide 4.
[374] *Trial of Lt Col Kanazawa Asao* (n 350) slide 4.
[375] *Trial of Lt Col Kanazawa Asao* (n 350) slide 3.
[376] *Trial of Col Tokunaga Isao and four others* (Part One) (n 174) slide 16.
[377] *Trial of Col Tokunaga Isao and four others* (Part One) (n 174) slide 30.
[378] Pritchard, 'The Historical Experience of British War Crimes Courts in the Far East' (n 2) 323.

## 5. Concluding Remarks

### 5.1 The Defence experience

To date, the assessment of British military courts in the Far East has been carried out mainly by Pritchard. His conclusions have been expressed in both absolute and relative terms. He has written that the military courts gave the Prosecution and the Defence 'sufficient time' to prepare their legal arguments;[379] that with few exceptions they scrupulously adhered to the principle of individual (as opposed to collective) criminal responsibility;[380] that they displayed 'a sensitivity to the rights of individual defendants which does credit to the humanity and even the chivalry of the legal officers responsible';[381] and that they were conducted 'with wonderful fairness in the vast majority of cases, and . . . justice was achieved to the fullest extent humanly possible',[382] or in any event at 'the highest standards of British justice'.[383] Some of Pritchard's assessments are expressed in more careful, relative, language. The British Far East trials, in this alternative view, were conducted according to procedures which would have been applied to offenders in the British armed forces 'without legal qualms';[384] and the professionalism of the judicial staff in the Far East zone stands in 'sharp contrast to the comportment of many of their better-remembered International and American counterparts'[385] and to 'the wretched partisanship shown in many of the American trials or in the comportment of Court Members . . . at the International Military Tribunals at Nuremberg and Tokyo'.[386]

A different conclusion is reached by Bloxham, whose focus is on the military courts in Germany. He finds much to be worthy of praise about the relatively large, drawn-out, IMT process (it was 'a competent exercise in being seen to be fair'[387]), but has only disdain for the British military courts: 'Unlike the more structured American trial programs, the Royal Warrant trials were basically enacted ad hoc . . . their frequency and subject matter were to a greater degree at the mercy of the ebb and flow of public and political opinion.'[388]

This chapter's examination of Britain's Hong Kong military courts shows that some of Pritchard's glowing assessments cannot be sustained. The requirement of the Army Act 1926 to show 'great latitude to the accused in making his defence',[389] which in principle applied unchanged to the military courts, was not adhered to. The accused in Hong Kong suffered significant relative disadvantage. The large

[379] Pritchard, 'The Historical Experience of British War Crimes Courts in the Far East' (n 2) 321.
[380] Pritchard, 'The Historical Experience of British War Crimes Courts in the Far East' (n 2) 318.
[381] Pritchard, 'The Historical Experience of British War Crimes Courts in the Far East' (n 2) 320.
[382] Pritchard, 'The Historical Experience of British War Crimes Courts in the Far East' (n 2) 326.
[383] Pritchard, 'The Historical Experience of British War Crimes Courts in the Far East' (n 2) 321.
[384] Pritchard, 'The Historical Experience of British War Crimes Courts in the Far East' (n 2) 317.
[385] Pritchard, 'The Historical Experience of British War Crimes Courts in the Far East' (n 2) 311.
[386] Pritchard, 'The Historical Experience of British War Crimes Courts in the Far East' (n 2) 320–1.
[387] Bloxham, 'British War Crimes Trial Policy in Germany, 1945–1957' (n 7) 97.
[388] Bloxham, 'British War Crimes Trial Policy in Germany, 1945–1957' (n 7 ) 119.
[389] Army Act, Rules of Procedure (1939) (n 10) art 60(C) and art 91(A).

joint trials, each and every one of them defended by a sole Counsel, seem like exercises in collective judgment. (It is also true that several of the accused in those trials were acquitted.) The use of Japanese Counsel conferred some benefits on the accused, but the downside was that the accused were defended by Counsel who were not familiar with the laws of England. These laws provided the backdrop of the military courts' procedure and stood in for some of the substantive law the judges applied. Many obstacles to procedural fairness were systemic—they went beyond the full control of the Presiding Judges. For example, cross-examination was not legally guaranteed: even the evidence of key Prosecution witnesses could be introduced in written form. Overall, speed was at least as important a consideration in the Hong Kong trials as the appearance of justice. Possibly the British government could not spare the resources to fund a better system; whatever the practical difficulties, though, we can be confident that the procedural standard experienced by the Japanese accused was much lower than that which applied to British servicemen at the time.

Besides the shortcomings in the process, the operation of British military courts was affected by a certain mentality, so foreign or inaccessible to us, I believe, as to place a part of that history beyond our comprehension. It was a mentality we would today call orientalism or racism. It was mixed in with a strong post-War emotion. The British *Manual of Military Law 1929 (as amended)* was itself not free of class prejudice, especially in its distinction between officers and privates. For example, 'allowance must be made for the coarse expressions which a man of inferior education will often use'.[390] When the British came in contact with the Japanese, a racial prejudice largely took the place of class-based concerns. In *Kishi et al*, the first of the Hong Kong trials, the Prosecutor submitted to the Court: 'every human being of whatever creed, race or colour, even a Japanese, is conscious in his own heart that to cut off a man's head without a fair trial is a crime.'[391] Lieutenant Haggan, the Defending Officer in *Matsuda*, argued in the course of his submissions on mitigation: 'The President and the Members of this Court are fully aware that the Japanese have not got the advantages of the upbringing, the idealism and the education of the right kind that we have.'[392] A Judge Advocate remarked upon the bias against senior Japanese personnel which was palpable at the time: 'A stigma clearly attaches to any man who has held high rank in the Kempeitai and/or the Gendarmerie and the fact that the accused succeeded to the command formerly held by the notorious Colonel Noma . . . no doubt had its effect on the minds of the Court.'[393] Emotions were still running high.

In his 2011 interview, Ormsby defended British superiority: 'this business of a lawful order, for instance. The Japanese do not know about such things. Ridiculous. How the hell does a Japanese know what that means? The Japanese peasant class, how do they know the difference between a lawful order and an unlawful

[390] *Manual of Military Law 1929 (as amended)* (n 12) 58–9.
[391] *Trial of Lt Kishi Yasuo and fourteen others* (n 62) slide 552.
[392] *Trial of Sgt Matsuda Kenichi* (n 201) slide 92.
[393] *Trial of Lt Col Kanazawa Asao* (n 350) slide 4.

order?'[394] 'You can't equate the Japanese mind, the soldier, the coolie, with say a British soldier.'[395] Ormsby was a judicial member in *Kishi et al.* When Stewart, the Presiding Judge in the case, pronounced the death sentence on two of the accused, this is what the courtroom heard from the President:

> Lieutenant Kishi, the unanimous sentence of this Court which is subject to confirmation is that you will suffer death by hanging. The Court has taken into consideration the fact that you belong to a black race from which little or no decency is expected, but by no conceivable standard of conduct is there any excuse for what you did.
>
> Lieutenant Matsumoto, the unanimous sentence of this Court which is subject to confirmation is that you will suffer death by hanging. The Court has taken into account that you belong to an evil race from which little decency is expected, but not according to any possible standard of conduct is there any justification for what you did.[396]

## 5.2 Justice or politics?

Can 'justice' administered by a victor in a war ever be seen in retrospect as justice? The notion of victor's justice is of course self-defeating, for if justice is desired, it must be desired equally for all situations, not just for those selected on the basis of national or ethnic distinction. The one-sided prosecution of the Japanese was not 'justice' in any sense that the British would have accepted as applicable to their domestic sphere. We could just as accurately refer to the aim of the Hong Kong trials by another term, including, broadly, politics. The political nature of victors' trials is clearer when we consider that the conduct of states on both sides of the Second World War wiped almost clean the slate of international humanitarian law. The indiscriminate Allied firebombing of German cities, the mindboggling bestiality of the Red Army in its final push through Poland and Germany, and the US nuclear attacks on Japan, when added to the unsurpassable crimes of the Nazi state and to those of Japan in China and elsewhere, mock the idea that a settled law of war existed, on the basis of which a criminal court could pass judgment on individual soldiers.

Even before the Hong Kong trials drew to a close in 1948, public pressure for clemency for the Japanese accused mounted.[397] Five petitions for clemency were submitted by relatives and friends of the accused Kinoshita after the outcome of his trial was confirmed in December 1948. They were received by the Judge Advocate, who advised the Confirming Officer that 'once the Proceedings of a War Crimes trial are confirmed, Petitions submitted on behalf of, or even by, convicted persons themselves are out of time . . . [it follows that] it is not incumbent on the confirming

[394] Linton,'Record of Two Interviews with Major Murray I. Ormsby' (n 35) 18.
[395] Linton,'Record of Two Interviews with Major Murray I. Ormsby' (n 35) 24.
[396] *Trial of Lt Kishi Yasuo and fourteen others* (n 62) slide 558. Pritchard, too, has commented on the racially charged remarks of the British military court judges: Pritchard, 'The Historical Experience of British War Crimes Courts in the Far East' (n 2) 325–6.
[397] Pritchard, 'British Postwar War Crimes Courts: The Gift of Clemency' (n 5) 17.

authority to take any action whatever on such Petitions'.[398] Around that time, however, a 'political' extension to the original procedure had been added. The Judge Advocate, aware of the new development, continued: 'the Secretary of State may consider that the proper course in this case would be for these Petitions to be referred in due course [to the] War Crimes Sentences Review Board.'[399]

The review board idea was first floated in May 1948. Review Boards were to be instituted in the relevant British commands to consider the cases with unexpired sentences that had been tried in those commands under the Royal Warrant. They were to examine the records of each case, the petitions received, and the reports of prison governors on the conduct and health of the prisoners.[400] The War Crimes Sentences Review Board for the Far East, alluded to above by the Judge Advocate, was established in January 1949.[401] Thus began a process which freed all convicted Japanese war criminals by 1957.[402]

As Pritchard explains in his useful history of the period, the British government came under considerable pressure from several quarters to end the Far East trials as quickly as possible and to release convicted war criminals, well before they had completed their sentences.[403] With the onset of the Cold War, Western countries wanted cordial relations with the new Japan. In November 1946, on the occasion of the promulgation of a revised Constitution for Japan, the Emperor issued a rescript pardoning all offences committed by members of the Japanese armed forces under the country's relevant criminal codes. In granting an amnesty by general pardon, the Emperor specifically included offences against POWs.[404] Mounting public pressure followed the rescript: petitions signed by hundreds of thousands of Japanese citizens and presented to the British embassy in Tokyo demanded the cessation of Britain's perceived degrading treatment of those enlisted men who supposedly had been made scapegoats for a war that everyone now deplored.[405] There was organized diplomatic pressure by Japan at every level.[406] By mid-1951, the British government had decided to put in place a process to repatriate all remaining Japanese persons serving time in British colonial prisons.[407]

We should perhaps resist judging the British military court trials by the events that followed them a few years later. Yet, we can also not entirely ignore the fact that the 22 Japanese nationals put to death in Hong Kong suffered, in a sense, disproportional punishment, when compared with those of their compatriots who received life terms or lengthy sentences of imprisonment, only to be sent back to

398 *Trial of Lt Gen Kinoshita Eiichi and Sgt Yoshida Bunzo* (n 118) slide 6.
399 *Trial of Lt Gen Kinoshita Eiichi and Sgt Yoshida Bunzo* (n 118) slide 6.
400 Pritchard, 'British Postwar War Crimes Courts: The Gift of Clemency' (n 5) 34.
401 Pritchard, 'British Postwar War Crimes Courts: The Gift of Clemency' (n 5) 35.
402 Bloxham, 'British War Crimes Trial Policy in Germany, 1945–1957' (n 7) 113; Linton, 'Record of Two Interviews with Major Murray I. Ormsby' (n 35) 31; Linton, 'Rediscovering the War Crimes Trials in Hong Kong, 1946–48' (n 6) 324.
403 Pritchard, 'British Postwar War Crimes Courts: The Gift of Clemency' (n 5) 16–17.
404 Pritchard, 'British Postwar War Crimes Courts: The Gift of Clemency' (n 5) 22.
405 Pritchard, 'British Postwar War Crimes Courts: The Gift of Clemency' (n 5) 24.
406 Pritchard, 'British Postwar War Crimes Courts: The Gift of Clemency' (n 5) 37–47.
407 Pritchard, 'British Postwar War Crimes Courts: The Gift of Clemency' (n 5) 29.

Japan, and be freed, within a few years. Virtually no Japanese war criminals convicted by the British courts to prison terms remained in custody longer than ten years.[408] Pritchard, who as we have seen is inclined to praise the trials when examining them close up, concludes that the subsequent events discredited them.[409] Their flimsy façade of judicial rectitude was taken down and mothballed in accordance with the dictates of international politics. Many years would pass before anything more was said about them.

[408] Pritchard, 'British Postwar War Crimes Courts: The Gift of Clemency' (n 5) 47. Even Kyoda, who was sentenced to just seven years' imprisonment for his role in the deaths of POWs on the *Lisbon Maru*, did not serve his full sentence but was sent back to Japan before it expired: Vine, 'Experiences as a War Crimes Prosecutor in Hong Kong' (n 36) 209.

[409] Pritchard, 'British Postwar War Crimes Courts: The Gift of Clemency' (n 5) 48.

# 3

# The Prisoner of War Camp Trials

*Yuma Totani*

## 1. Introduction

'After the fall of Corregidor and formal surrender by Gen. Wainwright of the forces of the USAFFE in the Philippines', Judge Brigadier General Calixto Duque read, 'the American prisoners of war and civilian internees were distributed in the different camps located at Cabanatuan, Davao, Fort McKinley, Camp Murphy, Pasay, Las Pinas, Clark, Lipa, old Bilibid Prisons, the Sto. Tomas University, Los Banos and other places.' It was 14 July 1949, when Judge Duque, President of the Philippine military commission at Manila, read out in the courtroom the rationale of guilty verdicts to accused Lieutenant General Kuroda Shigenori. Kuroda was the third of four Japanese generals who as commanding general of the Fourteenth Army had led military operations in the Philippines between May 1943 and September 1944. He faced a war crime charge that included 'the unlawful treatment of prisoners of war and civilian internees' and more specifically 'the inadequacy of food, quarters, clothing, medicine, medical care, hospitalization and other necessities, as well as the unlawful exaction of manual labour from prisoners of war and the commission of brutal atrocities on both prisoners of war and civilian internees alike'. The Prosecution's allegations were substantiated in most part, the Duque Court concluded, and declared that 'we are convinced of the occurrence of the specific complaints charged, their general pattern in all the camps and their monotonous consistency throughout'.[1]

The foregoing opinion by the Duque Court had special resonance with the findings made earlier at the British war crimes trials in Hong Kong (1945–48), where evidence showed that the Japanese treatment of prisoners of war ('POWs') at the neighbouring islands in the wartime Empire of Japan—namely,

[1] *PPI v Shigenori Kuroda—Rationale*, 6–7, in 'Shigenori Kuroda—Public Trial, vol 83' (Box 1702). Records of the General Headquarters Supreme Commander for the Allied Powers (SCAP), Records of the SCAP Legal Section, Prosecution Division—'Entry 1323: Philippines v Various Japanese War Criminals Case Files 1947–1949.' This record is part of RG 331 (Records of the Allied Operational and Occupation Headquarters, World War II). National Archives and Records Administration (NARA), College Park, MD, USA. The entire record of the Kuroda Trial is contained in Boxes 1699–1702/Entry 1323/RG 331.

Japanese-occupied British Hong Kong and colonial Taiwan[2]—was no different. One witness after another at the British courts attested, either in person or through affidavits, to the everyday life of POW camps at the two territories as consisting of inadequate rations, overcrowded and unhygienic quarters, withholding of medical supplies, neglect of the gravely sick, frequent beatings and other physical abuses, unlawful use of POW labour under trying and dangerous conditions, and many illnesses, injuries, and deaths resulting from the mistreatment. Each account was shocking and heart wrenching, although the cumulative effect of the voluminous witness testimony was—just as Judge Duque summarized with respect to the Kuroda case—almost that of monotonous consistency.[3]

The findings at the Manila and Hong Kong courts have another uncanny connection. The above-mentioned American general, Jonathan M Wainwright, and a number of US Army officers who capitulated to the Japanese at Bataan and Corregidor in the Philippines were subsequently transferred for segregated detention at camps in Taiwan, whereupon they experienced firsthand the cruelty of the Japanese POW administration. The British trial records show that the Japanese camp personnel paid little regard to the high status—or the relative advanced age of the officer detainees for that matter—and that they instead subjected the latter to a heightened level of humiliation, deprivation, and physical abuse. The British trials records further show that among the segregated detention were the highest-ranking Allied officers and civilian high officials from other theatres of war in the Pacific. They included Lieutenant General A F Percival, commander of the British forces in British Malaya; Brigadier Arthur S Blackburn, commander of the Australian forces in Java (then part of the Dutch East Indies, overrun by the Japanese); and Sir Mark Young, Governor of British Hong Kong.[4] They were made to salute the Japanese camp guards, endure beatings, carry out menial work, and undertake various other demoralizing tasks. The mistreatment of these special classes of Allied individuals continued at the last detention sites in Japanese-controlled Manchuria.

[2] Taiwan was a Japanese colony between 1895 and 1945 as a result of cession from Qing China to Imperial Japan in the aftermath of the Sino-Japanese War (1894–1895).

[3] There are a number of memoirs and research works that bring to light the lives of Allied POWs in Japanese custody in Hong Kong and Taiwan during the Pacific War. For representative publications, see G Wright-Nooth, *Prisoner of the Turnip Heads: Horror, Hunger and Humour in Hong Kong, 1941–1945* (Leo Cooper 1994); C G Roland, *Long Night's Journey into Day: Prisoners of War in Hong Kong and Japan, 1941–1945* (Wilfried Laurier University Press 2001); C Banham, *We Shall Suffer There: Hong Kong's Defenders Imprisoned, 1942–45* (Hong Kong University Press 2009); and C Barman, *Resist to the End: Hong Kong, 1941–1945* (Hong Kong University Press 2009). For representative accounts of *POW* incarceration in Taiwan, see J M Wainwright, *General Wainwright's Story: The Account of Four Years of Humiliating Defeat, Surrender, and Captivity* (Doubleday & Co 1946); D C James (ed), *South to Bataan, North to Mukden: The Prison Diary of Brigadier General W E Brougher* (University of Georgia Press 1971); L Beebe, *Prisoner of the Rising Sun: The Lost Diary of Brig Lewis Beebe* (University of Oklahoma Press 1993).

[4] Reference to high-ranking Allied military officers and civilian officials in Japanese custody is made in the record of *Trial of Col Nakano Junichi and two others* (HKWCT Collection, File No 235/1044) ('*Trial of Col Nakano Junichi and two others*'). See especially, Affidavit of Maj Gen Hervey Degge Wilmot Sitwell dated 10 December 1945, *Trial of Col Nakano Junichi and 2 others*, exhibit W, 1, slide 296; and Statement of Imamura Yaohachi dated 29 May 1946, *Trial of Col Nakano Junichi and two others,* exhibit J, 1, slide 261.

The day of liberation came at the War's end in August 1945, when the 'American parachutists and Russian tanks and Russian airborne troops' crossed the borders of the state of Manchukuo and descended upon the POW camps to carry out the rescue mission.[5]

Who was to blame for the widespread mistreatment of surrendered Allied military and civilian persons at the POW camps in Hong Kong, Taiwan, and many other Japanese-occupied territories in the Asia-Pacific region? Why did the camp facilities, medical supplies, and food conditions remain woefully inadequate? Should one attribute the primary responsibility to individual camp guards or those higher up in the military chain of command? Did the central government of Japan actually sanction unlawful policies regarding the treatment of POWs? What were the reasons behind incarcerating the high-ranking Allied military personnel and civilian officials in segregated camps in Taiwan and then in Manchuria?

The purpose of the present chapter is to address some of these questions by analysing as case studies a selection of British war crimes trials held in Hong Kong. The number of trials related to POW camps at Hong Kong is limited, but they are by no means unimportant. What makes the British Hong Kong cases particularly noteworthy is the inclusion in the groups of defendants a representative range of the Japanese camp authorities in wartime Hong Kong and Taiwan, thereby allowing an insight into structures, internal workings, and policy dimensions of the Japanese POW administration. Moreover, the trials enable us to have an in-depth appreciation of the general conditions of the camps as told in the immediate aftermath of the War by the former POWs themselves, the Japanese camp staff, their superior officers, representatives of the International Committee of Red Cross, civilian eyewitnesses in the camps' neighbourhood, and post-war Allied war crimes investigators.

This chapter will focus on the following four trials whose chief defendants were formerly the highest-ranking officers of the Japanese POW camps in the two territories: (1) the trial of Colonel Tokunaga Isao, who served as commandant of all POW camps in Hong Kong for practically the entire period of the Pacific War (January 1942–August 1945); (2) the trial of Colonel Nakano Junichi, the first of the three Japanese officers to serve as commandant of all POW camps in colonial Taiwan (July 1942–June 1943); (3) the trial of Colonel Sazawa Hideo, successor of Nakano (July 1943–March 1945); and (4) the trial of Major Uete Taichi, successor of Colonel Sazawa (March–September 1945).[6] All four accused were

[5] Affidavit of Maj Gen Christopher Michael Maltby dated 16 November 1945, *Trial of Col Tokunaga Isao and four others* (HKWCT Collection, File No 235/1012 Part Two) ('*Trial of Col Tokunaga Isao and four others (Part Two)*'), exhibit Z, 2, slide 75. ('*Trial of Col Tokunaga Isao and four others*'.) For a detailed account of liberation of the Allied officers from the camps in Manchuria, see Wainwright, *General Wainwright's Story* (n 3) chs 14–15. Japan assumed control over southern Manchuria since the Russo-Japanese War (1904–1905), and then the larger area of the region after the establishment of the state of Manchukuo (1932–1945).

[6] *Trial of Col Tokunaga Isao and four others* (n 5); *Trial of Col Nakano Junichi and two others* (n 4); *Trial of Col Sazawa Hideo and two others* (HKWCT Collection, File No 235/1029) ('*Trial of Col Sazawa Hideo and 2 others*'); *Trial of Maj Uete Taichi and seven others* (HKWCT Collection, File No 235/1105) ('*Trial of Maj Uete Taichi and seven others*').

prosecuted jointly with some of their wartime subordinates of varying ranks and positions, such as medical officers, commanders of branch camps, interpreters, and camp guards. The number of co-defendants ranged from two to seven. In addition to the four cases, this chapter will also analyse a trial involving civilian accused. The chief defendant was Toda Mitsugu, General Manager of the Japan Mining Company (*Nippon kōgyō*) at Kinkaseki, Taiwan, during the Pacific War. He and eight of the company employees were jointly prosecuted on the allegation that they collaborated with the Army in making unlawful and criminal use of POW labour.[7] By analysing these five trials, this chapter will assess the British courts' findings on the organizational and individual responsibility of the Japanese military and civilian authorities for the mistreatment of POWs.

## 2. The *Hong Kong POW Camps* Case

The trial of *Colonel Tokunaga Isao and four others* is arguably the most important of all POW cases that were held at the British Hong Kong courts. The chief defendant, Tokunaga, was the highest-ranking Japanese officer of the Hong Kong POW camp group, whose uninterrupted command made him the very face of the local camp authorities for the duration of the War. Moreover, many of the victims of atrocity at the Hong Kong camps were part of the local population, formerly being the members of the Hong Kong Volunteer Defence Corps (HKVDC) or the British armed forces stationed in the colony. The relative importance of the *Tokunaga* trial in the eyes of the Hong Kong public is evidenced by the fact that it started within a few months of V-J Day, on 17 October 1946, while the four high-profile POW cases related to Taiwan did not start until more than one and a half years later. The *Tokunaga* trial was the longest of the five as well; it consumed as many as 53 court days as opposed to 19.5 days on average with respect to the four cases related to Taiwan.

It may come as a little surprise, then, when one finds that overseas nationals figured prominently in the *Tokunaga* trial. The most noticeable group comprised of Canadian POWs. They were formerly members of the Royal Rifles of Canada, the Winnipeg Grenadiers, and their medical detachments. Why did these Canadians end up in Hong Kong, and how did they become prisoners of the Japanese? Charles G Roland in *Long Night's Journey into Day: Prisoners of War in Hong Kong and Japan, 1941–1945* (2001) provides relevant information.[8] The Canadian contingent had been hastily brought over at the request of the British government, which had persuaded the Dominion government in the fall of 1941 that two Canadian battalions would make it possible for Britain to defend its key Far Eastern colony, Hong Kong, in the eventuality of the Japanese invasion. This proved to be a gross underestimation. The Japanese assault forces overran the Crown territory in

[7] *Trial of Toda Mitsugu and eight others* (HKWCT Collection, File No 235/1028) ('*Trial of Toda Mitsugu and eight others*').

[8] Roland, *Long Night's Journey into Days of War in Hong Kong and Japan, 1941–1945* (n 3) 7–8.

a matter of weeks at the start of the Pacific War, turning more than 10,000 desperate defenders into prisoners of the Japanese.[9] The troops that had freshly arrived from Canada were among them. Notwithstanding the British prewar estimations, Canadians were unable to offer much help to repulse the Japanese, since they had little time to receive necessary military training or, for that matter, to overcome basic communication problems with their English-speaking counterparts in Hong Kong. (According to Roland, Canadian soldiers of the two units were mostly francophone.[10])

The language and/or nationality barriers appeared to continue alienating Canadians from the rest of the British Commonwealth soldiers in Japanese custody. Major General Christopher Michael Maltby, formerly General Officer Commanding the British troops in China based in Hong Kong, recalled that the Canadians were 'concentrated in the North Point Camp' in Hong Kong Island and that they 'remained as a separate body, officers and men being in the same camp'.[11]

The *Tokunaga* trial in many respects was a 'Canadian' event indeed; the visibility of Canadians in the court proceedings was great at any rate. The prosecuting officer, Major G B Puddicombe, was himself a Canadian and a member of the Victoria Rifles of Canada.[12] His Opening Address focused on outlining huge human losses that Canada was made to bear at the hands of the Japanese camp authorities. 'It will be proved beyond any doubt', he declared, 'that among Canadians alone, one hundred and twenty-eight deaths resulted', many of which could have been avoided if the accused Tokunaga and his chief medical officer and one of the co-defendants, Captain Saitō Shunkichi, 'had done their simple duty'.[13] The first Prosecution witness whom Puddicombe called to the stand was Lieutenant Colonel John Nieilson Brown Crawford, also Canadian, who was formerly a member of the Royal Canadian Medical Corps and a POW at Hong Kong for the duration of the War. While in Japanese custody, Crawford took charge of looking after the health of the Canadian POWs and communicating their medical needs to the Japanese camp authorities. He attested, among other things, that 101 men out of the total of 128 who perished at the Hong Kong camps 'need not have died', the causes of their deaths being preventable or treatable illnesses such as diphtheria, malnutrition, starvation, dysentery, and avitaminosis.[14]

[9] The figure 10,000 is taken from Utsumi Aiko, *Nihongun no horyo seisaku* (Prisoner-of-War Policies of the Japanese Military) (Aoki shoten 2005) 182.

[10] Roland, *Long Night's Journey into Day: Prisoners of War in Hong Kong and Japan, 1941–1945* (n 3) 8.

[11] Affidavit of Maj Gen Christopher Michael Maltby of 16 November 1945, *Trial of Col Tokunaga Isao and four others* (*Part Two*) (n 5) exhibit Z, 1, slide 74. Maltby was transferred in August 1943 to Camp Shirakawa in Taiwan, where he joined his brother, Air Vice Marshall P C Maltby of the Royal Air Force.

[12] *Trial of Col Tokunaga Isao and four others* (HKWCT Collection, File No 235/1012 *Part One*) ('*Trial of Col Tokunaga Isao and four others (Part One)*'), transcript 1, slide 40.

[13] Prosecutor's Opening Address, *Trial of Col Tokunaga Isao and four others (Part One)* (n 12) exhibit E, 2, slide 849.

[14] Testimony of Prosecution Witness Lt Col John Nielson Brown Crawford, *Trial of Col Tokunaga Isao and four others (Part One)* (n 12) transcript 28, slide 67.

Puddicombe further detailed in his Opening Address that Tokunaga was party to the arrest, interrogation, and extrajudicial killing in August 1942 of four Canadians and members of the Winnipeg Grenadiers. The four—Sergeant J O Payne, Lieutenant Corporal G Berzenski, Private J H Adams, and Private P J Ellis, as the victims were individually named in the charge sheet[15]—had been POWs at North Point, where they tried to fulfil 'the primary duty of Prisoners of War, that is, to escape'. They were recaptured shortly after breaking out of the camp, however, and interrogated in the presence of the camp Commandant, Tokunaga. The four were subsequently executed, although the report Tokunaga filed with Tokyo at the time indicated that the escapees 'had been shot while clambering through the wire enclosing the Camp'.[16] The actual circumstances of the killing surfaced only after the War by painstaking war crimes investigations and eyewitness accounts. Paying tribute to the four dead, Puddicombe characterized the doomed escape attempt as 'among the most romantic, if not the most tragic of all the stories which have come out of these terrible 44 months of imprisonment'.[17]

The episode of four Canadian escapees—whose general circumstances as outlined were corroborated by Tokunaga himself during examination-in-chief[18]—must have had a sympathetic hearing in the courtroom and especially at the bench. The president of the three-member panel (No 5 War Crimes Court) was Lieutenant Colonel R C Laming, a British barrister and a member of the Department of the Judge Advocate General (JAG) India; and the two associated judges were Captain K R Busfield, a British officer of the Royal Armoured Corps, and Major J T Loranger, a Canadian and a member the JAG Branch of the Canadian Army.[19] In all likelihood, the British authorities at the Hong Kong war crimes programme solicited the participation of a Canadian Judge in view of the preponderance of Canadian victims in the Tokunaga case.

The charges against Tokunaga and four co-defendants were articulated in 11 separate elements.[20] The first five concerned 'inhumane treatment' of British, Canadian, and Dutch POWs 'in violation of the laws and usages of war', by the 'members of the Prisoner-of-War Camp Staff under the command of the first named accused [Tokunaga], and responsible for the well being of' the prisoners. The mistreatment resulted 'in deaths of some and in physical sufferings to others'. It was alleged that Tokunaga, Saitō, and one or more of the remaining three co-defendants were criminally liable for mistreating the POWs at the following

[15] Charge Sheet, *Trial of Col Tokunaga Isao and four others (Part One)* (n 12) slide 12.

[16] Prosecutor's Opening Address, *Trial of Col Tokunaga Isao and four others (Part One)* (n 12) exhibit E, 3, slide 850.

[17] Prosecutor's Opening Address, *Trial of Col Tokunaga Isao and four others (Part One)* (n 12) exhibit E, 3, slide 850.

[18] Testimony of Col Tokunaga Isao, *Trial of Col Tokunaga Isao and four others (Part One)* (n 12) transcript 441–5, slides 482–6.

[19] Testimony of Col Tokunaga Isao, *Trial of Col Tokunaga Isao and four others (Part One)* (n 12) transcript 1, slide 40.

[20] Charge Sheet, Testimony of Col Tokunaga Isao, *Trial of Col Tokunaga Isao and four others (Part One)* (n 12) slides 11–12. The charges were read into the record of the trial at transcript 1–3, slides 40–2.

specified locations: the Sham Shui Po Camp (charge 1), the North Point Camp (charge 2), the Upper Argyle Street Officers Camp (charge 3), the Indian Military Hospital at Argyle Street (charge 4), and the Bowen Road Hospital (charge 5). The three to follow (charges 6–8) were principally against Tokunaga, charging him with 'maltreatment' and killing of camp escapees including the four Canadian POWs mentioned in the Prosecutor's Opening Address. Charge 9 was levelled against Tokunaga only and alleged that he 'misappropriate[d] for his own use and benefit[ted] Red Cross supplies of food, medicine, clothes and other comforts intended for the Prisoners-of-War interned in HONG KONG', and also 'permit[ted] and condone[d] the mis-appropriation of such Red Cross supplies by his staff'. The last two counts alleged that Tokunaga (charge 10) and a co-defendant, Lieutenant Tanaka Hitoshi (charge 11), were responsible for episodes of beating, torturing, and killing of Chinese civilians in Hong Kong. Tokunaga was found guilty of charges 1–3 and 5–9 but acquitted of charges 4 and 10. He received the death sentence.[21] The confirming authority subsequently reduced the sentence to life imprisonment due apparently to a petition submitted by the head of medical services of the Hong Kong government's Medical Department, who appealed for leniency in accordance with the 'British idea of justice'.[22]

The Court's guilty verdicts against Tokunaga were not explained, but the trial record allows one to reconstruct some of the basic reasoning. With respect to Tokunaga's responsibility as camp commandant in general, it was not a matter of controversy between the Prosecution and the Defence that the accused held control over the Hong Kong POW camps and over the camp personnel. Tokunaga himself testified during examination-in-chief that '[a]ll these camps were under my direct supervision and I appointed various officers to look after these camps, who were also under my direct control'.[23] He did try to downplay his power over the camp staff, however, arguing that he 'could be hardly to be held responsible for under-hand assault on POWs by his guards or interpreters' and that '[n]o one guard or

[21] With respect to charges 2 and 3, the Court found Tokunaga guilty except for the words 'in the deaths of some'. Record of Proceedings, *Trial of Col Tokunaga Isao and four others (Part One)* (n 12) 1, slide 8.

[22] The author of the petition was Dr Percy Selwyn Selwyn-Clarke, Director of Medical Services, Hong Kong Government Medical Department. The petition was addressed to Maj Gen G V E J Erskine, General Officer Commanding the Troops in China, China Command Headquarters, Hong Kong. It reported how 'about six weeks after the surrender he [Tokunaga] issued orders to the P.O.W. Camps and Military Hospital guards to allow parcels of food to be sent in weekly' as well as other relief items such as 'valuable drugs', which Clarke believed to have 'contributed very largely to the welfare of the inmates'. Tokunaga was 'lazy and greedy rather than deliberately sadistic', and was 'an oldish man and has been in prison awaiting trial for seventeen months'. The petitioner implored that 'justice will be met—our British idea of justice—by exercising your prerogative of mercy and commuting the sentence to one of imprisonment for life'. See Petition by Dr Selwyn-Clarke dated 17 February 1947, *Trial of Col Tokunaga Isao and four others (Part One)* (n 12) 1–2, slides 17–18. The reviewing Judge Advocate wrote that 'the confirming officer was probably influenced by the petition from Dr Selwyn Clarke'. See Judge Advocate's Report, Testimony of Col Tokunaga Isao, *Trial of Col Tokunaga Isao and four others (Part One)* (n 12) 14 July 1947, slide 6.

[23] Testimony of Col Tokunaga Isao, *Trial of Col Tokunaga Isao and four others (Part One)* (n 12) transcript 415, slide 456.

interpreter can be kept constantly observed in the off chance of his being caught in some act, which is not set down as his [Tokunaga's] duty' (the Closing Address for the Defence).[24] Tokunaga also stressed his limited authority within the overall chain of command, pointing out his subordinate position in relation to the chief of the Japanese military administration in the occupied territory of Hong Kong—or the 'Governor-General of Hong Kong', which was 'the Governor of the Expeditionary Area of HONG KONG', Tokunaga explained—under whose control the Hong Kong POW camps fell.[25] Tokunaga was a subordinate officer also in relation to the War Ministry in the central government, which took charge of determining basic rules and regulations concerning POW camp administration.[26] In the words of the Defence Counsel, Tokunaga should thus be understood as 'merely an executioner' of various instructions, regulations, and orders, and 'he could not go beyond the authority laid down in the regulations by the War Ministry or by the Governor General'.[27] This could be construed as a plea of superior orders and possibly that of 'bureaucratic responsibility'; the accused portrayed himself as a cog of a machine that simply fulfilled his ascribed functions in the chain of command of the Army.

It is not clear what opinion the Court formed concerning the responsibility of Tokunaga's superiors or the issues of organizational responsibility. The guilty verdicts and stern punishment that the Court handed down to the accused suggest, nonetheless, that the judges did not consider the Defence argument as exculpatory or mitigating factors. A few exchanges between the Court and Tokunaga during the trial actually point to the sceptical views of the judges about Tokunaga's downplaying of his authority. For instance, the Court once asked the accused, 'Did the Governor General, not the commander of 23 army, ever come and inspect the POW camps himself?' Tokunaga replied in the negative; whereupon the Court went on to ask if the successive chiefs of staff of the Governor-General inspected the camps instead. This time the reply was in the affirmative, although the further questioning revealed that the chiefs of staff visited the camps '[o]nly once' and that is, '[a]t the time of their appointment'.[28]

Tokunaga himself was a regular visitor to the Hong Kong POW camps, as evidenced by the Prosecution and Defence witnesses. For instance, the aforementioned Canadian medical officer at North Point, Lieutenant Colonel Crawford, testified that 'he [Tokunaga] made inspections at intervals of two to three months

[24] Closing Address for the Defence, *Trial of Col Tokunaga Isao and four others* (HKWCT Collection File No WO235/1012 part 3) ('*Trial of Col Tokunaga Isao and four others (Part Three)*'), exhibit M, 8, slide 646.

[25] Testimony of Col Tokunaga Isao, *Trial of Col Tokunaga Isao and four others (Part One)* (n 12) transcript 414–15, slides 455–6.

[26] Testimony of Col Tokunaga Isao, *Trial of Col Tokunaga Isao and four others (Part One)* (n 12) transcript 414, slide 455.

[27] Closing Address for the Defence, *Trial of Col Tokunaga Isao and four others (Part Three)* (n 24) exhibit M, 8, slide 646.

[28] Testimony of Col Tokunaga Isao (n 12) *Trial of Col Tokunaga Isao and four others (Part One)* (n 12) transcript 559, slide 600.

during the internment'.[29] Another witness, Captain J A G Reid of the Royal Canadian Army Medical Corps, similarly recounted in some detail an instance of Tokunaga's visit of the Canadian POW camp. Tokunaga is said to have delivered a speech during one such visit, in which he 'demand[ed] that all persons sign a document to the effect that they would not try to escape, making dire threats of what would happen if anyone refuse to sign them'. Tokunaga continued in the speech, Reid testified, 'that the prisoners should think of no appeal to international law as that no longer existed for them'. Instead 'there was only one law in the world, that being the Imperial Japanese Army Law'. According to Reid, one Canadian POW and a former member of the Royal Rifles of Canada refused to sign the non-escape oath. This person was promptly 'taken away to a Japanese prison and there [he] was tortured for about a week until he signed'.[30]

Captain Kenneth M A Barnett, a member of the Corps Artillery of the Hong Kong Volunteer Defence Corps and a former POW at the Sham Shui Po Camp, could relate to the Court yet another episode of Tokunaga's visit and his exercising of authority as camp commandant at a different location. According to Barnett's sworn statement, Tokunaga escorted to Sham Shui Po on a day in August 1944 Rudolf Zindel, the Hong Kong delegate of the International Committee of Red Cross (ICRC). POWs in the camp were not permitted to speak to the ICRC representative. Determined to have his voice heard, however, Barnett broke the rank and came standing face to face with Zindel. Thereupon Barnett is said to have cried out in French: 'Au Secours! M. le Délégué! Nous allons mourir de faim.' A Japanese interpreter rushed to him and demanded that Barnett state what he just said, to which the latter replied—this time in English—'We are not getting enough to eat.'[31] This abruptly ended the inspection tour, Tokunaga and his subordinates whisking the ICRC delegate away from the scene. The 'Barnett Incident', as it became known among the prisoners, cost Barnett seven consecutive days of severe beatings and solitary confinement, followed by further beatings while hospitalized[32] but it did bring about tangible improvement in the camp conditions. According to Lieutenant Colonel E J R Mitchell of the Hong Kong Volunteer Defence Corps, relief supplies from outside powers had rarely reached the prisoners but 'a fortnight after the BARNETT incident, we received 4 Canadian parcels each'.[33]

29 Testimony of Prosecution Witness Lt Col John Nieilson Brown Crawford, *Trial of Col Tokunaga Isao and four others (Part One)* (n 12) transcript 40, slide 79.

30 Extract from Sworn Statement of Capt J A G Reid dated 10 December 1945, *Trial of Col Tokunaga Isao and four others (Part Two)* (n 5) exhibit X, 1, slide 66.

31 Sworn Statement of Capt Kenneth Myer Arthur Barnett dated 23 March 1946, *Trial of Col Tokunaga Isao and four others (Part Two)* (n 5) exhibit L (2), 1, slide 254.

32 Sworn Statement of Capt Kenneth Myer Arthur Barnett dated 23 March 1946, *Trial of Col Tokunaga Isao and four others (Part Two)* (n 5) exhibit L (2), 2, slide 255.

33 Testimony of Prosecution Witness Lt Col E J R Mitchell, *Trial of Col Tokunaga Isao and four others (Part One)* (n 12) transcript 100, slide 139. According to Mitchell, his camp received Red Cross parcels on no more than two occasions prior to the Barnett Incident, in December 1942 and February 1943.

The ICRC delegate, Rudolf Zindel, confirmed in his postwar 31-page report to Geneva, the great difficulties he had faced when trying to access Allied POWs in Hong Kong and deliver them relief items. The difficulties were compounded by the fact that misappropriation of the ICRC packages was rampant among the Japanese camp members. Zindel believed that the misuse was committed 'with knowledge and co-operation of Colonel Tokunaga'[34] but he professed powerlessness, the reason being that Zindel had to maintain friendly relations with the local Japanese military authorities in order to ensure delivery of at least some of the relief supplies to POWs. He also felt his hands were tied because he could 'hardly question the integrity of a high-ranking Officer of the Japanese Army'—namely, Tokunaga—'without the risk of being accused of having committed "Lèse Majesté"'.[35] When assessing the validity of Tokunaga's plea of limited authority, the Court is likely to have weighed evidence such as the Zindel report, the Barnett Incident, and various other accounts attesting Tokunaga's personally exercising authority over camp administration, and concluded that the accused had effective control over the camps in Hong Kong.

Meanwhile, the trial record also indicates a degree of consensus between the Prosecution and the Defence that the War Ministry and the Governor-General's office were the ones with the policy-making power, not the Hong Kong camp commandant, and that the ultimate responsibility for the formulation of unlawful policies would rest with the Army authorities at the higher levels. Consider, for example, the Prosecution's allegation that Tokunaga forced POWs into signing an oath not to escape. The accused did not deny the fact, but made the point that the policy to use the non-escape pledge to prevent prisoners from escaping originated in the War Ministry at Tokyo. According to Tokunaga's testimony, he visited the POW Information Bureau in the central government prior to leaving for Hong Kong in January 1942 as newly-appointed camp commandant. Thereupon he received two instructions regarding the treatment of POWs. One was 'to treat the POWs in accordance with the International Law, that is, to treat them philanthropically; they should not be ill-treated'. But Japan having not ratified the Geneva Convention of 1929, Tokunaga is said to have been reminded that POWs would be treated 'according to the special circumstances of Japan'.[36] The second instruction from the bureau chief concerned control over POWs. Tokunaga is said to have been told that 'the POW might attempt escaping and it was the responsibility of the camp commandant to prevent any POWs escaping'. For the prevention of escape, he was instructed to take 'every possible means'.[37]

[34] Memorandum from Mr Rudolf Zindel, Delegate for Hong Kong of the International Red Cross Committee, to International Red Cross Committee, Geneva (Subject: Relief-Supplies for Allied Prisoners-of-War and Civilian Internees in Hong Kong Camps, dated 30 November 1945), *Trial of Col Tokunaga Isao and four others (Part Two)* (n 5) exhibit C(4), 6, slide 444.

[35] *Trial of Col Tokunaga Isao and four others (Part Two)* (n 5) exhibit C(4), 4, slide 442.

[36] Testimony of Col Tokunaga Isao, *Trial of Col Tokunaga Isao and four others (Part One)* (n 12) transcript 421, slide 462.

[37] Testimony of Col Tokunaga Isao, *Trial of Col Tokunaga Isao and four others (Part One)* (n 12) transcript 421, slide 462.

Documentary evidence introduced by the Defence corroborated in part the existence of this policy regarding prevention of POW escape. One document, titled, 'Detailed Prisoners of War Treatment Regulation', dated August 1943, contained the following rule:

> Article 5. A pledge of no escape shall be sworn by the Prisoner of War immediately after internment. The Prisoner of War refusing to make such a pledge shall be regarded as having intention of escaping and strict precautions shall be taken.[38]

When questioned by the Court about the timing of the War Ministry's issuance of this and other related regulations in evidence, Tokunaga explained that even though evidentiary material was dated 1943, the 'same sort of regulations were enforced' earlier as well, in 1942.[39]

It is not clear from the War Ministry's documents, however, if the 'strict precautions' in Article 5 should be construed as authorization to summarily execute recaptured POW escapees. Tokunaga attested that, in fact, he found himself in a legal and ethical quandary about his obligations. Concerning especially the four Canadian POWs who broke out of North Point, he informed the Court that, when determining their final disposition, he felt that 'shooting without trial seemed to me unreasonable'[40] and feared such action might 'cause a problem' also in relation to international law.[41] Why, then, did he order his subordinates to carry out the execution? His explanation was that a Major General Arisue, his immediate military superior and the chief of staff of the Governor-General, advised him on the occasion that it was 'not the time to talk about International Law'[42] and that the Hong Kong camp authorities as well as the Governor-General would 'lose face'[43] by the repeated escapes of POWs. It could not be separately verified whether or not Arisue made these remarks; he was killed in action before the termination of the War.[44] Even if Arisue had survived, however, Tokunaga may not have escaped conviction. The final guilty verdict—coupled with the death sentence—suggests that the Court ultimately rejected the accused's plea of superior orders as a defence.

38 Extracts from the Detailed Prisoners of War Treatment Regulation, Ministry of War Transmission No 29 dated 21 April 1943, *Trial of Col Tokunaga Isao (Part Three)* (n 24) exhibit W(4), slide 582.

39 Testimony of Col Tokunaga Isao, *Trial of Col Tokunaga Isao and four others (Part One)* (n 12) transcript 566, slide 607.

40 Testimony of Col Tokunaga Isao, *Trial of Col Tokunaga Isao and four others (Part One)* (n 12) transcript 445, slide 486.

41 Testimony of Col Tokunaga Isao, *Trial of Col Tokunaga Isao and four others (Part One)* (n 12) transcript 444, slide 485.

42 Testimony of Col Tokunaga Isao, *Trial of Col Tokunaga Isao and four others (Part One)* (n 12) transcript 444, slide 485.

43 Testimony of Col Tokunaga Isao, *Trial of Col Tokunaga Isao, and four others (Part One)* (n 12) transcript 443, slide 484.

44 Testimony of Col Tokunaga Isao, *Trial of Col Tokunaga Isao and four others (Part One)* (n 12) transcript 469, slide 510.

## 3. The Cases from Taiwan

More than one year after the conclusion of the *Tokunaga* trial, on 10 April 1947, the panel of three British Army officers sitting as judges at the No 7 War Crimes Court began hearing the case against Colonel Nakano Junichi, the first camp commandant of the POW camp group in Taiwan. The *Nakano* trial went into recess in mid-May, whereupon the same Court began hearing the case against Colonel Sazawa Hideo—Nakano's successor as camp commandant in Taiwan. The *Nakano* and *Sazawa* trials lasted for 13 and 14 court days respectively, and were completed by the end of July the same year. Meanwhile, the Laming Court—the No 5 War Crimes Court—became the venue for the trial of Toda Mitsugu and eight employees of the Kinkaseki Japan Mining Company. The *Toda* trial ended within the month of May 1947, lasting for 16 court days. A half-year later, the Laming Court heard the final case of the three high-profile trials related to the Taiwan POW camps: the trial of Major Uete Taichi—Sazawa's successor—and seven co-defendants. This trial turned out to be relatively time consuming, lasting for 35 court days.

Taiwan had been a colony of the Empire of Japan since the time of its cession from Qing China to Japan in 1895, and there were thus no Allied troops in the territory to be confronted with at the start of the Pacific War. Nonetheless, the Allied POWs came to make a large presence in Taiwan after eight months following the Pearl Harbor attack. From historical literature to date, one can learn that the new reality of the War—the combination of an acute labour shortage throughout the Empire of Japan on the one hand, and an unwieldy number of Allied POWs who fell under Japanese military control on the other—prompted the Japanese government to develop a new policy by which to authorize the relocation and usage of POWs as supplementary workforces. A policy paper by the War Ministry, dated 5 May 1942, outlined the basic principles of the use of POW labour (*Nanpō ni okeru furyo no shori yōryō no ken* [On Matters of the Outline of Prisoner-of-War Disposition in the Southern Area]). It read in part that the 'white' POWs should be transferred primarily to China, Korea, Manchuria, and Taiwan in order that they be 'utilized for expansion of production and war-related coolie labour'. As for 'non-white' POWs—presumably Asians, such as Indian soldiers in the British Army—they should be 'promptly declared liberated' and then used for labour 'preferably locally', in maritime and mainland Southeast Asia.[45]

The Imperial General Headquarters recorded that as many as 252,000 Allied soldiers surrendered to the Japanese and became POWs by April 1942.[46] A small portion of these persons was subsequently transferred to Taiwan. The full scope of the colonial government's policies concerning the use of POW labour is

[45] The text of the policy paper can be found in Utsumi, *Nihongun no horyo seisaku* (Prisoner-of-War Policies of the Japanese Military) (n 9) 204–5. A photostatic copy is reproduced in Chaen Yoshio, *Furyo ni kansuru shohōki ruishū* (Collection of Laws Concerning Prisoners of War) 57–8.

[46] Utsumi, *Nihongun no horyo seisaku* (Prisoner-of-War Policies of the Japanese Military) (n 9) 181.

understudied to date, but Kondō Masami's study shows that approximately 2,400 American and British POWs were brought over from the Philippines and Singapore in 1942, and that they were then utilized for digging, cultivating, transport, and so on, at the Taiwan Sugar Company, the Japan Mining Company, the Taiwan Shrine compounds, and other locations within the colony.[47] According to *Taiwan tōchi gaiyō* (Summary of Taiwan Governance), published by the Government-General of Taiwan in 1945, the Japan Mining Company had been the owner of a hugely successful gold-producing mine at Kinkaseki, Taiwan, since before the War.[48] It switched to copper production after the outbreak of the Pacific War, following the policy change of the government of Japan from promotion of gold to copper extraction. This made Kinkaseki the only mine in the colony with the ability to produce copper. The Japan Mining Company reportedly maintained an impressive level of productivity, making use of an array of subsidies, new infrastructure, and price control initiatives by the colonial government.[49] *Taiwan tōchi gaiyō* of 1945 does not discuss, however, what sort of workforces the Japan Mine Company utilized to maintain its wartime productivity.

The record of the *Toda* trial is helpful in this regard, as it brings to light the correspondence in 1942 between the local army authorities and the mining company concerning the use of POW labour. According to Colonel Yokota Hiroshi, a former staff officer of the Taiwan Army in charge of the affairs of POWs, in June 1942, his office contacted certain business and government organizations on behalf of the General Officer Commanding the Taiwan Army, General Andō Rikichi, 'with a view to employing Prisoners of War'.[50] The Japan Mining Company was among them. That this exchange took place was confirmed by accused Toda Mitsugu, who testified that his predecessor learned soon after the start of the War 'the wishes of the FORMOSAN Army' to transfer a number of POWs from Singapore and to allot them to various companies that could defray the costs of their accommodation. In view of the war situations of the Empire, 'the Company's opinion was to co-operate with the Japanese Army', which the head office of the Japan Mining Company in Tokyo approved.[51] Toda also testified that 'I personally did not wish to employ P.O.Ws.', since the Company 'did not feel any insufficiency in obtaining the working labour' and that he was also worried about 'such enormous expenses to be defrayed for the maintenance

[47] Kondō Masami, 'Taiwan no rōmu dōin', (Mobilization of Labor Forces in Taiwan), in Ōyama Tetsuya (ed), *Kindai Nihon no rekishiteki isō: kokka, minzoku, bunka* (Historical Topology of Modern Japan: Nation, Ethnicity, Culture) (Tōsui shobō 1999) 184. For a comprehensive study of the use of POW labour in Japan proper during the Pacific War, see Utsumi, *Nihongun no horyo seisaku* (Prisoner-of-War Policies of the Japanese Military) (n 9).

[48] *Kinkaseki* literally means 'golden gourd stones', indicating the abundance of gold at the Kinkaseki mine.

[49] Taiwan sōtokufu (Government-General of Taiwan), *Taiwan tōchi gaiyō* (Summary of Taiwan Governance) (Government-General of Taiwan, 1945) 401, 403.

[50] Statement of Col Yokota Hiroshi dated 6 September 1946, *Trial of Toda Mitsugu and eight others* (n 7) exhibit V(1), slide 380.

[51] Testimony of Toda Mitsugu, *Trial of Toda Mitsugu and eight others* (n 7) transcript 110, slide 118.

of P.O.W. Camps' as well as the likelihood of most prisoners' lack of experience in mine extraction work.[52]

In the end, a workforce of 300–500 POWs[53] appears to have been allotted to the mining company and used alongside regular Japanese mine workers, 'native coolies',[54] and 'criminals from Japanese prison at Taihoku [Taipei]'.[55] They dug and hauled copper ore under an extremely harsh work environment while also being subjected to violent flogging and beating by the mine foremen. Cho Kun Toku, a former Formosan squad worker supervisor and a co-defendant of Toda, almost daily beat the POWs using 'the mine hammer, the heads, not the handles'. according to another Formosan and a former squad worker supervisor.[56] With virtually no adequate safety precautions, and with daily exposure to the mine foremen's brutality, it was not infrequent that the POWs suffered injuries and illnesses—and at times, death—at the mine.[57]

Incidentally, the figure of 2,400 Allied POWs in Taiwan as cited by Kondō earlier may not take into account the officer-rank POWs even though many were, in fact, brought over to Taiwan from across the Pacific theatre.[58] The trial records indicate that the general policy of the Japanese authorities was to exempt officer detainees from work and not to count them as such unless they volunteered for labour. According to Utsumi Aiko's *Nihongun no horyo seisaku* (Prisoner-of-War Policies of the Japanese Military [2005]), the sheer inconvenience of keeping high-ranking Allied officers and civilian technocrats in war zones led the Japanese military to relocate them to the inner circle of the Empire,[59] and not necessarily because of their value as useful workforces. These special categories of individuals were removed further into Japanese-controlled Manchuria in the fall of 1944 when the War had turned decisively against Japan and when, anticipating imminent Allied aerial bombings and land invasion, Taiwan was no longer a secure location.

[52] Testimony of Toda Mitsugu, *Trial of Toda Mitsugu and eight others* (n 7) transcript 112, slide 120.

[53] Testimony of Toda Mitsugu, *Trial of Toda Mitsugu and eight others* (n 7) transcript 112, slide 120.

[54] Affidavit of Kameda Kanamatsu dated 29 March 1946, *Trial of Toda Mitsugu and eight others* (n 7) exhibit Y, 1, slide 309.

[55] Affidavit of Sannomiya Tsurumatsu dated 29 March 1946, *Trial of Toda Mitsugu and eight others* (n 7) exhibit X, 1, slide 307.

[56] Affidavit of Jo Sho Ki dated 16 April 1946, *Trial of Toda Mitsugu and eight others* (n 7) exhibit Z, 1, slide 311.

[57] *Trial of Toda Mitsugu and eight others* (n 7). For the general conditions of the mine working environment, see Testimony of Prosecution Witness WO John O Edwards, transcript 5–50, slides 13–58. Edwards was the Prosecution's key witness for the POW mistreatment at the Kinkaseki mine. He testified also at the *Trial of Col Sazawa Hideo and two others* as the first Prosecution witness, see Testimony of Prosecution Witness WO John O Edwards, *Trial of Col Sazawa Hideo and two others* (n 6) transcript 5–16, slides 15–26.

[58] Testimony of Lt Hioki Shiro, *Trial of Col Sazawa Hideo and two others* (n 6) transcript 160, slide 179. Lt Hioki Shirō—one of the co-defendants of Col Sazawa and formely Commander of the officer camp at Shirakawa—testified that the Allied POWs in segregated detention were made up of about 80 Generals, about 300 officers in the ranks below Major General, and around 100 other ranks.

[59] Utsumi, *Nihongun no horyo seisaku* (Prisoner-of-War Policies of the Japanese Military) (n 9) 207.

The life of the high-ranking Allied prisoners in Japanese custody was hardly that of luxury or comfort, however. The records of the British war crimes trials show that mistreatment was actually widespread. Consider, for instance, the experience of Major General Hervey Degge Wilmot Sitwell, formerly General Officer Commanding the British forces in Java. He became a prisoner of the Japanese in the wake of the Japanese invasion of the Dutch East Indies and transferred to the officer camp at Karenkō, Taiwan, in February 1943. Upon arrival, Sitwell is said to have been presented with a document that read in essence, 'I will obey all Japanese orders; I will not damage any Japanese property; I promise not to escape.' He was supposed to sign the document but refused to do so unless under duress, whereupon Captain Imamura Yayohachi—a co-defendant of Nakano and then commandant of the Karenkō camp—'got up and punched me on the jaw twice'.[60] This was followed by several hard kickings by the camp guards and 36-hour confinement in the guardhouse. At the end of this ordeal, Sitwell signed the document. The same was repeated with Brigadier Blackburn of Australia.[61] These kinds of brutality were a routine matter at Karenkō. The other prisoners were 'forced to work in the farm and also to salute all Japanese at all times', Sitwell recalled, and were often beaten up because of their 'failing to salute Japanese O.R.s'.[62] The camp was subsequently relocated from Karenkō to Shirakawa, where the situation turned from bad to worse. Sitwell characterized the new camp as a place where 'the policy of degradation of British Officers was carried out to the fullest extent'. Specifically, '[s]enior officers was [*sic*] forced to do coolie labour such as pulling out weeds, going on all fours to cut grass with razor blades, drawing water from the Japanese guards' bath'.[63]

Short rations and inadequate medical supplies for the most period of incarceration added to the officer detainees' difficulties. According to Colonel Kearie Lee Berry of the US Army, '[o]ur daily diet, per man, at Karenkō, consisted of ten ounces of dry rice, when cooked, made about thirty ounces, twenty-one ounces of vegetable soup, a small quantity of soya bean paste in the soup', which was supplemented by 'beans occasionally, and one half ounce of meat per week'.[64] This type of diet had debilitating effects on the health of the prisoners and particularly Colonel Paul D Bunker, formerly holding command of the 59th Coast Artillery of the US Army. He died in January 1943 due to starvation and lack of medical attention. '[H]is body was so swollen', Berry remembered the physical condition of Bunker in his last days, and 'he was in such poor condition

60 Affidavit of Maj Gen Hervey Degge Wilmot Sitwell dated 10 December 1945, *Trial of Col Nakano Junichi and two others* (n 4) exhibit W, 1, slide 296.

61 Affidavit of Maj Gen Hervey Degge Wilmot Sitwell, *Trial of Col Nakano Junichi and two others* (n 4) exhibit W, 1, slide 296.

62 Affidavit of Maj Gen Hervey Degge Wilmot Sitwell, *Trial of Col Nakano Junichi and two others* (n 4) exhibit W, 1, slide 296.

63 Affidavit of Maj Gen Hervey Degge Wilmot Sitwell, *Trial of Col Nakano Junichi and two others* (n 4) exhibit W, 2, slide 297.

64 Affidavit of Col Kearie Lee Berry dated 10 October 1945, *Trial of Col Nakano Junichi and two others* (n 4) exhibit FF, slide 316.

that he did not recognize me.'[65] General Wainwright, Bunker's former superior officer during the Battle of the Philippines, also remembered vividly the circumstances of the death. He wrote in his memoir that Bunker was 'a big, hearty, robust man and had been a great football player at West Point', but that he came to suffer 'moist beriberi' while a prisoner of the Japanese in Taiwan and his 'legs, feet, arms, and hands had swollen incredibly from the water with which he had tried to assuage his hunger'. Mourning his death, Wainwright and other officer prisoners cremated the body of the deceased 'in the rags in which he [Bunker] had carefully sewn a bit of the American flag he had had to pull down in Corregidor'.[66]

When debriefed after the V-J Day in late 1945, Brigadier General William Edward Brougher, formerly commanding the 11th Division of the Philippine Army at Bataan, ruminated over his wartime experiences as a prisoner of the Japanese.[67] He wondered aloud why the Japanese treated the officer detainees so brutally. 'It has always been a matter of great curiosity and interest to me', Brougher said to an investigative officer, 'as to why the Japanese adopted and pursued the policy that they did in dealing with their group of prisoners, of which I was a member, in the manner in which they did.' By the 'group of prisoners', Brougher was referring to 'the generals and colonels, with the detachment of enlisted men detailed as orderlies presumably to work for us and take care of us'.[68] Instead of respecting the rights of officer POWs, the Japanese camp authorities 'worked the generals and colonels under the same conditions that they did the enlisted men, and, at the same time, they fed us much poorer than they did the enlisted men'. The rations were so inadequate that '[t]hey starved the generals and colonels much worse than they did the enlisted personnel that were with us'.[69] Why this type of discriminatory treatment? Brougher's opinion was as follows:

> [T]hey classed the enlisted men as workers, without question. With regard to the status of the generals and colonels there was always doubt, even when we were working under their orders; that is, as to whether we were classed as workers or not, and given workers' rations. They never hesitated to give the enlisted personnel workers' rations.[70]

A sworn statement by accused Sazawa, taken after the War, supported Brougher's speculation. Sazawa explained that '[t]he scale of rations was based on four standards' at the camps, namely, (1) rations for men in 'very heavy work'; (2) rations for men in 'heavy work'; (3) rations for men in 'light work'; and (4) rations for men 'not doing any work at all'. The ones in the heavier work would receive

[65] Affidavit of Col Kearie Lee Berry, *Trial of Col Nakano Junichi and two others* (n 4) slide 317.

[66] Wainwright, *General Wainwright's Story* (n 3) 205.

[67] Perpetuation of Testimony of Brig Gen William Edward Brougher dated 10 November 1945, *Trial of Col Sazawa Hideo and two others* (n 6) exhibit X, 1–3, slides 313–316.

[68] Perpetuation of Testimony of Brig Gen William Edward Brougher, *Trial of Col Sazawa Hideo and two others* (n 6) 1, slide 313.

[69] Perpetuation of Testimony of Brig Gen William Edward Brougher *Trial of Col Sazawa Hideo and two others* (n 6) 2, slide 314.

[70] Perpetuation of Testimony of Brig Gen William Edward Brougher, *Trial of Col Sazawa Hideo and two others* (n 6) 2, slide 314.

better rations while those with no work, the least. Sazawa noted that '[o]fficers and patients' fell under the last category, viz. of 'not doing any work at all'.[71]

While serving as commandant of POW camps in Taiwan, Sazawa apparently attempted to change the work status of officer prisoners, although it is unclear whether he was motivated by humanitarian concerns or otherwise. According to Brougher's recollection, Sazawa 'made frequent visits to the prison camp' at Shirakawa and pressed the officer prisoners to vote on 'whether they would volunteer to work'.[72] Brougher guessed that the camp commandant was attempting to 'what-washing [white-washing] their (the Japanese) past record of having forced us to work without asking us one way or another, and of course, contrary to the Geneva Convention'.[73] When the prisoners refused to work on a voluntary basis, 'a program of reprisals against us' was set in place. The camp staff began forcing the prisoners to undertake various tasks in connection with camp sanitation that 'would not be classed as work'[74] but that still were physically demanding and mentally degrading. Air Vice Marshall Paul Copeland Maltby of the Royal Air Force confirmed the occurrence of this series of incidents. He attested in his affidavit that when the officers refused to 'volunteer' for work, the Japanese camp staff started a 'regime of progressive starvation and of indignity and restrictions'.[75]

An example of typical work that the officer detainees were made to do is given in the affidavit of Major General Albert Monmouth Jones, formerly commanding the First Philippine Corps at the time of surrender at Bataan. On a Saturday afternoon at the officer camp at Shirakawa, Jones was leading 'a detail of general officers under my command who had been required to haul water so that the Japanese privates could take a bath, although we could not take a bath ourselves'. On that occasion, he saw a group of ICRC representatives coming out of a meeting with Japanese camp staff. Jones promptly marched up 'the detail right over to them and looked at the biggest man there in the eye'. He then said to the visitor, '[W]hat do you think of we generals?'[76] Jones described the circumstances of the encounter as follows:

> We stood there naked except for breech clouts and wooden shoes, burned in the sun, dirty and sweat running off our backs from carrying water. I was the youngest man in the bunch and the group consisted of old, gray-headed men, weak and practically skeletons, carrying

[71] Sworn Statement of Col Sazawa Hideo dated 15 October 1945, *Trial of Col Sazawa Hideo and two others* (n 6) exhibit V, 1–2, slides 305–6.

[72] Perpetuation of Testimony of Brig Gen Wm Edward Brougher dated 10 November 1945, *Trial of Col Sazawa Hideo and two others* (n 6) exhibit X, 2, slide 314.

[73] Sazawa appears to have made this demand in light of the camp regulations, issued by the Taiwan Army in July 1942, according to which officer employment was permissible only on a voluntary basis. See articles 35–41 of Extracts from Service Regulations, Taiwan POW Camp, *Trial of Col Nakano Junichi and two others* (n 4) exhibit WWW, 2, slide 424.

[74] Perpetuation of Testimony of Brig Gen William Edward Brougher dated 10 November 1945, *Trial of Col Sazawa Hideo and two others* (n 6) exhibit X, 2, slide 314.

[75] Affidavit of A V M Paul Copeland Maltby dated 8 February 1946, *Trial of Col Sazawa Hideo and two others* (n 6) slide 392.

[76] Sworn Statement of Maj Gen Albert Monmouth Jones dated 11 January 1946, *Trial of Col Sazawa Hideo and two others* (n 6) exhibit EE, 6, slide 360.

these buckets, two men to a bucket slunk on a bamboo pole over their shoulders. It was obvious the suffering to which we had been and were being exposed.[77]

This confrontation startled the ICRC representatives but no words of consolation were forthcoming. This probably did not surprise Jones, who believed that these visitors had 'lived in Japan for many years, spoke Japanese fluently, and in my opinion, were pro-Japanese in sympathy'.[78] He could not but feel dejected, however, when months passed by after this incident without any improvement in the camp condition. 'This sort of thing took the spirit out of us', Jones recounted.[79]

The three principal accused in connection with the Taiwan POW camps—Nakano, Sazawa, and Uete—faced essentially the same charges except certain differences in the periods covered, the composition of the Taiwan camps under their control, and the frequency of POW deaths during their tenure as camp commandant. The charges typically read that the three accused and their co-defendants were 'in violation of laws and usage of war' in the 'ill-treatment' of POWs and civilian internees at camps in Taiwan despite their 'being responsible for the well-being' of the prisoners. The charges also read that the ill-treatment resulted 'in the deaths of some' or 'many' and also in 'causing physical sufferings to many'.[80]

The POW camp administration in Taiwan comprised of 5–6 semi-permanent camps that were established mostly in mid-1942, and a few temporary ones that were established in the last months of the War. The camps' names and their designations were as follows: the No 1 Branch Camp at Kinkaseki, later relocated to Kōkutsu; the No 2 Branch Camp at Taichū; the No 3 Branch Camp at Heitō; the No 4 Branch Camp at Karenkō, later transferred to Shirakawa; the No 5 Branch Camp at Tamasato (established in 1943); the Headquarter Camp/No 6 Camp at Daichoku, in the vicinity of Taipei; and temporary camps at Toroku, Yūboku, and Matsuyama.[81] The Prosecution alleged that mistreatment and death of POWs took place at most of these camps and that the three accused were individually responsible.[82] The cases against Nakano and Sazawa centred on the mistreatment and death of POWs primarily at the No 4 Branch Camp at Karenkō/Shirakawa where the Allied officers and civilian high officials met segregated detention, and the No 1 Branch Camp at Kinkaseki/Kōkutsu where POW labour for the Kinkaseki mines was accommodated. The centrepiece of the case against Uete, meanwhile, concerned the Yūboku temporary camp. According to court testimony by Captain E W Sowerby, a former POW and a member of the

[77] Sworn Statement of Maj Gen Albert Monmouth Jones, *Trial of Col Sazawa Hideo and two others* (n 6) exhibit EE, slide 360.

[78] *Trial of Col Sazawa Hideo and two others* (n 6) 5, slide 359.

[79] *Trial of Col Sazawa Hideo and two others* (n 6) 6, slide 360.

[80] Charge Sheet, *Trial of Col Nakano Junichi and two others* (n 4) slides 4–5; Record of Proceedings, *Trial of Col Sazawa Hideo and two others* (n 6) slide 3; Charge Sheet, *Trial of Maj Uete Taichi and seven others* (n 6) slides 5–6.

[81] To verify the list of Taiwanese POW camps, I also referred to Utsumi, *Nihongun no horyo seisaku* (Prisoner-of-War Policies of the Japanese Military) (n 9) 224.

[82] Charge Sheet, *Trial of Col Nakano Junichi and two others* (n 4) slides 4–5; Record of Proceedings, *Trial of Col Sazawa Hideo and two others* (n 6) slide 3; Charge Sheet, *Trial of Maj Uete Taichi and seven others* (n 6) slides 5–6.

268th Light Anti-Aircraft Regiment, Royal Artillery, Territorial Army, a total of 150 of the fittest POWs at the Daichoku Headquarter Camp were taken to Yūboku in the last few months of the War, only to be reduced to skeletons and barely alive when brought back to Daichoku after the V-J day. Sixteen of them died.[83]

The three accused contested all the charges by advancing the similar arguments as those made by Tokunaga. Each of them, however, was found guilty of part or all of the charges. Interestingly, the No 7 War Crimes Court handed down to Nakano and Sazawa relatively light sentences of 20 years and 15 years of imprisonment respectively, whereas the No 5 War Crimes Court sentenced Uete to death, along with two of his co-defendants. No explanation was given for the singularly heavy penalty, but the high attrition rate of prisoners at Yūboku may have been a determinant factor. It is also possible that the Court gave credence to the allegation—made by the Prosecution during the *Uete* trial—that the Taiwan POW camp authorities had a general plan to kill all prisoners in the case of the Allied invasion and that the gross mistreatment of prisoners at Yūboku resulted from such plan.

Oral evidence on related issues had been provided by Sowerby, the aforementioned Prosecution witness. A pertinent segment of his testimony appears in the transcripts of court proceedings as follows:

> Q [Prosecution]: When was the YUBOKU Hill camp opened and in what circumstances, do you know?
> A [Sowerby]: On the 15th May 1945 we were secretly informed that we were all to be shot when the American Forces landed in FORMOSA.
> Q: By whom?
> A: I was told by Capt. GIBBONS, who was informed by Mr YOSHIDA, who was the Japanese interpreter at the camp. This was confirmed by a Sgt. TANTO who was a Filipino Chinese who was taken prisoner in MANILA and he got the information from a Formosan sentry.
> Q: Yes and when did this camp open?
> A: The camp opened on the 12th June 1945 when one hundred men were sent to prepare it. I should explain the connection between this and my last remark was that we were informed that the Japanese authorities thought it would be difficult to shoot five hundred men at once and they were therefore going to split up into sub units.[84]

Sowerby's account was partly corroborated by an affidavit of Yoshida Hikosaku, the Japanese interpreter mentioned above. He stated: 'I heard on several occasions that in the event of an invasion of the island of Formosa by American Forces, all POWs were to be disposed of, that is, killed, in some way or another.'[85] Accused Uete himself disputed the allegation, and explained that the instructions he received from the War Ministry and the Taiwan Army were rather to ensure the

[83] Testimony of Prosecution Witness E W Sowerby, *Trial of Maj Uete Taichi and seven others* (n 6) transcript 89, slide 134.

[84] Testimony of Prosecution Witness E W Sowerby, *Trial of Maj Uete Taichi and seven others* (n 6) transcript 88, slide 133.

[85] Extracts from Affidavit of Yoshida Hikosaku dated 8 April 1946, *Trial of Maj Uete Taichi and seven others* (n 6) exhibit R, 4, slide 691.

safety of POWs.[86] This plea did little to help the accused, however, as the Court's stern decision indicates. The death sentences against Uete and two co-defendants were carried out on 6 and 7 April 1948, at Stanley Prison in Hong Kong.[87]

The defendants at the *Toda* trial came off with less dire outcomes when compared with the three high-profile cases related to Taiwan discussed thus far. The accused for this case consisted of Toda Mitsugu, General Manager of the Japan Mining Company at Kinkaseki, Taiwan; one of his immediate subordinate officials at the mining company; and a handful of former company employees of varying ranks, who used to supervise POW working parties at the mine. They were charged with war crimes in that they 'being on the staff of the KINKASEKI Nippon Mining Coy., and as such being responsible for the safety and welfare of the British and American Prisoners of War employed in the mine under their supervision, were, in violation of the laws and usages of war, concerned in the ill-treatment of the aforesaid Prisoners of War, contributing to the death of some of them and causing physical sufferings to the others'.[88]

This charge was vigorously contested by Toda during the trial, who argued that his company was, in fact, *not* responsible for the safety or welfare of the POWs at the mine. According to his testimony, Toda's own initial understanding was that POWs would be 'employed for the Company's work by the Company'.[89] However, the Army is said to have denied him repeatedly and explicitly the correctness of this understanding. Specifically, and according to Toda's recollection, the commandant of the No 1 Branch Camp at Kinkaseki told him from early on that 'the P.O.Ws. would not be employed by the Company at its discretion because these P.O.Ws. were prisoners in the custody of the Japanese Army'.[90] The branch

[86] Statement of Maj Uete Taichi dated 28 November 1946, *Trial of Maj Uete Taichi and seven others* (n 6) exhibit V, 2–3, slides 717–18.

[87] Record of Proceedings *Trial of Maj Uete Taichi and seven others* (n 6) 2, slide 4. Utsumi Aiko points out that the International Prosecution Section at the International Military Tribunal for the Far East (IMTFE, 1946–1948) presented corroborative evidence regarding the Taiwan POW camp administration's plan to kill POWs. Utsumi, *Nihongun no horyo seisaku* (Prisoner-of-War Policies of the Japanese Military) (n 9) 317–18. The evidentiary material she cites is Court Exhibit No 2015, which is an excerpt from the daily record of the Taiwan POW camp headquarters, dated 1 August. (It is unclear from the trial record whether this exhibit should be dated 1944 or 1945.) The exhibit recorded that 'in the case of grave emergency, prisoners of war shall be compressively confined at the present positions and under strict guard be prepared for the final disposition'. It went on to recommend the use of explosives, poison gas, poisoning, drowning, and beheading as methods of killing. It further read that 'no single soldier be allowed to escape under any circumstances; the main idea is to exterminate all and leave no trace'. The exhibit can be found in the transcripts of court proceedings: Nitta Mitsuo (ed), *Kyokutō kokusai gunji saiban sokkiroku* (Transcripts of the International Miltiary Tribunal for the Far East) Vol 4 (Yūshōdō 1968) 29. For the English-language version, see R J Pritchard and S M Zeide (eds), *The Tokyo War Crimes Trial*, vol 6 (Garland 1981) 14724–7. Utsumi discusses other evidentiary materials that point to the Amy's general plan to apply the same policy at other locations in the Pacific theatre. Utsumi, *Nihongun no horyo seisaku* (Prisoner-of-War Policies of the Japanese Military) (n 9) 317–20.

[88] *Trial of Toda Mitsugu and eight others* (n 7) transcript 3, slide 11.

[89] Testimony of Toda Mitsugu, *Trial of Toda Mitsugu and eight others* (n 7) transcript 116, slide 124.

[90] Testimony of Toda Mitsugu, *Trial of Toda Mitsugu and eight others* (n 7) transcript 116, slide 124.

camp commandant allegedly told Toda further that the same principle would apply to the company employees who would be detailed as supervisors of POW working parties. They 'could not be treated as civilians attached to the Army', so Toda testified as being told; instead, they would be 'regarded as Auxiliary Members of the Japanese Army'.[91]

The Prosecutor and the Court both followed up on Toda's testimony in order to ascertain the scope of the mining company's power and authority over POW labour. The Prosecutor, Major M I Ormsby, was especially interested in clarifying whether or not the company continued to maintain any control over the *hanchōs*—the 'group chiefs' or the 'unit chiefs' in English—who were company employees and mine foremen, detailed to supervise the work of POWs. 'Did you have any power whatever over HANCHOs?' Ormsby asked. Toda's reply was that of flat denial, saying, 'No, I have never.'[92] When cross-examined further, the accused explained that there was crucial difference between *hanchō*, which was 'only applied to the working party of P.O.Ws.', and *kantoku*—'supervisors' in English—which was the title the company usually attributed to its regular employees who worked as mine foremen. The *hanchōs* and *kantokus* were essentially 'the same rank',[93] and some of those who had previously served as *kantoku* for the company may have served during the War as *hanchō* for the Army. In this regard, the *hanchōs* still 'were employed by the Company' but they were nonetheless 'detailed to the P.O.W. Camp Authorities and their status was Auxiliary Members of the Army',[94] hence falling outside control of the company. But when Ormsby asked, 'Who paid them [*hanchōs*]?' Toda replied that '[t]hey were paid by the Company',[95] thereby acknowledging that the Company continued to have a degree of say over personnel issues.

The Court pursued the same line of inquiry shortly after. The judges were already satisfied that, during the War, Toda regularly received reports either weekly or monthly from subordinate company officials about 'the amount of work done, the amount of ore extracted, purchases of stones and expenditures and so on' of the Kinkaseki mine.[96] This admission—made by the accused—could be construed as Toda having access to information regarding the general work conditions and productivity including those of POW labour. Now that Toda confirmed to Ormsby that the *hanchōs* remained the company's paid employees, the Court asked, '*In the event*, could you dismiss one of such members of the P.O.Ws. staff

[91] Testimony of Toda Mitsugu, *Trial of Toda Mitsugu and eight others* (n 7) transcript 116, slide 124.

[92] Testimony of Toda Mitsugu, *Trial of Toda Mitsugu and eight others* (n 7) transcript 129, slide 137.

[93] Testimony of Toda Mitsugu, *Trial of Toda Mitsugu and eight others* (n 7) transcript 129, slide 137.

[94] Testimony of Toda Mitsugu, *Trial of Toda Mitsugu and eight others* (n 7) transcript 129, slide 137.

[95] Testimony of Toda Mitsugu, *Trial of Toda Mitsugu and eight others* (n 7) transcript 130, slide 138.

[96] Testimony of Toda Mitsugu, *Trial of Toda Mitsugu and eight others* (n 7) transcript 137, slide 145.

for incompetence or dishonesty or misconduct?'[97] (emphasis added). Toda's reply was as follows:

A [Toda]: Yes, I could do so [dismiss *hanchōs*] because it is clearly stipulated in the Regulation laid down by the Army authorities that whenever such employees were found disobedient or for any misconduct they shall be dismissed by the Company or punished by the Company because Army authorities themselves could not deal with them directly. However, these words were under the control of the Branch Camp commandant, so on this I received no report from the Camp Commandant and I could do nothing about it.[98]

In this reply, Toda readily admitted that he did indeed retain power to hire or fire the company employees no matter whether the latter's status was *hanchō* or otherwise. Yet he stressed that 'these words were under the control of the branch camp commandant' and therefore he 'could not do anything about it'. The meaning of this statement is not entirely clear, but Toda appears to be arguing that dismissal in practice by the company was impossible unless the Army supported it.

At the end of the day, the Court found Toda guilty as charged but handed down a surprisingly light penalty: one year's imprisonment. The remaining co-defendants received between two and ten years in prison.[99] How should one reconcile the stern verdict of guilty and short-term imprisonment? The Court offered no explanation. One could only surmise from the verdict and the sentence that the Court considered the high position of the accused in the mining company as not necessarily entailing his power to command or control the *hanchōs*, ie the supervisors of POW working parties.

This line of thinking had, in fact, been articulated by the Defence during the Closing Address. A Japanese defence lawyer, Yamana Toshio, argued that the Court ought to take into account differences between business and military organizations when reaching its opinion on individual responsibility. He made the following observation:

[S]upposing for a moment that we admit that there was some relation between the Manager and the HANCHOs, it would have been the normal relations of employer to employee under an ordinary business contract. The question of absolute obedience between superiors and juniors as we know it in the Army would not have entered into it.[100]

The Court may have held the same opinion and interpreted Toda's control over the *hanchōs*—and perhaps over the *kantokus* as well—in a far more restrictive manner than the Prosecution had; this can at least explain why the stern verdict of guilty could go hand-in-hand with a lenient penalty. Yet in the absence of the

[97] Testimony of Toda Mitsugu, *Trial of Toda Mitsugu and eight others* (n 7) transcript 137, slide 145.

[98] Testimony of Toda Mitsugu, *Trial of Toda Mitsugu and eight others* (n 7) transcript 138, slide 146.

[99] Record of Proceedings, *Trial of Toda Mitsugu and eight others* (n 7) slide 3. One of the co-defendants and a former *hanchō*, Yonemura Masatoshi, was acquitted.

[100] Closing Address for the Defence, *Trial of Toda Mitsugu and eight others* (n 7) exhibit K(2), 4, slide 445.

Court's explicit opinion, it remains an open-ended question as to what criteria of responsibility the Court applied in deciding Toda's case.

## 4. Concluding Remarks

This chapter has analysed a selection of British Hong Kong trials in order to shed light on the British courts' decisions concerning the organizational and individual responsibility of the Japanese for mistreating POWs during the Pacific War. First and foremost, the five cases discussed indicate the systematic and widespread nature of the Japanese mistreatment of POWs in violation of laws and customs of war. The massive relocation of more than 252,000 POWs and the use of their labour throughout the wartime Empire of Japan, indeed, would have been impossible had it not been for the overall planning, coordination, and monitoring by the central government and military authorities. The records of the British Hong Kong trials point to the War Ministry at the heart of planning process, whose policies were executed in collaboration with wide-ranging supporting agencies in the colonial governments, military administration in the occupied territories, and the business world throughout the wartime Empire of Japan.

The five case studies in this chapter have also brought to light the critical part that individuals fulfilled in the workings of POW administration. The rejection of the defence plea of superior orders by the British Hong Kong courts is significant in this respect, since it highlights how critical the acts of individual ranking Army officers and camp staff had been in sustaining the POW camp regime. A case in point would be Tokunaga's handling of four recaptured Canadian escapees in Hong Kong. If one were to take at face value Tokunaga's testimony, the accused had struggled to reconcile conflicting ethical and legal obligations when trying to determine the final disposition of the escapees in pursuit of his duties as camp commandant. He ultimately decided to take such steps to maintain the appearance of strict adherence to the War Ministry's policy while also ensuring that the local Hong Kong camp authorities 'saved face'. This episode illustrates the pivotal role that mid-level individual actors in the Army played in overcoming immediate practical obstacles in order to ensure the continuing functioning of the Japanese POW camp regime.

This chapter has explored a segment of the British Hong Kong trials, which, in turn, fall within a much larger group of some 330 war crimes trials that the British military authorities hosted in formerly Japanese-occupied British colonies in Southeast Asia between 1945 and 1948. The British trials themselves were part of an even larger pan-Pacific Allied war crimes programme, in which more than 2,240 trials of some 5,700 suspected war criminals were held.[101] Much of the records of these

[101] According to the Japanese data, the breakdown of the Allied war crimes trials in the Asia-Pacific is as follows: 456 American trials at Guam, Kwajalein, Manila, Shanghai, and Yokohama; 330 British trials in formerly Japanese-occupied British colonies in Southeast Asia including Hong Kong, Kuala Lumpur, Singapore, and Rangoon; 294 Australian trials in several different locations in the South

trials remain understudied to this day including the *Kuroda* trial, one of the capstone trials of the Philippine war crimes programme (1947–49) that this chapter touched on in its opening section. The challenge for researchers is to carry out a systematic analysis of these vast sources so as to reach a conclusive assessment of their jurisprudential legacy in the field of law today. A comprehensive study of these trials will allow us to have a fuller understanding of the principles of individual and organizational responsibility that arise from the Allied war crimes trials in the Asia-Pacific region. It is hoped that the case studies in the present chapter will serve as a stepping stone for the further advancement of WWII war crimes studies by the next generation of researchers.

Pacific such as Rabaul in East New Britain as well as at Hong Kong and Singapore; 448 Dutch trials at 12 separate locations in formerly Japanese-occupied Dutch East Indies including Batavia (present-day Jakarta); 39 French trials in Saigon; 72 Philippine trials in Manila; and 605 Chinese trials at ten different locations including Beijing, Nanjing, Guandong, Hankow, Shenyang, and Taipei. Tōkyō saiban handobukku henshū iinkai (Tokyo Trial Handbook Compilation Committee) (ed), *Tōkyō saiban handobukku* (The Tokyo Trial Handbook) (Aoki shoten 1989). The People's Republic of China carried out its own trials against select war crimes suspects in 1956. Data relative to the Soviet trials are unavailable except a special military trial held in Khabarovsk in December 1949.

# 4

# War Crimes

*Suzannah Linton*

## 1. Introduction

Hong Kong's war crimes process, adjudicating offences from Hong Kong and the New Territories, China (Taiwan, and also Shanghai and Waichow), Japan, and on the High Seas, resonates with the *leitmotif* of events in multiple jurisdictions across Asia as the Japanese forces swept through and conquered large swathes of Asia in the 1930s and 1940s. Some of the more notorious incidents were also considered by the International Military Tribunal in Tokyo ('IMTFE'),[1] which chronicled how the same crimes were committed over and over again, across vast tracts of invaded and occupied Asia: murder, torture, inhumane treatment and cruelty, arbitrary detention, disappearance, looting, and plundering. The victims included combatants, *hors de combat*, medical personnel and civilians, humanity itself.

This chapter's objective is to engage with the war crimes aspects of the trials held in Hong Kong, and to extract a deeper understanding from the cases themselves, a major task given the serious limitations that the lack of reasoned judgments poses. The author also faces the challenging reality that any chapter on war crimes is going to be very wide in its scope due to the large number of issues that should be examined. This is a chapter that could potentially run into hundreds of pages if full justice is to be done to all the war crimes issues in the cases. Necessity requires the author to balance the importance of bringing to light the previously untold stories of the war crimes trials held in Hong Kong, with the need to engage in more

[1] See the overview of atrocities across Asia in ch VII on Conventional War Crimes (Atrocities), in *IMT Tokyo Judgment*, in B V A Röling and C F Rüter (eds), *The Tokyo Judgment: The International Military Tribunal for the Far East (IMTFE) 29 April 1946–2 November 1948* (APA–University Press Amsterdam 1977) ('*IMTFE Judgment*'). Also see the many rich and insightful writings of R J Pritchard, including, 'The Historical Experience of British War Crimes Courts in the Far East 1946–1948' (1978) 6(1) *Int Rels* 311. For an overview of the rarely considered trials in British Malaya (including Singapore) and North Borneo, see A Narayanan, 'Japanese Atrocities and British Minor War Crimes Trials after World War II in the East' (2006) 33 *Jebat (Mal J Hist Pol St S)*. A helpful review of media coverage of the Asian trials is in P R Picigallo, *The Japanese On Trial: Allied War Crimes Operation in The East, 1945–1949* (University of Texas Press 1979).

detailed consideration and analysis. It is therefore longer than most of the other chapters in this collection, but not as long as it could be.[2]

The Hong Kong cases reveal that the term 'laws and usages of war' was employed to encompass a broad range of criminal acts in armed conflict and occupation. We see that the concept of war crimes was mainly used, in line with the categorizations described in the *Manual of Military Law 1929 (as amended)*[3] and the ALFSEA Instruction,[4] both discussed in detail in section 2, in relation to abuse of civilians (unlawful arrest and detention; torture; cruel, inhuman or degrading treatment); abuse of Prisoners of War ('POWs') (ranging from forced labour to poor working conditions to grossly sub-standard conditions of detention); and unlawful killing of both civilians and POWs. There were also a number of prosecutions involving crimes against *hors de combat*, ie sick and wounded combatants, and those caring for them. On a different level were the cases of stealing and pilfering, and also the forced swearing of oaths, which in themselves are clearly not of the same level of severity, and the appropriateness of the charge can be questioned on a case-by-case basis (it cannot, for example, be denied that sometimes food parcels kept people alive and their theft could lead to great suffering and possibly death by starvation). The charges in *Ito*, arising out of the invasion of Hong Kong island, show how the Prosecution divided out war crimes categories by group: killing and ill-treatment of Allied POWs and surrendered personnel in the first charge; killing and ill-treatment of wounded and sick members of Allied Forces that had fallen in the power of troops under the accused's command in the second charge;[5] the killing and ill-treatment of those engaged in the collection, transport, and treatment of the wounded and sick and in the administration of medical formations and establishments in the third

[2] For an introduction to the legal issues, and focus on four cases, see S Linton, 'Rediscovering the War Crimes Trials in Hong Kong, 1946–1948' (2012) 13(2) MJIL 284 ('Linton, "Rediscovering the War Crimes Trials in Hong Kong, 1946–1948"').

[3] The *Manual of Military Law* used in these trials was the 7th edition of 1929 (*Manual of Military Law*, 7th edn, Great Britain War Office 1929). This edition underwent two amendments before being replaced in an 8th edition in 1952. The amendments were the replacement of ch XIV (see Great Britain War Office, *Manual of Military Law 1929*, ch XIV (Amendment No 12 of 1936)); and an amendment to para 443 of ch XIV (see Great Britain War Office, *Manual of Military Law 1929*, Amendment No 34 of 1944). This author's use of the term *Manual of Military Law 1929 (as amended)* refers to the *Manual of Military Law 1929* and the two amendments of 1936 and 1944 collectively.

[4] Allied Land Forces South-East Asia, War Crimes Instruction No 1 (2nd edn) in File No WO 32/12197, UK National Archives [not part of the HKWCT Collection], as amended by Amendment No 1 of 12 June 1946, Amendment No 2 of 27 June 1946, Amendment No 3 of 16 July 1946, Amendment No 4 of 21 November 1946, Amendment No 5 of 4 December 1946, Amendment No 6 of 22 January 1947, Amendment No 7 of 14 March 1947 and Amendment No 8 of 26 March 1947 (collectively 'ALFSEA Instruction').

[5] See Geneva Convention Relative to the Treatment of Prisoners of War with Annex (opened for signature 27 July 1929, entered into force 19 June 1931) 118 LNTS 343 ('1929 POW Convention'). Under ch 1, art 2, the wounded and sick of an army who fall into the hands of the enemy were POWs, and the general principles of international law were applicable to them. Further to para 56(c) of the *Manual of Military Law (as amended)* (n 3), 'The following can claim to be prisoners-of-war if they fall into the hands of the enemy... Private enemy individuals and enemy officials whom a belligerent thinks it necessary to make prisoners.'

charge; and the killing and ill-treatment of civilian residents of Hong Kong in the fourth charge.[6]

There being no cases involving the means and methods of warfare, such as use of prohibited weapons, we can apply a contemporary understanding of war crimes in international humanitarian law and divide the cases into four categories similar to *Ito*, based on protected groups: war crimes against POWs;[7] war crimes against *hors de combat*[8] including surrendering or newly surrendered personnel, and sick and wounded personnel; war crimes against medical personnel;[9] and war crimes against civilians[10] and in the context of the Hong Kong trials, civilians in an occupied territory.[11] Working through these categorizations then allows for identification of what is most suitable for focus in this chapter, with the benefit of presenting the reader with the wider picture of the war crimes adjudicated.

[6] Schedule of Charges, *Trial of Lt Gen Ito Takeo* (HKWCT Collection, File No WO235/1107) ('*Trial of Lt Gen Ito Takeo*'), slides 4–5.

[7] See the position of the Prosecutor in *Trial of Maj Gen Tanaka Ryosaburo* (HKWCT Collection, File No WO235/1030) ('*Trial of Maj Gen Tanaka Ryosaburo*'), exhibit R(1), 1, slide 360. The Prosecutor's Closing Address there referred to POWs as 'Military personnel who have surrendered and have actually been taken into custody by their captors'.

[8] *Hors de combat* are those combatants who have, through unconsciousness, shipwreck, wounds or sickness been rendered incapable of combat or have clearly indicated an intention to surrender; see Hague Convention (IV) respecting the Laws and Customs of War on Land and its Annex: Regulations concerning the Laws and Customs of War on Land (opened for signature 18 October 1907, entered into force 26 January 1910) UKTS 9 ('1907 Hague Regulations'), art 23(c). The Hong Kong cases do show some overlap in the POW and *hors de combat* category, although divisions were clearly made between POWs, 'surrendered personnel' and 'medical personnel'. See Prosecutor's Closing Address, *Trial of Maj Gen Tanaka Ryosaburo* (n 7) exhibit R(1), 1, slide 360, where the Prosecutor explained that his charge concerning 'surrendered personnel' meant 'those who have signified their willingness to be taken captive but who have not, actually been taken into custody by their captors'. That case also shows that in addition to denial of quarter to captured combatants, sick and wounded were collapsed into 'surrendered personnel' and that battlefield *hors de combat* were treated as POWs (see First Charge against Maj Gen Tanaka Ryosaburo).

[9] Medical personnel, meaning those who care for the sick and wounded in armed conflict, and the shipwrecked, have, since the start of modern international humanitarian law, been protected from attack, as a corollary to the rule that the sick and wounded must be cared for and protected; see art 2 of the Convention for the Amelioration of the Condition of the Wounded in Armies in the Field (opened for signature 22 Aug 1864, entered into force 21 June 1865) 129 Consol TS 361; Convention for the Amelioration of the Condition of the Wounded and Sick in Armies in the Field (opened for signature 6 July 1906, entered into force 9 August 1907) 202 CTS 144 ('1906 Convention for the Amelioration of the Condition of the Wounded and Sick in Armies in the Field') arts 9–10; and Convention for the Amelioration of the Condition of the Wounded and Sick in Armies in the Field (opened for signature 27 Jul 1929, entered into force 19 June 1931)118 UNTS 303 ('1929 Red Cross Convention').

[10] Civilians are persons who are not members of the armed forces of a party to the conflict. This is the notion that comes through in the cases, although there was no specific litigation on the issue, other than in *Kishi et al*, discussed later in this chapter.

[11] Under Art 42 of the 1907 Hague Regulations (n 8) '[t]erritory is considered occupied when it is actually placed under the authority of the hostile army'. None of the cases raised the issue of when the occupation began, but a number of them, arising in the period after the Emperor's capitulation, did raise the issue of when, in accordance with the Royal Warrant, His Majesty stopped being engaged in 'war' with Japan. See for example, the *Trial of Lt Kishi Yasuo and fourteen others*, where the Defence argued that if a state of war no longer existed, 'it cannot also be true that the accused persons committed crimes in violation of the Laws and Usages of War' since a war crime can only be committed during a war. *Trial of Lt Kishi Yasuo and fourteen others* (HKWCT Collection, File WO235/993) ('*Trial of Lt Kishi Yasuo and fourteen others*'), exhibit A(1)[Not fully legible], 1, slide 736.

Professor Yuma Totani's chapter in this collection focuses on the POW camp cases, and it is therefore not necessary to revisit the issues here in this chapter, beyond emphasizing the following. The single case of WO235/1012 (*Trial of Colonel Tokunaga Isao et al*) shone a light on the several POW camps in Hong Kong, and is important for the insight it provides into war crimes and the concept of POWs and Japanese notions of humane treatment,[12] and the management of POW camps in the Japanese system. As in so many cases up to the present, the lines of authority were very much an issue in this trial, with the lead accused producing regulations and laws to emphasize the overarching responsibilities of the War Office in Tokyo, and the Chief of Staff and Governor-General as his superiors in the POW camp regime.[13] The case is also important for the evidence that it provides about how Japan did in fact draw conceptually from the 1907 Hague Regulations,[14] and the 1929 POW Convention.[15] We see from this how, despite her cultural antipathy towards surrender and capture, Japan established an Empire-wide regime creating and administering camps for the thousands of captured combatants that fell into her hands.[16] Finally, in this category of war crimes, we have the distinct and important *Kinkaseki Mining Company Case*, which involved what we would see in contemporary terms as forced POW labour in inhuman, slave-like conditions.[17] Under Article 6 of the 1907 Hague Regulations, Japan could utilize the labour of POWs according to their rank and aptitude, officers excepted, but the 'tasks shall not be excessive and shall have no connection with the operations of the war'. The Prosecutor's allegation that it was unlawful to force

[12] See Testimony of Col Tokunaga Isao, *Trial of Col Tokunaga Isao and four others* (HKWCT Collection File No W0235/1012 Part One) ('*Trial of Col Tokunaga Isao and four others, (Part One)*'), transcript 491, slide 532. Also see Translation of The Administrative Regulations for the Prisoners Of War (The Prisoners Of War Camp-Hong Kong), 1 April 17th Year of Showa (Col Tokunaga, Commander-in-chief, Prisoners of War Camp, Hong Kong, 1 April 1942), *Trial of Col Tokunaga Isao and four others* (HKWCT Collection File No W0235/1012 Part Three) ('*Trial of Col Tokunaga Isao and four others (Part Three)*'), exhibit Y(4), slides 584–607 ('*Translation of The Administrative Regulations for the Prisoners Of War (The Prisoners Of War Camp-Hong Kong)*'). Article 2 provided that POWs 'shall be treated by the authorities with the spirit of humanity; and their personality shall be respected'.

[13] Translation of Extract from Prisoner Of War Camp Regulation (Imperial Ordinance No 1182, 23 December 1941), *Trial of Col Tokunaga Isao and four others (Part Three)* (n 12) ('*Translation of Extract from Prisoner Of War Camp Regulation*'), exhibit V(4), 1, slide 581 (art II, art III); Translation, Extract from Prisoner Of War Camp Regulation, Imperial Ordinance No 1182, 23 December 1941, *Trial of Col Tokunaga Isao and four others (Part Three)* (n 12) exhibit V(4), 581.

[14] 1907 Hague Regulations (n 8).

[15] 1929 POW Convention (n 5).

[16] Documents in the *Trial of Col Tokunaga Isao and four others (Part Three)* (n 12) such as the following, offer much insight: (1) Translation of Extract from Prisoner Of War Camp Regulation (n 13); (2) Translation of The Administrative Regulations for the Prisoners Of War (The Prisoners Of War Camp-Hong Kong) (n 12); (3) Translation of Extract from Detailed Prisoners Of War Treatment Regulation (Ministry Of War, Transmission No 29, 21 April 1943), exhibit W(4), slide 582; (4) Translation of Extracts from the Prisoner of War Labour Regulation (Ministry Of War Ordinance No 22, 20 May 1943) (Amendments, Additions And Deletions, Ministry Of War Ordinance No 30 1943), exhibit X(4), slide 583; (5) Translation of 'Extracts from p 42, "The Collection of Various Regulations concerning POWs, the Prisoner of War Punishment Law, 9 March 1943, Law No. 41, amending Law No. 38 of 1905"', exhibit Z(4), slide 608.

[17] See Linton, 'Rediscovering Hong Kong's War Crimes Trials' (n 2) 328–35.

POWs to work in these conditions was not challenged. In this case, the Prosecutor told the Court there were no doubts about 'the overall and complete responsibility of the Camp Commandant of Kinkaseki Branch camp', and also the Japanese government, acting through the Army, for developing and implementing the illegal programme to use POWs as forced labour.[18] But, this was a case just against civilians, on the basis that the companies involved were not able to 'disclaim all responsibility over their new employees', he argued.[19] Here, although we do not know the reasoning of those who put the case together, we see the Prosecutor put forth an embryonic idea about corporate social responsibility, and that the forced labour was, strangely, seen as 'employment'. Even so, the crux of the matter, as discussed in Professor Yuma Totani's chapter, was who was responsible for the POWs when they went to work in the mine.

The two categories of war crimes against *hors de combat* and medical personnel were almost exclusively concerned with events during the invasion of Hong Kong island. In the first group, *hors de combat*, were crimes against sick and wounded, surrendering and freshly captured combatants such as already mentioned in *Ito*, but it also extended to crimes against the shipwrecked such as in the *Behar* case, which concerned the abuse and killing of shipwrecked captives from the afore-named torpedoed civilian vessel in the Indian Ocean at an advanced stage of the War. In the second group were crimes against medical personnel, committed on the battlefield, in the course of the storming of a medical post at the Salesian Mission, and against medical personnel at St Stephen's College, including the rape and murder of several nurses. In Hong Kong, three of the commanders involved in the battle for Hong Kong were to stand trial: Major General Shoji Toshishige,[20] Major General Tanaka Ryosaburo,[21] and Lieutenant General Ito Takeo.[22] Major General Shoji was acquitted of the allegations against him, and there were partial convictions (partial acquittals) for Major General Tanaka and Lieutenant General Ito. Neither of them received the death penalty.[23] None of the men below them, who were the direct perpetrators of the crimes, were brought to trial. In Nanking, the so-called 'Conqueror of Hong Kong', Lieutenant General Sakai Takashi, was convicted and executed for, among others, his role in the attack on Hong Kong and the atrocities committed in relation thereto.[24] One would have expected the

[18] Prosecution Closing Address, *Trial of Toda Mitsugu and eight others* (HKWCT Collection, File No WO235/1028) ('*Trial of Toda Mitsugu and eight others*'), exhibit L, 11, slide 459; Testimony of Prosecution Witness Col Nakano Junichi, transcript 93–4, slides 101–2.

[19] Prosecution Closing Address, *Trial of Toda Mitsugu and eight others* (n 18) exhibit L, 11, slide 459.

[20] *Trial of Maj Gen Shoji Toshishige* (HKWCT Collection, File No WO235/1015) ('*Trial of Maj Gen Shoji Toshishige*').

[21] *Trial of Maj Gen Tanaka Ryosaburo* (n 7).

[22] *Trial of Lt Gen Ito Takeo* (n 6).

[23] Maj Gen Tanaka Ryosaburo and Lt Gen Ito Takeo were sentenced to 20 and 12 years respectively.

[24] This author has, in relation to this case, which is discussed elsewhere in this chapter, relied on three translations of the judgment. Firstly, she relies on the Summary Translation of the 'Judgment of the Military Tribunal, Nanking, regarding Takashi Sakai, 27 August 1946' in File No WO311/563, UK National Archives. The case is summarized further in United Nations War Crimes Commission,

invasion cases to raise complex issues in the law of war crimes, but scrutiny of the files reveals that they were focused on establishing the facts, and in particular, the identity of the troops that committed the atrocities. The latter was to be a critical factor in the acquittals that were secured by the Defence. Legal issues certainly arose in relation to superior orders and modes of responsibility, which are covered in the chapters by Professors Bing Bing Jia and Nina Jørgensen. The law of war crimes was surprisingly peripheral in these cases. For this reason, the telling of the untold stories of the cases aside, there is no pressing need to focus on these two categories of cases.

It is the last category, war crimes against civilians, notably in an occupied territory, that this author has chosen to focus on. This choice is based on the considerations cited earlier, and on the reality that the majority of the Hong Kong cases actually involved war crimes against civilians. Furthermore, this category does raise some good substantive issues for closer consideration (involuntary displacement/deportation, torture and other ill-treatment, and unlawful killing of civilians). The reader should be aware that this study deliberately centralizes the Hong Kong cases; the objective is to excavate a forgotten legal process and shed light on the law of war crimes as it emerges from these cases. Thus, the exercise of detailed comparison with contemporary cases and current controversies is for another project in the future. In any event, Professor Roger Clark's chapter in the book situates the Hong Kong cases in a contemporary context.

The first thing we must now do, before moving to war crimes against civilians in occupied territory, is to establish the sources of the law of war crimes relied on in these Hong Kong trials.

## 2. The Sources of Law Used in the Hong Kong War Crimes Trials

Hong Kong's war crimes trials were regulated by a mixed regime of international law and domestic law. The four British military tribunals exercised jurisdiction over 'violation[s] of the laws and usages of war' committed during any war in which Britain was engaged since 2 September 1939, on the basis of the Royal Warrant of 18 June 1945, which had annexed to it Regulations for the Trials of War Criminals,[25] incorporating the *Manual of Military Law 1929 (as*

*Law Reports of Trials of War Criminals* vol III (HMSO 1948) 1–7. This author has also examined an informal translation of the original (reserved) judgment that is held by the National Archives Administration in Taiwan, China: *Judgment of War Criminal Takashi Sakai* [Michael Liu trans] (on file with the author). This judgment is more comprehensive than the UNWCC's report, with an exhibit of incidents that did not appear there. Ironically, the judgment is missing the page where the bulk of the Hong Kong atrocities are discussed. Together, the different versions are referred to as '*Sakai Judgments*'. The author thanks Professor Roger Clark, Professor Jingsi Wang and Judge Muchin Shih for their assistance in making this document available, and Michael Liu for his translation.

[25] Great Britain War Office, Regulations for the Trial of War Criminals (UK) AO 81/1945 ('Regulations for the Trial of War Criminals annexed to Royal Warrant').

*amended)*[26]. The *Manual* regarded the laws of war as the 'rules respecting warfare with which, according to international law, belligerents and neutrals are bound to comply'[27] and viewed the concept of 'laws and usages of war' as being comprised

> partly of customary rules, which have grown up in practice, and partly of written rules, that is, rules which have been purposely agreed upon by the powers in international treaties. Side by side with these customary and written laws of war there are in existence, and are still growing, usages concerning warfare. While the laws of war are legally binding, usages are not, and the latter can therefore, for sufficient reasons, be disregarded by belligerents. Usages have, however, a tendency gradually to harden into legal rules of warfare, and the greater part of the present laws of war have grown up in that way.[28]

In the *Manual of Military Law 1929 (as amended)*, war crimes were described as the 'technical expression for such an act of enemy soldiers and enemy civilians as may be visited by punishment or capture of the offenders'.[29] This conceptualization was given practical form in paragraph 442, which divided war crimes into four broad groups—violations of the recognized rules of warfare by members of the armed forces; illegitimate hostilities in arms committed by individuals who are not members of the armed forces; espionage and war treason; and marauding. Specific examples were provided—use of poisoned or otherwise forbidden arms and ammunition; killing of the wounded; refusal of quarter; bombardment of hospitals and other privileged buildings; ill-treatment of POWs; ill-treatment of inhabitants in occupied territory; abuse of the Red Cross flag and badge, etc.[30] Furthermore, Hong Kong fell within the command of Allied Land Forces South-East Asia ('ALFSEA'), based in Singapore. The ALFSEA Instruction,[31] was issued to supplement

[26] *Manual of Military Law 1929 (as amended)* (n 3).

[27] *Manual of Military Law 1929 (as amended)* (n 3) para 1. The IMT Nuremberg declared in its judgment that '[t]he law of war is to be found not only in treaties, but in the customs and practices of states which gradually obtained universal recognition, and from the general principles of justice applied by jurists and practised by military courts. This law is not static, but by continual adaptation follows the needs of a changing world. Indeed, in many cases treaties do no more than express and define for more accurate reference the principles of law already existing', *International Military Tribunal (Nuremberg), Judgment and Sentences*, reproduced in 'Judicial Decisions' (1947) 41 AJIL 172 ('*IMT Nuremberg Judgment*'), 219. The perspective laid out in the *British Manual of Military Law (as amended)* (n 3) and the sources of law that were used in the British war crimes trials, and of course, the product of the trials themselves, are part of the 'customs and practices of states' referred to by the IMT.

[28] *Manual of Military Law 1929 (as amended)* (n 3) ch XIV, para 2 (citations omitted). It is instructive to note the conceptualization of the time, by reference to H Lauterpacht (ed), *Oppenheim's International Law* (5th edn, Longmans, Green and Co 1937) vol 1, 25, para 17 (emphasis added) (citations omitted): 'Custom is the older and the original source of international law in particular as well as of law in general... International jurists speak of a *custom* when a clear and continuous habit of doing certain actions has grown up under the aegis of the conviction that these actions are, according to international law, obligatory or right.' As to the meaning of usages, Lauterpacht explained that 'international jurists speak of a *usage* when a habit of doing certain actions has grown up without there being the conviction that these actions are, according to international law, obligatory or right... a given course of conduct may be usual without being customary'.

[29] *Manual of Military Law 1929 (as amended)* (n 3) ch XIV, para 441.

[30] *Manual of Military Law 1929 (as amended)* (n 3) para 443.

[31] ALFSEA Instruction (n 4).

the basic procedures under the *Manual of Military Law 1929 (as amended)*. This provided further insight into what the British considered the main offences constituting war crimes to be:

1. Shooting and killing without justification.
2. Shooting and killing on the false pretence that the prisoner was escaping.
3. Assault with violence causing death, and other forms of murder or manslaughter.
4. Shooting, wounding with bayonet, torture, and unjustified violence.
5. Other forms of ill-treatment causing the infliction of grievous bodily harm.
6. Theft of money and goods.
7. Unjustified imprisonment.
8. Insufficient food, water, clothing.
9. Lack of medical attention.
10. Bad treatment in hospitals.
11. Employment on work having direct connection with the operations of the War, or on unhealthy or dangerous work.
12. Detaining Allied personnel in an area exposed to the fire of the fighting zone.
13. Making use of POWs or civilians as a screen; and such cases as attacks on hospitals or hospital ships, and on merchant ships without making provision for survivors.
14. Interrogation by 'third degree' or other forcible methods.[32]

This, then, was the British understanding of war crimes, the product of clearly serious violations of the laws and usages of war. As will be seen later, this is borne out in the Hong Kong cases.

But, as a matter of international law, we have, of course, to consider what 'laws and usages of war' actually bound sovereign Japan and her nationals. Outside of assertions about Japan's special approach to POWs, there was no dispute in the Hong Kong trials about the sources of the law of war crimes binding upon Japan. She was a party to the 1906 Convention for the Amelioration of the Condition of the Wounded and Sick in Armies in the Field, which did not apply as treaty law during the War in Asia, as China was only a signatory (it contained a *si omnes* clause).[33] Nevertheless, this treaty was incorporated by reference into

[32] ALFSEA Instruction (n 4) para 4.

[33] 1906 Convention for the Amelioration of the Condition of the Wounded and Sick in Armies in the Field (n 9). Japan (for itself and Korea) signed on 6 July 1906 and ratified on 23 April 1908 with a reservation to art 28. The UK ratified on 16 April 1907; the USA ratified on 9 February 1907; China signed on 6 July 1906 but did not ratify. Australia, New Zealand, and Canada were bound by reason of their being British Dominions at the time. Source: ICRC International Humanitarian Law—Treaties & Documents Database, <http://www.icrc.org/ihl> accessed 20 August 2012.

the 1907 Hague Regulations.[34] This 1907 convention, to which Japan was a party,[35] should have been *the* critical treaty, but it too contained a *si omnes* clause and it did not apply to the War in Asia as treaty law since China was not a party.[36] The two international military tribunals were, nevertheless, to hold that the 1907 Hague Regulations did apply as customary law.[37] The real problem came with the 1929 POW Convention which Japan had signed but not ratified, and so was not binding as treaty law.[38] Nevertheless, some of the agreements that Japan was bound by in treaty law supported or affirmed many of the same provisions and principles that were in the 1929 POW Convention. Notable are the 1907 Hague Regulations, already discussed, and the 1929 Red Cross Convention,[39] which did apply as treaty law to Japan's wars in Asia.[40]

A significant number of the Hong Kong cases involved abuse and killing of POWs. Japan had refused to become a party to the 1929 POW Convention, which

[34] 1907 Hague Regulations (n 8) art 21.

[35] Japan signed on 18 October 1907 and ratified on 13 December 1911 with a reservation made to art 44. The US and UK ratified on 27 November 1909. Australia, New Zealand, and Canada were bound by reason of their being British Dominions at the time. China acceded on 10 May 1917. Source: ICRC International Humanitarian Law—Treaties & Documents Database, at <http://www.icrc.org/ihl> accessed 20 August 2012.

[36] This was the finding of the *IMTFE Judgment* (n 1) 48. There does appear to be a discrepancy in relation to China's participation in the treaty, as the ICRC's website (Treaties and Documents) shows that China acceded on 10 May 1917. Source: ICRC International Humanitarian Law—Treaties & Documents Database, at <http://www.icrc.org/ihl> accessed 20 August 2012. This discrepancy may have been linked to the issue of the status and legitimacy of the Chinese representatives to bind China at a time of civil war and political chaos at home.

[37] One of the most famous determinations of the IMT at Nuremberg was that 'by 1939 the rules laid down in the [1907 Hague Regulations] were recognized by all civilized nations, and were regarded as being declaratory of the laws and customs of war'. See *IMT Nuremberg Judgment* (n 27) 248. The IMTFE followed the IMT Nuremberg on matters of law concerning the legality of exercise of jurisdiction over the accused and also agreed that the crimes set out in the Charter were 'the expression of international law' existing at the time of the IMT at Nuremberg's establishment. See *IMTFE Judgment* (n 1) 28.

[38] 1929 POW Convention (n 5). Japan signed on 27 July 1929, but did not become a party. Australia signed on 27 July 1929 and ratified on 23 June 1931. Canada signed on 27 July 1929 and ratified on 20 February 1933. China signed on 27 July 1929 and ratified on 19 July 1935. New Zealand signed on 27 July 1929 and ratified on 23 June 1931. The UK signed on 27 July 1927 and ratified on 23 June 1931. The USA signed on 27 July 1929 and ratified on 4 February 1932. Source: ICRC International Humanitarian Law—Treaties & Documents Database, at <http://www.icrc.org/ihl> accessed 20 August 2012.

[39] Convention for the Amelioration of the Condition of the Wounded and Sick in Armies in the Field (n 9). Japan signed on 27 July 1929 and ratified on 18 December 1934; the UK signed on 27 July 1929 and ratified on 23 June 1931; New Zealand signed on 27 July 1929 and ratified on 23 June 1931; Canada signed on 27 July 1929 and ratified on 20 February 1933; China signed on 27 July 1929 and ratified on 19 November 1935; the USA signed on 27 July 1929 and ratified on 4 February 1932; and Australia signed on 27 July 1929 and ratified on 23 June 1931. Source: ICRC International Humanitarian Law—Treaties & Documents Database, at <http://www.icrc.org/ihl> accessed on 20 August 2012.

[40] See F Kalshoven, 'The Undertaking to Respect and Ensure Respect in All Circumstances: From Tiny Seed to Ripening Fruit' (1999) 2 YIHL 3, 6–10 for discussion on whether the 1929 Red Cross Convention contained a *si omnes* clause proper. It is the view of the present author that it did not—art 25 provided that if a belligerent is not a party to the Convention, the Convention nonetheless continues to apply to all belligerents that are a party (to the exclusion only of the belligerent that is not a party).

strengthened some of the existing framework. She did not oppose the concept of the POW, having signed the relevant convention on 27 July 1929, but wished to preserve her distinct understanding about military honour and capture, as enshrined in her military honour code, the *Bushido*.[41] Illustrative of the mindset in this regard is the testimony of Major General Tanaka Ryosaburo, under cross-examination:

> Western people think that becoming a Prisoner of War is not shameful, and Japanese people think it is shameful. If a person thinks that becoming a Prisoner of War is not shameful and if any person thinks it is very shameful, then a big mistake may arise. I told my troops that it is better to die than become a Prisoner of War and also I told them that the Western people think if he has fulfilled his duty, to become a Prisoner of War is not shameful.[42]

We also see this approach explained by Colonel Tokunaga Isao, Commandant of Hong Kong's POW camps:

> According to a Japanese, not only military personnel but women and children will think it better to die than to become a POW. This principle was strongly taught [to] women and children and in this war, in the Pacific area, many women and children died rather than be POWs.[43]

There were also pragmatic considerations. As the IMTFE explained, in 1934, Japan had stated that under the 1929 POW Convention, POWs could not be as severely punished as Japanese soldiers, and that this would involve a 'revision of the Japanese Military and Naval Disciplinary Codes to put them on an equal footing, a revision which was undesirable in the interests of discipline'.[44] That tribunal observed that the real objection was that 'the Military desired to avoid any express commitments which would hinder their policy of ill-treatment of prisoners of war'.[45]

In the absence of reasoned judgments, the Hong Kong cases do not tell us about the rationale of the four British military tribunals in reaching their verdicts. However, in the POW camp cases from Hong Kong and Taiwan, China, convictions were entered on the basis of charges that appear to have been based on the 1929 POW Convention. We do know from the IMTFE that the convention was not applied to Japan as treaty law, but as customary law despite

[41] Some of the extensive literature on this includes Y Kita, 'The Japanese Military's Attitude towards International Law and the Treatment of Prisoners of War', in I Gow, Y Hirama, and J Chapman (eds), *The History of Anglo-Japanese Relations, 1600–2000: The Military Dimension* (Palgrave Macmillan 2003) vol 3, 256–60; E Ikegami, *The Taming of the Samurai: Honorific Individualism and the Making of Modern Japan* (Harvard University Press 1995); M Harries and S Harries, *Soldiers of the Sun: The Rise and Fall of the Imperial Japanese Army* (Random House 1994) 18; J W Dower, *War without Mercy: Race & Power in The Pacific War* (Pantheon Books 1986) 48–52; J Toland, *The Rising Sun: The Decline and Fall of the Japanese Empire 1936–45* (Random House 1970); Lord Russell, *The Knights of Bushido* (Cassell 1958) 53–8.

[42] Testimony of Maj Gen Tanaka Ryosaburo, *Trial of Maj Gen Tanaka Ryosaburo* (n 7) transcript 168, slide 181.

[43] Testimony of Col Tokunaga Isao, *Trial of Col Tokunaga Isao and four others (Part One)* (n 12) transcript 459, slide 500.

[44] *IMTFE Judgment* (n 1) 418–19.

[45] *IMTFE Judgment* (n 1) 419.

her obvious persistent objections; and that Japan was also held bound by her unilateral undertakings (see shortly) in relation to captives. One has to presume this was also the thinking in the Hong Kong trials, which preceded Tokyo.

In addition to treaty and custom, unilateral undertakings were a source of law binding on Japan. She had, in the course of the War, given certain formal assurances about how she would treat Allied POWs.[46] For example, in 1942, the Japanese government assured the Swiss Foreign Minister that Japan 'observes strictly the Geneva Convention of 27th July 1929, relative to the Red Cross, as a state signatory of that Convention'.[47] The IMTFE determined that this, and other assurances, constituted a legal obligation:

> Each undertaking given was a solemn agreement binding the government of Japan as well as the governments of the other combatants to apply the [1929 POW Convention] to [POWs] and civilian internees alike; to take into consideration the national and racial customs of those prisoners and internees when supplying them with food and clothing as required by the [1929 POW Convention] and not to force internees to work.[48]

English law was the final source of law relied on in Hong Kong, this being a process underpinned by the *Manual of Military Law 1929 (as amended)* and procedures determined by ALFSEA in Singapore, and also a process conducted by a colonial power returning to reassert her authority almost four years after being ousted. Some leading authorities have written about how the British trials under the Royal Warrant were international in nature. Lauterpacht argued that the *Manual of Military Law 1929 (as amended)* referred to violations of international law, not English municipal law[49] and Baxter argued that the Judge Advocates and legal members, 'with rare exceptions', emphasized the international substance of the proceedings, even declaring distinctions between murder and manslaughter to be irrelevant.[50] The Hong Kong trials do not conform to this depiction. It is clear that although these were about crimes under international law, and provisions of international law were cited from time to time, the parties relied heavily on the principles and approaches of domestic criminal law, with common law concepts such as murder, manslaughter, causation and others, feeding into their understanding of the notion of the war crime. *Archbold's Pleading, Evidence and Practice in Criminal Cases*[51] was the most commonly cited document[52] along with the *Manual*

[46] A Durand, *History of the International Committee of the Red Cross: From Sarajevo to Hiroshima* (Henry Dunant Institute 1984) 521, 543.

[47] Communication from Japanese Foreign Minister Togo Shigenori to Swiss Minister in Tokyo, 29 January 1942, in H S Levie (ed), *Documents on Prisoners of War*, International Law Studies (US Naval War College 1979) vol 60, 463.

[48] *IMTFE Judgment* (n 1) 424.

[49] H Lauterpacht, 'The Law of Nations and the Punishment of War Crimes' (1944) 21 BYIL 58, 64.

[50] R R Baxter, 'The Municipal and International Law Basis of Jurisdiction over War Crimes' (1951) 28 BYIL 382, 383.

[51] J F Archbold, R E Ross, and T R Fitzwalter Butler (eds), *Archbold's Pleading, Evidence and Practice in Criminal Cases* (29th edn, Sweet & Maxwell 1934).

[52] See for example, *Trial of Col Noma Kennosuke* (HKWCT Collection, File No WO235/999) ('*Trial of Col Noma Kennosuke*'), transcript 242, slide 248. Defence Counsel challenged the charges for

*of Military Law (as amended)*. According to the United Nations War Crimes Commission's commentary on the *Peleus Trial*, the *Manual* was not a source of law, but only a document setting out the law with 'no formal binding power'.[53] This was not so in Hong Kong, where the cases show that the parties relied heavily on it as a source of law. For example, the '*Manual of Military Law 1929*' was specifically cited as source of law for war crimes in the Prosecutor's Opening Statement in *Tanaka*[54] and as authority for the burden of proof in *Shoji*.[55] The Prosecutor in *Ito* cited the '*Manual of Military Law 1929*, ch XIV, para 56(c)' as a source of law.[56] The amendment on superior orders was cited as a source of law in several trials.[57] As to direct reliance on English (or common law) conceptions, examples abound. Counsel in *Noma* challenged the general, vague, and non-specific nature of the charge, citing *R v Yates*, *Archbold*, the compatibility of the procedure for handling of hostile witnesses with English law, and referred to *R v Harris* and Best on Evidence (*The Principles of the Laws of Evidence: With Elementary Rules for Conducting the Examination and Cross-Examination of Witnesses*).[58] In *Matsuda*, both Prosecution and Defence closed with references to Lord Hale on circumstantial evidence.[59]

For these reasons, the British trials in Hong Kong are more correctly described as being governed by a combination of international law, British military law, and English common law.

duplication, which was inadmissible under British law, citing Archbold's 29th edn at page 47. *Archbold* was also cited as authority for the procedure to follow in summing up the Prosecution's case, see Prosecution's Closing Address, *Trial of Maj Uete Taichi and six Others* (HKWCT Collection, File No WO235/1105) exhibit V, 5, slide 822.

[53] See commentary on *Trial of Kapitanleutnant Heinz Eck* (Peleus Trial), United Nations War Crimes Commission, *Law Reports of Trials of War Criminals* (HMSO 1947) Vol 1, 19.

[54] Prosecution's Opening Address, *Trial of Maj Gen Tanaka Ryosaburo* (n 7) exhibit E, 5, slide 267. See also transcript 526–7, slides 267–8, where he referred to the '*Manual of Military Law* ch XIV, para 56, exhibit to *Hague Convention* s 1 ch 1 art 1 cond 1' as a source of law.

[55] Prosecution's Reply to Defence Opening Address, *Trial of Maj Gen Shoji Toshishige* (n 20) transcript 110, slide 119, citing 'the Manual of Military Law, the chapter on evidence, chapter 6 in the Manual itself', with particular focus on para 12 on the burden of proof, and para 13 on shifting of the burden of proof.

[56] Prosecution Opening Address, *Trial of Lt Gen Ito Takeo* (n 6) exhibit E, 3, slide 251. He also cited to ch 1, art 1 of 'the *Sick and Wounded Convention*' [the 1929 POW Convention] and Hague Convention IV and its annexed Regulations, 's 1, ch 1, art 1, condition 1'.

[57] *Manual of Military Law 1929 (Amendment No 34 of 1944)* (n 3). See, eg, Prosecution Closing Address in *Trial of Col Tamura Teiichi and Two Others* (HKWCT Collection, File No WO235/1021) exhibit C(1), 6, slide 259, citing *Manual of Military Law 1929 (Amendment No 34 of 1944)*, ch XIV, para 443.

[58] *Trial of Col Noma Kennosuke* (n 52) transcript 243, slide 249. See W M Best, *The Principles of the Laws of Evidence: With Elementary Rules for Conducting the Examination and Cross-Examination of Witnesses* (11th edn, Sweet & Maxwell 1911).

[59] *Trial of Sgt Matsuda Kenichi* (HKWCT Collection, File No WO235/846) ('*Trial of Sgt Matsuda Kenichi*'), transcript 77–8, slides 88–9.

## 3. Focus on War Crimes against Civilians in an Occupied Territory

### 3.1 Ill-treatment of civilians through 'evacuation'/'compulsory evacuation'/'forced repatriation'/'deportation'/'banishment'/ 'forced displacement'[60]

When Hong Kong fell to the Japanese on Christmas Day 1941, it was already overrun with refugees from the War in China. An unofficial census by air raid wardens in 1941 estimated that the population of Hong Kong, bloated by the influx of refugees from the Mainland, had become 1,640,000; at the end of the War, the population was estimated to have been reduced to 600,000.[61] During the population bulge, residents faced hyper-inflation, serious food shortages, and there was even famine.[62] Testimony was provided in the Hong Kong trials about ailing people and dead bodies in the streets of Hong Kong.[63] The administration, under military Governor-General Sakai Takashi, devised a scheme to remove homeless persons to various places outside the territory, such as the Guangdong coast, Canton, and outlying islands.[64] It should here be pointed out that the involuntarily displaced persons, and those who 'volunteered', were sent from occupied Hong Kong to occupied China, and some of Hong Kong was still sovereign Chinese territory, having only been leased to the British.[65]

[60] A wide range of terminology was used by the Japanese, local Chinese, and non-locals to describe the phenomenon of the involuntary displacement or transfer that took place. The terms 'refugees' and 'undesirables' were both used when referring to those who were removed from the territory; and the displaced persons were said to have been held at 'refugee camps' before being removed from Hong Kong. An element of the displacements appears to have been formally voluntary, although under the coercive circumstances of the War and the Japanese occupation, rendering voluntariness highly suspect. For the purposes of this chapter, the author therefore refers to the action as *involuntary displacement* although preserving original terms used to the fullest extent possible, in quotation marks.

[61] S C Fan, 'The Population of Hong Kong' (The Committee for International Coordination of National Research in Demography Series 1974) 2. The Japanese estimated the population as being in excess of 1.8 million, see translation of extracts from 'Hong Kong under Military Administration' (Hong Kong Oriental Economics Co 1944), *Trial of Col Noma Kennosuke* (n 52) ('Hong Kong under Military Administration'), exhibit ZZ, 2, slides 664–6. The document was created under the auspices of the 'Information Dept., Office of Governor-Gen for Occupied Territory of Hong Kong'.

[62] S Y S Tsang, *A Modern History of Hong Kong* (I B Tauris 2004) 127–8; P Snow, *The Fall of Hong Kong: Britain, China and the Japanese Occupation* (Yale University Press 2003) ('Snow, *The Fall of Hong Kong: Britain, China and the Japanese Occupation*') 167.

[63] Testimony of Prosecution Witness Tang Kuen, *Trial of Col Noma Kennosuke* (n 52) transcript 85, slide 91; Testimony of Prosecution Witness Frederick Tyndall, *Trial of Col Noma Kennosuke* (n 52) transcript 217, slide 223.

[64] For more on the involuntary displacements over the years of the occupation, see Snow, *The Fall of Hong Kong: Britain, China and the Japanese Occupation* (n 62) 167–70, 208, 213–4, 223.

[65] China ceded the island of Hong Kong to Great Britain in perpetuity following the Treaty of Nanking, which ended the Opium War of 1839–1841 (see Treaty of Nanking, Nanking, 29 August 1842, Peace Treaty between the Queen of Great Britain and the Emperor of China, Ratifications Exchanged at Hong Kong, 26 June 1843. This was supplemented by a treaty in 1843, and renewed by a treaty of 26 June 1858, *Chinese Repository*, xiii (Aug. 1844), 437–46; p 521, (1844) LI 327; 30 B S P 389; 6 H C T 221; H B C T (1931) 55; 3 Martens (III) 484). China ceded Kowloon to the United Kingdom in perpetuity following the Convention of Peking ending the Second Anglo-Chinese War in 1862. The United Kingdom leased the New Territories from China for 99 years in 1898. See A Dicks,

Thus, the term 'deportation', in the sense of crossing international borders, was problematic.

Colonel Noma Kennosuke, the first and longest serving of the *Kempeitai* Commanders, testified that the purpose was:

> to cut down the population of the whole of the occupied territory of Hongkong, but it was mainly concerned with those within the town area of Hongkong and Kowloon.[66]

One source asserts that about 554,000 people were repatriated to China, to locations in Mirs Bay and Bias Bay, in the period of the military administration.[67] Another source claims that by October 1944, the Japanese had already repatriated nearly one million people from Hong Kong to occupied China.[68] An extract from the government-approved 'Hong Kong Under Military Administration'[69] submitted in evidence in the trial of Colonel Noma Kennosuke, and not challenged by the Prosecutor, revealed the following. The policy was developed at the beginning of the military administration of Hong Kong (ie under Lieutenant General Sakai Takashi).[70] Hong Kong's population had grown to nearly 2 million and it was an undesirable situation from an administrative perspective. The programme was developed to reduce the population, ridding the territory of

> those Chinese who are getting along in idleness and are not helpful for the establishment of Hong Kong, or who even hinder it . . . [and to] . . . repatriate either by persuasion and assistance, or, compulsorily, the vagabonds, the unemployed and the poorest people who are considered difficult to get job [sic] in Hong Kong in future, as well as the criminals.[71]

'Hong Kong Under Military Administration' revealed that there were three kinds of evacuation: evacuation by persuasion (free of charge), evacuation at own expense, and compulsory evacuation (free of charge). These confirm that the displacement was involuntary and 'voluntary' in a situation of some duress (that is, 'persuasion' or compulsory evacuation by a military occupier in a time of armed conflict and for reasons related to that situation can only be considered 'voluntary' by an extreme

'Grant, Usage or Sufferance? Some Legal Aspects of the Status of Hong Kong' (1983) 95 *The China Quarterly* 427.

66 Testimony of Col Noma Kennosuke, *Trial of Col Noma Kennosuke* (n 52) transcript 341, slide 347.

67 W T Han, 'Bureaucracy and the Japanese Occupation of Hong Kong', in W Newell (ed), *Japan in Asia: 1942–1945* (Singapore University Press 1981) 14. Former BAAG officer David Ronald Holmes testified that there came to be famine in the Bias Bay city of Tah Ping in 1943 and 'the condition was seriously aggravated by the arrival from time to time of large batches of refugees or deportees from Hong Kong', see Testimony of Prosecution Witness David Ronald Holmes, *Trial of Col Noma Kennosuke* (n 52) transcript 314–15, slides 320–1. According to the witness, the 'refugees' were all in very poor health and nutrition when they arrived, and came from the less wealthy class of people. Many died of starvation.

68 W T Han, 'Bureaucracy and the Japanese Occupation of Hong Kong', in W Newell (ed), *Japan in Asia: 1942–1945* (Singapore University Press 1981) 14.

69 'Hong Kong under Military Administration' (n 61) slides 664–7.

70 See *Sakai Judgments* (n 24).

71 'Hong Kong under Military Administration' (n 61) 2, slide 665.

stretch of the imagination). The total number of those who were 'evacuated' from the beginning of the Japanese occupation up till the end of September 1943 was said to be in excess of 973,000.[72] This included 576,000 'evacuated by persuasion', 16,000 'evacuated compulsorily', and 381,000 'evacuated at their own expense'.[73] In 'Hong Kong Under Military Administration', the Japanese regard these statistics, achieved in less than two years, to be a 'fine success'.[74]

The Japanese administration consulted with the local leadership committees and at both trials, they were, along with Colonel Noma and Lieutenant Colonel Kanazawa, to provide further insight into this scheme. Rice ration cards were issued according to the number of persons reported from the district bureaus based on those who had residence certificates. Those who did not have rice ration cards were not allowed to reside in Hong Kong; they were viewed as illegal immigrants. Prosecution witness Li Koon-Chun, the Secretary of the Co-operative Council (also called the Advisory Council) that liaised between locals and the regime of occupation, testified about the Japanese efforts first to secure 'voluntary repatriation', and then the scheme to reduce the population of Hong Kong by deporting those who did not possess rice ration cards.[75] According to the witness, others to be 'deported' were those who did not have a definite house to stay in, that is, those sleeping in the streets. The Gendarmerie assisted with the 'deportations', together with, and later replacing, the Civil Department's Repatriation Office; the garrison, the harbour authorities, and other official bodies were also involved. The witness testified that there were no proper investigations carried out as to whether the person possessed a rice ration or not, and that many people were arrested by mistake. These people were just arrested and then 'deported' without enquiries to ascertain if they had rice ration cards. The witness said he made representations to the Japanese, but with no result.

Sir Robert Kotewall,[76] the chairman of the Chinese Representative Council, testified how the original (first) scheme

> was the Government's intention to evacuate the unemployed and also vagrants and vagabonds and at the same time to encourage as much as possible with the assistance of the two Chinese Councils that voluntary evacuation of Chinese who had no employment in the Colony.[77]

He testified that there were three kinds of evacuees: 'voluntary evacuees, evacuees requiring some help from the Government, rogues and vagabonds and criminals'

[72] 'Hong Kong under Military Administration' (n 61) 2, slide 665.

[73] 'Hong Kong under Military Administration' (n 61) 3, slide 668.

[74] 'Hong Kong under Military Administration' (n 61) 2, slide 665.

[75] Testimony of Prosecution Witness Li Koon-Chun, *Trial of Col Noma Kennosuke* (n 52) transcript 264–5, slides 270–1.

[76] Testimony of Prosecution Witness Sir Robert Kotewall, *Trial of Col Noma Kennosuke* (n 52) transcript 273–83, slides 279–89.

[77] Testimony of Prosecution Witness Sir Robert Kotewall, *Trial of Col Noma Kennosuke* (n 52) transcript 275, slide 281. The transcript does not record the explanation of the second scheme.

(the latter regarded as undesirables).[78] The Chinese Representative Council also approached the Governor-General about the way that the 'evacuation' was being carried out, specifically the arrest of people in an arbitrary fashion and their maltreatment while in custody. Representations were made that those persons who were detained and awaiting 'deportation' should be given a chance to have their status further investigated. If they were indeed to be 'deported', the evacuees 'should be sent back to their native places or go to places near thereto'.[79] According to this witness, the Governor-General had acknowledged being aware that some abuses had been committed. Reading from minutes of a meeting between the Chinese Representative Council and the Governor of Hong Kong, the witness said that

> the Governor said that owing to the large population and scarcity of food he could not allow even people holding rice ration tickets but without employment to remain in Hongkong indefinitely. A time might come when they also had to go.[80]

Children who had rice ration tickets, but were caught stealing in the street, would also be 'evacuated' along with their parents, although there was discretion in this matter. The Governor-General, according to the witness, responded that malpractices and irregularities were not frequent, and those incidents were in the minority and should be sacrificed to the interest and welfare of the majority. Sir Robert also testified about the meeting that the community representatives had with Colonel Noma and the specific recommendations made for more humane handling of the 'evacuation' process.[81] People were being arrested without warrant or grounds, and were held in filthy cells where they were ill-treated. Some died in the cells and in the process of 'evacuation'. At a meeting, which was minuted, Colonel Noma said that he would make investigations and said he would welcome representations from the members of the two councils.

The testimony of one of the district bureau chiefs, Li Chung-Ching, who was involved in the public health and food aspects of the operation, was that

> [w]hen they [the Japanese] arrest people sometimes, they arrested many innocent people. For instance, when people picked up some wood from the hills, they were arrested too. Actually it was not a serious offence. We knew of this because we issued certificates for bailing these people. Actually many people were arrested innocently... When the gendarmes arrested people, we did not understand why they had to be arrested... They arrested everybody they came across in the streets.[82]

[78] Testimony of Prosecution Witness Sir Robert Kotewall, *Trial of Col Noma Kennosuke* (n 52) transcript 278, slide 284.

[79] Testimony of Prosecution Witness Sir Robert Kotewall, *Trial of Col Noma Kennosuke* (n 52) transcript 279, slide 285.

[80] Testimony of Prosecution Witness Sir Robert Kotewall, *Trial of Col Noma Kennosuke* (n 52) transcript 279, slide 285.

[81] Testimony of Prosecution Witness Sir Robert Kotewall, *Trial of Col Noma Kennosuke* (n 52) transcript 282, slide 288.

[82] Testimony of Prosecution Witness Li Chung-Ching, *Trial of Col Noma Kennosuke* (n 52) transcript 300, slide 306.

Mrs Tsang Mau-Ting testified for the Prosecution about how she, her husband, and others with rice ration cards were arrested, and taken to an air raid shelter in West Point.[83] They were later put on a boat with 100–200 people, and provided with '[a] can of rice, two loaves of bread and $10 National currency'.[84] The boat was towed out to sea by a launch, and then cut loose in a storm; the boat broke in half. The survivors were eventually rescued and taken to a nearby village. Prosecution witness Pang Yam-Sing testified to indiscriminate arrest and being expelled in inhumane conditions.[85] He was a local fisherman at the time. While on the way to the market to sell his fish, he was arrested by the commander of the Stanley Gendarmerie station and taken to the station and from there to the 'refugee concentration camp' at North Point. There, his name was registered, and he was held for 7 to 10 days together with some 800 people, none of whom knew why they had been arrested, or why they were being held. No one was interrogated. The people at this camp were then divided into two groups, and taken by boat to Nam O island. Several gendarmes and policemen, armed with guns, accompanied the boat. The conditions under which they were transported were extremely rough. Several people died, and some 40 to 50 were thrown into the sea. The witness was left on Nam O, others from the group were taken to an uninhabited island called Lo Chow Island. According to another witness:

> The refugees were brought to that uninhabited island and they were starved to death . . . it was said by the villagers of Hok Tsui Village that they were shouting for help, but after that time, about April the next year, I went by myself to that place and on this occasion I saw many dead bodies along the shore of that island.[86]

Was this involuntary displacement of civilians a legitimate administrative act with the greater good of the inhabitants of Hong Kong as its objective, or was it a war crime in itself, or was it a war crime for its detrimental effect on human life, and for the cruelty of its implementation? The first of the two *Kempeitai* heads, Colonel Noma Kennosuke, faced one single charge, covering the entire period of his service in Hong Kong, of being

> in violation of the laws and usages of war, concerned in the illtreatment of civilian residents, as a result of which numbers of them died or were unlawfully killed by members of the Japanese Forces, and many others underwent physical suffering.[87]

Copious evidence was brought in support of this, as well as the conduct of the *Kempeitai* across occupied Hong Kong, and the matter of their role in rounding up civilians for the mass 'deportation' scheme. The evidence suggested that the action

83 Testimony of Prosecution Witness Mrs Tsang Mau-ting, *Trial of Col Noma Kennosuke* (n 52) transcript 283–9, slides 289–95.

84 Testimony of Prosecution Witness Mrs Tsang Mau-ting, *Trial of Col Noma Kennosuke* (n 52) transcript 286, slide 292.

85 Testimony of Prosecution Witness Pang Yam-Sing, *Trial of Col Noma Kennosuke* (n 52) transcript 290, slide 296.

86 Testimony of Prosecution Witness Lai Kam-Shing, *Trial of Col Noma Kennosuke* (n 52) transcript 297, slide 303.

87 Schedule of Charges, *Trial of Col Noma Kennosuke* (n 52) slide 7.

was meant to be discriminatory in the sense of targeting particularly vulnerable persons seen as 'undesirable', but that it also became arbitrary in that everyone came to be at risk of being involuntarily or forcibly displaced. Colonel Noma was convicted of the single war crimes charge. This was regarded as the most high profile case of all those tried in Hong Kong, yet the Judge Advocate conducted a remarkably brief and inadequate review, and did not even comment on what the Prosecution argued as 'deportation'.[88] To return to the core issue: was this involuntary displacement of civilians legal or illegal, and was the way it was carried out legal or illegal, or at all relevant? How could this be linked to the accused? The Prosecutor's sole authority for arguing for jurisdiction over the involuntary displacement as a war crime was the IMT Nuremberg's Charter (in fact, both the IMTs Nuremberg and Tokyo considered as war crimes 'ill-treatment or deportation to slave labour or *for any other purpose* of civilian population of or in occupied territory').[89] The situation could, of course, be seen as transfer of persons resident in one part of an occupied territory to another. There was no argument in *Noma* on exactly what the elements of the crime were, but the Prosecutor submitted that

> [i]ts illegality consists in the fact that, at international law, it is a well authenticated war crime against humanity. If it was not already an established illegality it would not have been included in the list. . . . I would say the very idea is an affront to the feelings of any civilised community. Deportation is a historic measure for the punishment of crime. In that connection, you will call to mind Siberia, St Helens, Devil's Island, Sydney and the Andaman Islands.[90]

We can, of course, legitimately query some of this view, and ask whether the involuntary displacement in the acutely overcrowded Hong Kong situation can be equated with the extraordinary nature of the deportation to slave labour or industrialized killing, as occurred under Germany in occupied Europe. But, the Defence did not challenge this. For deportation to be established, a national border must be crossed, and as noted before, some of the British colony of Hong Kong was leased from China.[91] Thus, for some persons, they were not deported, but involuntarily or forcibly displaced back to their own country, falling outside the remit of the war crimes charge. This was not raised by the Defence. It did, however, indirectly challenge the rigidity of the prohibition, by reference to the fact that some people went voluntarily, and in principle, persons who were unlawfully present in Hong Kong and 'undesirables' such as thieves, beggars, and vagrants were legitimate targets of 'evacuation'.[92] The *Noma* Defence's 34-page Closing Address focused on challenging the evidence of witnesses, and did not engage in issues of the law on deportation as a war crime. Mistakes were inevitable, Counsel argued, given the size of the programme.[93] The acts of the *Kempeitai* were, 'as a

[88] Judge Advocate's Report, 18 April 1947, *Trial of Col Noma Kennosuke* (n 52) slide 5.
[89] Emphasis added.
[90] Prosecutor's Closing Address, *Trial of Col Noma Kennosuke* (n 52) exhibit EEE, 9, slide 714.
[91] See comments at (n 65).
[92] Closing Address, *Trial of Col Noma Kennosuke* (n 52) exhibit DDD, 25, slide 696.
[93] Closing Address, *Trial of Col Noma Kennosuke* (n 52) exhibit DDD, 25, slide 696.

whole, reasonable', given the kind of persons they arrested and removed from the territory and the locations that the persons were sent to.[94] Correct location of responsibility was with the Governor-General and the Civil Affairs Department, Counsel argued.[95] Obviously, given the conviction of Colonel Noma for a broad charge of 'ill-treatment', we cannot be 100 per cent sure that this included these involuntary displacements but it seems almost certain, given how overwhelming the evidence was, that involuntary displacement was carried out in an arbitrary, cruel, violent, and inhumane way. The verdict does not allow us to take a position on the illegality of the involuntary displacement programme in itself.

The second and last *Kempeitai* Commander, Lieutenant Colonel Kanazawa Asao, was convicted for his role in continuing the practices of his predecessor. Unlike Colonel Noma, he was specifically charged with the 'deportation': 'ill-treatment of civilian residents resulting in the death of many of them and in physical suffering to others, which ill-treatment included deportation from Hong Kong'.[96] The Prosecutor in *Kanazawa* submitted that the 'compulsory evacuation' was 'in its very essence' illegal, arguing, as in *Noma*, that this illegality consisted of 'the fact that at international law, it is a well authenticated crime against humanity' and that 'such well recognised illegality' was affirmed by its inclusion in the Charter of the IMT Nuremberg.[97] The *Kanazawa* Defence did not challenge the correctness of charging 'deportation' as a form of ill-treatment amounting to a war crime in the circumstances of Hong Kong. Counsel indirectly challenged the argument of inherent illegality by arguing that for blame to be allocated to the accused, the Prosecutor had to prove (1) whether 'innocent and bona fide residents were indiscriminately arrested'; (2) whether the accused ordered the arrests; (3) if the accused did not order the arrests, whether he took any steps in relation to the 'deportation'; (4) that people died while being 'deported'.[98] This put the focus on the way that the involuntary displacement was carried out, and the role of the accused. He was convicted of both charges, but support for the Defence came from the reviewing Judge Advocate. He disagreed with the conviction entered by the panel on the 'deportation' charge, and recommended that this finding not be confirmed. The Judge Advocate argued that there was 'nothing inherently illegal' in the 'deportation' of 'undesirable residents' from Hong Kong, and noted that

> as has already been pointed out the whole scheme was launched by the Governor with the qualified approval of the more responsible members of the population. There is no doubt that abuses occurred and that the conditions in which some of the deportees lived were bad. I am bound to say however that the weight of the evidence so far as it concerns the accused's own actions in the matter tends to prove that he did all that could reasonably be expected of

[94] Closing Address, *Trial of Col Noma Kennosuke* (n 52) 28, slide 699.

[95] Closing Address, *Trial of Col Noma Kennosuke* (n 52) 26–7, slides 697–8.

[96] *Trial of Lt Col Kanazawa Asao* (HKWCT Collection, File No WO235/1093) ('*Trial of Lt Col Kanazawa Asao*').

[97] Closing Address of the Prosecution, *Trial of Lt Col Kanazawa Asao* (n 96) exhibit AA, 7, slide 530.

[98] Closing Address in Defence of Lt Col Kanazawa, *Trial of Lt Col Kanazawa Asao* (n 96) exhibit Z, 5, slide 521.

him to ensure that the deportations were carried out humanely and to meet the wishes of the local populace.[99]

The General Officer Commanding Land Forces Hong Kong must have agreed with the argument that there was nothing inherently unlawful about the 'deportations', and the role of the accused, since he declined to confirm the conviction on this charge. Even so, Lieutenant Colonel Kanazawa's conviction on the first charge was upheld and he was hanged.

Case law from the Control Council No 10 trials, most notably *Krupp*[100]and *High Command*[101] raised different standards for evaluating involuntary displacement when civilians were forced across international boundaries within territory consolidated by the occupying power. They would have been helpful in *Noma,* but in all fairness, they came after that trial was completed and the Colonel was executed. For all we know, the military panels in *Noma* and *Kanazawa* may have been engaged in such considerations, but we can only speculate. The *Krupp* standard was broad, setting out three conditions for deportation in wartime to be unlawful: if it was done without legal title, where the purpose of the displacement was illegal (eg for forced labour), and where the displacement took place in disregard of 'generally recognised standards of decency and humanity'.[102] The *High Command* standard was much narrower; here the tribunal pointed out that international law did not permit the deportation or use of civilians against their will 'for other than on reasonable requisitions for the need of the army, either within the area of the army or after deportation to rear areas or to the homeland of the occupying power'.[103] These cases go to the parameters of when an otherwise permissible act becomes criminal.

Hong Kong's involuntary displacements were also the subject of litigation in China, with Lieutenant General Sakai Takashi, who initiated the scheme as the first military Governor-General of Hong Kong, being convicted of 'deportation of civilians'. The three translations of *Sakai*[104] do not reveal the Court examining the 'deportations' closely, and the Court seems to have viewed 'deportation' in itself as illegal, given how it was presented in the same way as torture and rape. Also in Nanking, former Governor-General Lieutenant General Isogai Rensuke, who oversaw the Hong Kong scheme for most of its life, was, convicted of the allegation that

he allowed his subordinates to arrest and deport non-army personnel to Bias Bay continuously, and without taking care about the safety of those being banished, 'causing the

[99] Judge Advocate's Report, 20 January 1948, *Trial of Lt Col Kanazawa Asao* (n 96) slide 4.

[100] *US v Alfried Felix Alwyn Krupp von Bohlen und Halbach* (The Krupp Case), Trials of War Criminals Before the Nuremberg Military Tribunal under Control Council Law No 10 vol IX (USGPO 1950) 1327 ('*US v Krupp*').

[101] *US v von Leeb*, Trials of War Criminals Before the Nuremberg Military Tribunal under Control Council Law No 10 vol IX (USGPO 1950) 462 ('*US v von Leeb*').

[102] *US v Krupp* (n 100) 1432, citing with approval Judge Phillips from the case of *US v Milch.*

[103] *US v von Leeb* (n 101) 603.

[104] *Sakai Judgments* (n 24).

old, weak, females and children to be homeless, resulting in deaths from starvation and exposure'.[105]

The tribunal noted that the former Governor was inconsistent in explaining the so-called 'banishments'. At trial, he 'suddenly denied his former evidence and said that such "banishments" were to get rid of thieves and robbers and to transport the Hong Kong residents back to their native villages'.[106] 'Such concealment cannot be believed', held the Court.[107] The judges observed that the 'banishment', was conducted with no attention to the safety of those being relocated, and held it to be a war crime in violation of Article 46 of the 1907 Hague Regulations and its annexed Regulations and Chinese laws. In other words, the 'banishment' itself was not unlawful, the way it was implemented was the problem. The tribunal accepted that his motive for these activities was due to the shortage of food in Hong Kong.[108] Lieutenant-General Isogai Rensuke was convicted and sentenced to life imprisonment, which suggests that the motive was taken into account in mitigation.

The involuntary displacements in Hong Kong were so similar to what was done in the Andaman Islands that it is instructive to examine the relevant case here. The 1946 trial in Singapore of Vice-Admiral Hara Teizo, the civilian Governor of the Andaman Islands, and eight Navy personnel, saw the accused charged with ill-treatment and killing of civilians.[109] The Judge Advocate's report is notably more thorough and considered than that in *Noma* and *Kanazawa,* and the following account draws from this report.[110] The situation, it was accepted by all parties, arose out of food shortages on the island. A conference at Naval Headquarters was held at the end of July 1945, and it was decided to transport certain 'undesirables' or 'bad' characters (the aged, infirm, women, children, and 'malcontents and idlers') who did not have ration cards owing to non employment by the Japanese authorities.[111] The Japanese described this as an 'emigration plan', an 'emergency measure'.[112] These persons were dispatched to Havelock Island (First Charge) and Tarmugli Island (Second Charge) in atrocious circumstances.[113]

Those sent to Havelock, an uninhabited but not barren island, were forced onto a boat (probably more than 300, at least 236), and forced ashore in circumstances where about 100 of them drowned. They were left without supplies, but eventually

105 File No WO325/135 in the UK National Archives contains, *inter alia*, a report by Captain F V Collison of No 14 War Crimes Investigation Team, Hong Kong, to his Officer in Charge, concerning the trial, which he attended as the official British observer. It also contains a 'rough translation' of the judgment of the Chinese Military Tribunal at Nanking, dated 22 July in the 36th year of the Chinese Republic (1947) ('*Isogai Rensuke Trial Judgment*').

106 *Isogai Rensuke Trial Judgment* (n 105) 3.

107 *Isogai Rensuke Trial Judgment* (n 105) 3.

108 *Isogai Rensuke Trial Judgment* (n 105) 4.

109 Opening and Closing Addresses for the Prosecution, *Trial of V Adm Hara Teizo and eight others* (UK National Archives, File No WO 235/839) ('*Trial of V Adm Hara Teizo and eight others*'). This case is not part of the HKWCT Collection, as it was tried in Singapore.

110 Judge Advocate's Report, 29 April 1946, *Trial of V Adm Hara Teizo and eight others* (n 109) 1.

111 Judge Advocate's Report, *Trial of V Adm Hara Teizo and eight others* (n 109) 1, 4.

112 Judge Advocate's Report, *Trial of V Adm Hara Teizo and eight others* (n 109) 1–2, 4–6.

113 Closing Address for the Prosecution, *Trial of V Adm Hara Teizo and eight others* (n 109) 1.

a small and inadequate amount of supplies was delivered. The Japanese even brought back some of the supplies, having considered that the deportees had enough to eat. According to the Judge Advocate, '[t]wo more had managed to escape on a raft. Of the rest, a certain number had been killed by Burmese raiders but the remainder had died of starvation or drowning.'[114] Only 11 persons survived and were eventually taken off the island. Investigators from the Allied Forces found the remains of 108 males, three females and three children on the island itself, and many more remains below the high water mark.

The Prosecutor argued that the accused failed to foresee the risks to the evacuees, who were landed on an island that was predictably prone to Burmese raids (for the wild pigs), and that

> such a lack of foresight in an allegedly carefully planned operation is criminal and the responsibility for the deaths of those who were killed by the Burmese must rest with those who planned the operation and failed to provide a guard for the civilians.[115]

He also argued that those junior officers who disobeyed orders must accept responsibility for the deaths that arose 'as a direct result of their disobedience or negligence'.[116] Vice-Admiral Hara should, the Prosecutor argued, have considered seven preliminary issues before approving the transportation, ranging from the suitability of the island to the provision of medical treatment to the 'possibility of finding other places which would cause less disturbance of the two people and permit them to keep their families with them'.[117] According to the Prosecutor, the two senior accused were under a duty to take steps to alleviate the situation:

> particularly as the plight of the people was a direct result of the occupation by the Japanese forces. In carry [sic] out this duty the authorities should have exercised the greatest tolerance and should have refrained from disturbing the liberty and rights of the people unless some disturbance was absolutely necessary in the interests of the people themselves or genuine and urgent military reason.[118]

The Japanese argued that this was an 'emigration plan', a lawful exercise in light of the food shortage on the island. Those who did not work did not get food rations, and since 'these undesirables would die of starvation unless they could steal rations they were considered a menace to the public peace'.[119] Emergency measures became necessary. Furthermore, proper provision was made for the evacuees to set up home in their new abode, and they were supplied with food from Port Blair. The Defence challenged the reliance on the notion of 'wilful neglect' as a basis for a war crimes prosecution. Counsel argued that paragraph 366 of the Manual of Military Law (1929 Edition) allowed the commander of an occupying force, so

[114] Judge Advocate's Report, 29 April 1946, *Trial of V Adm Hara Teizo and eight others* (n 109) 2.
[115] Closing Address for the Prosecution, *Trial of V Adm Hara Teizo and eight others* (n 109) 1.
[116] Closing Address for the Prosecution, *Trial of V Adm Hara Teizo and eight others* (n 109) 1.
[117] Closing Address for the Prosecution, *Trial of V Adm Hara Teizo and eight others* (n 109) 2.
[118] Accused's Petition, 21 April 1946 (Ref 10ZF No 2–21), *Trial of V Adm Hara Teizo and eight others* (n 109) para 12.
[119] Judge Advocate's Report, 29 April 1946, *Trial of V Adm Hara Teizo and eight others* (n 109) 2.

long as he observes the fundamental spirit of military law, to take any measures necessary to maintain his fighting strength, where he considers such measures necessary from a military point of view.[120] Thus, it was argued:

> [t]he measures adopted by the accused in connection with this case were purely administrative measures and were substantially free of criminal nature. Even if an administrative measure should result in a failure, against the expectations of the administration, could it be immediately concluded that the responsibility lies totally with the administration, in this case, the accused?[121]

The charge had, it will be recalled, alleged the ill-treatment and killing of civilians and the Prosecutor's case drew in a series of events associated with the involuntary displacement, from the rounding up, to the detention, to the transportation and then the abandonment of the civilians on Havelock and Tarmugli islands. The Judge Advocate's view was that it was clear that the intention was to remove persons who were 'not useful' to the Japanese, and the perpetrators were 'completely indifferent to their fate after removal, even if they did not positively intend them to starve'.[122] The senior officers conceived and organized the forced removal, although it was not clear if some of their subordinates acted in excess of orders (eg by throwing persons overboard). It does not appear that the Judge Advocate considered the scheme unlawful in itself, the illegality arising from the way it was carried out. The outcome indicates that the Court agreed with the Prosecutor's arguments. Convictions were entered and confirmed in relation to all but one accused, an interpreter; the sentences were six death penalties, two sentences of life imprisonment, and one term of three years.

Drawing all of this to the Hong Kong cases, it seems that the authorities there did have to balance their obligations to the occupied population under the 1907 Hague Regulations, and did face an extreme situation in relation to the pressure of an influx from mainland China in a time of wartime restrictions on food supplies. Article 43 of the 1907 Hague Regulations required Japan as occupier to 'take all the measures in his power to restore, and ensure, as far as possible, public order and safety', while Article 46 required that '[f]amily honour and rights, the lives of persons, and private property, as well as religious convictions and practice, must be respected'. The Japanese did have to take some measures to deal with the overcrowding as it came to impact on public order, wellbeing and safety. In itself, a scheme for the purpose of reducing the pressures of the huge wartime population would not be unlawful by Article 43 of the 1907 Hague Regulations. The evidence is that neither of the *Kempeitai* Commanders took part in the design of the programme, but were required to take part in its implementation. The cases surveyed further indicate that involuntary displacement not directly related to military operational factors can be lawful if it is conducted on legitimate grounds of public order, wellbeing, and safety, and one would presumably be able to say

120 Closing Address for the Prosecution, *Trial of V Adm Hara Teizo and eight others* (n 109) 12.
121 Closing Address for the Prosecution, *Trial of V Adm Hara Teizo and eight others* (n 109) 12.
122 Judge Advocate's Report, 29 April 1946, *Trial of V Adm Hara Teizo and eight others* (n 109) 4.

with confidence that genuine consent would also go towards providing legitimacy. But one has to question the voluntariness of consent in these circumstances. The cases support the position that where such activities are undertaken, there must be adequate precautionary measures taken to ensure compliance with Article 46 of the 1907 Hague Regulations. The 1948 *Krupp* case is instructive here, as the US Military Tribunal held that deportation becomes illegal 'whenever generally recognized standards of decency and humanity are disregarded... whenever the deportation is characterized by inhumane or illegal methods'.[123] One could certainly reach to the Martens Clause, drawing from the 'the rule of the principles of the law of nations, as they result from the usages established among civilized peoples, from the laws of humanity, and the dictates of the public conscience'.[124] The evidence suggests that both commanders were at fault (with more blame to Colonel Noma who was in office for most of the occupation, as the original commander implementing the programme of deportations), for their failures in foreseeing the risks during implementation, failing to take steps to ensure proper implementation, and then failing to respond adequately to information about how the involuntary displacement was not being carried out in a principled or humane way.

## 3.2 Ill-treatment: Torture and similar forms of severe maltreatment

Article 46 of the 1907 Hague Regulations speaks to the duty of the occupier to respect '[f]amily honour and rights, the lives of persons, and private property, as well as religious convictions and practice'. Probably all of the civilian maltreatment or ill-treatment with which the Hong Kong *Kempeitai* were charged would today be categorized as the war crime of torture or inhuman treatment. However, while torture was a term used repeatedly by witnesses and the parties, only two cases actually charged torture as a war crime.[125] There was, in these cases, no discussion of what torture of civilians as a war crime meant, and what distinguished it from ill-treatment of civilians as a war crime or maltreatment of civilians as a war crime. The case brought against *Kempeitai* Commander Colonel Noma did, however, suggest a distinction within the 'ill-treatment' he was charged with. Torture was associated with 'interrogation', 'inhuman practices', 'interrogators' pressure', and 'evil'; this was different from under-feeding, overcrowding in the cells, and lack of medical attention.[126]

The Hong Kong *Kempeitai* cases are rich in terms of volume and their range from the most senior commanders on the territory (Colonel Noma and Lieutenant Colonel Kanazawa) to mid-ranking officers in a supervisory role (Major Hirao Yoshio) to the lower ranks who actually committed the atrocities. In China, the former Governor-General, Lieutenant General Isogai Rensuke would stand trial

[123] *US v Krupp* (n 100) 1432.

[124] As stated in the preamble to the 1907 Hague Regulations (n 8).

[125] *Trial of WO Omura Kyoshi* (HKWCT Collection, File No WO235/893) and *Trial of Lt Kishi Yasuo and fourteen others* (n 11).

[126] Prosecution's Closing Address, *Trial of Col Noma Kennosuke* (n 52) exhibit EEE, 2–12, slides 707–17.

but be acquitted of responsibility for allowing the gendarmes in Hong Kong 'to arrest and torture Chinese and Foreign Residents'.[127] The standard *Kempeitai* case would involve persons taken into custody for suspicion of involvement in resistance activities, or black marketeering.[128] The persons would be physically abused and interrogated, sometimes over a period of days and weeks.[129] The same methods of torture would be used over and over again: 'water torture', 'aeroplane torture', beatings, burnings, and electrocution. The Hong Kong war crimes courts heard many first-hand accounts. One came from a Japanese-speaking businessman forced to become an interpreter at some of these interrogations. Jerome Edward Law testified that

> [a]t the interrogations, the gendarme who conducted them had the object of making the accused confess to his charges. To obtain these confessions, he invariably had recourse to torturing the accused . . . These tortures took the form of beatings with poles with electric wires. They also took the form of what was known as the aeroplane torture—hanging the accused up by the hands tied behind the back—and they also took the form of what was called the water torture—tying the accused to a frame, immobilising him and pouring water over his face . . . Other forms of torture were to starve the accused by giving them very poor food and insufficient at that and throwing them into cells that were unswept and insanitary and often leaving them in these cells for weeks on end without any questioning.[130]

The *Kempeitai* also used dogs, the Prosecutor alleged. One witness testified that 'I saw with my own eyes how these people were beaten up and how dogs were set upon them and tore their clothes off until they were bleeding. This I saw very, very many times.'[131] The ill-treatment varied, one witness testified about being held in a cage, of about 10 feet square to 12 feet square, with up to 19 people, in utterly squalid conditions, where the stench was such that 'the Indian guards coming in had to put handkerchiefs over their mouths and noses', and 'there was not enough

[127] *Isogai Rensuke Trial Judgment* (n 105). The Military Tribunal in Nanking held that the gendarmes were under a different chain of command, and also that it was not proven that the accused was connected with their atrocities.

[128] See for example, *Trial of Sgt Maj Yamada Kiichiro and Sgt Awa Isao* (HKWCT Collection, File No WO 235/887) ('*Trial of Sgt Maj Yamada Kiichiro and Sgt Awa Isao*') where some 30 Chinese from Tai Po in the New Territories were rounded up for questioning following the capture of a young boy bearing dispatches and the names of some of the locals involved in the ongoing communist and guerilla activities against the Japanese. Also, *Trial of WO Omura Kyoshi and four others* (HKWCT Collection, File No WO 235/1112) ('*Trial of WO Omura Kyoshi and four others*'), discussed in the text as a typical case.

[129] See for example, the testimony of Prosecution Witness Lam Chung-Sik, *Trial of Sgt Maj Yamada Kiichiro and Sgt Awa Isao* (n 128) transcript 32–8, slides 45–51 ('*Testimony of Lam Chung-Sik*'), detailing his own torture at the hands of the *Kempeitai* at Taipo Gendarmerie Headquarters, and also that of others, including the deaths in custody of some of his fellow detainees.

[130] Testimony of Prosecution Witness Jerome Edward Law, *Trial of Col Noma Kennosuke* (n 52) transcript 52, slide 57.

[131] Testimony of Prosecution Witness Dr S Ramler, *Trial of Col Noma Kennosuke* (n 52) transcript 33, slide 38. Denis Victor testified about how two dogs were set on him during interrogation, Testimony of Prosecution Witness Denis Victor, *Trial of Col Noma Kennosuke* (n 52) transcript 122, slide 128.

light to catch the lice which infested everyone in those cages'.[132] Sometimes, the persons would be released, sometimes they would be sent for trial, and sometimes they would die in custody. The facts were usually straightforward, and the only technical issues were to do with causation or with working out responsibilities and hierarchies within the *Kempeitai,* and the correct allocation of blame. For example, in the Trial of Warrant Office Omura Kyoshi et al, the technicalities turned on the role of Omura as Chief of the Special Branch of the *Kempeitai*, and his responsibility for the actions of his subordinates. The trials of Major Hirao, Colonel Noma, and Lieutenant Colonel Kanazawa were more complex because these were in essence command responsibility cases (although charged as 'being together concerned in'), and required looking at what was happening across Hong Kong.[133] But here too, it boiled down to what could actually be tied to the accused and what could not.

Scrutiny of the cases reveals that quite a number of persons were brought into custody on suspicion of having been spies and saboteurs working for the clandestine BAAG (British Aid Assistance Group)[134] or the Chinese resistance.[135] These persons came in for very harsh treatment.[136] As one petition for leniency pleaded, the actions of the accused were taken

> to inflict punishments to those who were engaged, in violation of the Laws of Land Warfare, in hostile activities against the Japanese. In the course of carrying out such countermeasures, however, the means and methods so applied were sometimes carried too far, and the excess so created has now become an object of criticism and judgement.[137]

Tellingly, in light of the charges and the evidence, the Defence in the Trial of Colonel Noma outlined the accused's duties as including the '[e]limination of the elements who obstructed the peace and order', although this was said to be accompanied by other duties, most notably the duty of '[a]voidance of infringement of basic human rights'.[138] Colonel Noma's motto was apparently 'Honesty, Kindness, and Good Results', and this was regularly impressed on his subordinates,

[132] Testimony of Prosecution Witness Cyril Munro Faure, *Trial of Col Noma Kennosuke* (n 52) transcript 90–1, slides 96–7.

[133] See the chapter by Professor Nina Jørgensen.

[134] The British Army Aid Group ('BAAG'), led by Col Lindsay Ride, who had escaped from a POW camp in Hong Kong, was known as MI9, and served as a unit gathering intelligence and assisting the escape of other POWs. See E Ride, *British Army Aid Group—BAAG: Hong Kong Resistance 1942–1945* (Oxford University Press 1981).

[135] These were organized as the East River Column, led by Gen Zeng Sheng, and comprised the Gangjiu Da Dui who were based on Lantau Island and the Dongjiang operating in the New Territories, and the Hong Kong Kowloon brigade. See generally, Tsang, *A Modern History Of Hong Kong* (n 62) 129–30. A case with strong elements of resistance activity is the *Trial of WO Omura Kyoshi and four others* (n 128).

[136] Testimony of Prosecution Witness Jerome Edward Law, *Trial of Col Noma Kennosuke* (n 52) transcript 52, slide 57. For a harrowing account of the torture by one such suspect, see Testimony of Prosecution Witness Beatrice Chan, *Trial of Col Noma Kennosuke* (n 52) transcript 106–11, slides 112–17.

[137] Petition on behalf of the Accused, *Trial of WO Omura Kyoshi and four others* (n 128) 4, slide 19.

[138] Defence Closing Submission, *Trial of Col Noma Kennosuke* (n 52) exhibit DDD, 32, slide 703.

he said.[139] The most important duty of the gendarmes was 'to fight against enemy spies behind the lines'.[140] The Defence argued that spies and the like were not entitled to be treated as civilians, and that the *Kempeitai* were engaged in legitimate 'fighting actions', but it provided no authorities in support of this.[141]

The Martens Clause affirms that nothing would have justified the abuse, torture, and sometimes outright murder of even these individuals.[142] As one Prosecutor argued in his Closing Address:

> [b]y no stretch of the imagination can it be conceded that the suspects could be ill-treated even if they admitted anti-Japanese activities nor that they would have saved themselves if they had admitted the allegations earlier. Every authority on international law advocates the necessity of a fair trial of any suspect whether a regular combatant or a non-uniformed guerrilla.[143]

*Kyoshi et al* involved the activities of the *Kempeitai* operating in Kowloon District, and reveals their modus operandi very clearly. The case was brought against five of its staff members for the ill-treatment and killing of civilians carried out in police stations within the District, and at the Kowloon Magistracy, in 1944 and 1945.[144] The *Kempeitai* were responding to resistance activities in the events covered by the charges. Local language interpreters were disappeared or attacked. Several Indians had been able, with assistance, to escape from occupied Hong Kong. There was resistance to the local *Kempeitai* in several areas, such as Tai Po. The railway bridge at Waterloo Road was one of the many places attacked. The *Kempeitai* actively investigated, focusing on those suspected of having been involved with the BAAG or the Chinese resistance. Three of the accused in this case were members of what was called the Special Branch of the *Kempeitai*, based at the Kowloon Magistracy. According to the Defence, the duties of the Special Branch involved 'anti-secret Warfare measures and anti-espionage measures'.[145] The first charge related to a major sweeping operation in the Sai Kung area of the New Territories in September 1944, and the abuse and interrogation of about one hundred villagers suspected of being involved in anti-Japanese activities. The second charge related to five separate arrests of several persons suspected of being involved with helping the BAAG in 1943 and 1944 (in particular over the escape of certain Indians from the territory), and the abuse and interrogation of these persons. The third charge related to another sweeping operation in December 1944, at Taipo village in the New Territories, with those taken into custody being abused and interrogated. In all of these charges, the standard form of torture emerged: beating and kicking, 'aeroplane torture', burning, and 'water torture'. Interrogation was often conducted

139 Defence Closing Submission, *Trial of Col Noma Kennosuke* (n 52) 30, slide 701.

140 Defence Closing Submission, *Trial of Col Noma Kennosuke* (n 52) 31, slide 702.

141 Defence Closing Submission, *Trial of Col Noma Kennosuke* (n 52) 31, slide 702.

142 Martens Clause (n 124).

143 Prosecution Closing Address, *Trial of WO Omura Kyoshi and four others* (n 128) exhibit W, 8, slide 431.

144 *Trial of WO Omura Kyoshi and four others* (n 128).

145 Closing Address on behalf of Omura, Nishida and Kawazumi, *Trial of WO Omura Kyoshi and four others* (n 128) exhibit V, 1, slide 409.

with the assistance of an interpreter. The conditions of detention were very poor, 'filthy and overcrowded', to quote from the Prosecution's Opening Address.[146] Several suspects died as a result of this treatment. Others were released, or were put through some kind of legal proceeding which in some cases resulted in the imposition of prison terms and in some cases, the death penalty.[147] The Prosecutor's Opening Address referred to torture in a way that indicated it was seen as interchangeable with the charge of ill-treatment.[148] The Prosecutor also claimed that the atrocities committed in this case 'can be classed as crimes against humanity and in direct contravention of existing rules of warfare regarding the position of a belligerent power towards the civilian population'.[149] The Defence comprised of challenging the allocation of responsibility by drawing on the structural divisions within the *Kempeitai* in Kowloon District, and challenging the evidence for its reliability and paucity. In closing, Defence Counsel argued that 'in war time it is permissible to take measures against espionage and to crush hostile activities and [it] is so acknowledged by international law'.[150] The final outcome, the Court's verdict, was mixed and therefore hard to assess: two 20-year sentences (one of which related to Kyoshi), one 12-year sentence, one death penalty, and one acquittal.

The vast majority of cases follow this pattern, which emerges in a different way for the more senior officers, where the focus went on proving their responsibility as commanders, albeit always under the rubric of being 'concerned in' war crimes. As Commanding Officer of the Kowloon *Kempeitai*, Major Hirao Yoshio was right in the middle of the Hong Kong *Kempeitai* structure, between the Commanders Noma and Asao and the *Kempeitai* on the ground. He was convicted of being

> concerned in the inhumane treatment by his subordinate staff, of Chinese and other civilians held in the custody of the said *Kempeitai* HQ and some of its substations which inhumane treatment consisted of killing some and ill-treating others.[151]

The Prosecutor brought evidence of much abuse by the Kowloon *Kempeitai* under the command of the accused, including one incident of alleged ill-treatment and an alleged beheading of ten Chinese suspects. The Defence challenged the claims of torture in the *Kempeitai* stations or of killings, by challenging the admissibility and reliability of witness testimonies.

[146] Prosecution's Opening Address, *Trial of WO Omura Kyoshi and four others* (n 128) exhibit E, 1, slide 381.

[147] Affidavit of Prosecution Witness Hui Shu Pui, *Trial of WO Omura Kyoshi and four others* (n 128) exhibit H, 1, slide 386: 'I and Ng Tai Hing were later sentenced to 3 years imprisonment whereas all the others I named received the death sentence and were all executed.'

[148] Prosecution's Opening Address, *Trial of WO Omura Kyoshi and four others* (n 128) exhibit E, 1, slide 381: 'In this charge, the prosecution will prove that all those [sic] men took part in the torture of those named in the charge and some unknown', and describing the various forms of torture used.

[149] Prosecution's Opening Address, *Trial of WO Omura Kyoshi and four others* (n 128) exhibit E, 1, slide 381.

[150] Closing Address on behalf of Omura, Nishida and Kawazumi, *Trial of WO Omura Kyoshi and four others* (n 128) exhibit V, 14–15, slides 422–3.

[151] *Trial of Maj Hirao Yoshio* (HKWCT Collection, File No WO235/1098).

Colonel Noma, as *Kempeitai* Commander of Hong Kong, was responsible for public order, the control of *Kempei* personnel and for the management of places of detention in Hong Kong; this was something the parties agreed on at trial. He was convicted of being

> concerned in the illtreatment of civilian residents, as a result of which numbers of them died or were unlawfully killed by members of the Japanese Forces, and many others underwent physical suffering.[152]

The Prosecution's theory of 'being together concerned in' (see the chapter by Professor Nina Jørgensen) was that Colonel Noma held command responsibility[153] for his subordinates' violations of the laws and customs of war, including mismanagement of places of detention resulting in overcrowding, starvation, torture, refusal of medical attention and consequential sufferings and deaths, illegal executions, and mass deportation of civilians from Hong Kong. The Prosecutor was eventually to convince the Court that through this command responsibility, he was guilty of 'being concerned in' war crimes. Many witnesses and affidavits were presented to attest to serious maltreatment and torture, sometimes killings, from across eight *Kempeitai* stations in Hong Kong, Kowloon, and the New Territories. This was a case where the accused acknowledged that there was always a risk of torture in detention, and that he therefore made a special effort to watch out for it himself. 'I was worried for it and I looked for it and I did not find such things', he testified in Court.[154] He claimed, in a statement under oath:

> I, having proper knowledge about 'Criminal Law' and Criminal and Procedure Law, as a specialist, warned repeatedly my subordinate Commanding officers strictly that confessions must not be obtained by forced means, especially by torture and that any torture, whatever means it might be, was firmly prohibited by my order.[155]

The Prosecutor provided many examples of *Kempeitai* abuse: beatings, inhumane treatment, torture, inadequate food and water, lack of or inadequate medical attention, and the use of dogs to harass and interrogate detainees. The Court found, from a test done during a site visit, that contrary to the Prosecutor's claim, he would not have heard the screaming of those being tortured at the Central Police Station (the Supreme Court building) from his office on the first floor.[156] There was evidence that he was present during some abuse of

[152] Oral delivery of verdict, *Trial of Col Noma Kennosuke* (n 52) transcript 459, slide 465.

[153] The Prosecution, in its Closing Statement, outlined a theory of command responsibility: where the commander knew of abuses by subordinates and either permitted them or failed to take adequate measures to prevent their continuation. Prosecution's Closing Address, *Trial of Col Noma Kennosuke* (n 52) exhibit EEE, 1–2, slides 706–7.

[154] Testimony of Col Noma Kennosuke, *Trial of Col Noma Kennosuke* (n 52) transcript 376, slide 362.

[155] Cited in Prosecution Closing Statement, *Trial of Col Noma Kennosuke* (n 52) exhibit EEE, 5, slide 710.

[156] Site visit with Prosecution witness Capt Rudy Choy, *Trial of Col Noma Kennosuke* (n 52) transcript 201–2, slides 207–8.

detainees, for example that of Prosecution witness Sykes.[157] The accused denied such evidence for being self-interested, unreliable, exaggerated, and biased against him personally or the Japanese as a whole. The Court obviously preferred to believe those witnesses, convicting him of all charges.

All but one of these cases of war crimes on civilians in the occupation period were committed by the *Kempeitai* in Hong Kong.[158] The Prosecutor was to argue 'a calculated policy of sustained cruelty, combined with the negative policy of starvation' under the regime of Colonel Noma.[159] The allegation of 'a calculated policy of sustained cruelty' was raised against Lieutenant Colonel Kanazawa, and like his predecessor, he too was convicted of the war crime of ill-treating civilians.[160] We can, indeed, see the hallmarks of crimes against humanity—widespread and systematic use of torture and other ill-treatment, including killings (see next) directed against civilians.[161]

## 3.3 Unlawful killing of civilians in an occupied territory

The Hong Kong cases abound with incidents of death in the custody of the *Kempeitai*. In the case of Colonel Noma, the Prosecutor alleged that the 'common occurrence' of deaths in custody—evidence of some 60 deaths in custody were raised during his trial—'seemed' to have been caused by

> a calculated policy of sustained cruelty, combined with the negative policy of starvation; and the evidence shows that the business lasted throughout the Accused's term of office, and throughout the area under his jurisdiction in eight different places, half of which were within a few miles of his own HQ.[162]

As already noted, Colonel Noma was convicted of the single charge against him, and evidence was brought about many deaths blamed on his subordinates (he did admit to ordering the execution of five guerrillas from the New Territories).[163]

[157] Testimony of Prosecution Witness Edward Davis Sykes, *Trial of Col Noma Kennosuke* (n 52) transcript 133–4, 140–3, slides 139–40, 146–9. This witness knew Col Noma and testified that he came into the interrogation room as he was being tortured, and did not intervene to stop it.

[158] The one non-*Kempeitai* case was that of the Silver Mine Bay Massacre, involving the Army. The accused in that case were charged with 'beating, torture and maltreatment' of civilians. The case, *Kishi et al*, is examined in the following section.

[159] Prosecution's Closing Address, *Trial of Col Noma Kennosuke* (n 52) exhibit EEE, 4, slide 709.

[160] Closing Address of the Prosecution, *Trial of Lt Col Kanazawa Asao* (n 96) exhibit AA, 3, slide 526.

[161] Para 6 of the ALFSEA Instruction (n 4) indicates that 'crimes against the laws of humanity' were in fact subsumed within war crimes.

[162] Prosecutor's Closing Address, *Trial of Col Noma Kennosuke* (n 52) exhibit EEE, 4, slide 709.

[163] Testimony of Col Noma Kennosuke, *Trial of Col Noma Kennosuke* (n 52) transcript 350, slide 356.

Some of the deaths of civilians at the hands of the *Kempeitai* were outright executions,[164] some were the result of torture,[165] and some were the result of the conditions in detention.[166] The Defence had much fertile ground to cast doubt on causation. For example, in the trial of Lieutenant Colonel Kanazawa, Counsel pointed out that four witnesses gave four different accounts of how a certain Mohinder Singh died in custody: overeating, poisoning, beri-beri and tuberculosis.[167] Sometimes the causes of death were unclear, including when deaths occurred shortly after release. The *Kanazawa* case saw discussion about the role that the torture played in the eventual death of Law Kim-Ching; he eventually died from cancer of the liver two months after his release.[168] Torture victim Yuan Po-to died soon after his release, and the doctor who treated him testified that he suffered from lung tuberculosis and a lung abscess, which had been brought about or aggravated by the ill-treatment he received in prison.[169]

[164] See the *Trial of SM Ito Junichi (No 1)* (HKWCT Collection, File No WO 235/914); *Trial of SM Ito Junichi (No 2)* (HKWCT Collection, File No WO 235/1048), a case involving the killing of local Chinese civilians at the Tsun Wan Gendarmerie. Also see Prosecution Witness A K Omar, *Trial of Col Noma Kennosuke* (n 52) transcripts 183, 187–91, slides 189, 193–7.

[165] Interpreter Noma Isame testified about how he was in the room when one Sgt Lloyd died after being beaten and then subjected to water torture for some 30 minutes, Testimony of Prosecution Witness Noma Isame, *Trial of Col Noma Kennosuke* (n 52) transcript 125, slide 131. Prosecution witness Tse Yao-Fong testified that he saw his uncle Tse Shek unconscious and wounded in the interrogation room; the uncle regained consciousness back in the cell and related what had happened but died after nine hours, see Testimony of Prosecution Witness Tse Yao-Fong (Tse Shek), *Trial of WO Omura Kyoshi and four others* (n 128) transcript 61, slide 104. Reviewing the convictions against accused Sgt Maj Yoshioko Eizo, the Judge Advocate concluded that the evidence of five witnesses 'appears to establish beyond reasonable doubt that the deaths of these three men were directly attributable to the ill-treatment and tortures to which they were subjected by this accused', Judge Advocate's Report, 20 May 1945, *Trial of WO Omura Kyoshi and four others* (n 128) 3, slide 33.

[166] See for example, Prosecution Witness Lam Chung Sik, *Trial of Sgt Maj Yamada Kiichiro and Sgt Awa Isao* (n 128) transcript 37, slide 50, testifying that when in detention at the Tai Po Gendarmerie, there was no doctor at all. 'When somebody suffered from sickness and someone asked the Chinese detectives whether they could get some medicines, it was refused by the Japanese.' Prosecution Witness Wan Tin-Cheung testified that his brother, detained with him, had told him that he had been beaten twice by one of the accused; the brother died at the Magistracy, not having received any medical treatment, see Testimony of Prosecution Witness Wan Tin-Cheung, *Trial of WO Omura Kyoshi and four others* (n 128) transcript 22, slide 65. See testimony of Prosecution Witness William Hong Sling, *Trial of Col Noma Kennosuke* (n 52) transcript 87, slide 93: 'There was no medical treatment supplied at all. I know that because towards the end of my imprisonment [165 days], I suffered from scabies. I tried to get medical treatment but they refused to allow me to see a doctor. Also a relative of mine who was arrested at the same time died in prison because no medical treatment was given to him.' There is also testimony about how medical care was sometimes provided, for example, A G Gardner testified that he contracted malaria and pneumonia, and after two days of asking for medication, was given some tablets; see Testimony of Prosecution Witness A G Gardner, *Trial of Col Noma Kennosuke* (n 52) transcript 99, slide 105. Witness Wan Tin-Cheung, *Trial of WO Omura Kyoshi and four others* (n 128) transcript 33, slide 76, discussed previously, also referred to the visit of a doctor in relation to the torture of another brother.

[167] Closing Address of the Defence, *Trial of Lt Col Kanazawa Asao* (n 96) exhibit Z, 2–3, slides 518–19.

[168] Summarized in the Closing Address of the Prosecution, *Trial of Lt Col Kanazawa Asao* (n 96) exhibit AA, 3, slide 526, referring to the testimony of his wife, Mrs Choy Lai-ching, and Dr Pang Tu-ki.

[169] Prosecution Witness Dr T P Wu, *Trial of Lt Col Kanazawa Asao* (n 96) transcript 109, slide 132.

Causation was, correctly, determined on a case-by-case basis. Decisions indicate that the courts were careful not to jump to conclusions about the causal link between ill-treatment and death. The Prosecutors were confident in their charging, and only a few cases alleged that the accused had been merely 'contributing to the death' of the victim. An example was the case of Niimori Genichiro, an interpreter for the Army.[170] In relation to one of the charges, the Prosecutor argued that the accused beat and kicked Canadian rifleman Peter Doucett, an already-ill POW being transported by ship to Japan, so severely as to contribute to his death. As it transpired, this caution was justified, for the accused was acquitted of 'contributing to the death of the said Rifleman Doucett' although not of his abuse.[171]

An example of a 'causing the death of' charge was the case against Sergeant Major Yamada Kiichiro, convicted of 'causing the death of Cheng Po and Lam Tin-Kau'.[172] The case arose out of Communist and resistance activities at Taipo. Witness Lam Chung-Sik testified about his own torture, and about what happened to Cheng Po, who was in his cell.[173] He did not see the abuse of Cheng Po, but related the condition that the man was in when he returned from his first interrogation ('He could not walk and was pulled back by several other people'; 'His clothes were wet'[174]) and the second interrogation ('He looked more serious and more weak on returning on the second occasion'; 'I saw blood coming from both his legs... He told me that a piece of brick was thrown at his legs and caused the blood to come out'; 'He told me that he was also given the aviation torture... the water torture and a beating up'[175]). The last time this witness saw Cheng Po, he assumed he was dead because he was lying still, with no movement in his eyes and he could not move. 'That was how I knew he was dead.'[176] Under questioning, he affirmed that 'I saw with my own eyes his dead body was carried out, and after an hour, the men who carried him out returned'.[177] This witness also testified that he saw torture victim Lam Tin-Kau dead in the cell.[178] Sergeant Major Yamada, who was convicted of being 'concerned as a party to the maltreatment' of numerous

[170] *Trial of Niimori Genichiro* (HKWCT Collection, File No WO235/892).

[171] The file contains neither a petition nor the Judge Advocate's Report.

[172] *Trial of Sgt Maj Yamada Kiichiro and Sgt Awa Isao* (n 128). The allegations against Sgt Maj Yamada and other *Kempeitai* were also litigated in the case against Col Noma Kennosuke. See for example, the testimony of Prosecution Witness Lam Kiu-Wai, *Trial of Col Noma Kennosuke* (n 52) transcript 48, slide 53.

[173] Testimony of Prosecution Witness Lam Chung-Sik, *Trial of Sgt Maj Yamada Kiichiro and Sgt Awa Isao* (n 128).

[174] Testimony of Prosecution Witness Lam Chung-Sik, *Trial of Sgt Maj Yamada Kiichiro and Sgt Awa Isao* (n 128) transcript 34, slide 47.

[175] Testimony of Prosecution Witness Lam Chung-Sik, *Trial of Sgt Maj Yamada Kiichiro and Sgt Awa Isao* (n 128) transcript 35, slide 48.

[176] Testimony of Prosecution Witness Lam Chung-Sik, *Trial of Sgt Maj Yamada Kiichiro and Sgt Awa Isao* (n 128) transcript 35, slide 48.

[177] Testimony of Prosecution Witness Lam Chung-Sik, *Trial of Sgt Maj Yamada Kiichiro and Sgt Awa Isao* (n 128) transcript 35, slide 48.

[178] Testimony of Prosecution Witness Lam Chung-Sik, *Trial of Sgt Maj Yamada Kiichiro and Sgt Awa Isao* (n 128) transcript 36, slide 49.

detainees, was also convicted of killing Cheng Po and Lam Tin-Kau, a somewhat tenous finding that was nevertheless supported by the Judge Advocate on review.[179]

An example of what is arguably excessive judicial caution was the decision in *Matsuda.* Sergeant Matsuda Kenichi worked for the *Kempeitai* in Hong Kong and Waichow, China. He was charged with committing the war crime of maltreating an arrested civilian, Li Kam-moon, resulting in Li's death.[180] On 20 May 1945, Li was arrested by Sergeant Matsuda and two Chinese detectives in Waichow. On 5 August 1945, his family were notified that he was dying. His badly maimed corpse was later buried by his two sisters in the grounds of Wai On Hospital, in Waichow. The trial came to turn on the conflicting accounts of Li's sister, Li Sau Chun, and Sergeant Matsuda Kenichi, about what happened to Li at the Wai On Hospital. A week after his arrest, the accused went to the Li family and asked them to bring certain toiletries to the Wai On Hospital. Li's sister testified about how she found her brother in a wounded and bruised condition, lying on a dirty bed without medical attention. She nursed her brother for ten days, during which time she often had to leave the room, and heard the accused interrogate her brother, and heard sounds of beating from the room where he was lying. Sergeant Matsuda argued that Li had tried to kill himself on two occasions, once stabbing himself in the abdomen with a sword.[181] According to him, Japanese medical personnel had operated on Li after that, but he eventually died of septic peritonitis. The three-man military court convicted Sergeant Matsuda of 'being concerned in' the war crime of maltreatment, but not of causing Li's death because 'the Prosecutor has failed to prove that Li Kam-moon died as a result of the ill-treatment which he received'.[182] A healthy young man went into the custody of the accused, and emerged dead, his body severely mutilated. The accused was convicted of his abuse, and this should have created a presumption, rebuttable of course, of responsibility for his death in custody. It is not convincing to learn from the Judge Advocate that the acquittal on the murder charge was sound because

> there were no eye-witnesses of his ill-treatment, which was deposed to by his sister who heard his screams during interrogation and the sounds of beating when he was in hospital. She also described his condition after interrogation. The witnesses who were applied for by the defence to support the accused's story of attempted suicide were not called, but if they had been called and had supported that story, it is clear that their testimony would not have affected the finding of the Court.[183]

[179] Judge Advocate's Report, 2 September 1946, *Trial of Sgt Maj Yamada Kiichiro and Sgt Awa Isao* (n 128), slides 7–8.

[180] Schedule of Charges, *Trial of Sgt Matsuda Kenichi* (n 59) slide 11.

[181] Testimony of Sgt Matsuda Kenichi, *Trial of Sgt Matsuda Kenichi* (n 59) transcript 48–9, slide 59–60.

[182] Delivery of the Court's verdict, *Trial of Sgt Matsuda Kenichi* (n 59) transcript 80, slide 91. In mitigation, the Defence submitted that the accused was responsible for security at a time when 'leakages' were occurring, resulting in the loss of Japanese lives. He argued that 'in interrogating Li Kam-moon, he did it not only in the interests of his own department but for his own people at heart'. See Defence submission in mitigation, *Trial of Sgt Matsuda Kenichi* (n 59) transcript 81, slide 92.

[183] Judge Advocate's Report, 20 June 1946, *Trial of Sgt Matsuda Kenichi* (n 59) 2, slide 6. Professor Alexander Zahar's chapter in this book observes how Matsuda's attempts to obtain witnesses to

There were many reported unlawful killings of civilians during the operational stages of the invasion and capture of Hong Kong,[184] but the focus here is on crimes against civilians during the occupation by Japan. There is one case that did involve the Army being engaged in operations against civilians, and it raised a number of substantial issues of law. The *Kishi et al* case, known as the *Lantau Island* or *Silver Mine Bay* case, involved 15 accused, from the Japanese Army. They were charged with being

> together concerned in the beating, torture and maltreatment of inhabitants of the SILVER MINE BAY district of LANTAU aforesaid and in the killing of nine of the said inhabitants.[185]

The events occurred in the tense period when the Japanese Emperor had capitulated, but he had not yet signed the instrument of surrender, and the British forces had not yet arrived back in Hong Kong to re-establish colonial authority. Chinese guerrillas, operating in the hills of Lantau Island, had attacked the small Japanese presence at Silver Mine Bay over a period of several weeks. The first accused, Lieutenant Kishi, was in charge of the company that arrived at Silver Mine Bay on 10 May 1945 to replace the exhausted Yasuhara Company. The Kishi Company also came under guerilla attack, and the events with which the indictment is concerned are to do with their response to these attacks, heading out into three nearby villages, burning and destroying them, rounding up villagers and bringing them down to the beach at Silver Mine Bay where several were killed, and others abused and maltreated.

The Prosecutor's case was that international law—'the Hague 1907 Convention'—obliged the occupying force to behave in a certain way towards the inhabitants of the territory (eg respecting their lives, not disturbing their domestic peace and honour etc); failing to do this would amount to a violation of the laws and usages of war.[186] Such dereliction, he alleged, had happened on Lantau Island. The Kishi defence was founded on justification of the actions of the accused, and involved more reliance on legal authorities than was usual in these cases. Lieutenant Kishi testified that he was instructed by his superiors not only to defend himself from attack, but also to use his weapons to the limit that he felt safe.[187] In closing, the Defence argued that the accused were convinced that 'they were executing Guerillas, and by that they meant Chinese villagers who had taken up arms against them'.[188]

substantiate his account were not facilitated by the Court, and we can speculate about how the verdict may have been affected by that reality.

[184] Even so, the only charges were in the *Trial of Lt Gen Ito Takeo* (n 6), in relation to killings at the Jockey Club and Blue Pool Road, charges on which he was acquitted.

[185] Schedule of Charges, *Trial of Lt Kishi Yasuo and fourteen others* (n 11) slide 23.

[186] Prosecution Opening Statement, *Trial of Lt Kishi Yasuo and fourteen others* (n 11) exhibit E, 3, slide 601.

[187] Testimony of Lt Kishi Yasuo, *Trial of Lt Kishi Yasuo and fourteen others* (n 11) transcript 261, slide 285.

[188] Defence Closing Address, *Trial of Lt Kishi Yasuo and fourteen others* (n 11) exhibit A(1) [Not fully legible], 1, slide 736.

The law enforcement argument, that the accused were justified in their use of force, and justified in the way that they used that force, linked back to one of the most controversial issues at the 1899 Peace Conference: the issue of what to do about civilian resistance to an occupying power. This could not be agreed, and the 1899 Convention with Respect to the Laws and Customs of War on Land along with its annexed Regulations, was silent on this matter. It is widely known that the Martens Clause was 'formulated especially with a view to the thorny problem of armed resistance in occupied territory'.[189] What seems clear was that at the time of World War II, civilians could be viewed as combatants if they engaged in armed activities, carried arms openly, and respected the laws and customs of war (see Articles 49 and 51 of the Lieber Code, Article 10 of the Brussels Declaration, and Article 2 of the 1907 Hague Regulations). Obviously, the nature of civilian participation in resistance activities during an occupation meant these requirements could rarely be satisfied. The problem could not be resolved in 1949 either. Article 1(4) of the 1977 Additional Protocol I, some 30 years after the Nuremberg and Tokyo processes, was at the time of its adoption and for some years afterwards, a highly controversial provision.[190] It is therefore no surprise that the Defence for Lieutenant Kishi and his co-accused in the *Lantau Island* case argued that, even in the period between capitulation and formal surrender, the Japanese in Hong Kong continued 'to exercise the rights and obligations of an occupying power in time of war'.[191] Under international law, they argued, the accused were allowed to take offensive measures against civilians who had taken up arms against the Japanese. 'It would be a mockery of international law if the inhabitants of Occupied Territory were allowed to snipe away at the troops of an Occupying Power with impunity.'[192] Counsel for the accused drew from three sources to justify the resort to force against such inhabitants:

1. Lassa Oppenheim as authority for the proposition that '[a]n occupant having Military authority over the territory, the inhabitants are under his Martial Law and have to render obedience to his commands'.[193]
2. Article 43 of the 1907 Hague Convention and its annexed Regulations, providing that one of the duties of the occupying power is to re-establish and ensure as far as possible, public order and safety.[194]

[189] F Kalshoven and L Zegveld, *Constraints on the Waging of War* (3rd edn, ICRC) 22.

[190] *Protocol Additional to the Geneva Conventions of 12 August 1949, and relating to the Protection of Victims of International Armed Conflicts*, opened for signature 8 June 1977, 1125 UNTS 3 (entered into force 7 December 1978).

[191] Defence Closing Address, *Trial of Lt Kishi Yasuo and fourteen others* (n 11) exhibit A(1) [Not fully legible], 1, slide 736 [citing page 301 of Oppenheim and sections 340–404 of the *Manual of Military Law (as amended)* as authority].

[192] Defence Closing Address, *Trial of Lt Kishi Yasuo and fourteen others* (n 11) 5, slide 740.

[193] Defence Closing Address, *Trial of Lt Kishi Yasuo and fourteen others* (n 11) 1, slide 736. The reference was to A McNair (ed), *Lassa Oppenheim's International Law* (4th edn, Longmans, Green and Company 1926 and 1928) vol II, 301.

[194] Defence Closing Address, *Trial of Lt Kishi Yasuo and fourteen others* (n 11) 1, slide 736.

3. Sections 340–404 of the Manual of Military Law (as amended) devoted to the Laws and Usages of War, which provide that the inhabitants of an occupied territory are forbidden to take part in the hostilities and are expected to refrain from any injury to the troops of the occupant. Following on from this, Counsel argued that '[i]nfringements of [t]he Martial Law of the occupant are punishable as war crimes'.[195]

However, Counsel went beyond arguing for the right of the occupier to respond to acts of resistance to its authority, and submitted that international law provided that guerrillas could be summarily executed. Counsel cited from Birkenhead's *International Law* and the US Lieber Code to justify summary execution 'as highway robbers or pirates' those persons who commit hostilities of the kind known as guerrilla warfare:

> Men or squads of men who commit hostilities . . . without commission, without being part and portion of the organised hostile Army, and without sharing continuously in the War, but who do so with intermitting return to their homes and avocations, or with the occasional assumption of the semblance of peaceful pursuit, divesting themselves of the character or appearance of soldiers—such men, or squads of men are not public enemies, and therefore if captured are not entitled to the privileges of prisoners of war, but shall be treated summarily as highway robbers or pirates.[196]

The Prosecutor's response, in his Closing Address, was that this was misplaced use of a specific reference to the American Civil War, one that could not be applied to the present case.[197] He argued, correctly, that summary treatment presupposed that there must be a trial, since 'in all [sic] and every case a trial is indispensable'.[198] The Prosecutor cited to the 'Manual of Military Law', and asserted that '[a]ccording to the Hague Convention 1899 previous trial is in every case indispensable and cannot for any reason or any pretext be dispensed with'.[199] The position that no one may be convicted or sentenced, except pursuant to a fair trial affording all essential judicial guarantees, is consistent with that adopted in other cases.[200]

As part of his argument that under international law, guerrillas could be summarily executed, Defence Counsel also cited to the Hague Convention of 1899, the 1907 Hague Convention and its annexed Regulations, and Article 9 of

[195] Defence Closing Address, *Trial of Lt Kishi Yasuo and fourteen others* (n 11) 1–2, slides 736–7.

[196] Defence Closing Address, *Trial of Lt Kishi Yasuo and fourteen others* (n 11) 3–4, slides 738–9.

[197] Final Address of Prosecuting Officer, *Trial of Lt Kishi Yasuo and fourteen others* (n 11) transcript 516, slide 542.

[198] Final Address of Prosecuting Officer, *Trial of Lt Kishi Yasuo and fourteen others* (n 11) transcript 517, slide 543.

[199] Final Address of Prosecuting Officer, *Trial of Lt Kishi Yasuo and fourteen others* (n 11) transcript 517, slide 543 referring to 'page 294 of the Manual Military Law'.

[200] See for example, Military Tribunal at Nuremberg, *In re Alstötter and others (The Justice Trial)*, Judgment of 4 December 1947, in *Annual Digest and Reports of Public International Law Cases*, vol 14 (1947), 278; Military Court at Almelo, *Trial of Otto Sandrock and Three Others (Almelo Trial)*, Judgment of 24–26 November 1945, in United Nations War Crimes Commission, *Law Reports of Trials of War Criminals*, vol I (HMSO 1947), 35; Military Court at Wuppertal, *Trial of Werner Rohde and Eight Others*, Judgment of 29 May–1 June 1946, in United Nations War Crimes Commission, *Law Reports of Trials of War Criminals*, vol V (HMSO 1948), 54.

the 1874 Declaration of Brussels, for the identification of persons who are subject to the laws, rights, and duties of the laws of war. The implication was that guerrillas did not meet the basic criteria (eg not carrying arms openly, and not being under responsible command) and were therefore not privileged combatants.[201] The Defence argued that civilians who take up arms against an occupying power are not entitled to combatant status and the protection of the mitigated usages of war, and those who attacked the Japanese at Silver Mine Bay 'cannot by any conceivable stretch of the imagination be considered as lawful combatants'.[202] Lassa Oppenheim was again cited as an authority, this time for the proposition that civilians who engage in armed hostilities commit war crimes 'not because they really are violations of recognised rules regarding Warfare, but because the enemy has the right to consider and punish them as acts of illegitimate Warfare', and as authority for the proposition that international law allowed the enemy to punish such illegal participation in hostilities to protect the safety of his troops.[203]

The Prosecutor responded correctly to this assertion. The villagers could not be killed outright. He argued, first of all, that the victims in this case did not take up arms against the Japanese, they were civilians and not guerrillas.[204] Secondly, he cited from the 'Manual of Military Law' that no law authorized an occupier to have private individuals engaged in hostilities shot without trial; they were responsible for their security of person and the decision on their fate is to be left to the competent authorities.[205] He argued, correctly, that 'international law forbids summary execution absolutely... under no circumstances may summary justice be meted to a person without a fair trial. He should be sent before a Court for examination. Nothing can be clearer than that.'[206]

Both the parties recognized that, regardless of whether the accused were entitled to use force, any such force would have had to be proportionate, or to use the words of Defence Counsel, the issue was 'whether they exceeded the limit of their power'.[207] The understanding of proportionality in a military context, Defence Counsel argued, was clear and it 'is a well known fact that it is not the amount of ammunition fired that causes casualties, but rather the accuracy with which the fire is directed'.[208] This was not adequately addressed by the Prosecutor, probably because the facts were so extreme as to make disproportionality a given: the Japanese had just one NCO injured in the attack on their garrison at Silver Mine

[201] Defence Closing Address, *Trial of Lt Kishi Yasuo and fourteen others* (n 11) exhibit A(1) [Not fully legible], 5, slide 740, citing 'Birkenhead's International Law (page 208)'.

[202] Defence Closing Address, *Trial of Lt Kishi Yasuo and fourteen others* (n 11) 7, slide 742.

[203] Defence Closing Address, *Trial of Lt Kishi Yasuo and fourteen others* (n 11) 5, slide 740, citing *Oppenheim's International Law*, 160, 413.

[204] Final Address of Prosecuting Officer, *Trial of Lt Kishi Yasuo and fourteen others* (n 11) transcript 517, slide 543.

[205] Final Address of Prosecuting Officer, *Trial of Lt Kishi Yasuo and fourteen others* (n 11) transcript 518, slide 544.

[206] Final Address of Prosecuting Officer, *Trial of Lt Kishi Yasuo and fourteen others* (n 11) transcript 518, slide 544.

[207] Defence Closing Address, *Trial of Lt Kishi Yasuo and fourteen others* (n 11) exhibit A(1) [Not fully legible], 3, slide 738.

[208] Defence Closing Address, *Trial of Lt Kishi Yasuo and fourteen others* (n 11) 6, slide 741.

Bay, yet for that, went on a rampage that resulted in the destruction of three villages and private property, mass unlawful arrest and detention, torture and other abuse, and ultimately, the killing of six persons.

The testimony of several of the accused clearly raised lack of choice, necessity, and also self-defence, in ways that often seemed to conflate them. Both superior orders and necessity can be seen in Lieutenant Kishi's testimony, repeated again during his address to the Court in mitigation: 'What I did on that occasion was within the orders of the commanding officer Shimakata and it was necessary to do so in order to save the lives of the other members of the company.'[209] As the Prosecutor acknowledged in his Final Address, everything that the accused Kishi did 'was done out of sheer necessity in order to save his unit, his men and himself from the kind of fate that had befallen Sergeant Yoshinori'.[210] At the same time, he stressed that the accused Kishi had admitted through his Defending Officer that he acted in self-defence, as if it were interchangeable with necessity.[211] Necessity with a touch of self-defence can also be seen in the testimony of the accused Mastumoto, in his final mitigating plea to the Court:

> The things which I have done . . . were inevitable . . . If we did not take such steps, I think we would have been attacked for the second and for the third time and on the worst circumstances, the whole of our company would be wiped out.[212]

Accused Uchida's explanation went towards the law and order justification: as he told the Court:

> Myself and other members of the Company concerning [sic] to [sic] our actions was [sic] concerned with preserving peace and order. I have nothing to regret or to be ashamed of on [sic] what we [sic] have done as a faithful soldier.[213]

The outcome of the case, with three acquittals, and 12 convictions (three death penalties, two 10-year sentences, one 8-year sentence, one 5-year sentence, and five 2-year sentences—later revised on review), is difficult to interpret. On the one hand, the convictions of 12 accused could suggest that the panel condemned attacks on, and abuse of, civilians in the course of anti-guerilla operations, and that the Court clearly did not accept that these villagers were guerillas. On the other hand, the relative lightness of the sentencing could also suggest the circumstances facing the Japanese were viewed as mitigating factors. Other factors, such as the low rank of all of the accused, and the existence of superior orders, could have had a role to play. The Judge Advocate, in conducting his review of the file, was not hostile to

[209] Delivery of the Court's verdict, *Trial of Lt Kishi Yasuo and fourteen others* (n 11) transcript 529, slide 556.

[210] Final Address of the Prosecuting Officer, *Trial of Lt Kishi Yasuo and fourteen others* (n 11) transcript 515, slide 541.

[211] Final Address of the Prosecuting Officer, *Trial of Lt Kishi Yasuo and fourteen others* (n 11) transcript 515, slide 541.

[212] Accused's statement in mitigation, *Trial of Lt Kishi Yasuo and fourteen others* (n 11) transcript 530, slide 557.

[213] Accused's statement in mitigation, *Trial of Lt Kishi Yasuo and fourteen others* (n 11) transcript 530, slide 557.

some of these arguments, but pointed out that 'while the Japanese were entitled to defend themselves against attack, they were not entitled to execute anyone without trial, least of all innocent villagers'.[214]

## 4. Concluding Observations

This chapter has drawn from the cases to paint a picture of some of the war crimes committed across Asia, and the resulting criminal proceedings held in Hong Kong. It has focused on the category of war crimes committed against civilians in an occupied territory. For all the obstacles faced in evaluating the cases, this chapter has provided insight into the anatomy of war crimes, and the fascinating process of an early attempt to bring allegations of violations of the laws and usages of war before a court of law. Some of the gaps in the war crimes prosecution strategy in Hong Kong remain unclear. Prosecutions for sexual violence, consistent with the practice of the time, were peripheral, although the rape of a number of nurses at St Stephen's College, the Jockey Club, and local civilians at Blue Pool Road were included in one of the Hong Kong island invasion cases.[215] The author has not located documentation to explain why there were no prosecutions of Japanese conduct during the taking of Kowloon and Victoria, about which there were many reports about the murder of civilians, looting, plunder, serious abuse, and sexual violence.[216] Former Governor-General Sakai Takashi was convicted by a military tribunal in Nanking for the invading forces' plundering of valuable books from the libraries of Hong Kong, but this was not charged in any of the cases tried in Hong Kong.[217] We also do not know why no one was prosecuted in relation to the maltreatment of Allied civilians interned at the camp at Stanley Prison.[218]

In relation to war crimes against civilians, the two Hong Kong involuntary displacement cases examined here, *Noma* and *Kanazawa*, indicate that such displacements are not in themselves illegal, but they can become illegal if they are not objectively justifiable, for example, by reference to public health and safety or

[214] Judge Advocate's Report, 11 June 1946, *Trial of Lt Kishi Yasuo and fourteen others* (n 11) 4, slide 7.

[215] *Trial of Lt Gen Ito Takeo* (n 6). The evidence on the identity of the troops committing the acts was very weak and the Defence was able to create sufficient doubt as to who was in charge of the operation. Lt Gen Ito was acquitted of these charges. Sexual violence was also part of the case against Lt Gen Sakai Takashi in Nanking. See *Sakai Judgments* (n 24).

[216] See, eg, Affidavit of Ramon Muniz Lavalle, 11 March 1943, reprinted in K Cambon, *Guest of Hirohito* (P W Press 1990) app 1, at <http://fourthmarineband.com/cambon8.htm> accessed 20 August 2012; Snow, *The Fall of Hong Kong: Britain, China and the Japanese Occupation* (n 62) 79–90, 308, referring *inter alia* to the 'glut' of half-Japanese children born in September–October 1942 after the Japanese 'orgy of rape' following the fall of Hong Kong. See also C G Roland, 'Massacre and Rape in Hong Kong: Two Case Studies Involving Medical Personnel and Patients' (1997) 32 *J Cont History* 43.

[217] See *Sakai Judgments* (n 24).

[218] See, eg, G C Emerson, *Hong Kong Internment, 1942 to 1945: Life in the Japanese Civilian Camp at Stanley* (Hong Kong University Press 2008) ch 1; J Gittins, *Stanley: Behind Barbed Wire* (Hong Kong University Press 1982).

imperative military necessity, or are carried out in a way that is arbitrary, and also cruel and inhuman. They would also be illegal if carried out without adequate consideration of the risks, and without contingency plans. The cases suggest a positive duty on the occupier engaged in displacement activities to ensure that the circumstances of its implementation including the conditions of the displacement are humane and in accordance with the duties imposed on an occupier. These positive duties would appear also to extend to provide some protection for those who 'volunteer' to be transferred, whether under duress or not. These suggestions become stronger when read together with the-then contemporaneous cases of *Sakai*, *Isogai* and the *Andaman Islands*, where there were two reasoned judgments (of a sort), and a careful Judge Advocate review.

As for the abuses by the *Kempeitai* of persons in custody, there were generally no disputes over the illegality of torture and inhumane treatment. No one stood up in court to say that torture or inhuman treatment was lawful, or culturally relative. The *Kempeitai* accused did, however, often raise issues of justification, given that some of the persons that they took into custody were believed to be engaged in criminal activity and armed resistance. The implication is a familiar one, even today: that it was imperative in the interests of public security to conduct rigorous interrogations (although, of course, not with torture, which they usually claimed never took place). The verdicts do not reveal any sympathy for this argument, in light of the fact that the crimes under review were of the utmost seriousness.

The cases of unlawful killings as war crimes raised the issue of causation, which was a matter of evidential sufficiency to satisfy the court. The more significant challenge in terms of law arose in the area of justification especially the issue of what an occupier could do in the face of armed resistance. Hague Convention IV and its annexed Regulations require balance between the occupying power's duty to return life to normality and ensure law and order, with the right to take punitive action against those civilians taking up arms against the regime of occupation. The outcome in *Kishi et al*, with convictions of nearly all the accused, suggests condemnation of attacks on, and abuse of, civilians in the course of anti-guerilla operations. The Court clearly did not accept that these villagers were guerillas. Even so, the sentencing, with only two receiving the death penalty following review, does suggest that there was sympathy for the reality that the Kishi Company faced that summer in 1945, their Emperor having capitulated, the increase in guerilla attacks, and the perceived support of the local population for them. It could also indicate sympathy for the low hierarchical position of the accused, who were acting pursuant to superior orders.

At one level, these proceedings were about the international crime that we know as the war crime. However, when one unpacks the cases and looks into the transcripts, pleadings, and documents, one sees that the legal drama that was being played out in the four courts was really a domestic one, to be more precise, a common law one. The British, Canadian, and Australian lawyers who took part were clearly not international lawyers, they were first and foremost domestic lawyers, and of course, also soldiers. On the Japanese side, there was a mixture of British officers acting as advisors (they were Defence Counsel in the early days, but the accused preferred to have Japanese lawyers) and Japanese lawyers, and of course, the accused. They struggled, not with the concept of the war crime, but with the British rules that governed the proceeding in which they were participating.

Through Major Murray Ormsby (see his interview in this book), we know that even the British officer corps had not been educated about war crimes as part of their training, and that not all the 'lawyers' in these proceedings were actually 'lawyers'. Even so, men like Major Ormsby and the other military personnel were clearly on familiar territory, and were able to operate easily in the no-nonsense, fact-driven, legally minimalistic process developed through the Royal Warrant and its annexed Regulations and the ALFSEA Instruction, which emphasized the summary nature of the proceedings, and required that this be 'borne in mind by all concerned, to the end that justice be administered promptly and efficiently'.[219]

Professor Alexander Zahar, in his chapter in this book, rightly challenges us on some of the procedural inadequacies of these war crimes trials, and the unfairness it caused the Japanese accused leading to some very serious consequences. We should always ask if justice was done in any process of accounting by the law, and especially with atrocities such as war crimes, which can have a terrible impact on, and going beyond, the immediate victims. This author's sense, from closely working through the cases and studying this historic situation for several years now, is that in the difficult circumstances of the post-war world in Asia, copious evidence was collated and brought before the four military courts, about the perpetration of war crimes. Sometimes the evidence was properly linked to the accused, and sometimes not. There were acquittals and convictions, and adjustment of verdicts and sentences following review. Some of the decisions seem correct on the weight of the evidence and in accordance with the applicable law, and some seem suspect. When we assess an effort such as this, do we look to the successes, or to the failings, or to the whole picture? In reflecting on that, we should also ask, what does justice mean in such a situation and who decides if justice was served? This author's conviction is that we should look at the whole picture and recognize the achievements without denying the stains on them. Perhaps, the way that the Hong Kong war crimes trials slipped into oblivion for half a century suggests that everyone concerned—victims, perpetrators, the public, the authorities—felt that justice for war crimes had, for better or for worse, been done and the chapter could be closed, and everyone could move on with life. What do we know about how those directly affected by these events feel? On 17 September 2010, this author interviewed torture survivor and former Prosecution witness, Stephen Tsui.[220] He indicated that he would, if the opportunity presented itself, tell his torturer, Warrant Officer Omura Kyoshi, that he recognized that the War made him a torturer. In other words, he understood. Stephen Tsui did not feel 'heavy or burdened' about what had happened to him all those years ago; for him, 'the war came and the war went'. He got on with life.

[219] ALFSEA Instruction (n 4) para 40.

[220] Suzannah Linton, 'Interview with Mr Stephen Tsui, 17 September 2010', Hong Kong War Crimes Trials Collection, at <http://hkwctc.lib.hku.hk/archive/files/img-y291702-0001_ac3a86c3ad.pdf> accessed 20 December 2012.

# 5

# On Being 'Concerned' in a Crime: Embryonic Joint Criminal Enterprise?

*Nina H B Jørgensen*

> It seemed to me just as wrong for us now to condemn Hara under a law which had never been his, of which he had never even heard, as he and his masters had been to punish and kill us for the transgressions of the code of Japan that was not ours. [...] He may have done wrong for the right reasons, but how could it be squared by us now doing right in the wrong way?[1]

## 1. Introduction

On the question whether joint criminal enterprise ('JCE') is the right or wrong way to address collective criminality, the 1999 decision of the Appeals Chamber of the International Criminal Tribunal for the Former Yugoslavia ('ICTY') in *Prosecutor v Tadić* and the 2010 decision of the Pre-Trial Chamber of the Extraordinary Chambers in the Courts of Cambodia ('ECCC') in *Ieng Sary*[2] stand out as historic. JCE has earned a reputation as the chilli pepper of modes of liability, refusing to be put to jurisprudential rest as reflected in the 11-year gap between *Tadić* and *Ieng Sary*.

The history of JCE does not begin with *Tadić*, and it may safely be said that it will not end with *Ieng Sary*. The *Tadić* decision relied heavily on selected cases from the trials that followed the Second World War from which it derived three categories of JCE. The *Ieng Sary* decision in turn relied heavily on *Tadić* and a further review of some of the underlying case law. Efforts to make accessible archive records from other war crimes trials both in Europe and the Asia-Pacific region have continued and the cases tried by British military courts in Hong Kong form part of

[1] L Van Der Post, *A Bar of Shadow* (William Morrow & Company 1956) ('Van Der Post, *A Bar of Shadow*') 54–5.

[2] *Prosecutor v Dūsko Tadić*, Case No. IT-94-1-A, Appeal Judgment, 15 July 1999 ('*Tadić JCE decision*'); *Charged Persons Ieng Thirith, Ieng Sary and Khieu Samphan*, Public Decision on the Appeals Against the Co-Investigative Judges Order on Joint Criminal Enterprise (JCE), PP 002/19-0902007-ECCC/OCIJ (PTC38) (20 May 2010) ('*Ieng Sary JCE decision*').

this broader historical picture. Customary international law, in whose temple JCE is said to dwell, is closely tied to these footsteps in history.

Turning back the clock, it is August 1945 and Lieutenant Kishi Yasuo of the Imperial Japanese Army is the Company Commander responsible for the Silver Mine Bay district of Hong Kong's Lantau Island. Kishi's company is attacked by Chinese guerrillas. In retaliation, Kishi's men, initially in his absence, raid several villages, burning and looting and carrying out arrests. The captives are beaten and several are beheaded by Kishi and others. The following year, Kishi and 14 co-accused are tried for a war crime in that they were 'together concerned in' the beating, torture, and maltreatment of the villagers and the killing of nine of those villagers.

The *Kishi* case illustrates the charging practice in the Hong Kong trials. All charges describe the accused's responsibility in terms of 'being concerned in' or 'together concerned in' the relevant crime, with the exception of a small number of allegations of direct responsibility for ill-treatment. Reading the charges together with the opening and closing arguments of the parties, as well as the summaries of the Judge Advocate, allows some light to be thrown on this characterization of the participation of the accused.[3]

This chapter will consider whether 'concern' in a crime constitutes 'embryonic' JCE when viewed in the context of related cases of the time, and if this impacts upon the future development of modes of liability addressing collective criminality. In order to understand the potential link between JCE and the framing of the charges in the Hong Kong cases, it is first necessary to provide a preview of how JCE is currently construed.

## 2. Joint Enterprise Liability in Modern International Criminal Law

Duško Tadić, a low-ranking member of the Serb armed forces operating in the Prijedor region of Bosnia-Herzegovina from May to December 1992, was found by the ICTY Trial Chamber to have participated in attacks on the villages of Sivci and nearby Jaskići, but not in the killing of five men in Jaskići. The Appeals Chamber overturned the latter finding on the basis that:

> [T]he only possible inference to be drawn is that the Appellant had the intention to further the criminal purpose to rid the Prijedor region of the non-Serb population, by committing inhumane acts against them. That non-Serbs might be killed in the effecting of this common aim was, in the circumstances of the present case, foreseeable. The Appellant was aware that the actions of the group of which he was a member were likely to lead to such killings, but he nevertheless willingly took that risk.[4]

[3] A preliminary motion filed in one case as to vagueness in the form of the charge related to the lack of particulars of the alleged maltreatment rather than the nature of the accused's involvement in it. *Trial of Sgt Hanada Zenji and three others* (HKWCT Collection, File No WO235/895) ('*Trial of Sgt Hanada Zenji and three others*').

[4] *Tadić JCE decision* (n 2) para 232.

Tadić was thereby convicted of the killings, despite the absence of any evidence of his direct, personal involvement. He received a prison term of 25 years in respect of the count alleging murder as a crime against humanity upon referral of the case to the Trial Chamber for sentencing; the highest of the sentences imposed in respect of the different counts.[5] This was reduced on appeal to 20 years due to his relatively low level in the command structure as compared to the architects of the ethnic cleansing.[6]

The ICTY, like the post-Second World War courts before it, faced the difficulty of responding to mass criminality and the particular problem of describing the participation of senior leaders in cases where the physical perpetrators were not on trial. It was a stated concern of the ICTY Appeals Chamber to link the moral gravity of the participation of decision makers, often divorced from the physical commission of criminal acts, with an appropriate level of responsibility. Hence the conclusion that 'international criminal responsibility embraces actions perpetrated by a collectivity of persons in furtherance of a common criminal design'.[7] The Appeals Chamber recognized the statutory embodiment both of the principle that nobody may be held criminally responsible for acts in which he has not participated and the principle that *all* participants in crimes should be held responsible for their personal contribution to the criminal conduct.[8] JCE as a mode of participation was seen to be consistent with the object and purpose of the ICTY's Statute as well as being warranted by the nature of the crimes, often amounting to 'manifestations of collective criminality'.[9]

The Appeals Chamber then turned to customary international law with the aim of discerning the objective and subjective elements of 'this category of collective criminality'.[10] Its analysis also served to affirm that 'the notion of common design as a form of accomplice liability is firmly established in customary international law and in addition is upheld, albeit implicitly, in the Statute of the International Tribunal'.[11] The Chamber drew the definitions of its three categories of JCE primarily from post-Second World War jurisprudence.

The first category refers to the situation in which all co-defendants, acting pursuant to a common design, possess the same criminal intention. In relation to this category it must be proved that the accused voluntarily participated in one aspect of the common design and, even if not physically committing the crime, nevertheless intended the planned result.[12] The second category, based on the

[5] *Prosecutor v Dŭsko Tadić* (Sentencing Judgment) IT-94-1-T *bis*R117 (11 November 1999) 17.

[6] *Prosecutor v Dŭsko Tadić* (Judgment in Sentencing Appeals) IT-94-1-A and IT-94-1-A*bis* (26 January 2000) paras 55–8.

[7] *Tadić JCE decision* (n 2) para 193.

[8] *Tadić JCE decision* (n 2) para 190.

[9] *Tadić JCE decision* (n 2) para 191.

[10] *Tadić JCE decision* (n 2) para 194.

[11] *Tadić JCE decision* (n 2) para 220.

[12] *Tadić JCE decision* (n 2), referring in support of the first category of JCE to: *Georg Otto Sandrock and others* (*Almelo trial*) (1945) in United Nations War Crimes Commission, *Law Reports of Trials of War Criminals* vol I (HMSO 1947) 35; *Hoelzer and others* (1946) in vol I 341, 347, 349 (RCAF Binder 181.009 (D2474)); *Gustav Alfred Jepsen and others* (1946) in (2007) 5 JICJ 228; *Franz Schonfeld and*

so-called 'concentration camp' cases, requires proof of active participation in the enforcement of a system of repression combined with knowledge of the nature of the system and the intent to further the common concerted design to ill-treat inmates.[13] The third and most controversial category, and the one in fact applied in *Tadić*, concerns a common design to pursue one course of conduct where one of the perpetrators commits an act which, while outside the common design, was nevertheless a natural and foreseeable consequence of the effecting of that design. In relation to this category the subjective element is defined as foreseeability that a crime other than the one agreed upon might be perpetrated by a member of the JCE and willingly taking that risk.[14]

The application of JCE liability quickly became commonplace at the ICTY.[15] The ICTR and Special Court for Sierra Leone followed suit although it was noted by the ICTR Appeals Chamber in the *Rwamakuba* case that:

> The post-World War II materials do not always fit neatly into the so-called 'three categories' of joint criminal enterprise discussed in *Tadić*, in part because the tribunals' judgements did not always dwell on the legal concepts of criminal responsibility, but simply concluded that, based on the evidence, the accused were 'connected with,' 'concerned in,' 'inculpated in,' or 'implicated in' war crimes and crimes against humanity.[16]

In *Ieng Sary*, a comprehensive challenge to the applicability of JCE before the ECCC was raised by the Defence. It was argued that the application of JCE would violate the principle of legality in that JCE was not recognized as customary international law before or during the period relevant to the alleged crimes (1975–79) or at the time the motion was filed, and that it was not otherwise recognized as being applicable before the ECCC. The Prosecution had urged the application of JCE before the ECCC, on the basis that the crimes were not the isolated acts of individual cadres 'but the result of deliberate criminal policies

*nine others* (1946) in United Nations War Crimes Commission, *Law Reports of Trials of War Criminals* vol XI (HMSO 1949) 64 ('*Schonfeld case*'); *Feurstein and others (Ponzano case)* (1948) in (2007) 5 JICJ 238 ('*Feurstein and others (Ponzano case)*'); *Otto Ohlendorf and others* ('*Einsatzgruppen case*') (1948) in Trials of War Criminals before the Nuremberg Military Tribunals under Control Council Law No 10 vol IV (United States Government Printing Office 1951) 3.

[13] *Tadić JCE decision* (n 2), referring in support of the second category of JCE to: *Martin Gottfried Weiss and others (Dachau Concentration Camp case)* (1945) in United Nations War Crimes Commission, *Law Reports of Trials of War Criminals* vol XI (HMSO 1949) 5; *Josef Kramer and others (Belsen trial)* (1945) in United Nations War Crimes Commission, *Law Reports of Trials of War Criminals* vol II (HMSO 1947) ('*Belsen case*') 1.

[14] *Tadić JCE decision* (n 2) para 228. Cases cited included *Eric Heyer and six others* (1945) in United Nations War Crimes Commission, *Law Reports of Trials of War Criminals*, vol 1 (HMSO 1947) ('*Essen Lynching case*'), *United States v Kurt Goebell and others* (*Borkum Island case*) (1946), and certain post-war cases before Italian courts.

[15] In the *Ojdanić*, case, the Appeals Chamber declined 'to revisit its finding in *Tadić* concerning the customary status of this form of liability', being satisfied that this status had been established. But, it emphasized the principle of legality and the need for the form of liability to be sufficiently accessible to the perpetrator at the time of acting. *Prosecutor v Milutinović, Šainović and Ojdanić* (Decision on Dragoljub Ojdanić's Motion Challenging Jurisdiction—Joint Criminal Enterprise) IT-99-37-AR72 (21 May 2003) para 29 ('*Ojdanić JCE decision*').

[16] *Rwamakuba v The Prosecutor* (Decision on Interlocutory Appeal Regarding Application of Joint Criminal Enterprise to the Crime of Genocide) ICTR-98-44-AR72.4 (22 October 2004) para 24.

designed and enforced by the *Khmer Rouge*'.[17] Further, the Prosecution asserted that the ECCC could only realize its mandate to try senior leaders and those most responsible if it were able to assign criminal responsibility to those who created and oversaw the implementation of policies.[18]

The Pre-Trial Chamber concurred with *Tadić* that the development of the forms of responsibility applicable to violations of international criminal law had to be viewed in the context of the very nature of such crimes, often carried out by groups of individuals acting in pursuance of a common criminal design.[19] The Chamber aimed to 'ascertain not only whether JCE existed under customary international law at the relevant time, thus being punishable under international criminal law, but also whether it was sufficiently accessible and foreseeable' to the suspects.[20] The jurisprudence relied upon in *Tadić* was discussed as well as additional cases cited in *Rwamakuba*, leading the Chamber to the conclusion that the first and second categories of JCE were 'recognized forms of responsibility in customary law' at the relevant time.[21] Since these categories also had underpinnings in the applicable Cambodian law of co-authorship, the test of foreseeability and accessibility to the accused was satisfied.[22]

A contrary conclusion was reached regarding the third category of JCE. There was found to be insufficient support for this category in the authorities relied upon in *Tadić*.[23] Turning to general principles of law, a consideration of which in the Chamber's opinion did not require a 'comprehensive survey of all the legal systems of the world',[24] the question addressed was whether it would be foreseeable to the suspects in 1975–79 that they could be held liable under the third category of JCE. The question was answered in the negative since no provision in Cambodian law would have given notice to them that they could be punished on this basis.[25]

The ECCC Pre-Trial Chamber therefore reinforced the status of the first and second categories of JCE while discrediting the third category. Shortly after the Pre-Trial Chamber issued its decision, the Trial Chamber in its judgment in the *Duch* case re-affirmed the applicability of the first two categories of JCE[26] and in an interlocutory decision in the *Ieng Sary* case confirmed that the third category was

[17] Charged Person *Ieng Sary* (Co-Prosecutors' Response to *Ieng Sary's* Motion on Joint Criminal Enterprise) 002/19-09-2007-ECCC/OCIJ (11 August 2008) para 13.

[18] Co-Prosecutors' Response to *Ieng Sary's* Motion on Joint Criminal Enterprise (n 17) paras 13–14. See also *Nuon Chea, Ieng Sary, Ieng Thirith and Khieu Samphan* (Co-Prosecutors' Request for the Trial Chamber to Consider JCE III as an Alternative Mode of Liability) 002/19-09-2007-ECCC/TC (17 June 2011).

[19] *Ieng Sary JCE decision* (n 2) para 55.

[20] *Ieng Sary JCE decision*, para 45, following *Ojdanić JCE decision* (n 15).

[21] *Ieng Sary JCE decision* (n 15) para 69.

[22] *Ieng Sary JCE decision* (n 15) para 72.

[23] *Ieng Sary JCE decision* (n 15) para 77.

[24] *Ieng Sary JCE decision* (n 15) para 86.

[25] *Ieng Sary JCE decision* (n 15) para 87.

[26] *Kaing Guek Eav alias Duch* (Judgment) 001/18-07-2007/ECCC/TC (26 July 2010) paras 511–13, stating that it was not necessary in the circumstances of the case to pronounce on the status of the third category of JCE.

neither customary law nor a general principle of law.[27] In the latter decision, some additional Second World War-era cases that another court—the Special Tribunal for Lebanon ('STL')—had referenced in its own discussion of JCE were considered without altering the Trial Chamber's conclusion.[28]

In the section that follows, the Hong Kong cases will be analysed with a view to assessing whether they provide support for *Tadić* or the re-appraisal in *Ieng Sary*.

## 3. Being 'Concerned' or 'Together Concerned' in Crimes in the Hong Kong Trials

### 3.1 Origins of the phrase 'being concerned in' crime

The phrase 'being concerned in' crime derives from English law and can be seen to provide a means both of formulating the charges in cases involving a plurality of offenders and of defining the scope of criminal participation in certain statutory offences.

English criminal law drew a distinction between principals in the first degree ('one who is the actor or actual perpetrator of the fact') and principals in the second degree ('those who are present, aiding and abetting, *at* the commission of the fact').[29] Presence could be constructive, where those not close enough to be eye witnesses nonetheless assisted by performing their assigned tasks. Further categories included accessories before the fact (those absent at the time of the felony who procure, counsel, command, or abet another to commit a felony) and accessories after the fact (one who receives, relieves, comforts, or assists the felon, knowing the felony to have been committed).[30] The term 'felony' refers to the graver indictable offences, below the degree of treason.[31] Where 'several persons combine for an unlawful purpose, or for a purpose to be carried into effect by unlawful means', and one of them in carrying out that purpose kills a person, all those involved in the killing would be considered principals to murder in the first degree as a consequence of their 'felonious participation in the design'.[32] In practice, principals in

[27] *Nuon Chea, Ieng Sary, Ieng Thirth, Khieu Samphan* (Decision on the Applicability of Joint Criminal Enterprise) 002/19-09-2007/ECCC/TC (12 September 2011).

[28] Interlocutory Decision on the Applicable Law: Terrorism, Conspiracy, Homicide, Perpetration, Cumulative Charging, STL-11-01/I, I (16 February 2011) ('STL, Interlocutory Decision on the Applicable Law'), fn 355. The cases considered by the ECCC Trial Chamber were *US v Ulrich and Merkle* and *US v Wuelfert* and were found not to support guilt based on JCE III.

[29] Sir John Jervis, *Archbold's Summary of the Law Relating to Pleading and Evidence in Criminal Cases* (11th edn, W N Welsby 1849) ('*Archbold's Summary of the Law*') 3, 4 emphasis added. See also Sir W M Oldnall Russell, 'Russell on Crimes and Misdemeanors', in W F Craies and L W Kershaw, *A Treatise on Crimes and Misdemeanors: vol 1* (7th edn, Stevens and Sons 1910) ('*Russell on Crimes and Misdemeanors*') writing after the adoption of the Accessories and Abettors Act 1861.

[30] *Archbold's Summary of the Law* (n 29) 7, 9.

[31] *Russell on Crimes and Misdemeanors* (n 29) 8. The distinction between felonies and misdemeanours was abolished by the Criminal Law Act 1967.

[32] *Archbold's Summary of the Law* (n 29) 5, 6. See also at 112–13.

the first and second degree and accessories before and after the fact could all be joined in the same indictment.[33]

The phrase 'being concerned in' allowed various degrees of involvement in crimes, especially serious crimes such as murder and riot/affray, to be reflected in the charges. The case of *Hyde v Cogan* addressed charges under the 1714 Riot Act in connection with the June 1780 anti-Catholic riots in London. A group of rioters had allegedly pulled down a dwelling house and demolished the goods therein. Justice Ashhurst, considering that the demolition of the goods was in pursuance of the riotous action, stated that even if one of the rioters had not been in the house, but had received some of the goods in the street from the others, 'he would have been guilty of felony, as being concerned in the riot'.[34] Those adjudged felons faced the death penalty under the Act. The Privy Council in the Indian case of *Calder v Halket* made reference to the charge of 'being concerned in' a riot brought against multiple offenders who were subsequently sentenced to various terms of imprisonment reflecting the degree of their involvement.[35]

The phrase 'being concerned in' appears in various statutes, such as the Foreign Enlistment Act 1870 (knowingly concerned in increasing or augmenting the warlike force of certain ships); Coinage Offences Act 1861 (being concerned in counterfeiting); and Customs Consolidation Act 1876 (being concerned in importing prohibited goods).[36] The Queensland Criminal Code Act 1899 refers, for example, in Article 334 to 'being concerned in the landing of [explosives]' and in Article 474 to being 'concerned in causing' communication of infectious diseases to animals. While the Slave Trade Act of 1824 refers directly to procurers, counsellors, aiders, and abettors to the prohibited acts, an 1826 treaty between Brazil and England prohibited (as piracy) 'being concerned in the carrying on of the African Slave Trade'.[37] Commenting on the case of *Serva* which analysed these instruments, Russell noted that the accused were tried for 'being concerned in the slave trade'[38] while the reported case indicates that they were charged as principals in the first and second degree. Finally, Article 39 of the Constitution of Ireland, enacted on 1 July 1937, includes in the definition of treason, 'taking part or being concerned in or inciting or conspiring with any person to make or to take part or be concerned in any [attempt by force of arms to overthrow the organs of government]'.[39]

The modern English statutory law usage of the phrase 'to be concerned in' as well as its interpretation in the cases is also informative. The 1971 Misuse of Drugs Act

[33] *Archbold's Summary of the Law* (n 29) 60. See also Accessories and Abettors Act 1861, s 6, stating any number of accessories to a felony may be tried together notwithstanding the absence of the principal felon.

[34] *Hyde v Cogan* (1781) 2 Douglas 699, 99 ER 445.

[35] *Calder v Halket* (1840) III Moore PC 28, 13 ER 12; [1835–42] All ER 306. See also *R v Pillay* [1922] All ER 437, accused charged with 'being concerned in' a housebreaking with three others.

[36] *Russell on Crimes and Misdemeanors* (n 29) 291, 346, 374–6.

[37] *The Queen v Serva, Majavel et al* (1845) 1 Denison 104, 169 ER 169, 174.

[38] *Russell on Crimes and Misdemeanors* (n 29) 48, note k.

[39] Constitution of the Republic of Ireland, at <https://www.constitution.ie/Documents/Bhunreacht_na_hEireann_web.pdf> accessed 6 May 2013.

makes it an offence for a person to be concerned in the production or supply of controlled drugs.[40] In *R v Hughes* the issue on appeal was precisely the meaning of the words 'concerned in'. The ingredients of the offence of being concerned in supply were held to be (1) the supply of a drug to another; (2) participation by the defendant in the enterprise involving such supply; and (3) knowledge by the defendant of the nature of the enterprise.[41] It was noted in *R v Blake* that the offence had been particularly widely drawn so as to involve persons who might be at some distance from the making of the offer to supply.[42]

The point of origin of joint enterprise in English common law is said to be the case of *Macklin* where, in 1838, it was held to be 'a principle of law that if several persons act together in pursuance of a common intent, every act in furtherance of such intent by each of them is, in law, done by all'.[43] But the concept appears to have much earlier origins. In *Lord Dacre's case* circa 1543, 'D and others came to steal deer in P's park, and one of the company killed the keeper in the park while D and the rest were in other parts of the park: Held this was murder in them all.'[44] The case was relied on in *Borthwick*, 1779, where it was accepted that principals in the second degree could be guilty of murder, even if presence was not proved, if 'they were of the same party, on the same pursuit, and under the same engagements and expectation of mutual defence and support with the person who did the fact'.[45]

The phrase 'being concerned in' may therefore be seen to provide a conveniently broad catch-all charge, especially in relation to serious crimes such as treason, slavery, murder, and riot or affray, and where the precise form of participation of each alleged offender is unknown. The 'exact degree of complicity'[46] of each offender would be expected to emerge at trial. There is an undeniable (but not necessary) connection between the use of 'being concerned in' and the notion of participation in an unlawful enterprise. The idea that several persons with a common unlawful purpose are 'concerned in the guilt'[47] of the one who 'happen[s] to kill a man'[48] may presumably be reflected in a charge of 'being concerned in' murder. All those found to be so concerned would be guilty as principals. The case of *Hughes*, although decided with reference to a specific statutory provision which postdates the Hong Kong trials, suggests that in certain contexts 'concern in' *requires* participation in an enterprise.

[40] Misuse of Drugs Act 1971, ss 4(2)(b), 4(3)(b)(c).

[41] *R v Hughes* (1985) 81 Cr App Rep, CA 344, 348.

[42] *R v Blake, R v O'Connor* (1978) 68 Cr App Rep, CA 1, 2.

[43] *Macklin, Murphy and Others* (1838) 2 Lew CC 225, 168 ER 1136 (Alderson B) in A Reed and B Fitzpatrick, *Criminal Law* (4th edn, Sweet & Maxwell 2009) ('Reed and Fitzpatrick, *Criminal Law*') 127.

[44] 1 Hale PC 439.

[45] *The King v John Borthwick and sixteen others* (1779) 1 Douglas 207, 99 Eng Rep 136, 139.

[46] *Russell on Crimes and Misdemeanors* (n 29) 104.

[47] *Russell on Crimes and Misdemeanors* (n 29) 759.

[48] *Russell on Crimes and Misdemeanors* (n 29) 759.

## 3.2 Procedures governing the Hong Kong trials

The Hong Kong trials were governed by the Royal Warrant of 18 June 1945 ('Royal Warrant') and the annexed Regulations for the Trial of War Criminals ('Regulations for the Trial of War Criminals').[49] Notably Regulation 8(ii) provided as follows:

> Where there is evidence that a war crime has been the result of concerted action upon the part of a unit or group of men, then evidence given upon any charge relating to that crime against any member of such unit or group may be received as prima facie evidence of the responsibility of each member of that unit or group for that crime.
>
> In any such case all or any members of such unit or group may be charged and tried jointly in respect of any such war crime and no application by any of them to be tried separately shall be allowed by the Court.

Regulation 8(ii) reflected the recommendation of the United Nations War Crimes Commission that those who had committed crimes collectively by groups, formations or units should be brought to trial either jointly or individually. The Regulation was a precursor of Articles 9 and 10 of the International Military Tribunal Nuremberg Charter, adopted on 8 August 1945, which dealt with responsibility for membership in a criminal organization.[50] Control Council Law No 10 of 20 December 1945, designed to establish a uniform legal basis in Germany for the prosecution of war criminals, continued this theme by providing in Article 2(2) that criminal responsibility would flow from a connection with plans or enterprises involving the commission of a crime or membership of an organization connected with such crime.[51]

The Hong Kong trials followed the procedure set out in the *Manual of Military Law 1929 (as amended)*. The *Manual* contains a section on responsibility for crime based on 'common intent':

> If several persons combine together for an unlawful purpose or for a lawful purpose to be effected by unlawful means, each is responsible for every offence committed by any one of them in furtherance of that purpose, but not for any offence committed by another member of the party which is unconnected with the common purpose, unless he personally instigates or assists in its commission. Thus, if a police officer goes with an assistant to arrest A in a house and all the occupants of this house combine to resist the arrest, and in the struggle the assistant is killed, the occupants are responsible. But if two persons go out to commit theft

[49] Royal Warrant 0160/2498, 18 June 1945, promulgated by the War Office, Army Order 81 of 1945 (Secondary legislation such as the Instructions issued by Allied Land Forces South-East Asia (ALFSEA) also applied: Allied Land Forces South-East Asia, War Crimes Instruction No 1 (2nd edn) (as amended) in File WO 32/12197, UK National Archives.

[50] *Belsen case* (n 13) 139.

[51] The ECCC Pre-Trial Chamber found clear support for the first and second categories of JCE in Article 6 of the IMT Nürnberg Charter and in Control Council Law No 10, see *Ieng Sary JCE decision* (n 2), paras 57–8, 61.

and one unknown to the other puts a pistol in his pocket and shoots a man the other is not responsible.[52]

Evidence of conspiracies is addressed in terms that are echoed by Regulation 8(ii).[53]

## 3.3 The Hong Kong cases

The case against Sergeant Kawamoto Kaname raises the preliminary question of the distinction in the charges between 'concerned in' and 'did ill-treat'. Kawamoto was attached to the Eastern District Gendarmerie as a Gendarmerie Sergeant and was tried alone on two charges of committing war crimes in that, in the first charge, he was 'concerned in the maltreatment' of a British prisoner resulting in the prisoner's death, and in the second charge, he 'did ill-treat' two civilians in custody.[54] In relation to the first charge, the Prosecution contended that the prisoner's death was wholly attributable to Kawamoto. The Judge Advocate commented that Kawamoto was the 'prime and only mover in the whole transaction' since, while others also participated, Kawamoto himself administered the water torture which led to the victim's death.[55] Under the second charge, Kawamoto was described by the Judge Advocate as the 'chief torturer' of both victims. The sentence of death was upheld. The phrasing of the first charge possibly reflects the fact that until the evidence was heard, the full extent of Kawamoto's 'concern' in the transaction vis-à-vis the other participants was not known.

Inouye Kanao was an interpreter charged with one count of being concerned in ill-treatment of prisoners of war ('POWs'), and two counts alleging that he 'did assault' them. The charge alleging that Inouye was 'concerned in' the ill-treatment was described by the Prosecutor as the more complicated charge.[56] In his Opening Address, the Prosecutor drew particular attention to the word 'concerned', and noted that 'in the great majority, if not all, the cases, the evidence produced will show that the accused was not merely "concerned in" but took a major active part in the ill-treatments'.[57] This suggests that those 'concerned in' a crime are all participants including the direct or chief perpetrator, who may himself be 'concerned' to a greater degree by taking a major active part. The Prosecutor confirmed this broad interpretation in his Closing Address. 'I think, and the Court can justly

[52] Great Britain War Office, *Manual of Military Law 1929* (7th edn, Great Britain War Office 1929) (Reprinted December 1939) (HMSO, 1940), as amended in 1936 (the replacement of ch XIV and in 1944 an amendment to para 443 of ch XIV). This chapter employs the short reference '*Manual of Military Law 1929 (as amended)*'. See col 17: this paragraph featured in the *1914 Manual* (89 col 18) in identical terms save the first phrase which referred instead to 'several persons' going out with 'a common intent to execute some criminal purpose'. The notion of 'common intent' was known to United States military law as well, see United States War Department *A Manual for Courts-Martial, Courts of Inquiry and of Other Procedure under Military Law* (Washington DC 1917) 34 col 69.

[53] *Manual of Military Law 1929 (as amended)* (n 52) 110 col 224.

[54] *Trial of Sgt Kaname Kawamoto* (HKWCT Collection, File No WO235/921).

[55] Judge Advocate's Report, 8 November 1946, *Trial of Sgt Kaname Kawamoto* (n 54) slide 5 para 1.

[56] *Trial of Inouye Kanao* (HKWCT Collection, File No 235/927).

[57] Prosecution's Opening Address, *Trial of Inouye Kanao* (n 56) exhibit F, slide 165.

say, that if the Accused *has anything whatsoever to do with* any of this ill-treatment he was concerned in [it].'[58]

Sato Chochi was charged in his capacity as Medical Officer at Stanley Gaol Hospital with one count of committing a war crime in that he was 'concerned in' the ill-treatment of prisoners who were patients at the hospital, by failing to provide them with adequate medical care, resulting in deaths and physical suffering.[59] In his Closing Address, the Prosecutor explained that:

> The expression 'concerned in' in the charge connoted that Lt. Sato was entrusted with the care and well-being of the sick British and Chinese prisoners at Stanley Gaol hospital, and as a medical officer, he [was] under obligation to render necessary medical aid and provide adequate diet for them, upon which laws of ethics, profession and Nations insist.[60]

Consequently, the only questions to be answered were whether the accused was responsible for looking after sick prisoners and whether the alleged ill-treatment occurred. In this case therefore, the 'concern' in the ill-treatment amounted to criminal negligence, in fact a direct form of responsibility, the deaths being attributable to neglect on the part of the accused who had charge of otherwise helpless prisoners.

The charge in *Lieutenant Kishi Yasuo and fourteen others*, alleged the commission of a war crime in that the accused at Lantau Island, between 18 and 26 August 1945, in violation of the laws and usages of war, were together concerned in the beating, torture and maltreatment of inhabitants of the Silver Mine Bay district, and in the killing of nine of those inhabitants.[61] Kishi admitted executing three Chinese villagers while his subordinate, Matsumoto, admitted giving orders to kill two further villagers. Uchida admitted killing two villagers but asserted that he was acting on Matsumoto's orders. The remaining accused argued that they were not present at or concerned in executions and/or maltreatment, or that the alleged maltreatment did not occur.

The Prosecution stressed in closing arguments that 'the execution of... all these villagers... was not a one man show'[62] and appeared to use Regulation 8(ii) as a centrepiece for its case:[63]

> the strength of the case against the accused does not lie in the fact that they have been each and everyone indicted with some act of barbaric cruelty against these Chinese civilians but it does lie in the fact [sic] and all the evidence before this court tends to prove that the cruelty, maltreatment, the torture and finally the murder of the unfortunate islanders was not the

[58] Prosecuting Officer's Closing Address, *Trial of Inouye Kanao* (n 56) transcript 133, slide 147 (emphasis added). Inouye's conviction was ultimately overturned, as it transpired he was a Canadian subject, and he was later convicted of high treason by the Supreme Court of Hong Kong.

[59] *Trial of Choichi Sato* (HKWCT Collection, File No WO235/1027) ('*Trial of Choichi Sato*').

[60] Prosecutor's Closing Address, *Trial of Choichi Sato* (n 59) exhibit N, 1, slide 340.

[61] *Trial of Lt Kishi Yasuo and fourteen others* (HKWCT Collection, File WO235/993) ('*Trial of Lt Kishi Yasuo and fourteen others*').

[62] Prosecution Closing Argument, *Trial of Lt Kishi Yasuo and fourteen others* (n 61) transcript 522, slide 548.

[63] Prosecution Closing Argument, *Trial of Lt Kishi Yasuo and fourteen others* (n 61) transcript 525, slide 551.

action of any one individual, however big a part he played in this crime, but was in actual fact the concerted action over a period of one week of a group of individuals belonging to one unit who acted jointly in the continued maltreatment of the civilian inhabitants in their custody and which group or unit having jointly and severally [sic] are thus jointly and severally responsible for the natural consequences of their actions which in this case was the cruel and untimely death of nine of the inhabitants of the said Lantau Island.[64]

Special emphasis was placed by the Prosecution on the assistance and moral support given by other members of the unit who were present at the time of the offence. The Prosecution added: 'The very fact that the accused have all been proved to be members of the one unit, namely the Kishi unit, is sufficient to support the Prosecution's contention that they were together acting jointly and severally and must for this reason accept full responsibility for the actions of their group.'[65] The Prosecution appeared to be suggesting that all of the accused should be treated as principals to the nine killings on the basis of their participation in a common design.

It is not evident that the Court adopted this approach to the responsibility of the accused, in particular the idea that all members of one unit acting in concert would be fully liable for the actions of the group. Kishi, Matsumoto, and Uchida were all found guilty of the charge and sentenced to death. Nine other accused were convicted of either the full charge or of being concerned in beating, torture, and maltreatment, and sentenced to various terms of imprisonment. It is clear, and it was also observed by the Judge Advocate, that the degree of 'concern' and therefore culpability was reflected in the sentences. Two members of the unit whose alibis were accepted were acquitted. Beyond actual presence, the Court appeared to require proof of individual acts of torture and maltreatment in order for guilt to be established.

The Prosecution attempted to give precision to the phrase 'together concerned' in the case against Sergeant Hanada Zenji, a Gendarme Lance-Corporal attached to the Hong Kong Island District Gendarmerie, and three other members of the Japanese Gendarmerie, charged with the maltreatment of certain civilians held under arrest at the Gendarmerie Headquarters.

This the prosecution takes to mean that all the accused were concerned in the crimes in so far as it affected one or other of the victims of maltreatments. To substantiate the charge as drawn it is not considered necessary to prove that each accused was concerned in the maltreatment of each victim. What will be proved in this regard, is that each accused, to a greater or lesser extent, maltreated one, more than one, or in at least one case all the victims.[66]

It is not clear what the Prosecution intended to be the consequence of demonstrating that each accused maltreated at least one victim, and whether it was envisaged

[64] Prosecution Closing Argument, *Trial of Lt Kishi Yasuo and fourteen others* (n 61) transcript 524, slide 550.

[65] Prosecution Closing Argument, *Trial of Lt Kishi Yasuo and fourteen others* (n 61) transcript 525, slide 551.

[66] Prosecutor's Opening Address, *Trial of Sgt Hanada Zenji and three others* (n 3) exhibit E, slide 212.

that each of the convicted accused would be responsible for the maltreatment of all the victims even if the individual accused's physical participation in the maltreatment was more limited. The sentences, which ranged from three to eight years' imprisonment, suggest that each accused's individual 'concern' in the crimes was considered separately rather than as a contribution to an unlawful purpose.

The head of the *Kempeitai* (Gendarmerie) in Hong Kong, Colonel Noma Kennosuke, was charged with being concerned in the ill-treatment and resultant deaths of civilian residents.[67] The Prosecutor stressed the importance of understanding clearly what was meant by the expression 'concerned in' which formed the basis of the indictment. The description offered was very specific to the factual circumstances of the case, Noma being charged as a commander in respect of the acts of his subordinates. Thus, 'concerned in' meant that Noma was 'so senior in rank and appointment, and yet so closely tied to the *Kempeitai* personnel in the chain of command, that whatever operations they undertook, his planning and guidance were present and paramount'.[68] Noma could therefore be found 'culpably concerned', in other words guilty, if his subordinates engaged in criminal operations. Noma was in fact found guilty and sentenced to death; his concern in the crime warranting the highest penalty. Thus, 'concern in' crime included the actions of senior commanders who might be one step removed from the physical commission of the crime yet in a position to control the acts of subordinates. The reference to 'culpable concern' suggests that such commanders were viewed as being complicit in the acts of their subordinates.

A similar outcome can be seen in the case of Captain Ushiyama Yukio and three other accused related to alleged ill-treatment at the Western *Kempeitai* Headquarters where Ushiyama was the Commanding Officer.[69] The pertinent question was said by the Prosecutor to be whether Ushiyama initiated or ordered criminal action against the prisoners or whether he acquiesced in it, connived at it, or knowingly failed to stop it. All these possibilities fell within the broad scope of the charge of being 'together concerned in' ill-treatment of prisoners. Ushiyama's case was the more difficult one as the other accused were alleged to have participated more actively in the ill-treatment. Perhaps to stress the significance of Ushiyama's contribution to the crimes, the Prosecutor told the judges: 'you will be asked to consider whether or not all the four accused were together concerned in carrying out a shameful system of a notorious organization like the Western *Kempeitai* Headquarters.'[70] Ushiyama was sentenced to death, suggesting that as the Commanding Officer his concern in any such system was critical. Two of his co-accused received prison sentences and one was acquitted.

The case of *Lieutenant General Kinoshita Kiichi and Sergeant Yoshida Bunzo* focused on the operations of the *Kempeitai* in Shanghai and also addressed the

[67] *Trial of Col Noma Kennosuke* (HKWCT Collection, File No 235/999) ('*Trial of Col Noma Kennosuke*').

[68] Prosecution's Closing Address, *Trial of Col Noma Kennosuke* (n 67) exhibit EEE, 1, slide 713.

[69] *Trial of Capt Ushiyama Yukio and three others* (HKWCT Collection, File No WO235/1041).

[70] Prosecution's Opening Address, *Trial of Capt Ushiyama Yukio and three others* (n 69) transcript 5, slide 71.

responsibility of commanders. The accused were charged jointly with committing a war crime in that in their respective positions of Major General (commanding the Shanghai District *Kempeitai*) and Corporal, they were concerned in the ill-treatment of civilian residents of Shanghai causing physical suffering and the death of one William Hutton.[71] It was explained by the Judge Advocate in his summing up that the case for the Prosecution was that Kinoshita was responsible overall for the alleged ill-treatment, while Yoshida actually took part in the torture of some of the victims. As in the case of Ushiyama, Kinoshita's responsibility presented greater difficulties than Yoshida's, hence in the arguments of the Prosecution 'concerned in' approximated to command responsibility in Kinoshita's case. The Prosecution also referred to Kinoshita's acquiescence in the torture of Hutton, while Yoshida was directly involved in the torture. Kinoshita was not a distant commander, however, as he appeared to have inspected the cells regularly where the ill-treatment was occurring.

The Judge Advocate observed in relation to Kinoshita that 'it was only with his acquiescence that the cruelty could have continued and therefore [. . .] he may be said to be responsible for and concerned in the numerous acts of cruelty practised by his subordinates'.[72] According to the Judge Advocate, the evidence indicated either that he knew of the ill-treatment, or that it was at least his duty to have known. He had furthermore admitted that even without that knowledge he owed a moral responsibility.[73] The Defence drew a distinction between moral responsibility and material responsibility for the ill-treatment, noting that 'although Kinoshita has been bound, as the then Commander of the Shanghai *Kempeitai*, to accept moral responsibility for these deplorable examples of inhumanity, the true material responsibility must rest with the various commanders of the *Kempeitai* branches in Shanghai'.[74] The Defence also took issue with the wording of the charge and, taking the hypothetical case of 'A' being concerned in a result 'B', argued that this could mean (i) A practised B; (ii) A ordered B; (iii) A suggested B; (iv) A acquiesced in B. According to the Defence, although the Prosecution had produced evidence proving ill-treatment of prisoners by specified or unspecified members of the Shanghai *Kempeitai*, no evidence had been produced to prove Kinoshita practised, ordered, suggested, or acquiesced in ill-treatment. On the contrary, it was asserted that he issued orders for correct behaviour.[75] The Defence argued further that it was a principle of English law that a term in a charge should be interpreted narrowly, and the Court should refrain from construing 'concerned in' broadly as 'responsible for'. The Judge Advocate found that there was no

[71] *Trial of Lt Gen Eiichi Kinoshita and Sgt Bunzo Yoshida* (HKWCT Collection, File No WO235/1116) ('*Trial of Lt Gen Eiichi Kinoshita and Sgt Bunzo Yoshida*').

[72] Judge Advocate's Report, *Trial of Lt Gen Eiichi Kinoshita and Sgt Bunzo Yoshida* (n 71) 23 December 1948, 4, slide 14, para 17.

[73] Judge Advocate's Report, *Trial of Lt Gen Eiichi Kinoshita and Sgt Bunzo Yoshida* (n 71) 23 December 1948, 5, slide 15, 5, para 21.

[74] Defence Closing Address, *Trial of Lt Gen Eiichi Kinoshita and Sgt Bunzo Yoshida* (n 71) exhibit WWW, 7, slide 550.

[75] Defence Closing Address, *Trial of Lt Gen Eiichi Kinoshita and Sgt Bunzo Yoshida* (n 71) exhibit WWW, 10, slide 553.

substance to this last argument, although it is not entirely clear what 'responsible for' was taken to mean in this context.[76] Arguably, the assertion was that responsibility for the conditions of detention and treatment of prisoners was being conflated with 'concern in' ill-treatment or that moral responsibility without a criminal *mens rea* was taken to be sufficient. Both Kinoshita and Yoshida were convicted. They were sentenced to life and 12 years' imprisonment respectively.

Captain Shibata Shigeo, who was the Officer-in-Charge of the Eastern *Kempeitai* Headquarters in Hong Kong and a member of his staff, Sergeant Major Oba Takao, were charged with committing a war crime in that they were 'together concerned in the ill-treatment of civilian residents' held in custody at the Headquarters causing deaths and physical suffering.[77] In his Opening Address, the Prosecutor indicated that the key questions were (i) whether Shibata ordered the criminal acts, making him liable for all the consequences which flowed from them; (ii) whether he was instrumental in carrying out the policy of deliberate mistreatment emanating from a superior authority so that he completely identified himself with such a policy, again making him liable for all the consequences which flowed out of it; or (iii) whether he acquiesced in such acts, connived at them, or knowingly failed to stop them.[78] In relation to Oba, the question was whether he personally ill-treated and tortured suspects. The allegation was that Oba, by his active participation in ill-treatment and prolonged attachment to the Eastern *Kempeitai* Headquarters, 'was a consenting party to a continuous and systematic persecution of such prisoners and was in fact a part of the wider organization which made such tortures possible'.[79] In his Closing Address, the Prosecutor considered the meaning of the expression 'concerned in' and related it expressly to the notion of command responsibility:

> The expression 'concerned in' in the charge connoted that Shibata was senior in rank and appointment at the Eastern *Kempeitai* HQs. In fact, he was in command of all *Kempeitai* personnel and as such was unquestionably responsible for their actions. When actions of his subordinates were the negation of legality as would be the case when tortures and ill-treatment were frequently perpetrated, then clearly Shibata could be said to be concerned in the misdeeds and charged accordingly. The alleged violation of the laws and usages of war had in all instances been carried out by Shibata's subordinates at the Eastern *Kempeitai* HQs during the period with which we are concerned. Therefore, the Court has to decide that measure of responsibility which a senior officer must accept for the acts of his subordinates.[80]

[76] Judge Advocate's Report, *Trial of Lt Gen Eiichi Kinoshita and Sgt Bunzo Yoshida* (n 71) 23 December 1948, 5, slide 15, para 22.

[77] *Trial of Capt Shibata Shigeo and Sgt Maj Oba Takao* (HKWCT Collection, File No WO235/1007) ('*Trial of Capt Shibata Shigeo and Sgt Maj Oba Takao*').

[78] Opening Address by the Prosecution, *Trial of Capt Shibata Shigeo and Sgt Maj Oba Takao* (n 77) transcript 5, slide 12.

[79] Opening Address by the Prosecution, *Trial of Capt Shibata Shigeo and Sgt Maj Oba Takao* (n 77) transcript 5, slide 12.

[80] Closing Address of the Prosecutor, *Trial of Capt Shibata Shigeo and Sgt Maj Oba Takao* (n 77) 1, slide 360.

In the event, the evidence was insufficient and Shigeo was acquitted, although the Judge Advocate was of the opinion that a conviction on the grounds of Shigeo's general responsibility as a commanding officer could have been sustained. Oba received a sentence of three years' imprisonment on a reduced charge which excluded responsibility for causing deaths. The courts were very much in uncharted territory when it came to marrying the evolving notion of command responsibility with a charge of 'being concerned in' ill-treatment, but the broad scope of the charge appeared to permit the inclusion of all those 'culpably concerned' whether as principals or accessories. The reference to 'concern in the misdeeds' by the Prosecutor suggests, as in the case of *Noma*, that commanders were viewed as accomplices to the crimes of their subordinates. Notably, it was apparently not seen fit to approach these cases as concerted action in pursuance of a common unlawful purpose despite the challenges of assigning responsibility to the more senior commanders.

As Totani and Linton affirm in this collection, the leading case relating to ill-treatment of POWs is that of *Colonel Tokunaga Isao and four others*. Under the first of 11 charges, it was alleged that all five accused committed a war crime in that they, when members of the POW Camp Staff at Sham Shui Po under the command of Tokunaga, were 'together concerned in the inhumane treatment' of POWs resulting in deaths and physical suffering.[81] In his Opening Address, the Prosecutor stated that the 'accusations against Tanaka, Tsutada and Harada besides the implications against them personally will point up the general policy of ill-treatment and calculated humiliation which was the apparent policy of the Camps Commander'.[82] Specific evidence of the formulation of such a policy and any planning phase does not appear to have been presented. The Judge Advocate, in his summing up, noted generally that the sentences reflected the degree of guilt attributable to each accused. Tokunaga's death sentence was commuted to life imprisonment. Saito was found guilty of criminal neglect of the highest degree, but since his crimes were those of omission rather than commission, the Judge Advocate recommended commutation of the death sentence and a sentence of 20 years' imprisonment was imposed instead.[83] The other three accused were also found guilty of the first charge, although they were found not to be implicated in the deaths. There was no suggestion that their personal contribution to the 'general policy of ill-treatment and calculated humiliation' could have made them liable for the deaths as foreseeable consequences of the implementation of that policy. Although the case contained elements of the second category of JCE as defined in *Tadić*, it was not ultimately treated in that way.

Another case relating to POW camps, this time in Taiwan, China, is that of *Colonel Sazawa Hideo and two others*. Sazawa was in command of several camps and

[81] *Trial of Col Tokunaga Isao and four others* (HKWCT Collection, File No WO235/1012, Part One).

[82] Prosecutor's Opening Address, *Trial of Col Tokunaga Isao and four others* (n 81) 2, slide 848.

[83] Judge Advocate's Report, *Trial of Col Tokunaga Isao and four others* (n 81) 9 May 1947, 4, slide 16.

was charged together with Hioki Shiro, Commandant of the Shirokawa camp and Matsumura Yoshio, a medical orderly, with being 'together concerned in the ill-treatment of prisoners-of-war and civilians resulting in physical sufferings to many of them'.[84] The Prosecutor, in his Opening Address, referred to 'a deliberate policy of starvation'.[85] There were several strands to the alleged culpability of the accused. First, 'by their individual positions of authority they were instrumental in carrying out a shameful system'. Second, 'they either actively committed the various offences, or condoned them'. Finally and alternatively, they were liable 'because they failed to carry out the duty imposed upon them by the laws and usages of war towards the prisoners under their charge'.[86] The Defence viewed the Prosecution's allegations as being based on the premise that the fundamental policy of the Japanese military authorities towards the POWs was one of deliberate ill-treatment and that Sazawa was a willing participant in the execution of this policy.[87] Indeed, in relation to the second charge against Sazawa alone, the Prosecutor stated 'the administration of prisoners-of-war camps under Sazawa... ran true to a pattern'[88] which included inadequate food and beatings. But, the Defence argued that 'nothing is so erroneous and dangerous as the reasoning, which follows the premise while the premise has not been proved to be true'.[89] Here, the Defence strikes at a general weakness in the Prosecution's case in terms of evidence of the underlying policy and plan. However, the Prosecution did not appear to follow through on any assertions as to the accused's willing participation in the execution of a policy. In his Closing Address, the Prosecutor indicated that the modes of liability to be applied with respect to both Sazawa and Hioki were (a) ordering, (b) conniving at or condoning the crime, or (c) command responsibility using the precedent of *Yamashita*. All three accused were sentenced to various terms of imprisonment.

The facts of the case relating to ill-treatment of workers in the copper mines of Taiwan, China allow some parallels to be drawn with JCE especially where there is systematic mistreatment. Toda Mitsugu and nine other accused were all civilians in the service of the Imperial Japanese Army on the staff of the Kinkaseki Nippon Mining Company. The six POW camps in the vicinity of the mine supplied manpower, and prisoners were forced to work under appalling conditions. Toda was the general manager of the mine, Nakamura was the chief of the mining department, Yonemura was a liaison officer between the POWs and the mining company, and all the other accused were foremen working in the mine and in charge of operations. The accused were charged jointly with committing a war

84 *Trial of Col Sazawa Hideo and two others* (HKWCT Collection, File No WO235/1029).

85 Prosecutor's Opening Address, *Trial of Col Sazawa Hideo and two others* (n 84) transcript 5, slide 15.

86 Prosecutor's Opening Address, *Trial of Col Sazawa Hideo and two others* (n 84) transcript 5, slide 15.

87 Closing Address by Defence Counsel Tanaka Yutake, *Trial of Col Sazawa Hideo and two others* (n 84) transcript 424, slide 432.

88 Prosecution Closing Address, *Trial of Col Sazawa Hideo and two others* (n 84) transcript 444, slide 452.

89 Closing Address by Defence Counsel Tanaka Yutake, *Trial of Col Sazawa Hideo and two others* (n 88) transcript 424, slide 432.

crime in that they were 'concerned in' the ill-treatment of the POWs at the mine causing physical suffering and deaths.[90] In his Opening Address, the Prosecutor pointed out:

> It will be seen that all accused are charged with causing suffering over lengthy periods. In many instances individual instances stand out and are described. But the most serious thing is the everyday practice of sustained cruelty, calculated to make a misery of men's lives who had no come-back and no physical stamina.[91]

There is no particular discussion of the meaning of 'concerned in' and it is therefore difficult to deduce whether the 'everyday practice of sustained cruelty' was alleged to form part of a system of cruelty impacting on the manner in which the accused were held responsible. Sentences for the eight convicted accused were low and six of them were explicitly absolved of liability in respect of the allegation of causing deaths contained in the charge.

The cases relating to the High Seas offer some further explanation of the term 'concerned in'. Niimori Genichiro was charged with seven counts of committing a war crime in that he was 'concerned in the ill-treatment' of POWs, including in the first charge the battening down of the prisoners in the hold of the *Lisbon Maru* after it had been torpedoed and was sinking, resulting in deaths and physical suffering.[92] The Prosecutor emphasized, relying on the Oxford Dictionary definition,[93] that 'concern' meant 'to take part in or had a part in' the ill-treatment of POWs and argued that the ill-treatment included the battening down of the hatches but was not restricted to that. 'The battening down includes ordering the POWs below, threatening them with shooting if they endeavoured to get out of the holds and thirdly covering of the hatches. I submit the participation in any of these three is sufficient to show a taking part in.'[94] It was also alleged that Niimori was responsible for the wellbeing of the POWs. However, 'the ingredient of the charge is "concerned in" the ill-treatment. It has nothing to do with responsibility.'[95] Thus the Prosecutor suggested that there was no need to demonstrate that the accused was responsible for the wellbeing of the POWs in order to prove that he was concerned in their ill-treatment. This helps to clarify the meaning of 'responsible for' in the *Kinoshita* case. The analysis was accepted by the Court which found the accused guilty of the first charge but exempted therefrom the words 'and responsible for the well-being of the said prisoners-of-war'. 'Concern in' was given its ordinary meaning of 'to take part in'; in other words, any involvement would suffice for liability potentially to follow.

[90] *Trial of Toda Mitsugu and eight others* (HKWCT Collection, File WO235/1028).

[91] Prosecutor's Opening Address, *Trial of Toda Mitsugu and eight others* (n 90) exhibit E, 3, slide 302.

[92] *Trial of Niimori Genichiro* (HKWCT Collection, File No 235/892).

[93] Prosecution's Closing Address, *Trial of Niimori Genichiro* (n 92) transcript 292, slide 301.

[94] Prosecution's Closing Address, *Trial of Niimori Genichiro* (n 92) transcript 236, slide 305. The Prosecutor stressed 'being concerned in' as taking or having part again at transcript 298, slide 307.

[95] Prosecution's Closing Address, *Trial of Niimori Genichiro* (n 92) transcript 296, slide 305.

Another case concerning events on the High Seas is that of *Rear Admiral Sakonju Naomasa and Captain Mayazumi Haruo*, charged in their respective capacities as Commanding Officer of the 16th Squadron and Officer-in-Command of the *Tone* with committing a war crime in that they were together concerned in the killing of approximately 65 survivors from the sinking of the British vessel the *Behar*.[96] The *Tone*, in accordance with instructions to disrupt Allied communications in the Indian Ocean, sank the *Behar* on 9 March 1944 rescuing almost everybody aboard. Sakonju allegedly issued an order to dispose of all but a few prisoners but Mayazumi failed to comply, keeping all prisoners alive until the *Tone* left from Batavia for Singapore on 18 March 1944, whereupon some of the prisoners were killed. The Prosecutor's theory was that Mayazumi became 'concerned in' and a party to the crime by acknowledging the order to dispose of the prisoners and eventually agreeing to obey it despite knowing it to be an illegal order. 'Together concerned in' in this case appears to mean little more than that Sakonju issued an order and Mayazumi carried it out. This is further evident from the fact that the Defence argued superior orders strongly on behalf of Mayazumi. The two accused were convicted and Sakonju was sentenced to death while Mayazumi received a sentence of seven years' imprisonment.

On its face, the case of Tamura Teiichi, Hirano Noboru, and Fujino Nasazo has all the ingredients of a classic joint enterprise. Tamura was Commanding Officer of the 426th Regiment which formed part of the 147th Infantry Division of which Hirano was a Staff-Officer. Fujino was an Officer of the 426th Regiment and adjutant to Tamura. All three accused listened to the Emperor's speech of surrender on 15 August 1945, giving them a possible vengeful motive for the action that followed. The 426th Regiment reported the capture of Fred Hockley, a British pilot who set out on a sortie from the aircraft carrier HMS Indefatigable on the morning of 15 August 1945 and was forced to bale out over Japanese territory. When captured, he was handed over to the 426th Regiment. The capture was reported to the 147th Division where Hockley should have been transported for interrogation. However, a telephone conversation ensued and on Hirano's instruction, an order was given to the Regiment to 'dispose of' (*shochi se*) Hockley themselves. The conversation was reported to Tamura who ordered Fujino to kill Hockley that same night, which Fujino did. The three accused were charged with a war crime in that they were 'together concerned in the killing' of Hockley.[97]

The case was not treated as a joint enterprise, perhaps because the events evolved as a series of orders rather than as three individuals coming together to form a common intent. The Prosecution asked the Court to find the three accused guilty 'in a greater or lesser degree of being together concerned in this killing'.[98] Tamura

[96] *Trial of R Adm Naomasa Sakonju and Capt Haruo Mayazumi* (HKWCT Collection, File No WO235/1089).

[97] *Trial of Col Tamura Teichi and two others* (HKWCT Collection, File No WO235/1021).

[98] Prosecution Closing Address, *Trial of Col Tamura Teichi and two others* (n 97) exhibit C(1), 6, slide 259.

and Hirano were sentenced to death while Fujino received a penalty of 15 years' imprisonment, superior orders apparently affording some mitigation.

The meaning of 'concerned in' based on this overview of selected Hong Kong cases may be summarized as follows. The *Kawamoto* case suggests that the phrase is broad enough to cover direct if not sole responsibility and this is supported by the *Ushiyama*, *Kinoshita*, *Sakonju*, and *Shibata* cases where superiors were jointly charged with physical perpetrators. Command responsibility is also included, as indicated in *Shibata*, *Sazawa*, and *Noma*, as well as ordering, conniving at, or condoning criminal acts. According to *Sato*, an accused will be concerned in crime where there is a duty of care and the accused is criminally negligent in performing that duty. The case of *Kishi* suggests that Regulation (ii)-type concerted action by members of a unit is potentially covered, though the implications were not spelt out. *Zenji* and *Tamura* support the notion that within a joint charge, individual accused may be concerned to different degrees and with respect to different victims, and according to *Tokunaga* and *Toda*, a charge can be split so not all jointly charged accused are convicted of being concerned to the full extent of the charge where for example ill-treatment resulted in deaths. That all these forms of participation come under the broad umbrella of 'being concerned in' crimes is supported by *Niimori* which defines the phrase as 'to take part in', and *Inouye* which includes within its scope anyone having 'anything whatsoever to do with' the crimes.

While the charge may have covered any involvement whatsoever in criminal activity, the prosecutors nevertheless appeared careful to characterize each accused's involvement with as much specificity as possible. Extra care was taken where the accused were not themselves physical perpetrators in explaining their particular concern in the crimes. The phrase 'concerned in' hints at a joint venture but appears to have been used primarily to indicate that the accused was implicated in crimes for which he was not necessarily exclusively liable. This is consistent with the common law use of the phrase as a means of casting a wide net over perpetrators who may either be equally culpable or involved to various degrees in the offence.

There is a risk of reading too much into the phrase 'together concerned in', more commonly used in joint trials. Regulation 8(ii) and the notion of common intent were available to the courts but the former received only passing reference and in no case was responsibility based explicitly on the latter. As a Judge Advocate summing up a contemporaneous case in Germany observed, there is 'nothing magic about a joint charge except that it enables you to try more than one person at one time'.[99] This observation arose from the more creative use of Regulation 8(ii) and JCE-related notions such as conspiracy in other post-Second World War trials held elsewhere. What follows does not purport to be a comprehensive assessment of all those other cases that included the charge of being 'concerned in' crimes. Rather,

[99] Summing up in the trial of *Georg Tyroltarid and others* before a British Military Court (1946) cited in the case notes on *Max Wielen and seventeen others*, (*Stalag Luft III case*) (1947) in United Nations War Crimes Commission, *Law Reports of Trials of War Criminals* vol XI (HMSO 1949) 31, 45, fn 1.

the aim is to highlight some of the cases tried by British military courts that assist in putting the Hong Kong cases in context.

## 3.4 Being 'concerned' in crime in other post-Second World War trials

The *Ponzano* case is instructive as the Judge Advocate summarized the meaning of the phrase 'concerned in' in a manner which is consistent with the broad interpretation in the Hong Kong cases:

[T]o be concerned in the commission of a criminal offence [. . . ] does not only mean that you are the person who in fact inflicted the fatal injury and directly caused death, be it by shooting or by any other violent means; it also means an indirect degree of participation, that is to say, a person can be concerned in the commission of a criminal offence, who, without being present at the place where the offence was committed, took such a part in the preparation for this offence as to further its object; in other words, he must be the cog in the wheel of events leading up to the result which in fact occurred. He can further that object not only by giving orders for a criminal offence to be committed, but he can further that object by a variety of other means, and the person who so furthers an object, the result of which is the commission of a criminal offence, can be guilty of that offence not only by an act of commission but also by an act of omission. In other words, a person is guilty not only if he does a positive act but he is also guilty if he does nothing in a case where there is a legal duty upon him to do something.[100]

All possible forms of indirect participation appear to be included. The trial of *Karl Adam Golkel and thirteen others* by the British Military Court at Wuppertal supports this broad interpretation.[101] The accused were charged with committing a war crime in France in that they were concerned in the killing of eight named members of a British Air Service Regiment. The victims were captured parachutists who were questioned, imprisoned, and then taken to a wood and shot. None of the accused was proved to have taken part in the actual shooting but there was evidence of prior planning, such as choosing the site for the shooting and the assignment of tasks such as driving the lorry and digging the grave. The trial has been said to illustrate the various courses of action which have been held to make an accused guilty of the war crime of being 'concerned in the killing' of POWs.[102] The Judge Advocate, in his summing up, stated:

It is for the members of the Court to decide what participation is fairly within the meaning of those words. But it is quite clear that those words do not mean that a man actually had to be present at the site of the shooting; a man would be concerned in the shooting if he was 50 miles away if he had ordered it and had taken the executive steps to set the shooting in motion. You must consider not only physical acts done at the scene of the shooting, but

[100] *Feurstein and others (Ponzano case)* (n 12) 239.

[101] *Karl Adam Golkel and thirteen others* (1946) in United Nations War Crimes Commission, *Law Reports of Trials of War Criminals* vol V (HMSO 1948) 45.

[102] *Karl Adam Golkel and thirteen others* (n 101) 53.

whether a particular accused ordered it or took any part in organizing it, even if he was not present at the wood.[103]

This corresponds both with the common law notion of constructive presence and the idea of participation in an unlawful enterprise although the emphasis is placed on ordering and organizing. Further, it emphasizes the Court's flexibility in determining exactly what counts as participation in the context of the charge. The facts are similar to those of the *Tamura* case except that in *Tamura*, the direct perpetrator was also charged. The element of prior organization or a common plan was not brought into clear focus in either of these cases.

In the trial of *Franz Schonfeld and nine others*[104] before the British Military Court at Essen, the accused were charged with committing a war crime in that they were concerned in the killing of three members of the Allied air force. The case-note indicates that a question of major interest in the trial was the finding of guilt against three accused, *in addition to* the sole physical perpetrator of the killings. In his summing up, the Judge Advocate in fact referred to a rule of English substantive law in terms similar to the definition of 'common intent' in the *1929 Military Manual* as follows:

In our law if several persons combine for an unlawful purpose or for a lawful purpose to be effected by unlawful means, and one of them, in carrying out the purpose, kills a man, it is murder in all who are present, whether they actually aid or abet or not, provided that the death was caused by a member of the party in the course of his endeavours to effect the common object of the assembly.[105]

Apart from the theory of common purpose, the Judge Advocate went on to explain the notion of 'concerned in' killing in terms of the law relating to parties to an offence including aiders and abettors. It is not clear whether the judges ultimately opted for the common purpose theory or the rules on accessories and aiders and abettors. However, as the case-note points out, no other accused would have been found guilty had the guilt of the physical perpetrator himself not been proven. The physical perpetrator, Rotschopf, was described by the Judge Advocate as 'the axle upon which the wheel of this case turns'.[106]

In the case of *Max Wielen and seventeen others* before the British Military Court at Hamburg, the Judge Advocate confirmed that presence at the scene of the crime was not required, and defined the term 'concerned in the killing' in this manner:

I do not think the prosecution can ask you to consider a case of a minor official who was concerned with some administrative matter. What they had in mind is that the persons concerned must have been part of the machine doing some duty, carrying out some performance which went on directly to achieve the killing, that it had some real bearing

[103] *Karl Adam Golkel and thirteen others* (n 101) 53.

[104] *Franz Schonfeld and nine others*, British Military Court, Essen, 11–26 June 1946 (Case No 66), published in United Nations War Crimes Commission, *Law Reports of Trials of War Criminals* vol XI (HMSO 1949) 64 ('*Schonfeld case*').

[105] *Schonfeld case* (n 104) 68.

[106] *Schonfeld case* (n 104) 70.

on the killing, would not have been so effective or been done so expeditiously if that person had not contributed his willing aid.[107]

The case-note points to the broad nature of the charge encompassing participants who gave the order or fired the fatal shot themselves or acted as an escort or kept off the public. This is reminiscent of the common law approach of including in one charge principals in the first and second degree as well as accessories, especially where it is not known who fired the fatal shot. The prominence of the participation was reflected in sentencing.

In *Werner Rohde and eight others*, the accused were charged with being concerned in the killing of four POWs, but none of them had physically killed any of the victims. The Judge Advocate indicated: 'If two or more men set out on a murder and one stood half a mile away from where the actual murder was committed, perhaps to keep guard, although he was not actually present when the murder was done, if he was taking part with the other man with the knowledge that that other man was going to put the killing into effect then he was just as guilty as the person who fired the shot or delivered the blow.'[108] This clear recognition of the principle elucidated as far back as *Borthwick*, demonstrates the availability of the notion of joint enterprise to the Hong Kong courts had they chosen to apply it.

The *Essen Lynching* case,[109] heard by the British Military Court at Essen, in which seven accused were jointly charged with committing a war crime on the basis that they were, with other persons, concerned in the killing of three unidentified British prisoners, was a major focus of the *Tadić* JCE decision. It is sufficient to note that it demonstrates the practice of bringing broad charges under the phrase 'concern in killings' to include (particularly in the context of a lynching) those who gave orders, incited the crowd, gave blows, and inflicted ill-treatment, though it was not known precisely which blows caused the deaths. Aside from the context of a lynching, the case reflects the approach taken in contemporaneous cases of individualizing guilt so that, for example, the accused Heyer, who did not himself take any physical action against the prisoners, received a sentence of death in respect of incitement ('words that kill' making him more responsible than anyone else concerned).[110] The guard, Koenen, was sentenced to five years' imprisonment in respect of his omission (failing to secure the safety of the prisoners) which,

[107] *Max Wielen and seventeen others* (*Stalag Luft III case*), British Military Court, Hamburg, Germany, 1 July–3 September 1947 (Case No 62), published in United Nations War Crimes Commission, *Law Reports of Trials of War Criminals* vol XI (HMSO 1949) 31, 46. A broad conspiracy was also alleged and incorporated into a charge of 'being concerned together and with others in killings' of 50 Royal Air Force Officers. The case-note observes that the Court apparently found insufficient evidence that all accused knew what had been planned at a higher level or what was happening outside their region and consequently they could not be found to have been together concerned in all 50 of the killings as charged.

[108] *Werner Rohde and eight others* (1946) in United Nations War Crimes Commission, *Law Reports of Trials of War Criminals* vol V (HMSO 1948) 54, 56.

[109] *Essen Lynching case* (n 14).

[110] *Essen Lynching case* (n 14) 89.

consistent with the trend in the Hong Kong cases, such as *Sato*, was seen to be less grave than taking an active part.[111]

The Hong Kong cases mainly addressed 'concern in ill-treatment' sometimes resulting in deaths, as opposed to 'concern in killings'. This may explain the more cautious use of notions analogous to joint enterprise which were more prominent historically in murder cases. The military courts in Hong Kong also exercised restraint in the use of Regulation 8(ii) despite the evidence of concerted action in terms of a system of ill-treatment in cases such as *Kinoshita*, *Shibata*, and *Tokunaga*. The *Kishi* case, which included a charge of being together concerned in killings among other acts, was one case in which the Prosecutor did attempt to put Regulation 8(ii) forward, apparently without success.

Regulation 8(ii) was invoked more actively in the parallel proceedings.[112] The *Killinger* case, which presented a factual scenario similar to the Hong Kong prison camp cases, was heard by the British Military Court at Wuppertal and concerned five former officers of the *Luftwaffe* who were charged with being together concerned as parties in the ill-treatment of British POWs.[113] The Prosecution quoted Regulation 8(ii) in connection with the phrasing of the charge and, when asked whether a commandant of POW camp who was ignorant of the ill-treatment of prisoners but negligent in the supervision of his subordinates would be a party to the ill-treatment on the basis of such negligence, responded that 'a man might be concerned as a party either through intention, where "malice—a designated plan" was present, or through [. . .] the type of recklessness and complete disregard of the situation necessary to prove a major crime such as manslaughter'.[114] The Defence argued that there was no Prosecution suggestion or evidence of a plan in the sense of a method of treatment. The Court, announcing its interpretation of the phrase 'were concerned together as parties to the ill-treatment of British prisoners of war', stated that negligence was insufficient to bring a person within the category of a party as defined in the particulars of the charge. The word 'parties' meant that some degree of knowledge was required together with deliberately refraining from stopping such practice, at least as a principal in the second degree or aider and abettor as these terms were used in the criminal law of England.[115] The Prosecution in its Closing Address returned to Regulation 8(ii), and attempted to demonstrate its relevance by asserting that each accused was concerned, in his respective capacity on the staff of Dulag Luft, as a party to the ill-treatment of POWs, and concerned with sufficient proximity to make him criminally responsible on the ordinary standards of criminal responsibility in English law. The only difference between these ordinary standards and the law to be applied in the trial lay in Regulation 8(ii)

[111] *Essen Lynching case* (n 14) 90.

[112] Contrast with cases alleging a common design or conspiracy in more direct terms rather than through the medium of a charge of 'being concerned in', such as *Josef Alstötter and others* (*Justice trial*) (1947) in United Nations War Crimes Commission, *Law Reports of Trials of War Criminals* vol VI (HMSO 1948) 1.

[113] *Erich Killinger and four others (Killinger case)* in United Nations War Crimes Commission, *Law Reports of Trials of War Criminals* vol III (1948) 67.

[114] *Killinger case* (n 113) 69. [115] *Killinger case* (n 113) 69.

and that the evidence regarding one accused might be treated as evidence against another.[116] The case-note points out, however, that the Court was careful to explain the charge exclusively in terms of the law relating to parties to a crime (specifically aiders and abettors) without reference to Regulation 8(ii). 'It therefore remains possible to assume that a prior conspiracy to commit a war crime must be proved before Regulation 8(ii) can become effective, and that it is not enough to show that certain accused acted as aiders and abettors.'[117] Similar to the Hong Kong cases, the emphasis was on the traditional (English law) understanding of principals and accessories, and the suggestion is that Regulation 8(ii) was inadequately presented by the Prosecution and of little assistance to the judges.

An interpretation of Regulation 8(ii) as requiring proof of a prior conspiracy was put forward in the *Belsen* case, which addressed the question of joint responsibility in the context of Bergen-Belsen and Auschwitz concentration camps. The charges used the phrase 'together concerned as parties to' in alleging ill-treatment against members of the camp staff resulting in deaths and physical suffering. The Prosecutor claimed that all the accused were parties to a general conspiracy (also described as 'concerted action', 'joint action', or 'unit'). It was argued that anyone who was 'one of a body of people who were habitually ill-treating the persons under their care' and who 'took an active part, however small, in the conspiracy' would be guilty as parties to the whole offence, irrespective of the significance of their participation.[118]

According to the Judge Advocate:

> The case for the Prosecution was that all the accused employed on the staff at Auschwitz knew that a system and a course of conduct was in force, and that, in one way or another in furtherance of a common agreement to run the camp in a brutal way, all those people were taking part in that course of conduct. They asked the Court not to treat the individual acts which might be proved merely as offences committed by themselves, but also as evidence clearly indicating that the particular offender was acting willingly as a party in the furtherance of this system. They suggested that if the Court were satisfied that they were doing so, then they must, each and every one of them, assume responsibility for what happened.[119]

The case-note on the *Belsen* trial clarifies that Regulation 8(ii) was relevant primarily for the purpose of assessing evidence and not as a provision relating to substantive law. This was so, despite both parties agreeing that before Regulation 8(ii) could operate against an accused, it must be proved that he knowingly took part in a common plan to ill-treat the POWs in the camps. It appeared impossible to state whether and how far the Court acted on Regulation 8(ii) in convicting the various accused.[120] The responsibility of each member of the unit or group still had to be proved, even where Regulation 8(ii) was applicable. The case appears to go further than the Hong Kong POW camp cases, however, in emphasizing the systematic

[116] *Killinger case* (n 113), 69.
[117] *Killinger case* (n 113) 70.
[118] *Belsen case* (n 13) 108, 109.
[119] *Belsen case* (n 13) 120.
[120] *Belsen case* (n 13) 138–41.

nature of the acts and suggesting that all those who 'took part' would be guilty of the offence.

The notes appended to the *Franz Schonfeld* case offer three alternative bases for the ultimate decision to convict Rotschopf and three others, namely (i) that the three other accused were principals in the second degree in the murders committed by Rotschopf as principal in the first degree; (ii) that the three accused were acting in pursuance of a common plan to commit murder, and were therefore liable for the offence even though the actual killing was committed by Rotschopf; or (iii) that the rule of evidence set out in Regulation 8(ii) was applicable.[121] Regulation 8(ii) was said to require (a) 'evidence that a war crime was the result of *concerted action*', although the aim of such action need not be illegal nor need it be the commission of the offence which was in fact committed, and (b) that 'the war crime must have been in some way the *result* of such concerted action', though 'not necessarily the intended result'.[122] The notes explain the possible basis under Regulation 8(ii) as follows:

> In the present case, *(a)* it was shown that there had been a plan at the very least to make arrests, and *(b)* the killing was the result of such a plan, in the sense that had the raid never taken place the murder would not have been committed. The Court may therefore have taken the view that the evidence against Rotschopf could, under Regulation 8(ii), be taken as *prima facie* evidence against the other three who were found guilty, and that the evidence produced in defence of the three men was not strong enough to rebut the presumption that they too were responsible for the crime.[123]

This selection of cases heard by British military courts addressing the charge of 'being concerned in' killings or ill-treatment indicates that attempts by prosecutors to bring in the notion of conspiracy or a common plan, especially via Regulation 8(ii), were not always warmly embraced by the courts. As demonstrated by the *Franz Schonfeld* case, Regulation 8(ii) was viewed essentially as an evidentiary rule, distinct from the common law notion of common intent, although its use appeared dependent on prior proof of a common plan. Of the cases addressed here, *Ponzano* and *Schonfeld* were deemed in *Tadić* to support the first category of JCE, *Belsen* the second, and *Essen Lynching* the third. The cases confirm the broad scope of the charge of being concerned in crimes. Anyone who was 'part of the machine doing some duty' which had some real bearing on the crime or a 'cog in the wheel of events' was liable on this basis. There was little explanation of the precise *mens rea* and little preoccupation with the classification of principals and accomplices. What is clear is that the significance of the contribution found expression in sentencing with military superiors suffering harsher penalties than the 'small cog in the machine of destruction'.[124]

[121] *Schonfeld case* (n 104) 71.

[122] *Schonfeld case* (n 104) (emphasis in original).

[123] *Schonfeld case* (n 104).

[124] *Robert Mulka* (*Auschwitz trial*) 1965, cited in H Friedlander, 'Nazi Crimes and the German Law', in N Stoltfus and H Friedlander (eds), *Nazi Crimes and the Law* (Cambridge University Press 2008) 15, 31.

### 3.5. Being 'concerned' in crimes as embryonic joint criminal enterprise.

It has emerged that a charge of 'being concerned', or 'together concerned in', killing or ill-treatment is not, per se, embryonic JCE. In its submissions before the ECCC, the Prosecution footnoted a number of post-Second World War cases additional to those cited in *Tadić* that purportedly applied the common plan concept, including cases from German courts applying Control Council Law No 10.[125] These cases were neither presented fully by the Prosecution nor analysed by the Pre-Trial Chamber. The list included cases such as *Killinger*, *Rohde*, and *Wielen* which can only at a stretch be described as JCE cases.

However, when the 'baby JCE was born'[126] in *Tadić*, it was not born of nothing. The charges in the Hong Kong cases were broad enough to encompass a common intent doctrine, whether understood in common law terms or read into Regulation 8(ii) and, outside the Hong Kong context, some convictions were based on such a doctrine although its parameters were ill-defined. Most importantly, and as reflected in the sometimes harsh penalties, the charge of 'being concerned in' achieved a similar goal to JCE in allowing military superiors to be held responsible as principals alongside or even separately from physical perpetrators.

In *Tadić* itself it was recognized that in many post-Second World War trials in different countries, courts 'did not rely upon the notion of common purpose or common design, preferring to refer instead to the notion of co-perpetration',[127] in connection with crimes in which two or more persons participated with different degrees of involvement. The ECCC Pre-Trial Chamber noted that the first and second categories of JCE resembled the traditional civil law notion of co-perpetration recognized in the applicable *Cambodian Penal Code*, but distinguished this notion from JCE, finding that both co-perpetration and JCE constituted forms of 'committing' a crime and were potentially applicable before the ECCC.[128] Nevertheless, the *Ieng Sary* decision reads as a check on whether *Tadić* was correctly decided, albeit without delving into the relationship between JCE and co-perpetration in any detail.

The ICC has indicated a preference for co-perpetration over what has come to be its competitor, JCE, as a means of including within the notion of principals, as opposed to accessories, 'those who, in spite of being removed from the scene of the crime, control or mastermind its commission because they decide whether and how

[125] Co-Prosecutors' Supplementary Observations on Joint Criminal Enterprise, 002/19-09-2007-ECCC/OCIJ (31 December 2008) para 19, fn 47–48.

[126] W Schomburg, 'Jurisprudence on JCE—Revisiting a Never Ending Story', *Cambodia Tribunal Monitor*, 3 June 2010, at <http://www.cambodiatribunal.org/blog/2010/06/jurisprudence-jce%E2%80%94revisiting-never-ending-story> accessed 16 January 2013 ('Schomburg, "Jurisprudence on JCE"').

[127] *Tadić JCE decision* (n 2) para 201.

[128] *Ieng Sary JCE decision* (n 2) para 102.

the offence will be committed'.[129] In the *Lubanga* case, the Pre-Trial Chamber, interpreting Article 25(3)(a) of the Rome Statute, took the view that the concept of co-perpetration was based on 'the idea that when the sum of the coordinated individual contributions of a plurality of persons results in the realisation of all the objective elements of a crime, any person making a contribution can be held vicariously responsible for the contributions of all the others and, as a result, can be considered as a principal to the whole crime'.[130] The Chamber rejected both an objective focus, whereby the distinction between principals and accessories is based on the level of contribution viewed in terms of the objective elements of the crime, and a subjective focus, whereby this distinction is based on the state of mind in which the contribution to the crime was made.[131] The concept of co-perpetration based on joint control over the crime was said to be:

> rooted in the principle of the division of essential tasks for the purpose of committing a crime between two or more persons acting in a concerted manner. Hence, although none of the participants has overall control over the offence because they all depend on one another for its commission, they all share control because each of them could frustrate the commission of the crime by not carrying out his or her task.[132]

The ICTY Appeals Chamber in *Stakić* apparently thought a choice had to be made between JCE and co-perpetration, finding that co-perpetration as defined by the Trial Chamber in that case 'does not have support in customary international law or in the settled jurisprudence of this Tribunal'.[133] The ICC has been less concerned with custom, preferring to rely on general principles and legal theory while stressing that the Statute is the primary source of law.[134]

JCE is undoubtedly a 'unique concept' combining features from different legal traditions and being applied and shaped by actors from various legal back-

[129] *The Prosecutor v Thomas Lubanga Dyilo* (Decision on the Confirmation of the Charges) ICC-01/04-01/06 (29 January 2007) ('*Lubanga*, Decision on Confirmation of Charges'), para 330. See also, discussion in *The Prosecutor v Thomas Lubanga Dyilo* (Judgment Pursuant to Article 74 of the Statute) ICC-01/04-01/06 (14 March 2012) paras 917–1018.

[130] *Lubanga*, Decision on Confirmation of Charges (n 129) para 326. The notion of common purpose as a type of accessorial liability is included in Article 25(3)(d) of the Rome Statute.

[131] *Lubanga*, Decision on Confirmation of Charges (n 129) para 329.

[132] *Lubanga*, Decision on Confirmation of Charges (n 129) para 342. See further, para(s) 343–5 and 349–67 for the objective and subjective elements.

[133] *Prosecutor v Stakić* (Appeal Judgment) IT-97-24-A (22 March 2006) para 62.

[134] The Defence argued that the Prosecutor's theory was not supported by customary international law or by general principles of law but the Pre-Trial Chamber did not conduct an analysis similar to the one in the *Tadić JCE decision* (n 2), being content to conclude that concept of control over the crime is 'applied in numerous legal systems' (*Lubanga*, Decision on Confirmation of Charges (n 129) para 330). Similarly in *Katanga*, the Defence argued that the concept of co-perpetration as defined in *Lubanga* was not supported by customary international law. However, the Pre-Trial Chamber concluded, citing various sources, that '[t]he control over the crime approach has been applied in a number of legal systems, and is widely recognized in legal doctrine'. *The Prosecutor v Germain Katanga and Mathieu Ngudjolo Chui* (Decision on the Confirmation of the Charges) ICC-01/04-01/07 (30 September 2008) ('*Katanga and Chui*, Decision on the Confirmation of the Charges'), para 485, fn 647. The Chamber said later in its decision, 'the question whether customary law admits or discards "the joint commission through another person" is not relevant for this court' (para 508).

grounds.[135] Like JCE, the concept of co-perpetration as construed by the ICC addresses situations which 'almost inevitably concern collective or mass criminality'.[136] The translation of co-perpetratorship into JCE by the Appeals Chamber in *Stakić* suggests that in most cases either mode of liability is capable of leading to the same result, namely linking the moral gravity of the accused's involvement in crimes with the appropriate degree of responsibility.

The Hong Kong cases do not reveal a subjective focus on the state of mind in which the contribution to the crime was made, being more interested in the division of actual contributory tasks. At the same time, a requirement of control over the crime does not appear to be envisaged as 'taking part in' or performing an act that has a real bearing on the crime is not equivalent to taking on an essential task. Notably, the Judge Advocate in the *Ponzano* case, considering the question of causation, rejected the idea that an accused would not be concerned in a crime if the crime would have been carried out even without his participation.[137] While the Hong Kong cases do not align themselves strictly with either a JCE or co-perpetration theory, the influence of English law is clearly predominant.

## 4. Conclusion

It has been remarked in relation to English law that '[i]f prizes were awarded for the most convoluted and opaque branch of the criminal law then joint enterprise principles would be a strong contender for first place'.[138] Difficulties arise precisely in third category JCE-type cases involving the commission of a 'collateral' offence that falls outside the common purpose, where 'substantial uncertainty still exists over the definition of *mens rea* required to secure a conviction' for that offence.[139]

In *Tadić*, reference is made to case law reflecting 'customary rules of international *criminal* law'.[140] The nature of the relevant case law was also seen to be significant by the ECCC Pre-Trial Chamber, in that it reflected an authoritative interpretation of the military courts' own constitutive instruments which themselves reflected customary law, and could therefore be relied upon to determine the state of customary international law with respect to the existence of JCE as a mode of liability.[141] Notably the same two cases—*Essen Lynching* and *Borkum Island*—are persistently presented in support of the third category of JCE.[142] Even assuming they provided unambiguous support for the third category, and even

[135] *Ieng Sary JCE Decision* (n 2) para 40.

[136] *Katanga and Chui*, Decision on the Confirmation of the Charges (n 134) para 501.

[137] *Feurstein and others (Ponzano case)* (n 12) 239–40.

[138] Reed and Fitzpatrick, *Criminal Law* (n 43) 148.

[139] Reed and Fitzpatrick, *Criminal Law* (n 43) 128.

[140] *Tadić JCE decision* (n 2) para 226 (emphasis added).

[141] *Ieng Sary JCE decision* (n 2) para 60, citing *Prosecutor v Kupreškić*, Case No IT-95-16-T, Judgment, 14 January 2000, paras 540–1.

[142] See also R C Clarke, 'Return to Borkum Island, Extended Joint Criminal Enterprise Responsibility in the Wake of World War II' (2011) 9 JICJ 839–61, discussing American and Australian post-Second World War trials which provide some further, limited support for third category JCE.

accepting the species of custom labelled customary international *criminal* law, the third category of JCE appears to be a common law-inspired progressive development first explicitly asserted in *Tadić*. That it has not yet fully developed is evident in the uncertainty over its applicability to specific intent crimes. The ICTY allows convictions under the third category of JCE for crimes such as genocide, while the STL doubts this approach and excludes the possibility for the crime of terrorism.[143] The argument that in most cases the evidence will show that the specific intent crime became part of the enterprise so as to allow a conviction under the first category of JCE does not resolve the theoretical conundrum.

The STL Appeals Chamber has admitted that the third category of JCE 'is founded on considerations of public policy'.[144] Lord Hutton was of the opinion in the leading English case of *Powell* that there is 'an argument of considerable force that the secondary party who takes part in a criminal enterprise [. . .] with foresight that a deadly weapon may be used, should not escape liability for murder because he, unlike the principal party, is not suddenly confronted by the security officer so that he has to decide whether to use the gun or knife or have the enterprise thwarted and face arrest'.[145] Also touching on public policy considerations, Lord Steyn noted: 'Experience has shown that joint criminal enterprises only too readily escalate into the commission of greater offences. In order to deal with this important social problem the accessory principle is needed and cannot be abolished or relaxed.'[146] Applying the arguments raised in *Powell* by analogy, it may be asked whether it should be possible for senior leaders to hide behind commanders making decisions on the ground where the criminal extent of those decisions is foreseeable and willingly accepted. In situations where acts on the ground escalate from ethnic cleansing to genocide, for example, should the decision makers be permitted to escape liability for genocide where it is foreseeable and acceptable to them that the hatred they inspire will be translated into a specific intent to eradicate a group?

These may be important policy questions but they should not serve to undermine the principle of legality which has been held up as a torch in post-Nuremberg processes. Moreover, it is difficult to see how a mode of liability whose equivalent at common law is multi-faceted and in a state of flux can have been accessible and foreseeable to perpetrators pre-*Tadić*. The Hong Kong cases do nothing to make third category JCE more accessible. The charge of 'being concerned in' crime is certainly broad and itself embodies considerations of public policy in that all those who 'take part in' and incur culpability for international crimes are considered to be punishable. The Hong Kong courts may have applied modes of liability more familiar to the victors than the accused, but were careful not to stretch domestic law principles too far.

While the ICTY (and in turn the ICTR and SCSL) has taken a definite stance in favour of all three categories of JCE, the ECCC has the possibility to consider JCE

143 STL, Interlocutory Decision on the Applicable Law (n 28) para 249.
144 STL, Interlocutory Decision on the Applicable Law (n 28) para 245.
145 *R v Powell; R v English* [1997] 4 All ER 545, 562 (Lord Hutton).
146 *R v Powell; R v English* (n 145) 551 (Lord Steyn).

and co-perpetration in tandem. The Civil Parties had appealed the part of the Co-Investigating Judges' original order on JCE that referred to autonomous liability regimes for domestic and international crimes meaning that JCE was only applicable to international crimes. However, the Pre-Trial Chamber found that the arguments on appeal failed to demonstrate an error.[147] If JCE is considered to apply only to international crimes while co-perpetration applies to the domestic crimes under Cambodian law, the two modes of liability could potentially stand face-to-face in the same case. The ECCC should seize the opportunity to answer the Prosecutor's assertion that JCE, specifically, is necessary to hold responsible those who create and oversee the implementation of criminal policies.

Judge Mohamed Shahabuddeen, one of the ICTY Appeals Chamber judges in *Tadić*, has written that as an exercise in judicial creativity he prefers JCE over co-perpetration, considering that one or the other theory is needed if the ICTY is to fulfil its mission of administering international criminal justice.[148] He notes that, unlike co-perpetration which 'restricts criminal liability to cases in which there was control', JCE 'does not know of that limitation and accordingly provides room for growth'.[149] The prospect of growth or the capability of 'indefinite extension'[150] is precisely what concerns critics of the JCE concept and tests the principle of legality. Judge Wolfgang Schomburg prefers co-perpetration, describing JCE as an unnecessary and even dangerous invention.[151] The Hong Kong cases are essentially neutral in this debate but by virtue of their neutrality at least hint at the correctness of the reappraisal in *Ieng Sary*. Caution is warranted, as it can be no answer to say:

> You can try to think only with all your heart, Hara-san, that unfair and unjust as this thing which my people are doing seems to you, that it is done only to try and stop the kind of things that happened between us in the war from ever happening again.[152]

[147] *Ieng Sary JCE decision* (n 2) para(s) 98–102.

[148] Schomburg, 'Jurisprudence on JCE' (n 126) 2–3.

[149] M Shahabuddeen, 'Judicial Creativity and Joint Criminal Enterprise', in S Darcy and J Powderly (eds), *Judicial Creativity at the International Criminal Tribunals* (OUP 2010) 184, 200.

[150] In relation to the early notion of conspiracy, it has been said that '[t]he doctrine was expressed so widely or loosely, that it became in course of time a head of law of great importance, and capable of almost indefinite extension'. Sir J F Stephen, *A History of the Criminal Law of England: Volume II* (Macmillan 1883) 229.

[151] Schomburg, 'Jurisprudence on JCE' (n 126) 2.

[152] Van Der Post, *A Bar of Shadow* (n 1) 56.

# 6

# The Plea of Superior Orders in the Hong Kong Trials

*Bing Bing Jia*

## 1. Introduction

The plea of superior orders, though well-known to present-day international law,[1] may not, as yet, be free of the controversy that has existed since the beginning of its life as a feature of international criminal law. The point of dispute lies in its categorization either as a mitigating factor in sentencing or as a defence excluding criminal responsibility. In a sense, the two differing functions of the plea can both stake a claim to reflect customary law, as chiefly derived from the post-World War II military trials. It will, however, be clear from the present discussion that the law at the time of the Hong Kong trials admitted of only one version of it, even though various tribunals had ventured to suggest alternatives in the light of the factual circumstances of the cases before them. However, it is not thought that that version of plea was the only one that found expression in subsequent practice; in fact, another version of the plea, mainly developed through judicial decisions since 1945, has seen a revival in contemporary international law, to the extent that it has been consummated in the Rome Statute of the International Criminal Court ('Rome Statute').[2] In those trials, as in today's criminal proceedings involving international crimes, it may also happen that the plea is initially raised as a defence, but later transforms to a mitigating factor. The spectrum of the appeals to the plea displays a variety that turns on the circumstances of each case in which it has been pleaded.

On a doctrinal level, the plea may also be considered from the angle of either a justification or that of an excuse, but this differentiation is not central to this

[1] This has much to do with the frequency with which the plea was used in the military trials conducted after the Second World War: see the many cases in the *Law Reports of Trials of War Criminals* selected and prepared by the United Nations War Crimes Commission over the period 1947–1949 ('*Law Reports of Trials of War Criminals*'), notably vol XV (1949).

[2] Rome Statute of the International Criminal Court, UN Doc A/CONF.183/9 (as corrected by the procès-verbaux of 10 November 1998, 12 July 1999, 30 November 1999, 8 May 2000, 17 January 2001, and 16 January 2002) art 33.

chapter.[3] The development of the plea to this level of sophistication—despite the point of dispute mentioned previously—has by no means been a smooth process; on the contrary, it has encountered unceasing challenges, due mainly to a somewhat abrupt change of rule regarding the effect of the plea in the course of World War II.[4] At the time, the change gave rise to questions regarding *ex post facto* law, but the rule that action taken in accordance with a superior order was not a defence was held to be 'a rule of a fundamental criminal justice that has been adopted by civilized nations extensively'.[5] It further led to argumentation in court proceedings over the link between this plea and that of duress. But the primary contention that survived the trials remains that of its nature as either a defence or an attenuating factor in sentencing.[6] In the extreme conditions of a total war, with many countries involved to varying degrees in violation of the laws and customs of war, could international law still expect a soldier, being a member of a gigantic machine of armed forces—often numbering millions at the height of a world war—to retain his own judgment as to the legality or otherwise of an order that commanded him to kill prisoners of war ('POWs') or civilian detainees, or other orders of lesser hue of unlawfulness? Law sets standards such that the ordinary citizen can reasonably be expected to act in accordance with them. If some of the standards are in demand of considerable personal sacrifice in the conditions of a war, they would demand a *moral* choice to be made by the person facing them on the spur of the moment. On that account, the International Military Tribunal at Nuremberg ('IMT Nuremberg') once reasonably asserted:

> That a soldier was ordered to kill or to torture in violation of the International Law of war has never been recognized as a defence to such acts of brutality, though, as the Charter here provides, the order may be urged in mitigation of the punishment. The true test, which is found in varying degrees in the criminal law of most nations, is not the existence of the order, but whether moral choice was in fact possible.[7]

[3] M Scaliotti, 'Defences before the International Criminal Court: Substantive grounds for excluding criminal responsibility-Part 1' (2001) 1 ICLR 111, 118. However, see K Ambos, 'Defences in International Criminal Law', in B Brown (ed), *Research Handbook on International Criminal Law* (Edward Elgar 2011) ('Ambos, "Defences in International Criminal Law"') 299, 300–1.

[4] It may be stressed that the change was confined to British and American military law. Nevertheless, it had already featured in German military law since 1882: L C Green, 'Superior Orders and Command Responsibility' (1989) 27 CYIL 167, 177. For the *Llandovery Castle* trial at Leipzig in 1921, see *Annual Digest of Public International Law Cases*, vol 2 (1923–1924) 436 (in which the 1882 German Military Penal Code was applied by the German Supreme Court).

[5] *In re List* (Hostages Trial) (1948) 15 (1948) *Annual Digest of Public International Law Cases* 632, 649–51 (the previous view that superior orders were a complete defence was deemed by the tribunal as 'a decidedly minority view'). Also see, G Schwarzenberger, *International Law as Applied by International Courts and Tribunals: the Law of Armed Conflict* vol ii (Stevens & Sons 1968) 516–17.

[6] War Department, *Field Manual 27–10, The Law of Land Warfare* (Department of the Army 1956) para 509. Even at the time of the post-World War II military trials, it may be noted, the applicable law was by no means uniform among the Allies, and Canada's relevant regulations are an example: L Green, *Superior Orders in National and International Law* (Sijthoff 1976) ('Green, *Superior Orders in National and International Law*') 184 (referring to the War Crimes Regulations 1945 and the War Crimes Act 1946).

[7] *International Military Tribunal (Nuremberg), Judgment and Sentences,* reproduced in 'Judicial Decisions' (1947) 41 AJIL 172 ('*IMT Nuremberg Judgment*') 221.

The statement shows that the plea of superior orders not only expects the recipient to perceive the brutality and illegality of certain action as ordered by his superiors, but often arises in circumstances which involve an element of compulsion. This gives rise to the question as to whether the plea itself should have a rather limited scope, in that it is one that solely concerns the question of orders and their effect upon the recipient, with no consideration for the element of compulsion. Otherwise, the plea of duress would be redundant. The Hong Kong trials, to be discussed later, tend to show that the plea in its pure form had little chance of success before a military court, but that it could have a marked effect of mitigation when accompanied by compulsion due to such factors as the well-organized disciplinary structure of an army of which the recipient is a member, training, cultural background, urgency of the situation, etc. Indeed, compulsion does not always come with a gunpoint or the edge of a sword. It is therefore necessary to distinguish compulsion caused by environment, habit, or external force that is imminently palpable or contained in threats.

The Hong Kong trials dealt with crimes committed within the jurisdiction of the Allied Land Forces South-East Asia Command ('ALFSEA') and they were conducted before British military courts convened by the Commander of Land Forces Hong Kong.[8] The review of the proceedings was provided under Regulation 10 of the 1945 Royal Warrant, with the Commander of Land Forces of Hong Kong given the power to confirm or not confirm any convictions and sentences.

These trials provide the background for this chapter, and the overall impression from reading the files of the cases is that the applicable law for the trials was well settled in the minds of the judges—who were usually British officers—admitting of few, if any, new interpretations that could vary the rule concerning the plea. On the other hand, decisions from the trials, being included in dossiers for review by higher military authorities, are not in the form of fully reasoned opinions, although they contain verdicts, sentences, and a summary of the proceedings of the trials. This renders difficult the analysis in this chapter of the impact of the plea of superior orders upon the trials. All cases referred to in the following pages bear that unfortunate mark. It is often impossible to know precisely the degree to which they relied on such rules.

Before the Hong Kong trials are examined, a word must be said of the applicable law for the trials conducted by the military courts in Hong Kong.

## 2. Superior Orders—The Applicable Law

### 2.1 The Royal Warrant of 1945

The main source of law for the British war crimes trials held immediately after World War II was the Royal Warrant dated 14 June and promulgated on 18 June

[8] Royal Warrant 0160/2498, 18 June 1945, promulgated by the War Office, Army Order 81 of 1945 ('Royal Warrant'). It allowed, by Regulation 5, the establishment of mixed inter-Allied military courts, but the courts so established remained 'a British municipal court': *Law Reports of Trials of War Criminals* (n 1) vol II 127. For more on this instrument, see section 2.1, later in the chapter.

1945 ('Royal Warrant'), and its annexed Regulations ('Regulations for the Trial of War Criminals annexed to Royal Warrant').[9] There is no need to recount the appropriateness of using a Royal Warrant, as distinct from a statute, to found the jurisdiction of British military courts in this regard.[10] The prerogative instrument, however, contained an important provision that 'the Court shall take judicial notice of the laws and usages of war'.[11] It signifies the fundamental importance of international law to those trials, as that law was effectively treated as part of British law. In the Royal Warrant, there was no reference to the plea of superior orders,[12] despite its pivotal role in war crimes trials.[13] The plea must therefore be considered as a matter of general international law, evidenced by the general practice of nations of the world. The source of that law, as understood and applied by British military courts, lay with the successive editions of the *Manual of Military Law* ('*Manual of Military Law*'), published by the British War Office. The *Manual*, especially the edition published in 1951, including amendments made during World War II, directly bears on an examination of the military trials held in Hong Kong. As will be shown later, the question as to what the *Manual of Military Law* sought to present—domestic practice or international law—was one of the issues for debate that occupied the House of Lords in a session in 1952.

Under the Royal Warrant, the rules of procedure were defined as those applicable in a Field General Court Martial of the British Army, where appropriate, and the rules of evidence were set forth partly in Regulation 8.[14] There was also a procedure for review of the proceedings, but no right of appeal. Regulation 10 provided:

> The accused may within 14 days of the termination of the Proceedings in Court submit a Petition to the Confirming Officer against the finding or sentence or both provided that he gives notice to the Confirming Officer within 48 hours of such termination of his intention to submit such a Petition. The accused shall have no right to submit any Petition otherwise than as aforesaid.
>
> Provided that if such Petition is against the finding it shall be referred by the Confirming Officer, together with the Proceedings of the trial, to His Majesty's Judge Advocate General or to any Deputy of his approved by him for that purpose in the Command overseas where the trial took place for advice and report.

[9] Regulations for the Trial of War Criminals annexed to Royal Warrant 1945 (UK) AO 81/1945 ('Regulations for the Trial of War Criminals annexed to Royal Warrant'). For the salient points of the regulations, see *Law Reports of Trials of War Criminals* (n 1) vol I 105–10.

[10] A P V Rogers, 'War Crimes Trials under the Royal Warrant: British Practice 1945–1949', (1990) 39 ICLQ 780 ('Rogers, "War Crimes Trials under the Royal Warrant: British Practice 1945–1949"') 788–9.

[11] Regulations for the Trial of War Criminals annexed to Royal Warrant (n 9), Regulation 8(iii).

[12] The lack of statutory reference to the plea in British law had been a fact until as late as the 1970s: Green, Superior Orders in National and International Law (n 6) 31.

[13] *Law Reports of Trials of War Criminals* (n 1) vol XV 157.

[14] Other rules were equally relevant: *Law Reports of Trials of War Criminals* (n 1) vol I 107–8.

It is noted that the Royal Warrant applied to the trials conducted under the aegis of ALFSEA, involving Japanese war crimes, and that it was for the Judge-Advocate General in Singapore to prepare the cases.[15]

## 2.2 Manual of Military Law

The version of the *Manual of Military Law* used in these trials was the 7th edition (1929), as amended ('*Manual of Military Law 1929 (as amended)*').[16] The manual was frequently referred to in the British war crimes trials as an embodiment of the relevant part of contemporary international law, and whether a British military court accepted or rejected the content of the *Manual of Military Law* would depend 'on its merits', in the sense that it stated, or failed to state, the law correctly. This view was typically set forth in the Judge Advocate's advice to the Court in the *Peleus* case.[17] In the same case, the Judge Advocate also advised that, where a statement in the *Manual of Military Law* was inconsistent with 'the view of most writers upon the subject and also with the decision of the German Supreme Court in the case of the Llandovery Castle', there was no obstacle, legal or otherwise, to correcting the mistake in the statement of law, and to proceeding on the basis of the law as thus elucidated.[18] In the instant case, the Judge Advocate accepted the law regarding superior orders as stated in Amendment No 34 of 1944 on superior orders, and he advised the Court on that basis. Here, a digression is necessary to recall the process whereby the amendment occurred and its repercussions.

The 1944 amendment on superior orders marked a drastic change in British military law with regard to the plea of superior orders, although its impact reached well beyond that law. Prior to that, the consistent position had been that soldiers were not to be held responsible for their acts done in the service of armed forces:

> It is important, however, to note that members of the armed forces who commit such violations of the recognised rules of warfare as are ordered by their Government or by their commander are not war criminals and cannot therefore be punished by the enemy. He may punish the officials or commanders responsible for such orders if they fall into his hands, but otherwise he may only resort to the other means of obtaining redress which are dealt with in this chapter.[19]

[15] See United Nations War Crimes Commission, *History of the United Nations War Crimes Commission and the Development of the Laws of War* (HMSO 1948) 381–2; *Law Reports of Trials of War Criminals* (n 1) vol XV 28–9.

[16] See Great Britain War Office, *Manual of Military Law 1929* (7th edn), as amended by Great Britain War Office, *Manual of Military Law 1929*, ch XIV (Amendment No 12 of 1936) and Great Britain War Office, *Manual of Military Law 1929*, ch XIV (Amendment No 34 of 1944) (collectively '*Manual of Military 1929 (as amended)*', the 1944 amendment is referred to as '*Amendment No 34 of 1944 on superior orders*').

[17] *Trial of Kapitenleutnant Heinz Eck and four others* (The Peleus Trial), *Law Reports of Trials of War Criminals* (n 1) vol I 19. This was the first British trial completed in the British Zone of Control in Germany on 20 October 1945: Rogers, 'War Crimes Trials under the Royal Warrant: British Practice 1945–1949' (n 10) 789, fn 51.

[18] *Law Reports of Trials of War Criminals* (n 1) vol I 19.

[19] *Amendment No 34 of 1944 on superior orders* (n 16).

Paragraph 443 of the *Manual of Military Law* in this form contained a nearly literal repetition of what was stated by Professors Oppenheim and Lauterpacht in the first five editions of *Oppenheim's International Law* treatise. However, Lauterpacht seemingly had a change of mind in this regard, when the sixth edition of the treatise came out in later 1944, following upon his article published in the *British Yearbook of International Law* in the same year.[20] In the sixth, revised edition of the treatise, he settled on the following view:

> ... subject to these qualification, the question is governed by the major principle that members of the armed forces are bound to obey lawful orders only and that they cannot therefore escape liability if, in obedience to a command, they commit acts which both violate unchallenged rules of warfare and outrage the general sentiment of humanity.[21]

This view was duly reflected in the eighth edition of the *Manual of Military Law*, published in 1951 ('*Manual of Military Law (8th ed)*'), which reflected the full body of rules that were applied by the British military courts since 1944.[22] In this edition, it was stated that:

> The better view appears to be, however, that an order to do or make an act or omission which is illegal, even if given by a duly constituted superior whom the recipient is bound to obey and whether the act or omission is manifestly illegal or not can never of itself excuse the recipient if he carries out the order although it may give rise to a defence on other grounds, e.g. by establishing a claim of right made in good faith in answer to a charge of larceny, or by negativing a particular intent which may be a complete defence or reduce the crime to one of a less serious nature, or by excusing what appears to be culpable negligence.[23]

In the chapter on the laws and usages of war on land, the *Manual of Military Law (8th ed)* further stated:

> The fact that a rule of warfare has been violated in pursuance of an order of the belligerent Government or of an individual belligerent commander does not deprive the act in question of its character as a war crime; neither does it, in principle, confer on the perpetrator immunity from punishment by the injured belligerent. Undoubtedly, a court confronted with the plea of superior orders adduced in justification of a war crime is bound to take in consideration the fact that obedience to military orders, not obviously unlawful, is the duty of every member of the armed forces and that he latter cannot, in conditions of war discipline, be expected to weigh scrupulously the legal merits of the order received.[24]

[20] H Lauterpacht, 'The Law of Nations and the Punishment of War Crimes' (1944) 21 BYIL 58. The background of the article was explained in United Nations War Crimes Commission, *History of the United Nations War Crimes Commission* (HMSO 1948) ('*History of the United Nations War Crimes Commission*') 275–7.

[21] L Oppenheim, *International Law* (6th edn, Longmans, Green and Co 1944) 453 s 253.

[22] Great Britain War Office, *Manual of Military Law*, part 1 1951 (HMSO 1952) ('*Manual of Military Law (8th ed)*').

[23] *Manual of Military Law (8th ed)* (n 22) ch v 116 para 23.

[24] *Manual of Military Law (8th ed)* (n 22) pt ii 1951, ch xiv para 433.

This amended paragraph 443, Chapter XIV, was issued in April 1944.[25] The amendment would eventually give rise to interesting debates in the House of Lords, to be dealt with shortly.

But before embarking on that, two comments are made of the statements quoted earlier from the *Manual of Military Law (8th ed)*. First, the approach of the first statement, from paragraph 23, seems to suggest that the plea of superior orders could give rise to a proper defence, if it is part of the circumstances in which the alleged crime and the plea were concerned. Secondly, according to paragraph 443, the lawfulness *vel non* of the order in question is to be the test against which the recipient's responsibility is to be assessed. This reading is strengthened by the remainder of paragraph 443, which repeats the passage quoted earlier from the sixth edition of *Oppenheim's International Law*, setting forth the 'major principle' emphasized by Professor Lauterpacht in the treatise.

In 1951, the proposed revision of the *Manual of Military Law*, in light of Amendment No 34 of 1944 on superior orders, was subject to a motion in the House of Lords that it be reviewed by persons of suitable authority and experience of military command. This was tabled by some of the Lords who had had military experiences or simply had sympathies towards the servicemen and women in the British Armed Forces. The concerns were expressed especially on the rationale for the change wrought in the law existing up to 1944 and, if the change were to be effected nevertheless, on the clarity of the changed law.[26] While some serious doubts were reserved for Professor Lauterpacht, the author of the Amendment in question, with regard to his suitability to write the new law in the *Manual of Military Law*,[27] there were voices calling for mitigation on the basis of the function of a text writer in stating the law as it is, not what it ought to be.[28]

In addition, the debates in the House also showed some interesting points in respect of the effect of superior orders upon the servicemen, past or present. First, it was suggested that, in a battle area of any kind, 'the duty of every man is to carry out his orders as efficiently as he can both mentally and physically'.[29] To allow doubt to arise in his mind from fear for the possibility of war crime charges in future, after the change in the military law on superior orders, would undermine the morale of the soldier, his peers and officers alike, who would be uncertain as to the expectations of orders passed down a command chain. Secondly, it was pointed out that Amendment No 34 of 1944 on superior orders did not refer to military necessity, besides war crimes prohibited by international law.[30] The point sought to be argued was that, at the time, participation in a war crime was considered by

[25] *Amendment No 34 of 1944 on superior orders* (n 16). Also see HL Deb 14 May 1952, vol 176, col 956 (Earl of Cork and Orrery).

[26] HL Deb 14 May 1952, vol 176, cols 959–60.

[27] HL Deb 14 May 1952, vol 176, col 962. Similarly, cols 985–986 (Lord Hankey (sometime Secretary of the Imperial War Cabinet)).

[28] HL Deb 14 May 1952, vol 176, col 970 (Earl Jowitt (sometime Lord Chancellor)).

[29] HL Deb 14 May 1952, vol 176, col 961.

[30] HL Deb 14 May 1952, vol 176, col 964 (Lord Wilson), speaking from the Army's point of view.

many as a crime against humanity.[31] That point obviously would become difficult in its application when the recipient of an order, being a low-ranking officer or soldier, might need to Judge the validity and force of an order based in military necessity, which only required the person issuing the order to be well-informed of the reasons behind it. This delay on the part of the recipient of the order was not supposed to happen in a well-organized army, as the general presumption was that the commander took action which he himself deemed to be 'reasonable for the safety or security of his command'.[32] Thirdly, the *Manual of Military Law* was perceived, rightly or wrongly, as a textbook, and 'it has no authority'.[33] The new version in question actually *reflected* what British law always upheld in respect of the plea of superior orders.[34] This view was further explained by another Law Lord, who stated that the *Manual of Military Law* had the same measure of authority as established textbooks in the British legal system, that it was seen overseas as a statute, and that, at military trials conducted under the Royal Warrant of 1945, no alternative statement of military law existed to guide the courts.[35] More support came from yet another former Lord Chancellor, who considered that the previous editions of the *Manual of Military Law* did not reflect the correct law on this matter, thus creating the issues for the debate.[36] Fourthly, an interesting point was broached several times during the debate about the legality of an order for reprisal, the action ordered under which, but for the order, would otherwise be illegal under the law of war and customs.[37] The point was not that superior orders of this type might not be manifestly unlawful, but that it would be very difficult for the addressee, often a low-ranking officer or a soldier, to know that the orders were for the sole purpose of reprisal, thus being completely beyond reproach. Fifthly, some language in connection with Amendment No 34 of 1944 on superior orders, such as 'general sentiment of humanity', used in *Oppenheim's International Law*, 6th edition, was obviously conducive to confusion if used as a standard to assess the legality *vel non* of a certain order.[38] Lastly, it was forcefully pointed out that the *Manual of Military Law*'s new version could not simply change again due to the concerns aired during the debate, and that it was supposed to be a 'true interpretation of international law'.[39] In other words, 'it must be in the stream of jurisprudence which affects all armies and all peoples'.[40] It is to international law that our attention must turn next.

[31] HL Deb 14 May 1952, vol 176, col 964.

[32] HL Deb 14 May 1952, vol 176, col 964.

[33] HL Deb 14 May 1952, vol 176, col 970 (Earl Jowitt).

[34] HL Deb 14 May 1952, vol 176, col 971.

[35] HL Deb 14 May 1952, vol 176, col 974 per (Viscount Maugham (sometime Lord Chancellor)). There was a time when officers had to be examined on it: cols 980–1(Lord Hankey).

[36] HL Deb 14 May 1952, vol 176, col 1004 (Viscount Simon—he was probably correct in saying so, considering what Stephen said in 1883). See Y Dinstein, *The Defence of Obedience to Superior Orders in International Law* (Sijthoff 1965) ('Dinstein, *The Defence of Obedience to Superior Orders in International Law*').

[37] HL Deb 14 May 1952, vol 176, col 988 (Earl Wavell (a former Army officer)).

[38] HL Deb 14 May 1952, vol 176, col 994 (Lord Winster).

[39] HL Deb 14 May 1952, vol 176, col 1008 (Lord Ogmore).

[40] HL Deb 14 May 1952, vol 176, col 1011 (Lord Ogmore).

## 2.3 Customary international law

The question after the preceding discussion would be with 'the laws and usages of war', of which judicial notice should be taken by the British military courts convened at the time of the Hong Kong trials, in accordance with the 1945 Royal Warrant. It is not likely that they applied the *Manual of Military Law* literally, which had no legal force per se.[41] But the manual's statement of the international law of superior orders has not been found by British military courts, Judge Advocates, or even Defence Counsel, to be so incorrect as to justify a deviation from it.[42] As the chapter by Linton in this collection shows, the parties relied on the *Manual of Military Law* as a direct source of law, contrary to the view expressed in the *Peleus* trial. In fact, the new paragraph 443, changed through Amendment No 34 of 1944, was directly cited in numerous cases. The laws and usages of war at the time were reflected to a considerable extent by the Charter of the International Military Tribunal at Nuremberg ('Nuremberg Charter'),[43] and other instruments relevant to war crime trials. To be precise, the development of the international law of war already took place with the adoption of the IV Hague Convention in 1907[44], and the Nuremberg Charter reflected customary law as of 1939, which in turn reflected the rules of the 1907 convention.[45] The instruments, starting with the Nuremberg Charter, invariably contain a rule on superior orders. Under the Nuremberg Charter, Article 8 provides:

> The fact that the Defendant acted pursuant to order of his Government or of a superior shall not free him from responsibility, but may be considered in mitigation of punishment if the Tribunal determines that justice so requires.[46]

With slight changes, the rule appeared in Control Council Law No 10:

> The fact that any person acted pursuant to the order of his Government or of a superior does not free him from responsibility for a crime, but may be considered in mitigation.[47]

In the Charter of the International Military Tribunal for the Far East, Article VI provided,

[41] *Law Reports of Trials of War Criminals* (n 1) vol I 19.

[42] *Law Reports of Trials of War Criminals* (n 1). Also see *Trial of Max Wielen et al* (the *Stalag Luft III case*), *Law Reports of Trials of War Criminals* (n 1) vol XI 46–7.

[43] *IMT Nuremberg Judgment* (n 7) 248.

[44] Hague Convention (IV) respecting the Laws and Customs of War on Land and its Annex: Regulations concerning the Laws and Customs of War on Land, opened for signature 18 October 1907, (1910) UKTS 9 (entered into force 26 January 1910).

[45] *IMT Nuremberg Judgment* (n 7) 248–9.

[46] Charter of the International Military Tribunal, attached to the Agreement by the US, France, UK and USSR for the Prosecution and Punishment of the Major War Criminals of the European Axis, 8 August 1945 in L Friedman (ed), *The Law of War: A Documentary History,* vol 1 (Random House 1972) ('Friedman, *The Law of War*') 883, 887.

[47] Friedman, *The Law of War* (n 46) 908. Control Council Law No 10, Punishment of Persons Guilty of War Crimes, Crimes against Peace and against Humanity, 3 *Official Gazette Control Council for Germany* 50–5 (1946), 20 December 1945, art II(4)(b).

> Neither the official position, at any time, of an accused, nor the fact that an accused acted pursuant to order of his government or of a superior shall, of itself, be sufficient to free such accused from responsibility for any crime with which he is charged, but such circumstances may be considered in mitigation of punishment if the Tribunal determines that justice so requires.[48]

The principle, as so provided by these important instruments, was reaffirmed in the *Principles of International Law Recognized in the Charter of the Nürnberg Tribunal and in the Judgment of the Tribunal.*[49] On 11 December 1946, the United Nations General Assembly ('UNGA') adopted resolution 95(I) to affirm the principles of international law recognized by the Nuremberg Charter and the *IMT Nuremberg Judgment*. By resolution 177 (II) of 21 November 1947, the UNGA, having established the International Law Commission (ILC) by resolution 174 (II) of the same date, requested the ILC to formulate the principles and to start work on a Draft Code on Offences against the Peace and Security of Mankind. At its second session held in 1950, the aforementioned principles were adopted by the ILC. Principle IV provided that the fact that a person acted pursuant to orders of his Government or of a superior does not relieve him from responsibility under international law, provided a moral choice was in fact possible to him. The report containing the principles was submitted to the UNGA in 1950. The principles were examined by the Sixth Committee of the UNGA, but there was a division of opinions.[50] The divide ran so sharp that the UNGA did not reaffirm the principles as formulated, but invited governments of the member states to furnish their observations thereon.[51] The formulation of the principles was based on a thorough consideration of the Nuremberg process, and the failure of the UNGA to reaffirm those principles could only mean that the law from Nuremberg was no longer dominant in state practice in this field. It may be said that Principle IV in fact highlighted another reading of Article 8 of the Nuremberg Charter, given by the *IMT Nuremberg Judgment*.

It may be recalled that in the *IMT Nuremberg Judgment*, the tribunal held that the denial of superior orders as a defence was in conformity with 'the law of all nations'.[52] In addition, it pointed out that many of the accused had made 'a mockery of the soldier's oath of obedience to military orders', using it to their advantage as a defence in contrasting situations.[53] Where the alleged crimes 'had been committed consciously, ruthlessly, and without military excuse or justification', the plea was rejected by the IMT even as a mitigating factor.[54] However, the

[48] Charter of the International Military Tribunal for the Far East, TIAS No 1589 at 3, 4 Bevans 20, 19 January 1946, amended 26 April 1946.

[49] Report of the International Law Commission, covering the work of its Second Session, *Yearbook of the International Law Commission* 1950, vol II, UN Doc A/1316, 363, 374.

[50] Dinstein, *The Defence of Obedience to Superior Orders in International Law* (n 36) 238.

[51] Formulation of the Nurnberg Principles, UN Doc A/RES/488 (V), 12 December 1950.

[52] *IMT Nuremberg Judgment* (n 7) 221.

[53] *IMT Nuremberg Judgment* (n 7) 271–2.

[54] *IMT Nuremberg Judgment* (n 7) 283.

IMT did not completely close the door to the plea being invoked as a defence, where a moral choice became impossible.[55]

The International Military Tribunal for the Far East followed the conclusions of the *IMT Nuremberg Judgment* in this regard.[56]

Without repeating the volumes of war crimes trials in which the plea of superior orders has been invoked, it may be submitted, on the one hand, that between 1944 and 1948, the effect of the plea of superior orders was clearly defined under statutory instruments for military trials, to the extent that it was not a defence as such.[57] But the case law of the war crimes trials seems to show a marked lack of uniformity as to whether the plea could ever stand alone as a defence, and as to the extent to which the plea mitigated the scale of the defendant's sentence. This state of uncertainty was due to the fact that the plea was not totally dismissed as a defence in the military trials, whose invocation, subject to certain conditions, in those trials was allowed by judicial bodies, and reference is made to the remarkable fact that all but one of the US military tribunals established under Control Council Law No 10 adopted this conditional liability approach to the plea of superior orders.[58] As one of the leading writers on the subject has noted, the legal position—after his survey of jurisprudence—at the time of the post-World War II military trials seemed to be that the plea was accepted as a defence when the recipient believed in the order's lawfulness, and not as such when the order concerned was obviously illegal or the recipient knew it to be criminal.[59] It must be clear that the approach to the plea, as described so far, was initiated, deliberately or otherwise, in the *IMT Nuremberg Judgment*. A cursory look through the instruments listed earlier would also show that the instruments, as interpreted in judicial practice, could result in quite different results for defendants subject to the instruments. This is particularly the case with the content of Principle IV as formulated by the ILC in 1950, from the wording of which the possibility for the plea to become a defence could not be excluded. While the principle closely reflected the conclusion of the *IMT Nuremberg Judgment*, by its resolution of non-committal, however, the UNGA undermined the principle as part of the then international law. The point, despite this uncertain situation, is that the importance of the *IMT Nuremberg Judgment*'s implicit allowance for this defence,[60] in spite of Article 8 of the Nuremberg Charter, should not be overlooked, as it would enjoy longevity after its delivery.[61]

[55] *IMT Nuremberg Judgment* (n 7) 221.

[56] In *Hirota and others* (Judgment 12 November 1948) (1948) 15 *Annual Digest of Public International Law Cases* 356, 363 (in 'complete accord').

[57] *Law Reports of Trials of War Criminals* (n 1) vol XV 158–9.

[58] K J Heller, *The Nuremberg Military Tribunals and the Origin of International Criminal Law* (Oxford University Press 2011) ('Heller, *The Nuremberg Military Tribunals and the Origin of International Criminal Law*') 301.

[59] M Greenspan, *The Modern Law of Land Warfare* (University of California Press 1959) ('Greenspan, *The Modern Law of Land Warfare*') 495.

[60] Greenspan, *The Modern Law of Land Warfare* (n 59) 494–5. *US v Otto Ohlendorf et al* ('*Einsatzgruppen case*') (1948) *Law Reports of Trials of War Criminals* (n 1) vol IV 90–1.

[61] See, however, the contrary view held by, for instance, Ambos, 'Defences in International Criminal Law' (n 3) and Greenspan, *The Modern Law of Land Warfare* (n 59) 322–3.

On the other hand, there was, and still is, no doubt that the plea could be combined with other factors in a case to form *another* defence recognized in state practice. Here, the problem is with the necessity to preserve the independence of the plea of superior orders, in view of its obviously ancillary and evidentiary function, in this combination of factors.

But the reason for an independent plea of superior orders is also forceful, because it has been a special feature of military law, inherent in the nature of the organization and structure of armed forces. This independence has always been recognized in international law, with good reason.[62]

Apart from the aforementioned points of ambiguity, it seems that the case law of the military trials then settled on three tests against which to determine whether the plea could be open to a defendant as a defence, namely:

> whether an order, *illegal* under international law, on which an accused has acted was or must be presumed to have been known to him to be so illegal, or was obviously so illegal ... or should have been recognized by him as being so illegal.[63]

To add to this what has been said by Greenspan, referred to in the text accompanying footnote 61, it seems that the following interesting point would emerge with respect to the state of customary law at the time of the Hong Kong trials. The plea of superior orders may constitute a defence, if the recipient did not believe it to be unlawful, either after his own assessment or without making such assessment due to the urgency of the situation in which the order was issued to him, provided that the order was not obviously/manifestly illegal, or should not have been so in his view as a reasonable person. The case law thus upheld the illegality prerequisite, as well as the knowledge on the part of the recipient of superior orders, before it allowed the plea to stand as a defence. In addition, there was, usually, no element of compulsion included,[64] which means that, at trial, the defendant did not produce evidence of that element when pleading superior orders.

Where the plea was not accepted as a defence, it might be considered as: (1) a factor that, in conjunction with other factors present in a case, contributed to the formation of another separate defence;[65] or (2) a mitigating factor in sentencing. But the case law also shows some further muddles in this regard, in that even when invoking the plea as a mitigating factor, the defendant may still have to show that he did not realize the illegality of the order in question.[66]

The hesitation of courts in determining the effect of the plea referred to earlier was also shown in the Hong Kong trials. But the conclusion is that, substantively,

[62] See section 5 later in the chapter.

[63] *Law Reports of Trials of War Criminals* (n 1) vol XV (1949) 158.

[64] Heller's survey of the 12 US military trials under Control Council Law No 10 has shown support for this point. See Heller, *The Nuremberg Military Tribunals and the Origins of International Criminal Law* (n 58) 301–2.

[65] For instance, it may be a factor that helps substantiate a plea of duress or necessity: *Law Reports of Trials of War Criminals* (n 1) vol XV (1949) 155–7.

[66] *US v Karl Brandt et al* (Medical Case) (1947) *Trials of War Criminals Before the Nuernberg Military Tribunals Under Control Council Law No 10* (USGPO 1947) vol II 227.

customary international law as reflected in the *Manual of Military Law* had been applied in those trials. At this juncture, caution is called for in respect of the preceding conclusion. It is not claimed that the British or American practice in relation to the plea would be in itself sufficient for the purposes of proof of the then customary law, even though that practice has since been the predominant (and readily available) source of state practice on this very topic. The international instruments referred to in this section provide another relevant source of evidence of practice. Both sources point to one inference that customary law entertained two strains of thought with regard to the nature of the plea of superior orders.[67]

Two matters need be separated in this light. First, what the British courts deemed to be the applicable law for the Hong Kong trials or other similar trials conducted after World War II was confined within the terms of the *Manual of Military Law* and the Royal Warrant and perhaps, legal doctrines recognized therein. The version of international law of which judicial notice was taken by British military courts might reflect the true state of international law prevalent at the time, as believed by the authors of the *Manual of Military Law* in particular. Secondly, the belief of the *Manual of Military Law*'s authors might not be a *complete* reflection of the state of customary law at the time, as amply shown in the practice of judicial bodies that were more readily to accommodate the plea as a defence under suitable conditions. The most that can be said in view of the two matters is that customary law was not settled on the plea's nature at the time of the Hong Kong trials. But, the British courts that conducted trials no doubt subscribed to the view of the law as presented in the *Manual of Military Law*, which had enough authority over the views of the judges or Judge Advocates. If so, the Hong Kong trials are not considered in order to discover new understandings of the *Manual of Military Law*'s version of the law; even less should they be examined for the purposes of affirming or disproving the true state of international law. They remain a step in a long process of evolution of the plea of superior orders in ICL.

## 3. The Plea of Superior Orders Raised as a Defence

### 3.1 The plea as a defence without an element of duress

The plea may be raised without any alleged coercion accompanying it. In reality, it is entirely possible that not every superior order comes with the penalty of death, even in wartime; besides, chaos or defeats may seriously disrupt the disciplinary structure in armies so that enforcement of orders is impossible, thus rendering ineffective the threat or penalty attached to the orders. The plea may be raised in various forms under this heading. It could be raised in reference to the general atmosphere in a unit of the armed forces, which adheres to a strict tradition of

[67] For a contrary position, see 'Report of the Deputy Judge Advocate for War Crimes, European Command, June 1944 to July 1948, 46–49', in M Whiteman, *Digest of International Law*, vol XI (USGPO 1968) 941.

compliance with superior orders. It could be raised with the argument that it would be against training or culture in the armed forces to dissent from such orders. It may be said that the plea so raised relies on the force of habit of obeying orders. When the plea was raised in this form in the Hong Kong trials, it was never treated as a complete defence but might, considering other factors, result in mitigation of sentences.

This has been shown in, among others, the record of the trial against *Yamada Kiichiro and Awa Isao*.[68] The accused were non-commissioned officers of the *Kempeitai,* or the Military Police, of the Japanese Army.[69] The trial was held in Hong Kong between 17 and 22 July 1946. The accused were charged with a war crime against civilians at Tai Po, New Territories, between 28 December 1944 and 8 January 1945, which had resulted in the death or physical suffering of several civilians. The acts of ill-treatment took place when the locals were arrested on suspicion of helping guerrillas. In the course of the trial, Yamada pleaded superior orders as a defence, on the ground that the arrest and interrogations that led to the ill-treatment were ordered by his superiors.[70] The trial ended with a death penalty against Yamada and an acquittal for Awa.[71] On review, the verdicts and sentences were all confirmed.

If the plea of superior orders was only raised in a general way by claiming an environment in an army that itself induces compliance with orders, either by way of training or of discipline or of tradition, it was not likely to receive favourable treatment from the military courts. In the trial against Suzuki Nobuo, Tahara Iwao, Furuo Tatsuo, and Nakajima Mitoshi, the accused were all members of the Japanese Army.[72] The accused were charged with two war crimes involving ill-treatment of POWs at two camps in Taiwan, China between 1 January and 5 September 1945, causing suffering to the victims.[73] Under the first charge, the ill-treatment took place on two occasions: one after some POWs were caught stealing sugar at the Kokutsu Camp, and the other, during the evacuation of the said camp. The second charge alleged ill-treatment by dispatching unfit POWs to work at a mine in harsh working conditions near the Kinkaseki Camp, Taiwan, China.[74] The accused were serving as staff of the two POW camps when the alleged crimes were committed. At the trial, all the accused pleaded not guilty to the charges against

[68] *Trial of Sgt Maj Yamada Kiichiro and Sgt Awa Isao* (HKWCT Collection, File No WO235/887) ('*Trial of Sgt Maj Yamada Kiichiro and Sgt Awa Isao*').

[69] *Trial of Sgt Maj Yamada Kiichiro and Sgt Awa Isao* (n 68).

[70] Judge Advocate's Report, 2 September 1946, *Trial of Sgt Maj Yamada Kiichiro and Sgt Awa Isao* (n 68) 1–2, slides 7–8.

[71] It may be noted that death penalties were imposed in war crimes trials at the time, without any requirement that the crimes had resulted in the death of the victims of such crimes. This implies that the severity of the crimes—which might not have resulted in deaths—would be sufficient in determining the scale of the sentence: *Law Reports of Trials of War Criminals* (n 1) vol XV 200.

[72] Judge Advocate's Report, 30 January 1947, *Trial of Lt Suzuki Nebuo and three others* (HKWCT Collection, File No WO235/954) ('*Trial of Lt Suzuki Nebuo and three others*'), 1–2, slides 4–5.

[73] Judge Advocate's Report, 30 January 1947, *Trial of Lt Suzuki Nebuo and three others* (n 72).

[74] Prosecutor's Opening Address, *Trial of Lt Suzuki Nebuo and three others* (n 72) transcript 2, slide 14.

them, and pleaded superior orders as a general defence in their cases.[75] The Court found them all guilty on the charges.[76] The trial ended with a sentence of seven years' imprisonment each against Suzuki and Tahara, ten years' imprisonment against Furuo, and three years' imprisonment against Nakajima.[77] The verdicts and sentences were all confirmed. The gravity of the alleged crimes, although they did not result in deaths, appears to be critical in the assessment of individual guilt and of the severity of punishment. In addition, it is felt that specificity is necessary to provide the plea of superior orders with some degree of credibility and extenuating effect.[78] For each of the preceding two propositions, there is a relevant case in support.

With respect to the gravity point, reference is made to the trial against Ito Junichi, Sergeant-Major of the *Kempeitai* in the Japanese Army.[79] The accused was charged with the commission of a war crime at Tsun Wan on or about 17 August 1945, which involved the killing of two Chinese civilians in his custody. The killing took place after certain local residents were arrested on suspicion of being guerrillas. In the course of his trial, the accused admitted to the crime of shooting, but pleaded that the executions were carried out in compliance with the so-called 'taking suitable steps to all suspects' order issued by his superior.[80] The trial ended with a guilty verdict and a death penalty by shooting; on the advice of the Judge Advocate, on review of the proceedings, the Commander of Land Force Hong Kong did not confirm the guilty verdict because of procedural irregularities in relation to the plea, and ordered a re-trial.[81] The gravity of the alleged crimes was plain to see, and it may be said with some certainty that the plea of superior orders invoked by the accused clearly did not mitigate, as the order to shoot was apparently not addressed to him but to another *Kempeitai* sergeant.[82] In any case, the plea had no bearing on the order for re-trial.

With regard to the proposition regarding specificity, in the trial against Major Hirao Yoshio, Commanding Officer of the Kowloon *Kempeitai*, the accused was charged with war crimes committed at Kowloon between September 1942 and September 1945; the case was chiefly concerned with the ill-treatment by his subordinates of Chinese civilians that caused death to some and physical suffering

[75] Defence Closing Address, *Trial of Lt Suzuki Nebuo and three others* (n 72) exhibit S, 7–9, slides 159–61.

[76] Judge Advocate's Report, 30 January 1947, *Trial of Lt Suzuki Nebuo and three others* (n 72) 1, slide 4.

[77] Judge Advocate's Report, 30 January 1947, *Trial of Lt Suzuki Nebuo and three others* (n 72) 1, slide 4.

[78] The relevance of the plea was shown in the reference to the plan for POWs to work certain mines which, though carried into effect by Suzuki, was made and enforced by the Headquarters of the Japanese Army in Taiwan, China and the Japanese War Ministry: Accused's Petition (Suzuki), 30 January 1947, *Trial of Lt Suzuki Nebuo and three others* (n 72) slide 6.

[79] *Trial of SM Ito Junichi (No 1)* (HKWCT Collection, File No WO 235/914) ('*Trial of SM Ito Junichi (No 1)*').

[80] Accused's Petition, *Trial of SM Ito Junichi (No 1)* (n 79) 1–2, slides 5–6.

[81] Judge Advocate's Report, 28 October 1946, *Trial of SM Ito Junichi (No 1)* (n 79) 1, slide 4.

[82] Accused's Petition, *Trial of SM Ito Junichi (No 1)* (n 79) 1–2, slides 5–6.

to the others.[83] The incidents of ill-treatment took place when civilian residents were taken into custody at the *Kempeitai* Headquarters and sub-stations under Hirao's command. In the course of the trial, the accused pleaded superior orders as one of his defences, on the ground that his superior officer, Colonel Noma, was a meticulous person and never invested any power in subordinates, and that the accused could not act at his own discretion but only obey the instructions of the Colonel, since he was nothing but an intermediate officer with the mere function of conveying orders.[84] He stated that the determination of his criminal responsibility should rely on how far he performed his supervisory duty faithfully in the light of the concrete conditions, and that while he had tried his best to prevent ill-treatment, the circumstances relating to the War and occupation impeded him from performing his duty.[85] The trial ended with a guilty verdict, and the accused was sentenced to death by hanging. On review, the verdict was confirmed, together with the sentence,[86] and the sentence was carried out on 24 February 1948.

In some cases, the plea could make a difference in terms of the severity of sentences handed down by the military courts, to the same extent that a partial defence may achieve in a domestic felony case to which a mandatory penalty is attached by statute. In the trial against Tamura Teiichi, Hirano Noboru, and Fujino Masazo—all members of the Imperial Japanese Army—held in Hong Kong between 30 May and 13 June 1947, the Court was composed of two Indian officers and a Canadian officer.[87] The accused were charged with a war crime for the killing of a member of the Royal Naval Volunteer Reserve at Ichinomiya, Japan, on or about 15 August 1945.[88] The victim, airman Fred Hockley, was captured by a civil defence unit and turned over to a military unit, of which Tamura was the commanding officer with Fujino as his adjutant, and which formed part of a division, in which Hirano was an intelligence officer.[89] After the Japanese Emperor's surrender speech, Hirano allegedly ordered the captured victim to be 'disposed of', and the execution was later carried out by Fujino under the command of Tamura, who was informed of the gist of Hirano's order.[90] Tamura and Fujino both pleaded superior orders as a defence, and Hirano denied having ordered the killing of the victim, contending that his instructions had been misconstrued.[91] The Court, having found the accused guilty, handed down death penalties against Tamura and Hirano, and 15 years' imprisonment for

[83] Judge Advocate's Report, 19 January 1948, *Trial of Maj Hirao Yoshio* (HKWCT Collection, File No WO235/1098) ('*Trial of Maj Hirao Yoshio*'), 1–2, slides 5–6.

[84] Accused's Petition, *Trial of Maj Hirao Yoshio* (n 83) 1–2, slides 7–8.

[85] Accused's Petition, *Trial of Maj Hirao Yoshio* (n 83) 1–2, slides 7–8.

[86] Judge Advocate's Report, 19 January 1948, *Trial of Maj Hirao Yoshio* (n 83) 1–2, slides 5–6, confirmed by the Reviewing Officer.

[87] *Trial of Col Tamura Teiichi and two others* (HKWCT Collection, File No WO235/1021) ('*Trial of Col Tamura Teiichi and two others*').

[88] Judge Advocate's Report, 27 August 1947, *Trial of Col Tamura Teiichi and two others* (n 87) 1–3, slides 6–8.

[89] Accused's Petition, *Trial of Col Tamura Teiichi and two others* (n 87) 1, slide 6.

[90] Accused's Petition, *Trial of Col Tamura Teiichi and two others* (n 87) 1–3, slides 6–8.

[91] Accused's Petition, *Trial of Col Tamura Teiichi and two others* (n 87) 1–3, slides 6–8.

Fujino.[92] In reviewing the Court's decision, the Judge Advocate was in no doubt as to the correctness of the convictions of Colonel Tamuro and Captain Fujino. He advised that:

> Superior Orders [were] not of course a ground of defence for an offence such as this but the Court evidently considered that they afforded some mitigation in the case of [FUJINO] and accordingly refrained from sentencing him to death.[93]

On review, the Commander of Land Forces confirmed the findings made by the Court.[94]

The trial against Colonel Tokunaga Isao, Captain Saito Shunkichi, and three others, all officers of the Japanese Army in charge of various POW camps in Hong Kong, was held in Hong Kong between 17 November 1946 and 14 February 1947.[95] The accused were charged with a total of 11 war crimes, which involved the ill-treatment of POWs and civilians in the camps in Hong Kong between 1942 and 1945, causing deaths and physical sufferings to many of them, in addition to the misappropriation of certain Red Cross supplies.[96] All accused pleaded not guilty. All of the accused bar Captain Saito, the medical officer, and Lieutenant Tanaka, the chief of intelligence, pleaded superior orders as a defence, with Colonel Tokunaga (who was at the material time in charge of all POW camps in Hong Kong) pleading this defence in respect of charges seven and eight concerning the execution of recaptured POWs after escape as well as those only attempting escape. Having found all the accused guilty on at least some of the 11 charges, the Court handed down death penalties against Tokunaga and Saito, and various terms of jail for the other accused.[97] The Judge Advocate's Report noted that, with regard to the defence of superior orders put forward by the fourth and fifth of the accused, 'this could only influence the court in mitigation of sentence'.[98] In his petition to the Commander of Land Forces Hong Kong, Tokunaga repeated the defence by claiming that the execution of the escapees or those attempting escape from the POW camps was carried out on superior orders.[99] On review, the death penalty against Tokunaga was commuted to a life sentence, and that against Saito to 20 years' imprisonment.[100] The Judge Advocate indicated that this was most likely to have been because of a petition from Dr Selwyn Clarke, the Chief British

[92] Accused's Petition, *Trial of Col Tamura Teiichi and two others* (n 87) 1–3, slides 6–8.

[93] Accused's Petition, *Trial of Col Tamura Teiichi and two others* (n 87) 2, slide 7.

[94] Record of Proceedings, *Trial of Col Tamura Teiichi and two others* (n 87) slide 3.

[95] Judge Advocate's Report, 9 May 1947, *Trial of Col Tokunaga Isao and four others* (HKWCT Collection, File No W0235/1012 Part One) ('*Trial of Col Tokunaga Isao and four others (Part One)*'), 1–4, slides 13–16.

[96] Schedule of Charges, *Trial of Col Tokunaga Isao and four others (Part One)* (n 95) slides 11–12.

[97] Judge Advocate's Report, 9 May 1947, *Trial of Col Tokunaga Isao and four others (Part One)* (n 95) 1, slide 13.

[98] Judge Advocate's Report, *Trial of Col Tokunaga Isao and four others (Part One)* (n 95) 3, slide 15.

[99] Accused's Petition, *Trial of Col Tokunaga Isao and four others (Part One)* (n 95) slides 23–4.

[100] Letter from Judge Advocate to Attorney General's Office, 14 July 1947, *Trial of Col Tokunaga Isao and four others (Part One)* (n 95) slide 6.

Medical Officer in Hong Kong, affirming that the accused did what he could in the circumstances.[101]

In the trial against Colonel Kanazawa, held in Hong Kong between 26 September and 30 October 1947, the accused was the Head of the *Kempeitai* in Hong Kong, succeeding Colonel Noma.[102] He was charged with two war crimes for (1) the ill-treatment of Hong Kong civilians between 10 February and 15 August 1945; and (2) as commander of the *Kempeitai*, ill-treatment of civilians in the form of deportation from Hong Kong, between 1 June and 31 August 1945. The first crime allegedly took place when certain civilian residents were taken into custody by the *Kempeitai* under Kanazawa's command. The second charge was concerned with the compulsory evacuation arising from a shortage of food in Hong Kong, discussed in further detail in Suzannah Linton's chapter. In the course of the trial, with regard to the second charge, the accused pleaded superior orders as one of his defences, on the basis that deportation was the policy of the Japanese Governor-General, and the Gendarmerie was merely in charge of arresting and guarding of people to be deported.[103] The Court convicted him on both charges, complete with a sentence of death by hanging. On review of the proceedings, the second verdict was not confirmed, *partly* due to the existence of superior orders of the Governor-General.[104] The factual circumstances alleged in the second charge were clearly in the accused's favour; as the Judge Advocate pointed out, he did all that could reasonably be expected of him as commander in complying with the policy of the Governor-General, thus relieving his personal responsibility for the abuses that occurred during the deportation process.[105] The role of the superior orders was not dominant in respect of the second charge.

## 3.2 The plea, when raised at trial, contained an element of duress

One premise of this chapter is that the distinction between the plea of superior orders and the defence of duress is clear: there are orders and orders.[106] As the *IMT Nuremberg Judgment* shows, the question of duress may come into the assessment of the role of superior orders when the orders leave the recipient no moral choice.[107] It was implied that where a choice was possible, the plea could not succeed at trial for any purpose. It is acknowledged that, in war crimes trials, the plea of superior orders was not infrequently invoked with the element of

[101] Letter from Judge Advocate to Attorney General's Office, 14 July 1947, *Trial of Col Tokunaga Isao and four others (Part One)* (n 95) slide 6.

[102] Judge Advocate's Report, 20 January 1948, *Trial of Lt Col Kanazawa Asao* (HKWCT Collection, File No WO235/1093), ('*Trial of Lt Col Kanazawa Asao*'), 1–3, slides 4–6.

[103] Judge Advocate's Report, 20 January 1948, *Trial of Lt Col Kanazawa Asao* (n 102) 2, slide 4.

[104] Judge Advocate's Report, 20 January 1948, *Trial of Lt Col Kanazawa Asao* (n 102) 1–2, slides 3–4. Also see Testimony of Col Kanazawa Asao, transcript 337–41, slides 361–5.

[105] Judge Advocate's Report, 20 January 1948, *Trial of Lt Col Kanazawa Asao* (n 102) 1–2, slides 3–4.

[106] Dinstein, *The Defence of Obedience to Superior Orders in International Law* (n 36) 53–4.

[107] *IMT Nuremberg Judgment* (n 7) 221.

compulsion, which would enhance the status of the plea as a defence.[108] But then, the question becomes one of duress rather than superior orders. The general question would be whether there is any need for a separate category of superior orders that is accompanied by compulsion, from the one that is not. It is suggested that compulsion or duress has always been a separate part of international law by reason of 'general principles of law recognized by civilized nations'. As such, the plea of superior orders can be relied on independently of the plea of duress. On the other hand, when the two are jointly brought up at trial, it appears that the defendant would have a better chance to have the mixed plea considered favourably by the Court. However, it is not always possible to disentangle these two elements in the strenuous and chaotic circumstances of a wartime situation. It is natural that duress creeps in when hostilities reached the intense moments, in that obeying or disobeying orders would be regarded as a step that was critical for the survival or destruction of the unit, to which the recipient belonged, in the circumstances. On this point, a word will be said later in this chapter.

The Hong Kong trials include examples where the plea of superior orders, clearly influenced by an element of duress, was relied on by defendants as a defence. However, the element of duress was sometimes referred to in a cursory manner, without adding much to the other grounds offered to refute charges. That did not enhance the force of the plea in exonerating the pleading party.

Inouye Kanao was an interpreter in the Imperial Japanese Army.[109] He was charged with three war crimes for his role in the ill-treatment of two Canadian POWs by assault, when he was interpreter at Sham Shui Po POW camp, and the ill-treatment of several Hong Kong civilians resulting in the death of four civilians and physical suffering to the others.[110] The accused pleaded not guilty to all charges. At the trial, he raised superior orders as one of his defences, claiming 'I was under orders', that 'I had to obey these orders', and that he did what he did because he was ordered to do so.[111] The Court found the accused guilty on all charges, and sentenced him to death by hanging.[112] The defendant filed a petition, again claiming superior orders, disobedience to which would have been like suicide on his part.[113] The penalty was not carried out, on the ground that 'it transpired after the trial that the accused was a Canadian subject', and the case was transferred to the jurisdiction of the civilian courts, where he was convicted of treason despite the superior orders plea, and eventually executed.[114]

On occasion, a mixture of pleas of superior orders and duress may result in a lenient sentence, but it is not always clear whether the court in question opted for

[108] *US v Otto Ohlendorf et al* ('*Einsatzgruppen case*'), (n 60) 480. See also Greenspan, *The Modern Law of Land Warfare* (n 59) 497–8.

[109] *Trial of Inouye Kanao* (HKWCT Collection, File No WO235/927 ('*Trial of Inouye Kanao*'). The accused contended that he was a civilian employed as an interpreter and nothing more: Closing Address by the Defence, slide 158.

[110] Charge Sheet [Schedule of Charges], *Trial of Inouye Kanao* (n 109) slide 4.

[111] Closing Address by the Defence, *Trial of Inouye Kanao* (n 109) 1–2, slides 157–8.

[112] Record of Proceedings, *Trial of Inouye Kanao* (n 109) slide 3.

[113] Accused's Petition, *Trial of Inouye Kanao* (n 109) slide 7.

[114] Judge Advocate's Report, 14 September 1946, *Trial of Inouye Kanao* (n 109) 1–3, slides 3–5.

the lenient punishment on account of the circumstances of duress or of something else. Reference is here made to the trial of Rear Admiral Sakonju Naomasa and Captain Mayazumi Haruo, who were officers of the Japanese Navy.[115] The accused were charged with a war crime for the killing of survivors from a sunken British vessel on the High Seas at or about midnight of 18 or 19 March 1944. In the killing incident, the 16th Squadron of the Japanese Navy was carrying out an operation in the Indian Ocean, with Sakonju in command on board the *Aoba*. The naval vessel *Tone*, under the command of Captain Mayazumi, was attached to the squadron. There was then an operational order in force for the squadron, which required that, if captured ships could not feasibly be taken to a friendly port, they were to be sunk, and a minimal number of prisoners were to be taken.[116] The *Tone* then sank a British merchant vessel, the *Behar*, but rescued almost everyone on board. After reporting this incident to the Rear Admiral on board the *Aoba*, the *Tone* received two orders for disposal of the survivors, but Captain Mayazumi did not comply with the orders. The vessel later arrived in Tanjung Priok, the port for Batavia, on 15 March and a debriefing session was held the day after. On 18 March, the *Tone* departed for Singapore, with Captain Mayazumi in charge. All the survivors of the *Behar* on board were killed during the voyage (some survived, having been taken off the vessel at Tanjung Priok).

At the trial, Captain Mayazumi pleaded not guilty on the following three grounds. First, he pleaded superior orders, in that he acted against his own conscience in the killing incident.[117] The orders to dispose of the survivors came from his superior. In the Japanese Navy, it was impossible to appeal to a higher-ranking officer than the one who issued the orders. Secondly, he tried his best to change the orders, but to no avail, which left him with no alternatives.[118] Thirdly, he relied on the existence of coercion and duress at the time, by arguing that he knew of the rumours that, after the War, military personnel would be executed for dissents against superior orders during the War.[119] He assumed that he could well be punished for disobeying the disposal orders.

Admiral Sakonju denied any responsibility in the killing. First, the word '*shobun*' included in the operational order meant that whether to carry out executions of the survivors was a matter that was left to the discretion of the commanding officer who, in this case, was the accused Captain.[120] Secondly, he claimed that he received no report from Captain Mayazumi at the squadron base, where they could easily

[115] *Trial of R Adm Sakonju Naomasa and Capt Mayazumi Haruo* (HKWCT Collection, File No WO235/1089) ('*Trial of R Adm Sakonju Naomasa and Capt Mayazumi Haruo*').

[116] Judge Advocate's Report, *Trial of R Adm Sakonju Naomasa and Capt Mayazumi Haruo* (n 115) 17 December 1947, 1–3, slides 10–12.

[117] Accused's Petition (Mayazumi), *Trial of R Adm Sakonju Naomasa and Capt Mayazumi Haruo* (n 115) 1–2, slides 21–2.

[118] Accused's Petition (Mayazumi), *Trial of R Adm Sakonju Naomasa and Capt Mayazumi Haruo* (n 115) 1–2, slides 21–2.

[119] Accused's Petition (Mayazumi), *Trial of R Adm Sakonju Naomasa and Capt Mayazumi Haruo* (n 115) 1–2, slides 21–2.

[120] Accused's Petition (Sakonju), *Trial of R Adm Sakonju Naomasa and Capt Mayazumi Haruo* (n 115) 3, slide 16.

have met, nor did he issue any order to the Captain before the killing occurred.[121] Thirdly, when the *Tone*'s crew killed the survivors on 18 March, Admiral Sakonju was no longer in command of the vessel nor its Captain.[122] Additionally, he pleaded superior orders as one of his defences, by claiming that based on the practice of the Japanese Navy and the nature of the operation of the squadron, the disposal orders could conceivably be deemed as reflecting the intention of the Commander-in-Chief, Takasu.[123] The trial was concluded with a sentence of death by hanging upon Vice-Admiral Sakonju, and of seven years' imprisonment upon Captain Mayazumi. On review, the verdicts and the sentences were confirmed, and the death penalty was carried out on 21 January 1948.[124] The Captain's case was helped by the combination of superior orders and the circumstances in which he received the orders in question, and what seemed to be a genuine desire to save the lives of the captives in spite of his orders. But the weak argument of the Admiral that his orders reflected the intention of his superior did not help his defence at all.

The trial against Sergeant Major Ogasawara Haruji and Sergeant Kawai Hisao, both members of the Imperial Japanese Army, was held in Hong Kong between 20 and 31 March 1947.[125] The accused were charged with a war crime, in that they were allegedly concerned in the killing of three civilian residents in Taipo, and Ogasawara was additionally charged with a war crime for the ill-treatment of two civilian residents, resulting in the death of one of them.[126] The first charge concerned what happened after several civilian residents of Taipo were arrested, when Ogasawara was given the order to have them sent for trial, which, however, was cancelled and replaced by an order to have them killed instead.[127] The second charge alleged ill-treatment by beating, hanging, and water torture.[128] Ogasawara was then in charge of a *Kempeitai* detachment at Taipo, and Kawai worked under him when the alleged crimes took place.[129] Ogasawara pleaded superior orders as a defence to the first charge, whereas Kawai denied any part in the ill-treatment or

[121] Accused's Petition (Sakonju), *Trial of R Adm Sakonju Naomasa and Capt Mayazumi Haruo* (n 115) 5, slide 18.

[122] Accused's Petition (Sakonju), *Trial of R Adm Sakonju Naomasa and Capt Mayazumi Haruo* (n 115) 5, slide 18.

[123] Record of Proceedings, *Trial of R Adm Sakonju Naomasa and Capt Mayazumi Haruo* (n 115) slide 6.

[124] Record of Proceedings, *Trial of R Adm Sakonju Naomasa and Capt Mayazumi Haruo* (n 115) slide 6.

[125] Judge Advocate's Report, 22 May 1947, *Trial of Sgt Maj Ogasawara Maruji and Sgt Kawai Hisao* (HKWCT Collection, File No WO235/1011) ('*Trial of Sgt Maj Ogasawara Maruji and Sgt Kawai Hisao*'), 1–2, slides 5–6.

[126] Judge Advocate's Report, 22 May 1947, *Trial of Sgt Maj Ogasawara Maruji and Sgt Kawai Hisao* (n 125) 1–2, slides 5–6.

[127] Judge Advocate's Report, 22 May 1947, *Trial of Sgt Maj Ogasawara Maruji and Sgt Kawai Hisao* (n 125) 1–2, slide 5.

[128] Judge Advocate's Report, 22 May 1947, *Trial of Sgt Maj Ogasawara Maruji and Sgt Kawai Hisao* (n 125) 1–2, slide 5.

[129] Judge Advocate's Report, 22 May 1947, *Trial of Sgt Maj Ogasawara Maruji and Sgt Kawai Hisao* (n 125) 1–2, slide 5.

that he was present at the time.[130] The Court found Ogasawara guilty of both charges, with, however, a specific finding that negated the causality between his act and the civilian death implicated in the second charge.[131] The trial ended with a ten-year sentence of imprisonment against Ogasawara and an acquittal for Kawai.[132] Ogasawara submitted a petition repeatedly pleading superior orders as his defence, claiming that, had he disobeyed the order to shoot the civilians, he 'would have been brought to trial on a charge of mutiny' and 'would have brought disgrace and severe punishment to [him]self'.[133] For him, it was a habit to comply with orders after ten years in the Army.[134] There was indication in his testimony at the trial that the orders in question were received by him accompanied by coercion imposed by the Army regulations.[135] The verdict was eventually confirmed on review. It could be surmised that the Court at first instance took the plea of superior orders into account, and meted out a lenient sentence on that account.

In the trial against Captain Yoshimi Taneyoshi, Corporal Yamaguchi Kiyoshige, and five others, the accused were all of the Imperial Japanese Army in Taiwan, China.[136] The trial was held in Hong Kong between 17 November and 11 December 1947. The accused were charged with war crimes committed at the Daichoku Camp, Taiwan, China, between November 1942 and 15 August 1945. Yoshimi was the doctor to all POWs in the camp, and Yamaguchi was one of the staff members of the camp. All the accused were alleged to have been concerned in the ill-treatment of the POWs, resulting in some deaths and physical suffering. The acts of ill-treatment took place when all the accused were responsible for the wellbeing of British and Allied POWs in the camp. In the course of the trial, Yoshimi pleaded superior orders as one of his defences, on the ground that he was vested with no power other than that to provide medical advice to his superior (who was a co-accused in this case), and that, being a low-ranking officer in the army, he had no choice but to follow superior orders.[137] Yamaguchi also pleaded superior orders as a defence, on the ground that his alleged offences against three POWs were committed under the compulsion of his superiors, such that he had to obey the orders against his own will, or he would be treated as a traitor and be severely

[130] *Trial of Sgt Maj Ogasawara Maruji and Sgt Kawai Hisao* (n 125) 1–2, slides 5–6. Also see Testimony of Sgt Maj Ogasawara Haruji, transcript 85–8, slides 96–9; Testimony of Sgt Kawai Hisao, transcript 126, 129, slides 137, 140.

[131] Judge Advocate's Report, 22 May 1947, *Trial of Sgt Maj Ogasawara Maruji and Sgt Kawai Hisao* (n 125) 1, slide 5.

[132] Judge Advocate's Report, 22 May 1947, *Trial of Sgt Maj Ogasawara Maruji and Sgt Kawai Hisao* (n 125) 1, slide 5.

[133] Petition of Accused (Ogasawara), 22 May 1947, *Trial of Sgt Maj Ogasawara Maruji and Sgt Kawai Hisao* (n 125) slide 7.

[134] Petition of Accused (Ogasawara), 22 May 1947, *Trial of Sgt Maj Ogasawara Maruji and Sgt Kawai Hisao* (n 125) slide 7.

[135] Testimony of Sgt Maj Ogasawara Maruji, 22 May 1947, *Trial of Sgt Maj Ogasawara Maruji and Sgt Kawai Hisao* (n 125) transcript 86–7, slides 97–8.

[136] Judge Advocate's Report, 4 February 1948, *Trial of Captain Yoshimi Taneyoshi and six others* (HKWCT Collection, File No WO235/1099) ('*Trial of Captain Yoshimi Taneyoshi and six others*'), 1–3, slides 4–6.

[137] Accused's Petition (Yoshimi), *Trial of Captain Yoshimi Taneyoshi and six others* (n 136) 2, slide 8.

punished.[138] The Court found all the accused guilty as charged, sentencing Yoshimi and Yamaguchi to seven and eight years' imprisonment respectively.[139] On review, the verdicts and sentences were both confirmed.

These cases show that the element of duress may not need to reach the same level of stringency as in other war crimes trials held at the same time. In the *Einsatzgruppen* case, the US military tribunal stated the following:

> In order successfully to plead the defence of superior orders the opposition of the doer must be constant. It is not enough that he mentally rebel at the time the order is received. If at any time after receiving the order he acquiesces in its illegal character, the defense of superior orders is closed to him.[140]

Whether this was a correct interpretation of Control Council Law No 10 is not certain. It has, however, opened a gap in the law, for what it intended to convey would have to rely on the establishment of several presumptions. For instance, it may have to be presumed that the resistance of the recipient of the orders in question must be maintained, even after a warning of severe punishment against him. It may also need to be presumed that after he showed sustained resistance, the superior brought an imminent penalty to bear on him, for threats of punishment might not be enough for compliance. It would be then a clear case of duress, with the initial order becoming secondary in the assessment of the desperateness of the situation. Then, the question would be why there is any need to infuse the factor of compulsion in the plea of superior orders.[141]

## 3.3 The plea raised in conjunction with other factors

In some of the Hong Kong trials, the plea of superior orders was raised by the defendants in conjunction with other factors present at the time when the alleged crimes were committed. The plea was often accepted for mitigating purposes, but the issuers of the orders so pleaded would be dealt with severely.

In the trial against Lieutenants Kishi Yasuo and Matsumoto Chozaburo, and 13 others, held in Hong Kong between 28 March and 25 April 1946, the accused were low-ranking officers and soldiers of the Imperial Japanese Army.[142] They were charged with a war crime in that they were together concerned in the beating, torture, and maltreatment of the inhabitants of Silver Mine Bay district of Lantau,

[138] Accused's Petition (Yamaguchi), *Trial of Captain Yoshimi Taneyoshi and six others* (n 136) 1, slide 12.

[139] Judge Advocate's Report, 4 February 1948, *Trial of Captain Yoshimi Taneyoshi and six others* (n 136) 1, slide 4.

[140] *Law Reports of Trials of War Criminals* (n 1) vol IV 481.

[141] Some trials did mix these factors. In *Law Reports of Trials of War Criminals* (n 1) vol XV 156, it was noted that the case-law, including that of *Einsatzgruppen*, showed that the recognition of the illegality in a certain order by subordinates was not enough for the subordinates to ignore the order, as the implementation of such order was often made under compulsion. So, the subordinates were faced with the two factors of superior orders and duress.

[142] Judge Advocate's Report, 11 June 1946, *Trial of Lt Kishi Yasuo and fourteen others* (HKWCT Collection, File No WO235/993) ('*Trial of Lt Kishi Yasuo and fourteen others*'), 1–4, slides 4–7.

Hong Kong, in August 1945, as well as the killing of nine of the inhabitants.[143] The alleged acts of ill-treatment took place when the company to which the accused belonged proceeded to three villages after repelling an attack by Chinese guerrillas, and the villages were burned and looted, and some of the villagers were killed while others were arrested.[144] The ill-treatment included severe beatings and executions by beheading.[145] The accused pleaded not guilty to the charge. The defence for the five non-commissioned officers and soldiers concerned with the actual killings was that of superior orders.[146] Only Sergeant Major Uchida Hiroshi received the death penalty, with the remaining four receiving jail terms of less than ten years.[147] Upon review, the Commander of Land Forces Hong Kong determined that the death penalty against Uchida should be remitted to ten years' imprisonment, and that the sentences of two years' imprisonment against two other accused were reduced to one year each.[148]

This case shows that even in the confusing circumstances of multiple accused trials, the relevant court would consider the plea of superior orders strictly in accordance with existing law as was known to it. Gravity aside, the plea would be given suitable weight in the scale of sentencing. The review by the confirming authority further reduced sentences of three of the accused who pleaded superior orders. It may be noted that Uchida's petition was successful, probably due to the mixing of superior orders with duress in the form of the presence of his commanding officer at the scene of execution and right behind him.[149]

In the trial against Major Uete Taichi, Lieutenant Kuruta Iwao, Lieutenant Kawaida Susuma, and five others, held in Hong Kong between 13 November 1947 and 16 January 1948, the accused were either officers or civilians in service of the Imperial Japanese Army in Taiwan, China.[150] They were charged on five counts of war crimes, all involving maltreatment of Allied POWs held at various camps in Taiwan, China, between November 1942 and September 1945. The charges alleged that Allied POWs were detained under the control of the accused and subjected to ill-treatment. In the course of the trial and the review, Uete pleaded superior orders as one of his defences, on the basis that even if certain casualties among the POWs were caused by the evacuation of the camp under his command carried out by his charges, the evacuation was consequential upon the order of the

[143] Judge Advocate's Report, 11 June 1946, *Trial of Lt Kishi Yasuo and fourteen others* (n 142) 1, slide 4.

[144] Judge Advocate's Report, 11 June 1946, *Trial of Lt Kishi Yasuo and fourteen others* (n 142) 1, slide 4.

[145] Judge Advocate's Report, 11 June 1946, *Trial of Lt Kishi Yasuo and fourteen others* (n 142) 1–2, slides 4–5.

[146] Judge Advocate's Report, 11 June 1946, *Trial of Lt Kishi Yasuo and fourteen others* (n 142) 2–4, slides 5–7.

[147] Judge Advocate's Report, 11 June 1946, *Trial of Lt Kishi Yasuo and fourteen others* (n 142) 1, slide 4.

[148] Decision of the Confirming Officer, *Trial of Lt Kishi Yasuo and fourteen others* (n 142) slide 24.

[149] Accused's Petition (Uchida), *Trial of Lt Kishi Yasuo and fourteen others* (n 142) slide 13.

[150] Judge Advocate's Report, 3 March 1948, *Trial of Maj Uete Taichi and six others* (HKWCT Collection, File No WO235/1105) ('*Trial of Maj Uete Taichi and six others*'), 1–3, slides 12–14.

Commanding Officer of the Japanese Army in Taiwan, China.[151] Kuruta pleaded superior orders, on the ground that he acted in compliance with Uete's order.[152] Kawaida also pleaded in the course of the review that due to the Japanese Army's regulations, a superior officer should be responsible for the acts of his subordinates, since the regulations demanded full obedience by subordinates of superior orders.[153] The judgment contained guilty verdicts against these three accused, accompanied with the penalty of death by hanging for each. On review, both the verdicts and sentences were confirmed.[154]

### 3.4 The plea raised by civilian officials

The Hong Kong trials also saw civilian officials plead superior orders for their action during the War when they were attached to the military.

The trial against Kyoda Shigeru, a civilian shipmaster in the service of the Japanese Army, took place in Hong Kong between 23 October and 29 November 1946.[155] The accused was charged with a war crime for what happened over 1–2 October 1942, when he was the captain of a Japanese military vessel, SS *Lisbon Maru*, on the High Seas on its way from Hong Kong to Japan. The allegation was that, on those dates, British POWs were battened down in the ship's holds after the ship was torpedoed, and he failed to provide them with boats and life jackets when the ship was sinking. Both acts resulted in deaths, as well as physical and mental suffering. In the course of the trial, the accused pleaded not guilty mainly on the ground that a civilian master of a Japanese troopship had no authority to issue orders to the military personnel on board; on the contrary, he had to obey orders from the military officer in charge.[156] The trial ended with a guilty verdict and the accused was sentenced to seven years' imprisonment, and both were confirmed on review.[157] The circumstance of a civilian in charge of navigation, but the military in charge of transport of POWs, must have weighed on the mind of the judges to allow the plea in mitigating the sentence against Kyoda, as the shipmaster had no authority over the military on board.

Reference is also made to the trial of Niimori Genichiro, a civilian interpreter attached to the Imperial Japanese Army.[158] The accused was charged with war crimes committed, *inter alia*, aboard the *Lisbon Maru* on the High Seas in late

[151] Testimony of Maj Uete Taichi, *Trial of Maj Uete Taichi and six others* (n 150) transcript 161–2, slides 206–7; Accused's Petition (Uete), slide 35.

[152] Testimony of Lt Kuruta Iwao, *Trial of Maj Uete Taichi and six others* (n 150) transcript 223–4, slides 268–9, 301; Petition of Accused (Kuruta), slide 31.

[153] Petition of Accused (Kawaida), *Trial of Maj Uete Taichi and six others* (n 150) slide 26.

[154] Record of Proceedings, *Trial of Maj Uete Taichi and six others* (n 150) slides 7–9.

[155] *Trial of Kyoda Shigeru* (HKWCT Collection, File No WO235/1114) ('*Trial of Kyoda Shigeru*').

[156] Judge Advocate's Report, 11 February 1947, *Trial of Kyoda Shigeru* (n 155) 3, slide 9.

[157] Judge Advocate's Report, 11 February 1947, *Trial of Kyoda Shigeru* (n 155) 1, slide 7; Record of Proceedings, *Trial of Kyoda Shigeru* (n 155) slide 5.

[158] *Trial of Niimori Genichiro* (HKWCT Collection, File No WO235/892) ('*Trial of Niimori Genichiro*').

September 1942, involving acts of ill-treatment of POWs.[159] The first and third charges of ill-treatment, therefore, involved acts against British and Canadian POWs on the High Seas, resulting in one death. Other charges involved the ill-treatment of British POWs in Shanghai, and of Canadian POWs in Hong Kong, resulting in physical sufferings. In the last charge, the accused was alleged to have stolen Red Cross parcels and the property of POWs at the Happy Valley Racecourse Camp.[160] At the trial, the accused pleaded not guilty to all charges. He pleaded superior orders as one of his defences, arguing that he, as a low-ranking civilian official in the military, 'was always responsible to the military personnel', and that 'no matter how high the civil official [was] in the line of administration he could never command military personnel... not even to a private soldier'.[161] Niimori also contended that it was the orders issued by military officials that led to the ill-treatment. The fact that he 'did not mention the names of his superiors' when he passed down the orders, and that he 'was apt to adopt a self-important attitude' towards the POWs, made him seemingly appear to be the one giving the orders.[162] The point seemed to be that he did not issue the orders to ill-treat the victims, as he did not have that authority, but that his actions, savage as they were, stemmed from the orders he received or passed down.[163] The plea of superior orders was not accepted as a defence, but clearly played a role in his rather lenient sentence of 15 years' imprisonment, being 'one of the most notorious of Hong Kong War Criminals'.[164] The verdict and sentence were confirmed on review.

## 4. The Plea of Superior Orders as a Mitigating Factor

In the Hong Kong trials, the plea of superior orders was also raised by the defendants as a mitigating factor. This different approach revealed the understanding of the nature of the plea among the defence lawyers at the time, who had pinned little hope on the insistence of the plea as a complete defence.

Thus, in the trial against Sergeant Major Yokohata Toshiro, the defendant approached the plea in this way.[165] The accused was a member of the Shanghai-based *Kempeitai*.[166] The accused was charged with a war crime on the basis that, while being stationed in Shanghai between 1 September and 30 November 1942, he was involved in ill-treatment of certain civilian residents, causing them physical suffering. To that, the accused pleaded guilty, but his plea was altered to not guilty

159 Schedule of Charges, *Trial of Niimori Genichiro* (n 158) slide 4.

160 Schedule of Charges, *Trial of Niimori Genichiro* (n 158) slide 4.

161 Defence Closing Submission, *Trial of Niimori Genichiro* (n 158) exhibit A (P), 1, slide 378.

162 Defence Closing Submission, *Trial of Niimori Genichiro* (n 158) 2, slide 379.

163 Defence Opening Address, *Trial of Niimori Genichiro* (n 158) transcript 114, slide 123; Prosecution Closing Address, *Trial of Niimori Genichiro* (n 158) slide 379.

164 Judge Advocate's Report, *Trial of Niimori Genichiro* (n 158) 1, slide 2.

165 *Trial of Sergeant Maj Yokohata Toshiro* (HKWCT Collection, File No WO235/1117) ('*Trial of Sergeant Maj Yokohata Toshiro*').

166 Judge Advocate's Report [date illegible], *Trial of Sergeant Maj Yokohata Toshiro* (n 165) 1, slide 4.

by the Court.[167] It was clearly established at trial that acts of ill-treatment took place when the civilians were detained by the *Kempeitai* in Shanghai on suspicion of being involved in espionage for the Allies.[168] The accused pleaded superior orders as a ground for mitigation.[169] The trial ended with a guilty verdict and the accused was sentenced to 15 years' imprisonment. On review, the verdict and the sentence were both confirmed.[170]

## 5. Remarks: The Hong Kong Trials and the Subsequent Development Surrounding the Plea of Superior Orders

The survey carried out in this chapter suggests that the plea of superior orders did not create much of a problem for the British military courts conducting the Hong Kong trials. The courts had a fairly clear conception about the applicable law and the effect of the plea. It was, of course, not a process of mechanical application of the 1945 Royal Warrant and the *Manual of Military Law*'s embodiment of international law. But, the weight of the existing international law concerning superior orders as expounded by the *Manual of Military Law* was rather overwhelming, so that there was little trace of a successfully raised defence based on this plea alone. The trials discussed so far might have provided further evidence to the trend of denying the plea the status of a defence. However, the ambiguity left by the *IMT Nuremberg Judgment* and other judicial pronouncements in parallel to these trials has not vanished; rather, it resurfaced in time to influence the drafting of one monumental instrument of international criminal law of our times. This is why the law on superior orders as developed in the 1940s must be compared with the law in its contemporary form, in order to show the extent of development during the intervening years.

The advent of Article 33 of the Rome Statute is a clear indicator that the Nuremberg Charter's rule in this respect was not deemed, in 1998, to be sufficient for the purpose of contemporary international law. On the contrary, the *IMT Nuremberg Judgment*'s reasoning on the issue of superior orders, which preserved the possibility that the plea could be accepted as a defence, has been revitalized.[171]

[167] Judge Advocate's Report [date illegible], *Trial of Sergeant Maj Yokohata Toshiro* (n 165) 1, 1, slide 4.

[168] Judge Advocate's Report [date illegible], *Trial of Sergeant Maj Yokohata Toshiro* (n 165) 1, 1, slide 4.

[169] Judge Advocate's Report [date illegible], *Trial of Sergeant Maj Yokohata Toshiro* (n 165) 1, 2, slide 5.

[170] Record of Proceedings, [date illegible], *Trial of Sergeant Maj Yokohata Toshiro* (n 165) 1, slide 3.

[171] A quick look at the debates of the 1974–1977 Geneva Diplomatic Conference, which produced the two Additional Protocols to the 1949 Geneva Conventions on IHL, would show that the revitalization of that defence actually enjoyed the support of the majority of the delegations in Committee I when voted upon: 38:22:15 (CDDH/405/Rev.1, Report of Committee I, 21 May 1977, OR, vol x, 181). The relevant draft article was however rejected by the Plenary for failing to obtain the two-thirds majority, as the vote ended as 36 in favour, 25 against, and 25 abstentions: CDDH/SR.45, 30 May 1977, OR, vol vi, 307. The reason for the failure was apparently the different treatment of grave breaches and other breaches. According to the draft article, the plea was only relevant to the former.

The gist of Article 33 is that the plea of superior orders can be invoked as a defence, subject to the conditions laid down therein. It provides that:

1. The fact that a crime within the jurisdiction of the Court has been committed by a person pursuant to an order of a Government or of a superior, whether military or civilian, shall not relieve that person of criminal responsibility unless:
   (a) The person was under a legal obligation to obey orders of the Government or the superior in question;
   (b) The person did not know that the order was unlawful; and
   (c) The order was not manifestly unlawful.
2. For the purposes of this article, orders to commit genocide or crimes against humanity are manifestly unlawful.

The terms of the article reflect a compromise reached at the Rome Conference in 1998,[172] in that genocide or crimes against humanity are regarded as two categories of crime that are manifestly unlawful, thus being excluded from the defence of superior orders. But the door is left open for persons charged with war crimes to successfully plead the defence.[173]

It has been noted that national and international law differed in approach on this point prior to the Rome Statute, with the former inclined to the conditional-liability interpretation of the plea.[174] However, the view is not shared that the defence of superior orders cannot succeed in cases of grave crimes even under national law, which upholds the conditional liability model.[175] Whether the plea fails to be accepted as a defence by a court may in fact turn on the failure by the pleading party to meet the requirements of the defence, substantively or in evidentiary terms, and not because the plea simply cannot be a defence to war crimes. Looking back at the post-World War II military trials surveyed earlier in the chapter, and the instruments under which they were conducted in particular, it is hard not to think that Article 33 closely reflects Principle IV of the Nuremberg Principles, which in turn originated in the *IMT Nuremberg Judgment*. The pedigree of the article as such may render it difficult to completely discredit it as a reflection of international law, since it is solidly based in a judicial decision of the highest authority,[176] and well supported by other decisions and subsequent state practice,

State practice prior to the Rome Statute was not that straightforward in respect of the nature of the plea of superior orders.

[172] P Saland, 'International Criminal Law Principles', in R Lee (ed), *The International Criminal Court: The Making of the Rome Statute* (Kluwer Law International 1999) ('Saland, "International Criminal Law Principles"') 210–12.

[173] For the role of the US delegation in the making of this article, which allows superior orders to be invoked as a defence under certain conditions: UN Doc A/CONF.183/C.1/WGGP/L.2, 16 June 1998 (containing a US proposal on relevant articles of the draft Rome Statute).

[174] P Gaeta, 'The Defence of Superior Orders: The Statute of the International Criminal Court versus Customary International Law' (1999) 10 EJIL 172 ('Gaeta, "The Defence of Superior Orders"') 174–81.

[175] Gaeta, 'The Defence of Superior Orders' (n 174) 183, 186.

[176] *History of the United Nations War Crimes Commission* (n 15) 287.

thus signifying perhaps another version of international law on this matter. It may be argued that Article 33 bucks the trend in the development of one version of the customary law in this regard,[177] as exemplified by the statutes of the ad hoc tribunals for the former Yugoslavia and Rwanda.[178] But on further examination, it may also be pointed out that the provision is entitled to claim a basis in customary law, as evidenced by a not inconsiderable number of instances of national practice[179] and judicial precedents from the post-World War II trials. The Rome Statute itself, after all, remains a treaty that has emerged from years of development of customary law. Ultimately, it is always open to States to agree to a new rule that is different from customary law, if any, if their agreement is reached in the midst of such an exercise as the Rome Conference that combined acts of law-making and codification.[180] There is no stopping States bent on making new law from achieving it on such occasions.[181] Law advances to meet the needs of its subjects; it sometimes does so in leaps.

However, based on what has already been said, the content of customary law, albeit in constant development, clearly recognizes two approaches to the issue of superior orders, and has yet to settle on either of them. It may not, therefore, be necessary for the ICC to bring its interpretation of Article 33 in line with the version of customary law as represented by the Nuremberg Charter, Control Council Law No 10, right up to the statutes of the ad hoc international tribunals for the former Yugoslavia and Rwanda. For Article 33 reflects the state of customary law as represented by the *IMT Nuremberg Judgment*, national military law after World War II, and the debates at the Rome Conference that eventually produced the article.[182]

As for the potential of the plea invoked in conjunction with other factors in a certain case, it is probably correct to see it as a mitigating factor in terms of Rule 145(2)(a)(i) of the Rules of Procedure and Evidence for the ICC,[183] or one of the factors that produce the combined effect of another, independent, defence.

A word is added here to support the continued independence of the plea of superior orders in international criminal law. The special defence established under Article 33 reflects the special nature of a plea that cannot be subsumed by parallel defences of mistake of law or duress, which are recognized under the Rome Statute.[184] Destruction of *mens rea*, which would be the common effect likely to

[177] Gaeta, 'The Defence of Superior Orders' (n 174) 190–1.

[178] Art 7(4), Statute of the ICTY; Art 6(4), Statute of the ICTR.

[179] Gaeta, 'The Defence of Superior Orders' (n 174) 176–7.

[180] M Arsanjani, 'The Rome Statute of the International Criminal Court', (1999) 93 JIL 22, 25.

[181] Article 33 of the Rome Statute was initially based in the proposals from Canada and France, which were couched in more lenient terms than those of the relevant provisions of the statutes for the ICTY and ICTR. See Saland, 'International Criminal Law Principles' (n 172) 211.

[182] Schabas has a slightly different view of the basis for this view, which he nonetheless endorses: W Schabas, *The International Criminal Court: A Commentary on the Rome Statute* (Oxford University Press 2010) 507–8, 512.

[183] G-J A Knoops, 'The Diverging Position of Criminal Law Defences before the ICTY and the ICC: Contemporary Developments', in J Doria, H-P Gasser, and M C Bassiouni (eds), *The Legal Regime of the International Criminal Court* (Martinus Nijhoff Publishers 2009) 779, 781.

[184] It is true that a cross reference to Article 33 is included in Article 32 (2) of the Rome Statute.

result from the presence of any of these defences, may happen in very different ways, as evidenced by the defences of, for instance, intoxication or mental disease included under Article 31(1) of the Rome Statute, with each containing elements that are not to be found in the other. Superior orders may lead to the destruction of *mens rea*, but in its own way that can be known only to the soldier on the battlefield. That singularity,[185] engendered by the special nature of armed forces, would dissuade one from merging it with other established defences in criminal law.[186] In that light, Article 33 has clarified the concept and effect of superior orders in international law, rather than made a new rule out of it. The customary law of superior orders is still evolving.

[185] As Stephen once noted, 'A soldier should be protected by orders for which he might reasonably believe his officer to have good grounds', quoted by L C Green, 'Superior Orders and Command Responsibility' (2003) 175 MLR 309, 314.

[186] But see Y Dinstein, *War, Aggression and Self Defence* (4th edn, Cambridge University Press 2005) 87.

# 7

# Concluding Thoughts

*Roger S Clark*

## 1. Introduction

It falls to me to try to place the Hong Kong trials in their contemporary perspective alongside the International Military Tribunal trials in Nuremberg and Tokyo, and to make some modern comparisons, based especially on the contents of the Rome Statute of the International Criminal Court ('Rome Statute')[1] and the early decisions of the International Criminal Court ('ICC').

## 2. War Crimes in a Narrow Sense

It should be understood first that the Hong Kong trials, in common with other post-War British proceedings in Asia and Europe, were prosecutions for war crimes in the narrow sense, breaches of the laws of armed conflict. The acts or omissions that gave rise to criminal responsibility took place in Hong Kong, Kowloon, the New Territories, China (Taiwan and on the mainland), on the High Seas, and in Japan. Many of the victims in the Hong Kong trials were described as 'Chinese', so the jurisdictional theory was a territorial one. To the extent the cases were 'extraterritorially' based, they relied essentially on a theory of passive personality jurisdiction since the victims in those cases were British or Commonwealth citizens. No universal jurisdiction theory was necessary. The concepts of crimes against humanity[2] and genocide that were later to play such a prominent role in

[1] Statute of the International Criminal Court (1998) (entered into force 1 July 2002) 2187 UNTS 3 ('Rome Statute').

[2] Occasional references in the material to 'the laws of humanity' appear to be references to the 'Martens clause' of the preamble to the Hague Convention (IV) respecting the Laws and Customs of War on Land and its Annex: Regulations concerning the Laws and Customs of War on Land, opened for signature 18 October 1907, (1910) UKTS 9 (entered into force 26 January 1910) ('1907 Hague Regulations'), a residual class of customary law of armed conflict:

> Until a more complete code of the laws of war has been issued, the High Contracting Parties deem it expedient to declare that, in cases not included in the Regulations adopted by them, the inhabitants and the belligerents remain under the protection and the rule of the principles of the law of nations, as they result from the usages established among civilized peoples, *from the laws of humanity*, and the dictates of the public conscience. (emphasis added)

international criminal law are not to be found in the Royal Warrant of 18 June 1945 ('Royal Warrant')[3] which provided for the establishment of the British military courts. Moreover, the Crime against Peace, prominent at Nuremberg[4] and Tokyo,[5] was not included in the Royal Warrant.[6] So, no one was prosecuted in the proceedings discussed in this book for the act of aggression itself that was the invasion of Hong Kong.[7]

The Royal Warrant's definition of war crimes, over which the military courts had jurisdiction, was stunning in its simplicity and generality: 'a violation of the laws and usages of war committed during any war in which His Majesty has been or may be engaged at any time since the 2nd September 1939'.[8] This is close to the equally

While Japan was a party to the 1907 Hague Regulations, China was not. Thus, because of the *si omnes* clause in the Convention, it did not apply *qua* treaty law to the conflict in Asia, but was applied in Hong Kong as customary law.

[3] Royal Warrant 0160/2498, 18 June 1945, promulgated by the War Office, Army Order 81 of 1945 (1945) ('Royal Warrant') and annexed Regulations for the Trial of War Criminals ('Regulations for the Trial of War Criminals'). The 44 trials in Hong Kong were among over 500 trials conducted worldwide pursuant to the Warrant in the period 1945–49. A useful discussion of the European trials is A P V Rogers, 'War Crimes Trials Under the Royal Warrant: British Practice 1945–1949' (1990) 39 ICLQ 780 ('Rogers, "War Crimes Trials Under the Royal Warrant"'). Professor Totani, this volume (n 101), relates figures suggesting that there were 330 British trials in Southeast Asia, including Hong Kong, Kuala Lumpur, Singapore, and Rangoon. She has interesting figures too for American, Australian, Dutch, Philippine, and French trials in Southeast Asia, as well as the Chinese trials.

[4] Charter of the International Military Tribunal, annexed to Agreement by the Government of the United States of America, the Provisional Government of the French Republic, the Government of the United Kingdom of Great Britain and Northern Ireland, and the Government of the Union of Soviet Socialist Republics for the Prosecution and Punishment of the Major War Criminals of the European Axis; Judgment of the International Military Tribunal for the Trial of German Major War Criminals, (1946) *Cmd* 6964 ('IMT Nuremberg Charter'). Several of the United States trials held subsequently in Nuremberg pursuant to Control Council Law No 10, Punishment of Persons Guilty of War Crimes, Crimes against Peace and against Humanity (1946) 3 *Official Gazette Control Council for Germany* 50–5, 20 December 1945, also included charges of crimes against humanity and crimes against peace. The United Kingdom did not, in its numerous European trials or elsewhere, avail itself (as it might have done as a party to it) of the definitions of crimes set out in Control Council Law No 10, prosecuting instead simply for war crimes.

[5] Charter of the International Military Tribunal for the Far East, TIAS No 1589 at 3, 4 Bevans 20, 19 January 1946, amended 26 April 1946 ('IMTFE Charter'); B V A Röling and C F Rüter (eds), *The Tokyo Judgment: The International Military Tribunal for the Far East (IMTFE) 29 April 1946–2 November 1948* (APA–University Press Amsterdam 1977) ('*IMTFE Judgment*'). Indeed, under article 5 of the Charter, the Tokyo Tribunal had jurisdiction *only* over those 'charged with offences which include Crimes against Peace'.

[6] The IMT Nuremberg Charter (n 4), with its broader field of subject-matter jurisdiction, was agreed upon in London on 8 August 1945, after the Royal Warrant, but no move was made subsequently to expand the jurisdiction of the courts created by the warrant to crimes against humanity or crimes against peace.

[7] See Professor Linton's chapter in this work for a discussion of the *Sakai Takashi* case, a prosecution in Nanking, where the Chinese military tribunal exercised jurisdiction over the crime of aggression. The death sentence did not apparently include the invasion of Hong Kong, as it could have on the facts. See also R S Clark, 'The Crime of Aggression: From the Trial of Takashi Sakai, August 1946, to the Kampala Review Conference on the ICC in 2010', forthcoming in G Simpson and K Heller (eds), *Untold Stories: Hidden Histories of War Crimes Trials* (Oxford University Press 2013).

[8] Royal Warrant (n 3) reg 1. Regulation 1 added that '[a]ny expression used in these Regulations has the same meaning as in the Army Act or the Rules of Procedure made pursuant thereto'. The military courts were set up by the Executive in application of the residual prerogative powers of the Crown; they

general statement in the IMTFE Charter[9] and only a slightly stripped-down version of what appears in the IMT Nuremberg Charter.[10] Slightly more detail would appear in the statutes of the tribunals for Former Yugoslavia[11] and Rwanda,[12] although the material there was still remarkably open-ended and the offences wide open to judicial creativity. It remained for the Rome Statute to provide a closed itemization of the war crimes (and Crimes against Humanity and genocide) over which the Court would have jurisdiction.[13] The Rome Statute also contributed a detailed 'general part' of criminal law, something totally lacking in the Royal Warrant.[14]

For the Hong Kong cases, and others in Southeast Asia, the Allied Land Forces South-East Asia ('ALFSEA') office in Singapore issued instructions spelling out some of the details.[15] While the ALFSEA Instruction was mostly a bureaucratic collection of forms and procedures, dealing with issues such as the chain of command, how to conduct an execution (and spirit away the remains), and rations for Japanese prisoners and Defence Counsel, it also provided a list of 14 examples of what the Command regarded as the main applicable war crimes offences (see Professor Linton's chapter). It is, in this respect, an interesting example of executive 'legislation', codifying the offences thought relevant by the military legal people for the Hong Kong and related trials.[16] It is probably the case that standards for the principle of legality, or *nullum crimen sine lege*, have become more demanding since

were not the work-product of Parliament, although, as reg 1 indicates, some parliamentary material was incorporated by reference.

9 IMTFE Charter (n 5) art 5 b: '*Conventional War Crimes*: Namely, violations of the laws or customs of war.' 'Conventional' in this sentence meant 'ordinary', that is common or garden, rather than crimes against peace and crimes against humanity—it was not limited to treaty-based norms.

10 IMT Nuremberg Charter (n 4) art 6(b):

> War crimes: namely violations of the laws or customs of war. Such violations shall include, but not be limited to, murder ill-treatment or deportation to slave labour or for any other purpose of civilian population of or in occupied territory, murder or ill-treatment of prisoners of war or persons on the seas, killing of hostages, plunder of public or private property, wanton destruction of cities, towns or villages, or devastation not justified by military necessity.

11 Statute of the International Criminal Tribunal for Former Yugoslavia, adopted by Security Council Res 827 (1993), articles 3 (grave breaches of the Geneva Conventions of 1949) and 4 (violations of the laws or customs of war).

12 Statute of the International Criminal Tribunal for Rwanda, adopted by Security Council Res 955 (1994), article 4 (violations of article 3 common to the Geneva Conventions and of Additional Protocol II).

13 Rome Statute (n 1) art 8 (war crimes). The definition runs about five printed pages in most editions of the text, rather more detail than the simple phrase in the 1945 Royal Warrant. Amendments to the Statute, adopted in Kampala in 2010 but not yet in force, add a detailed definition of the crime of aggression to the Statute (resolution RC/Res.6; see Official Records of the Review Conference of the Rome Statute of the International Criminal Court, Kampala, 31 May–11 June 2010 (International Criminal Court publication, RC/11), part II)).

14 See Rome Statute (n 1) arts 22–33 ('General Principles of Criminal Law').

15 Allied Land Forces South-East Asia, *War Crimes Instruction No 1, 2nd Edition* (4 May 1946), File No WO 32/12197, UK National Archives ('ALFSEA Instruction').

16 As to 'crimes against the laws of humanity' (p 2), the ALFSEA Instruction notes, at 2, that '. . . crimes and atrocities committed by Japanese or satellite enemy nationals against civilians of whatever nationality during the continuance of hostilities will be reported as war crimes'.

1945, although the Hong Kong accused must have found it hard to deny that most of the kinds of activities mentioned in the ALFSEA Instruction were illegal when perpetrated against persons protected by the laws of armed conflict, primarily civilians and POWs. Professor Linton's clear summary, in modern language, of what was actually alleged against individual accused demonstrates the basic and fairly uncontroversial lines within which the Prosecution confined itself:

> [A]buse of civilians (unlawful arrest and detention; torture;[17] cruel, inhuman or degrading treatment); abuse of Prisoners of War ('POWs') (ranging from forced labour to poor working conditions to grossly sub-standard conditions of detention); and unlawful killing of both civilians and POWs. There were also a number of prosecutions involving crimes against *hors de combat*, ie sick and wounded combatants, and those caring for them. On a different level were the cases of stealing and pilfering, and also the forced swearing of oaths, which in themselves are clearly not of the same level of severity, and the appropriateness of the charge can be questioned on a case by case basis (it cannot, for example, be denied that sometimes food parcels kept people alive and their theft could lead to great suffering and possibly death by starvation).[18]

## 3. Finding the Applicable Law

The Royal Warrant[19] provided that the Court 'shall take judicial notice of the laws and usages of war'. But it must have been very difficult for those involved in the proceedings, Prosecution, Defence, judges and Judges Advocate, who evidently did not have access to significant library resources, to be sure that they had it right. Not surprisingly, they seem to have relied mostly for their law on what they obviously had available, the British War Office's *Manual of Military Law*, ('*Manual of Military Law 1929 (as amended)*')[20] and occasional references to international law scholars.[21] Professor Jia[22] points out that in the *Peleus* case, in Germany,[23] also prosecuted under the Royal Warrant, the Judge Advocate advised the members of the Court that, where the statement of law in the *Manual* did not accurately state

[17] In a chilling foreshadowing of the present, those hanged for torture included some who had engaged in waterboarding.

[18] See Professor Linton's chapter in this volume. By the same token, not all the individual war crimes in the lengthy catalogue contained in article 8 of the Rome Statute will always be of supreme importance. Discretion exercised by the Prosecutor or a Pre-Trial Chamber will no doubt keep most such cases from coming to trial.

[19] Reg 8 (iii).

[20] Great Britain War Office, *Manual of Military Law* (7th edn 1929) (reprinted 1939), with 1936 and 1944 amendments ('*Manual of Military Law 1929 (as amended)*'). One is reminded, in this respect, of the enormous influence wielded in American and other British colonial legal history by William Blackstone's 1765 work, *Commentaries on the Laws of England*, in the absence of extensive libraries.

[21] A McNair (ed), *Lassa Oppenheim's International Law* (4th edn, Longman Green and Co 1926 and 1928); F E Smith, *International Law* (1st edn, London 1900), Smith F E, *International Law* (2nd edn, Edinburgh University Press 1903) and later editions; H Wheaton and A B Keith, *Wheaton's Elements of International Law* (7th edn, Stevens 1944).

[22] See chapter 6 by Professor Jia.

[23] Judgment, *United Kingdom v Eck and four others (Peleus Trial)*, in United Nations War Crimes Commission, *Law Reports of Trials of War Criminals* vol 1 (1947) 19.

the law, 'there was no obstacle, legal or otherwise, to correcting the mistake in the statement of law, and to proceeding on the basis of the law as thus elucidated'. I found no instance where the Hong Kong judges took the plunge and departed deliberately from the *Manual.*

Since most of the legally qualified persons involved in the process had practised in English or Commonwealth courts, it was also not surprising that there should be numerous references made on procedural and evidentiary matters to the Bible of British criminal procedure, *Archbold's Pleading, Evidence and Practice in Criminal Cases*[24] and to another classic, *Best on Evidence.*[25]

There is, indeed, a strong flavour of English law in the proceedings and the *Manual of Military Law 1929 (as amended)* discusses mostly British legal sources. Bear in mind, though, that International Criminal Law was in the mid-1940s, even more than it is now, a work in progress, so gap-filling from domestic law was to be expected. There was, it should be noted, not much English domestic law available with respect to war crimes as such since, as was (and is) also the case in the United States, British nationals who were court-martialled for offences against 'enemy' civilians or military were normally charged with 'domestic' crimes such as murder, rape, or assault rather than with a breach of the laws of armed conflict.[26] That has now changed some for the future in the United Kingdom as a result of the International Criminal Court Act 2001.[27] Enacted to give effect to the Rome Statute, it encourages charges under British law in line with the Statute. So, as in other state parties to the Rome Statute, a domestic British jurisprudence, geared to war crimes, is likely to develop. In this development, more attention is likely to be given to the elements of the offences, including such jurisdictional questions, glossed over in the Hong Kong trials, as how particular victims are protected by such laws of armed conflict as the Hague and Geneva Conventions in their Rome Statute manifestation.

Another aspect of the military manual model appeared again (creatively) in the negotiations on the ICC. United States military representatives in the negotiations pressed for the requirement that became article 9 of the Rome Statute, namely the mandate to develop 'Elements of Crimes' to 'assist the Court in the interpretation and application of articles 6, 7 and 8 [of the Statute—the provisions defining the substantive crimes]'. When it came to considering the details of the Elements at the Preparatory Commission for the Court, it became clear that the military lawyers had in mind provisions in American military manuals that set out the elements of

24 The edition available in Hong Kong seems to have been by J F Archbold, R E Ross, and T R Fitzwaller Butler (eds) (29th edn, Sweet and Maxwell 1934). Archbold went through 42 editions between 1822 and 1992 and now appears annually. Given its huge commercial and forensic success and citation even in modern international prosecutions, it is not surprising that in 2003 Sweet and Maxwell began publication of a spinoff: R Dixon, K A A Kahn, and R May, *Archbold, International Criminal Courts: Practice and Procedure.* The power of a well-established brand name!

25 W M Best, *The Principles of the Laws of Evidence: With Elementary Rules for Conducting the Examination and Cross-Examination of Witnesses* (11th edn, Sweet and Maxwell 1911).

26 Rogers, 'War Crimes Trials Under the Royal Warrant' (n 3) 781.

27 International Criminal Court Act 2001 (UK).

crimes subject to court-martial jurisdiction.[28] Setting out details in manual form made great sense in a military context where the 'judges', like those in Hong Kong, would not necessarily have legal training and would not have ready access to a law library. There was certainly some debate in Rome and beyond about whether the professional judges of the ICC would need such guidance, but nevertheless the decision was made to 'assist' them.[29]

## 4. The Proceedings Were of a Summary Nature

It also bears noting that, compared with Nuremberg and Tokyo and the late 20th and early 21st century trials, these were summary proceedings, designed to be expeditious and inexpensive. The ALFSEA Instruction underscored what it called the 'nature of the trials': 'The summary nature of trials by British Military Courts will be borne in mind by all concerned, to the end that justice be administered promptly and efficiently.'[30] As Professor Zahar notes in his chapter, which is very critical of the process, '[t]he 44 cases consumed a total of 595 court days, or an average of 13.5 days per case and 5 days per accused. The most rapid of the trials (*Junichi Ito No 2*) was over in two days, while the lengthiest (*Tokunaga et al*) ran for 53 days.'[31] There were no judgments, and the Judge Advocate reports (they reviewed the cases for the Confirming Officer) comprised a few paragraphs. Compare that with the IMT Nuremberg trial that ran for nearly ten months, followed by an adjournment of almost a month for writing the judgment that dealt both with the merits and with the sentences, a judgment that ran to 190 pages. Or compare the Tokyo trial that ran for a year and nine months plus another seven months to write the judgment, and whose majority judgment consumed some 1,281 mimeographed pages. The five dissenting judgments ran several hundreds of pages more, including that by Justice Pal of India who devoted 1,235 pages to explicating his belief that the whole proceedings were legally misconceived.[32] The first completed trial in the ICC took over three years to complete, plus another

[28] The British *Manual of Military Law 1929 (as amended)* (n 20) has never stated the 'elements' as starkly as the American materials do, but the UK negotiators of the Rome Statute Elements of Crimes understood the American analysis with little difficulty.

[29] The indication in the *Peleus* case (n 23) that the judges might exercise their own judgment on the content of international law is suggestive of an approach for the International Criminal Court ('ICC') judges to the Elements of Crimes. Article 9(3) of the Rome Statute (n 1) insists that the Elements of Crimes 'shall be consistent with this Statute'. The reference to the Statute can include, in appropriate cases, reference to other treaties and to customary usages. So, like judges acting under the Royal Warrant (n 3), ICC judges should no doubt give significant deference to what is stated in the Elements of Crimes, but feel free to strike it down when it finds 'the law' to be different. Article 8*bis* of the 2010 amendments (n 13) adds appropriate Elements for the crime of aggression.

[30] ALFSEA Instruction (n 15) para 14.

[31] See chapter 2 by Professor Zahar.

[32] The Hong Kong trials were conducted in courts set up after the event and were open to similar arguments about ex post facto law to those made (and rejected) in Nuremberg and Tokyo. The Royal Warrant, reg 6, was aimed at precluding attacks on the jurisdiction. It provided: 'The accused shall not be entitled to object to the President or any member of the Court or the Judge Advocate or to offer any special plea to the jurisdiction of the Court.'

seven months to write the opinion, and resulted in a judgment of 593 pages (plus a 14-page separate opinion and a 17-page partial dissent)[33] followed by 52 more pages on sentencing the lone convicted person and another 94 pages on principles of reparation. In only a few cases, such as WO235/1012 (*Trial of Colonel Tokunaga Isao et al*), are the transcripts of the evidence and the arguments for the Prosecution and Defence—the meat of these files—anywhere near the length of the judgments at Nuremberg, Tokyo, or The Hague.

Unlike the modern cases, where the judgments are replete with references to national and international precedents, the Hong Kong cases are thin on doctrine. What legal gems the cases contain have to be gleaned from the arguments of Counsel and the summing up of the Judge Advocate, a functionary contemplated by Regulation 5 of the Royal Warrant who was a feature of British court-martial procedure, but whose function was significantly modified here.[34] The verdicts themselves contain no discussion of the details of the evidence given by individual witnesses or any comments on their credibility. Nor do they contain any significant discussions of the legal issues involved. They consist merely of a conclusory statement, geared to the charges made against the individual in question, recording which parts of the accusation had been found to be proved. They normally came either immediately following the conclusion of the prosecution and defence cases, or the next day. Convictions were typically followed by an adjournment of a few minutes for 'deliberation' and then a sentence was imposed. As was the case at Nuremberg and Tokyo, there was no right of appeal. Convicted persons (and others with an interest in them) were, however, entitled to make a petition which was considered by the Judge Advocate in making a recommendation to the Confirming Officer. The recommendations were usually to confirm the conviction and sentence. The decisions of ICC Pre-Trial Chambers (a modern innovation)[35] confirming the charges run far longer and contain far more legal explication than the decisions in Hong Kong deciding guilt or innocence, life or death. Then, at the ICC, as was the case with the tribunals for Former Yugoslavia and Rwanda, there is the almost inevitable appeal.

## 5. 'Modes of Participation'

Most of the international instruments providing for war crimes prosecution, beginning with the IMT Nuremberg Charter, make some effort to deal with the problem of 'modes of participation' or 'parties to offences', that is to say, the responsibility not only of those who physically do the deed, but those to

[33] *Prosecutor v Lubanga Dyilo* (Judgment) ICC-01/04-01/06 (14 March 2012) ('*Dyilo Judgment*').

[34] As Professor Zahar points out, in ordinary British court-martial practice, the Judge Advocate participated in the process to give impartial legal advice which might benefit both sides. In the Hong Kong trials, the Judge Advocate was not present at trial; he merely reviewed the written record afterwards.

[35] None of the documents I have seen concerning the Hong Kong trials set out any criteria for deciding who would go to trial and the decisions were obviously purely executive ones.

whom responsibility is to be attributed. Thus the IMT Nuremberg Charter[36] asserted that:

> Leaders, organizers, instigators and accomplices participating in the formulation or execution of a common plan or conspiracy to commit any of the [crimes within the jurisdiction of the Tribunal] are responsible for all acts performed by any persons in execution of such plan.

I was surprised that there was no discussion of this provision of the IMT Nuremberg Charter in the Hong Kong proceedings. 'Leaders, organizers, instigators and accomplices' are words that are consistent with the Anglo-American concepts of principals and accessories, concepts linking the responsibility of those who engage together in criminal activity. The reference to a 'common plan' and a 'conspiracy' are, to my mind, early antecedents of what was to become joint criminal enterprise.[37] 'Common purpose' is a more English idea,[38] while 'conspiracy' is linked to the more American notion that a conspirator is liable for reasonably foreseeable acts of a co-conspirator done in the course of the conspiracy.[39] The nearest thing to a description of modes of responsibility in the Royal Warrant, however, was Regulation 8 (ii); it took a procedural rather than a substantive approach. It said that where there was evidence that a war crime had been the result of concerted action upon the part of a unit or group of men, then evidence given upon any charge relating to that crime against any member of such unit or group may be received as *prima facie* evidence of the responsibility of each member of that unit or group for that crime. It added, through an amendment adopted on 4 August 1945,[40] that in any such case, all or any members of such unit or group may be charged and tried jointly in respect of any such war crime and no application by any of them to be tried separately shall be allowed by the Court. I have not been able to ascertain whether the evidentiary rule ('*prima facie*' evidence) constituted effectively a reversal of the burden of persuasion by requiring the Defence to affirmatively rebut it in some fashion.[41] This would most emphatically be impossible under article 67(1)(i) of the Rome Statute which includes among the 'rights of the accused' the right '[n]ot to have imposed on him or her any reversal of the burden of proof or any onus of rebuttal'. It is fair to say that, in the mid-1940s, the British and Commonwealth courts were still trying to work out all the ramifications of the decision in

[36] IMT Nuremberg Charter (n 4) art 6.

[37] See chapter by Professor Jørgensen.

[38] The *Manual of Military Law 1929 (as amended)* (n 20) discusses this concept at 107:

> If several persons combine together for an unlawful purpose or for a lawful purpose to be effected by unlawful means, each is responsible for every offence committed by any one of them in furtherance of that purpose, but not for any offence committed by another member of the party which is unconnected with the common purpose, unless he personally instigates or assists in its commission.

[39] *See Pinkerton v US* (1946) 328 U.S. 640.

[40] Army Order 127, 1945. This amendment was obviously designed to cut off applications by defendants to sever trials in order to side-step the evidentiary presumption created in the first place.

[41] Again, the decisions are unhelpful.

*Woolmington v DPP*[42] to the effect that it is for the Prosecution to establish the guilt of the accused beyond reasonable doubt. So it is perhaps not surprising that military courts would not be on the clear end of the explanatory spectrum. Indeed, in international negotiations, it was left to the Rome Statute drafters to articulate clearly the prosecutorial obligation to prove guilt beyond a reasonable doubt and the concomitant refusal to place any reversal of the burden on the accused.

Procedure, in the typical event where there were several parties, was thus covered in the Royal Warrant; the substantive law concerning the responsibility of those parties was left to improvization. As Professor Jørgensen points out in this volume,[43] all of the charges in the Hong Kong cases 'describe the accused's responsibility in terms of "being concerned in" or "together concerned in" the relevant crime, with the exception of a small number of allegations of direct responsibility for ill-treatment'. Professor Jørgensen accurately catalogues the random usages of these formulas in English common law (and occasionally treaty and statutory law). There is no general statute (or even a discussion in a treatise) explicating whatever theory the language entails. Where exactly 'concerned in' came from on the immediate occasion to populate the Hong Kong indictments is something that I have not discovered. Nonetheless, it is clear that it catches what the common law would have called principals and accessories, including those who command, counsel, procure, or aid and abet the person who actually does the deed.[44] It was also interpreted to include a nascent version of the doctrine of command responsibility[45] which was to secure itself a place in International Criminal Law under the aegis of the United States decision in *Yamashita*[46] and the holding of the Tokyo Tribunal.[47] I agree with Professor Jørgensen that it is too much of an extrapolation to see the Hong Kong cases as providing much support for the birth of that strange beast 'joint criminal enterprise'.

42 [1935] AC 462. The *Manual of Military Law 1929 (as amended)* (n 20) contains, at 72–3, a discussion of burden of proof and presumptions that was at the least unhelpful in a post-*Woolmington* world.

43 See ch 5 by Professor Jørgensen.

44 Rogers, 'War Crimes Trials Under the Royal Warrant' (n 3) at 794, says, in respect of the European trials under the Royal Warrant where a similar approach was taken:

> The British practice was to charge an accused with 'being concerned in' the committing of a specific war crime and the English law relating to principals and accessories was often set out by the Judge advocate and counsel as providing analogies on which the court might act.

He does not explain where the practice came from and I have found no other source. The *Manual of Military Law 1929 (as amended)* (n 20) includes, at 106–8, a discussion of aiders and abettors and instigators but does not have any discussion of 'concerned in' that I could find.

45 None of the humanitarian treaty instruments extant at the time of the World War had anything like a clear statement on command responsibility, nor do the 1949 Geneva Conventions. Article 86 of the First Protocol of 1977 to the 1949 Conventions is the first time that such a provision makes an appearance. Protocol Additional to the Geneva Conventions of 12 August 1949, and relating to the Protection of Victims of International Armed Conflicts (entered into force 7 December 1978) 1125 UNTS 3.

46 *In re Yamashita*, (1946) 327 US 1.

47 *IMTFE Judgment* (n 5). See also Rome Statute (n 1) art 28 ('Responsibility of commanders and other superiors'), the current manifestation of the issue.

One other thing about modes of participation is apparent from these trials, and provides a suitable transition into the next section of this overview. Sentencing was not an issue that turned on whether the accused was what might be called a principal or an accessory, or a primary or secondary party. In many of the cases where a prisoner or civilian was killed, the foot-soldier who did the actual killing and the officer who ordered it, or who was in command, were tried and convicted jointly, but when it came to sentencing, the officer was often regarded as having more responsibility and thus sentenced more harshly. Thus the 'principal' might sometimes be punished less than an 'accessory before the fact'. Having said that, one notes that of the four POW camp commandants who were tried in Hong Kong, just one got the ultimate penalty—Major Uete Taichi (Colonel Tokunagao Isao's death penalty was commuted to a life sentence and the others, from the Japanese Imperial Army in Taiwan, China also escaped the death penalty). The two *Kempeitai* Colonels, Noma Kennosuke and Kanazawa Asao, were both sentenced to death. Rear Admiral Sakonju Naomasa (Commanding Officer of the 16th Squadron, South-West Area Fleet) and Colonel Tamura Teiichi (Commander of the 426th Regiment Infantry Regiment) also received the death penalty.

## 6. Sentencing

So far as sentencing was concerned, the Royal Warrant's Regulation 9 provided, laconically, that a person found guilty by a military court of a war crime might be sentenced to death (either by hanging or shooting), imprisonment for life or for any less term, confiscation, or fine. It added that where the war crime consisted wholly or partly of the taking, distribution, or destruction of money or other property, the Court could as part of the sentence order the restitution of such money or other property and in default of complete restitution award a penalty equal in value to that which has been taken, distributed or destroyed, or not restored. It is interesting to note, by way of comparison with the Rome Statute, that, in the Royal Warrant, it is only in the case of crimes against property that there is any consideration given to compensation or restitution. The Rome Statute, echoing the 1985 General Assembly Resolution on Basic Principles Reparation for Victims of Crime and of Abuse of Power,[48] not only contemplates that the defendant may ultimately be required to pay reparations to the victim or the victim's family,[49] but also provides for the participation of victims in the prosecution.[50] The proceedings in Hong Kong were quintessentially in the mould of common law proceedings of their day; they had no room for any (substantive or sentimental) participation by victims, other than as witnesses for the Prosecution.

No further substantive criteria for sentencing were provided for the Court, although the Regulation stated that a sentence of death could not be passed without the concurrence of all those serving on the Court if it consisted of not more than

[48] GA Res 40/34 (1985). [49] Rome Statute (n 1) art 75.
[50] See, especially, Rome Statute (n 1), art 68.

three members, including the President, or without the concurrence of at least two-thirds of those serving on the Court if the Court consists of more than three members, including the President. No 'guidelines' or 'principles of sentencing' to channel judicial discretion were contained in the Royal Warrant and I found no indication that the Court articulated any general considerations.[51]

Some interesting analogies may be made with the ICC. The Rome Statute itself hardly provides much more by way of guidance to the sentencers than the Royal Warrant did. Its most helpful words are that 'the Court shall, in accordance with the Rules of Procedure and Evidence, take into account such factors as the gravity of the crime and the individual circumstances of the convicted person'.[52] My impression is that this very abstract generality reflected something like what the Hong Kong judges did, that is, consider the characteristics of both the crime and the criminal. The ICC's Rules of Evidence and Procedure are somewhat more forthcoming than the Rome Statute itself and a number of the matters included therein have a familiar ring when one thinks about what must have been going on in Hong Kong. Thus, Rule 145 of the Rules of Procedure and Evidence provides that the sentence 'must reflect the culpability of the convicted person' and 'balance all the relevant factors, including any mitigating and aggravating circumstances both of the convicted person and of the crime'.[53] It also insists that the Court should give consideration, *inter alia*, 'to the extent of the damage caused, in particular the harm caused to the victims and their families, the nature of the unlawful behaviour and the means employed to execute the crime; the degree of participation of the convicted person; the degree of intent; the circumstances of manner, time and location; and the age, education, social and economic condition of the convicted person'. 'Degree of participation' is a very significant criterion here. Whatever is to be made of the debate about modes of complicity and article 25(3) of the Statute,[54] the way is wide open to regard a 'principal' (one who pulls the

[51] The *Manual of Military Law 1929 (as amended)* (n 20) was, itself, rather thin on sentencing principles. It did, however comment, at 61 (in the context of courts-martial):

> A non-commissioned officer should, as a rule, be more severely punished than a private soldier concerned with him in the commission of the same offence, while the instigator of an offence should receive a more severe sentence than the person who was instigated to commit it.

The tone of this perhaps supports the instinct of the Hong Kong courts to impose higher sentences on officers and even on NCOs than on footsoldiers.

[52] Rome Statute (n 1) art 78(1).

[53] Rules of Procedure and Evidence, adopted by the Assembly of State Parties, First Session, New York, 3–10 September 2002, Official Records ICC-ASP/1/3, rule 145.

[54] In the *Dyilo Judgment* (n 33), the Pre-Trial Chamber and the majority of the Trial Chamber insisted on characterizing the situation of the military and political leader there as a co-perpetrator and suggesting a hierarchy of seriousness in the order in which the various modes of liability were listed. Compare the Separate Opinion of Judge Fulford in that case and the Concurring Opinion of Judge Van den Wyngaert in the Trial Chamber's 2012 acquittal rendered in *Prosecutor v Ngudjolo Chui* (Concurring Opinion of Judge Van den Wyngaert) ICC-01/04/12 (18 December 2012). Judges Fulford and Van den Wyngaert find a hierarchical approach, and much of the reasoning on which the theory of co-perpetration is based, inconsistent with the plain meaning of art 25(3). I must confess that, as one involved in the negotiations that led to the adoption of art 25 at the Rome Conference, it never occurred to me that it made any difference to sentencing in itself whether the accused was a

trigger, for example) as less, even much less, responsible than the officer who orders the pulling or hands the weapon to the foot soldier (a 'secondary' party in traditional usage). It is not the category of participation that is important, but the relative degree of guilt. This notion was one with which the Hong Kong tribunals were perfectly comfortable, and indeed the typical charge in the indictment that the accused was 'concerned' in the crime easily shifted the categorization of the accused's responsibility from the 'guilt' phase to the 'how much guilt' phase of the trial, from guilty or not guilty to 'how guilty'.

In ICC Rule 145, the Court is required to take into account mitigating or aggravating circumstances. A non-exclusive list of such matters is provided. Aggravating circumstances are said in the Rule to include: any relevant prior criminal convictions for crimes under the jurisdiction of the Court or of a similar nature; abuse of power or official capacity; commission of the crime where the victim is particularly defenceless; commission of the crime with particular cruelty or where there were multiple victims; commission of the crime for any motive involving discrimination on the ground referred to in article 21, paragraph 3 of the Statute, namely age, race, colour, language, religion or belief, political or other opinion, national, ethnic or social origin, wealth, birth or other status.

The mitigating circumstances include the 'convicted person's conduct after the act, including any efforts by the person to compensate the victims and any cooperation with the Court' and 'circumstances falling short of constituting grounds for exclusion of criminal responsibility, such as substantially diminished mental capacity or duress'. There is a close analogy here between the ICC Rule's mitigation role for defences such as diminished capacity or some kinds of duress that do not quite meet the standards for a complete exclusion of responsibility and the way in which the Hong Kong courts dealt with the defence of superior orders. Ultimately the Hong Kong tribunals held in effect that 'superior orders' and 'duress' fell short of being a complete defence,[55] but it is clear that orders from above were nonetheless often treated as a mitigating circumstance, as Professor Jia explains.[56]

Professor Jia has also done an admirable job elucidating the change in the British doctrine of superior orders represented by the 1944 amendment to the *1929 Manual of Military Law* (7th edition), to say nothing of the confusion generated by the apparent flat denial of any role for that defence in the Nuremberg Charter[57]

principal, an accessory before the fact, an aider or abettor, or was involved by means of a common purpose. The real question was that particular person's degree of responsibility—admittedly an elusive concept. The majority's co-perpetrator theory in *Lubanga Dyilo* required that the offender's contribution be 'essential', which seems to mean a substantial 'but for' contribution. 'Being concerned', as used in the Hong Kong cases, does not require a substantial or 'but for' connection between the accused and the events in question. In accordance with the basic English approach to complicity, the causal connection between the accused and the event may be quite minimal. A minimally connected defendant may be 'guilty' but less 'responsible' at the penalty stage. The penalty is ultimately some apothecary's blend of 'individual evil' and 'contribution' to the prohibited event.

55 Under the Rome Statute (n 13) arts 31(1)(d) and 33, duress and superior orders may provide complete exoneration (at least, in the case of superior orders, for war crimes).

56 See pp 194–195 of Professor Jia's chapter.

57 See pp 177–181 of Professor Jia's chapter.

but the Tribunal's opening of the door a little.[58] Professor Richard Baxter some years ago treated the question of superior orders as a poster-child for a discussion of 'ill-conceived' codification.[59] Article 33 of the Rome Statute, its latest manifestation, is probably destined to sow even more confusion in the minds of the unfortunate judges who try to work out its practical implications. Be that as it may, I suspect that they will find it necessary to invoke the power to mitigate, especially in respect of the Rome Statute's apparent denial of the defence to genocide and crimes against humanity. At Hong Kong, superior orders made a regular appearance as a matter of mitigation.

More, perhaps, needs to be said about the concept of mitigating circumstances, since it seems to have played a prominent role in the ultimate resolution of penalties in the Hong Kong military courts. The 'plea in mitigation' is an important feature of life in everyday criminal courts and so it was post-conviction in Hong Kong. The provoked punch ('provocation is no defense to assault')[60]; the starving thief ('necessity is no excuse for stealing'); mental illness short of that leading to a complete acquittal on the ground of insanity ('insanity is all-or-nothing, not a continuum'); eating the cabin boy to stave off starvation in the longboat a thousand miles from land ('die rather than yield to temptation'),[61] all are losers as total excuses or justifications. But they find some sympathy at the punishment phase of a trial. It is not surprising therefore that many of the Hong Kong courts felt sympathy for the recipient of orders, especially for the hapless foot soldier or non-commissioned officer who was required to do the dirty work. Again, an ICC analogy is perhaps illuminating. In a commendable effort at transparency, the first Prosecutor of the Court offered some thoughts on his prosecutorial strategy. He suggested that the Office of the Prosecutor had 'adopted a policy of focusing its efforts on the most serious crimes and on those who bear the greatest responsibility for those crimes'.[62] All the players in the criminal justice system find themselves with some discretion on whether or not to apply the letter of the law. Dare I suggest that one of the factors affecting penalty in Hong Kong was the instinct about whether a particular

[58] See ch 6, by Professor Jia, pp 177–81.

[59] R R Baxter, 'The effects of ill-conceived codification and development of international law', in *Recueil d'études de droit international en homage à Paul Guggenheim* (Tribune 1968) 146.

[60] The *Manual of Military Law 1929 (as amended)* (n 20) has an interesting take at 61 when it comments that 'a court would be justified in awarding a more lenient sentence to a soldier who has been provoked into striking his superior officer than to one who had deliberately struck his superior officer without provocation'.

[61] *The Queen v Dudley and Stephens* (1884) 14 QBD 273 (albeit there that, with the punishment for murder being mandatory, it was left to the Royal Prerogative for the exercise of mercy). The Royal Warrant of 1945 delegated that prerogative down the military chain of command. There were a few occasions when the Confirming Officer, in this instance the Commander of Land Forces of Hong Kong, exercised a power of mercy very similar to that exercised by Her Majesty in *Dudley and Stephens*, although, unlike the Queen, who acted on the advice of Her Ministers, the Commander made his own call. The subsequent commutation decisions, when punishment fatigue and realpolitik took over, were made by the Executive, on decidedly general political grounds, rather than some appeal to the equities of particular situations. See R J Pritchard, 'British Postwar War Crimes Courts: The Gift of Clemency Following British War Crimes Trials in the Far East, 1946–1948' (1996) 1 CLF 15.

[62] Office of the Prosecutor, International Criminal Court, Report on Prosecutorial Strategy, September 2006, available at <http://www.icc-cpi.int/> accessed 24 January 2013.

offender was or was not one who 'bore the greatest responsibility'. The higher officers often fit that category.

Capital punishment is, of course, an extreme penalty, to which 22 of the 108 accused convicted in the Hong Kong trials were ultimately subjected. This might reasonably be compared with the 11 death sentences issued in Nuremberg and the seven in Tokyo where the highest level of criminals were tried, to suggest that something harsh was going on here. Alexander Zahar makes the point that '[w]e should perhaps resist judging the British military-court trials by the events that followed them a few years later'. But, he adds:

> Yet we can also not entirely ignore the fact that the twenty-two Japanese nationals put to death in Hong Kong suffered, in a sense, disproportional punishment, when compared with those who received life terms and other long sentences of imprisonment, only to be sent back to Japan, and freed, within a few years.[63]

One is reminded that at the Nuremberg trials it was similarly assumed, even by the Chief United States Prosecutor, Justice Robert Jackson, himself an abolitionist, that there would be some executions. As Professor Schabas notes, when Uruguay, an early abolitionist country, objected to the inclusion of the death penalty in the IMT Nuremberg Charter, 'it was accused of having Nazi sympathies'.[64] Nonetheless, at Tokyo, the position was more controversial. While the Charter provided for capital punishment, both the Australian President of the Tribunal and the Soviet member voted against all the death sentences. None of the Hong Kong judges seems to have had any such qualms. Indeed, those executed in Hong Kong were unlucky in a way other than the grant of clemency to those imprisoned. They were among the last to be executed for war crimes. A sea change in attitudes to capital punishment took place in the ensuing decades as all of Europe, Canada, Australia, and New Zealand joined the ranks of abolitionists. It was plain when the United Nations Security Council was adopting the statutes for the tribunals for Former Yugoslavia and Rwanda in the early 1990s that the European members of the organization would never accept tribunal statutes including the death penalty. And in the negotiations on the Rome Statute, many European and Latin-American states noted that they even had constitutional and human rights qualms about the imposition of life imprisonment, at least unless it included the possibility of parole. The upshot is that the Statute permits the imposition of imprisonment for a term of years, which may not exceed a maximum of 30 years, and life imprisonment 'when justified by the extreme gravity of the crime and the individual circumstances of the convicted person'. This is a far cry from the Hong Kong of the 1940s.

I searched in vain for any indication in the materials that the appropriateness of the imposition of the death penalty received any serious debate, in general, or in specific cases. Indeed, in the specific cases, five or six minutes of deliberation, with

[63] See chapter 2 by Professor Zahar.

[64] W A Schabas, *The Abolition of the Death Penalty in International Law* (3rd edn, Cambridge University Press 2002) 1.

no articulated reasons, often sufficed for making the decision.[65] I take it that those making the decision made some sort of *gestalt* calculation that 'the worst' should hang, but they articulated no criteria for explaining who fitted that category. I had hoped, again in vain, that the cases might contain some discussion of the aesthetics of hanging rather than shooting war criminals. The received wisdom is that, at least in Anglo-American usage, death by shooting is more honourable than death by hanging (at least death by firing squad rather than by a bullet in the back of the head which is still a common method of dispatching miscreants in retentionist countries). It is a 'soldier's' rather than a 'common criminal's' death. These options were open to the tribunals, although hanging became the norm. In one case, that of *Ito Junichi*, an initial conviction led to a sentence of death by shooting.[66] This was one instance where a new trial was recommended—because the procedure had gone awry following an initial guilty plea. Alas for the accused, the second trial resulted in a sentencing decision (which took an adjournment for all of 15 minutes to arrive at) for death by hanging. The sentence was duly carried out.[67] Neither decision contains any discussion of the relative merits of the options or whether the accused had any preference.

The problem of determining who are the worst of the worst is still very much with us, but the casual acceptance of capital punishment found in the Hong Kong cases is a thing of the past.

[65] See chapter 2 by Professor Zahar, fns 329–34.

[66] *Trial of SM Ito Junichi (No 1)* (HKWCT Collection, File No WO 235/914), slide 914.

[67] *Trial of SM Ito Junichi (No 2)* (HKWCT Collection, File No WO 235/1048), slide 1048.

APPENDIX

# Major Murray Ormsby: War Crimes Judge and Prosecutor 1919–2012

*Suzannah Linton*

In the course of excavating Hong Kong's War Crimes Trials, I have had many extraordinary and enriching experiences, and have been privileged to touch the past in ways that I never imagined when I conceived the idea of a research project into Hong Kong's legal history. I have been approached by people from all over the world, with links to wartime Hong Kong and seeking information or assistance. I have been drawn into the lives of people who have passed on, but whose families have reached out to me. I have had the amazing experience of meeting some people, now elderly, who took part in the events that I, as a scholar, have been chronicling. Of these wonderful people who have touched my life and become part of my world, Major Murray Incell Ormsby is the most important to this compilation.

One day in May 2011, Dr Donal Lowry, Reader in Imperial and Commonwealth History, and Irish History, at Oxford Brookes University, contacted me to say that he had read about my work, and that he knew a gentleman who had been a war crimes Prosecutor in Hong Kong. I was ecstatic about this news, as my numerous efforts to find former judges, prosecutors, and lawyers had not borne fruit. Through Dr Lowry, I met Major Murray Incell Ormsby, formerly of the West Yorkshire Regiment, and his wonderful wife, Chris. Major Ormsby had been, from 1946–1948, a panel member (Judge) and then a prosecutor of War Crimes Court No. 7 in Hong Kong. Major Ormsby was involved in 27 of the 46 trials that were held in Hong Kong. As a member of the panel, he sat on the earliest cases such as the Lantau Island case (Silver Mine Bay case) and the trial of *Kempeitai* Colonel Noma Kennosuke. As a Prosecutor, he prosecuted two of the 'Invasion of Hong Kong' trials (Major General Tanaka Ryosaburo and Lietenant General Ito Takeo), and the trial concerning the execution of Sub-Lieutenant (A) Fred Hockley, FN, a Fleet Air Arm pilot, shot down over Tokyo Bay on the day of the Emperor's capitulation to the Allies, following the atomic bombings of Nagasaki and Hiroshima.

Major Ormsby was 92 years old when I interviewed him at his home on 21 and 22 July 2011, and conducted a follow-up interview by telephone on 4 August 2011. I taped my interviews with Major Ormsby, and transcribed them; the complete versions are publicly available, with his consent, at the website of the Hong Kong War Crimes Trials Project: <http://hkwctc.lib.hku.hk/exhibits/show/hkwctc/accountsoftrials/oral>. The precision and consistency of Major Ormsby's long-term recollections about his extraordinary adventure as a young man in his twenties was very impressive. Our first interviews were in a relaxed setting, his family home, and were conversational. Our follow-up telephone interview was also along the same lines. I posed questions in a variety of ways so as to trigger his recollections, and engaged in discussions to extract as much information as possible. While I followed a clear structure in my questioning, the interviews were conducted in a way that was dynamic and responsive. Some questions were open-ended, some were not. Sometimes I presented what I already knew, sometimes I left it to the interviewee to bring up issues, and then probed on what I already knew. The transcripts, I believe, provide a first-hand account of a remarkable person's role in an important process of dealing with some of the wrongs of the Second World War in Asia, and a priceless window into the past. Sadly, Major Ormsby's memory and health deteriorated rapidly in the months after we first met, and he passed away peacefully at home on 6 December 2012 aged 93. The obituaries in The Times on 1 February 2013 and the Daily Telegraph on 26 March 2013 were based on our interviews.

What follows is a lightly edited consolidated transcript of our interviews, drawn together in a way that is conducive to a more general readership. The edits have been limited to deletions of background information, and irrelevant material, and occasional insertions to explain a point that may not be entirely clear. I preferred this approach to paraphrasing our interviews into an article, as it offers the true account of our discussions.

The transcript opens at a point of the interview where we discuss how his journey to Hong Kong, after the War ended, was by way of Singapore's War Crimes Trials.

## Interview with Major Murray Ormsby

### 21 and 22 July 2011—interview at home

[...]

SL: How was it that you went from Burma to Singapore?

MO: I ended up in Moulmein in Burma, which is South Burma and near the railway [the Burma Railway].

[...]

It was there that the CO called me in and said he had to provide a Major because they're forming War Crimes courts from Singapore. He said 'I've nominated you'. I said 'Oh yes? You want to get rid of me, Sir?' He said 'Look, you're going to retain your rank of Major and if you don't go down there, the whole of this unit is disbanding [anyway] so you'll lose your rank and will be posted somewhere as a Captain. If you go on this War Crimes trial you'll retain your rank.' So, I was sent down there to Singapore and stayed in this transit hotel which I can never remember the name of.

SL: At this stage, did you know what War Crimes were?

MO: Yes. In this hotel I used to walk to the Supreme Court in Hong Kong where the War Crimes were being held.

SL: Hong Kong or Singapore?

MO: Singapore. I used to walk down to the Supreme Court and used to sit in on these War Crimes trials, although I was nothing to do with the War Crimes at that stage. But, I did go down every day. I think I was probably noticed: 'Who's this officer who keeps coming into the court?' I had a feeling that they found me there because next minute I was told I was going to be Defence Advisory Officer to the General who had ordered the troops to dig their latrines in the barracks square, that sort of thing. I was assigned to be Defence Advisory Officer on procedure. Not on the defence of the person but advising on procedure [for example, saying:] 'Now you can get up', 'You can cross examine now', 'You can re-examine now'. That sort of thing.

SL: How did you know about the procedure? Did you learn that sort of thing at Sandhurst?

MO: Well, that's true. I've always thought about that myself. How was I to know the court martial procedure? I had a bit of experience but of course most of my experience of court martial came afterwards as a result of this War Crimes tribunal. We knew we were going to be on the War Crimes court somewhere, I could have settled anywhere. Everybody was in this transit hotel.

SL: How many were there for the trials? When you say everybody, can you remember how large a group it was?

MO: They weren't all War Crime people. Singapore was the headquarters of the Command and a very important headquarters. Mountbatten was still there.

SL: How did you find out you were going to Hong Kong?

MO: In the bar one evening, I met this half colonel and he suddenly said 'would you like to come to Hong Kong? I've got to form a War Crimes court.' So, I said 'yes, please'.

SL: It was a colonel who had asked you? Can you remember his name?

MO: Stewart.

SL: It was Colonel Stewart?

MO: What do you know about Colonel Stewart?

SL: He was the head of the panel, of the War Crimes panel. He headed Court No. 7. So, Colonel Stewart went round forming his team?

MO: We met in this bar in the transit hotel and he took a fancy to me I suppose! He said 'Would you like to come to Hong Kong?' I said 'Yes, sir!' He said 'I'm forming a court and I've got to get another member, got to get a Major.' I said 'Ooh yes, rather! Hong Kong!' Even if I'd stayed in Rangoon, for instance, it would have been a pleasure from soldiering in the sticks somewhere. So that's how that happened.

SL: Did you get any training in Singapore before they sent you off?

MO: No, no training. I used to sit in the War Crimes court in Singapore where they noticed me. It was fascinating because you could hear the procedure and all.

SL: So, there was no actual training provided for you? At this stage, you'd had no experience; you'd never sat on a court martial before?

MO: No. Nothing, no.

SL: Was Colonel Stewart a lawyer?

MO: Yes, he was a lawyer. Never forget that you had two divisions in Burma and mostly national service. There weren't many regulars. It was 90 per cent national service. A reservoir, of course, of learning lawyers or would-be lawyers or trained lawyers who could be inveigled to join the War Crimes court.

[...]

SL: So, he was a Lieutenant-Colonel?

MO: Yes, this was part of the act. The President of the Court would be a half-Colonel, a Major would be the senior member which was me and a junior member. Most of the junior members were Indians. Ours was an Indian; he was a great chap. Bajendra Nath Kaul of the Frontier 4th Rifles.

[...]

SL: What were your first impressions?

MO: The centre of Hong Kong had two hotels, the Hong Kong Hotel and the Gloucester, we were billeted at the Gloucester at one stage and the Japanese had this flooring, matting. The floor itself bounced, it was bouncy. You could lie on it and fall asleep quite easily. It had just enough give. The Japanese liked to sleep on the floor. In this hotel, they had the rooms still equipped for the Japanese.

SL: So, you were billeted in a 5-star hotel?

MO: Yes, we started off in Kowloon and were billeted in the Gloucester.

SL: You were involved with the formation of the Court. You were the forerunners. You really set up the whole thing.

MO: That's right.

SL: Can you remember much about that or did Colonel Stewart handle all that side of things? When you were there the other member was there, Captain Kaul?

MO: Bajendra Nath Kaul.

SL: Right. And did you meet any of the Prosecutors at this stage? Did you meet McGregor at this stage?

MO: The Prosecutor was a Glaswegian, a corporal. We opened up with a great flurry in Hong Kong Supreme Court. It was the first time. There were 12 accused. It was the Lantau case.

SL: It was the largest one that they ever did.

MO: That's right, yes.

SL: And the first one [they did]. How did they select that one as the first one?

MO: I don't know. I really don't know why they selected that one. We were told to just get on with it. Stewart was unable at one stage to go back into court and I had to go there and say 'the court is adjourned sine die' owing to the indisposition of the Colonel. I had to say the court is adjourned for the rest of the day—sine die.

SL: So, this was during the Lantau case?

MO: Lantau, yes. That was the first case.

SL: Do you think it could be possible that that case went first because it was so important for the British, having lost face, to show to the locals that they were taking that case, which was involving the locals as victims, and bringing that case first?

MO: Yes, could be. There was great publicity. It was the first War Crimes trial, you know. But it didn't last. We were sent out to Causeway Bay in one of the godowns. We were in a godown for dry goods. The packaging was quite clean. It was perfectly positioned. There was an office one end of the godown which of course was perfect so we'd have the table there and come out of a door and go back into the office—there were two offices behind. It was very convenient actually. Very convenient and out of the way just where the midday gun was fired. Exactly there.

SL: Yes, there's now a hotel there.

MO: Is there? A hotel? Would that be in the godown?

SL: The godown is not there any more, they tore it down. It is all skyscrapers there. That area is called Causeway Bay and it is now a massive shopping area with hotels.

MO: Well, this is where it was. There was a passageway outside where the witnesses could reside before coming in.

SL: Now that was Court No. 7. Where was Court No. 5 sitting?

MO: I don't know. I simply don't know how that came about.

SL: Did No. 5 start work first?

MO: I don't know.

SL: Well, logically No. 5 should come first . . .

MO: The first one was in the Supreme Court. There was big publicity and everyone in Hong Kong was there including [Colonel] Stewart.

SL: And the team that worked on the panel, the three of you, did you have any legal advisors or young officers helping you with anything? There was a lot of paperwork and a heavy schedule . . .

MO: Yes, we had an admin chap, but really he was more concerned with pay and making sure there were chairs and all of that sort of thing. He was in the office in the back of the court.

SL: So, he would presumably be organising the stenographers and making sure there were copies of documents made available for the Defence and the different parties. Was that his role?

MO: That's right. As you know, we used these reporters. At that stage we had these Indian Army girls as stenographers.

SL: So, at the beginning you had two ladies from the Indian Army as stenographers and…

MO: WACI—Women's Army Corps India, something like that. Anyway, Indian ATS.

SL: And they were eventually replaced by professional journalists?

MO: Yes. I remember we had this case in the New Territories where we had to go, some of it was very much China with the bund and the rice fields and we had to go out there and these girls they could hardly make it.

SL: So, the ladies had to come along with their typewriters?

MO: Yes, that's right. They sat below.

SL: That must have been quite exciting, going to a crime scene. You were going to a crime scene. The court was going to the scene of a crime.

MO: Yes, that's right. The whole court. And, of course all of these girls didn't appreciate walking through the rice fields.

SL: So, you replaced the ladies with some men who didn't mind traipsing through the fields?

MO: No, it was only once we had to do it and they complained about having to walk through the fields.

SL: If you cast your mind back to the courtroom can you describe what the courtroom looked like when you were on the bench.

MO: At one end you had the offices. And we had this platform with a table on top. It was very convenient. It was very well placed. You had the offices when you came out of the door, straight on to the raised the platform, the dais.

SL: And Colonel Stewart was in the middle?

MO: Yes.

SL: And you were to his left as the senior officer?

MO: Quite right. I was to his left and the junior was on his right. That's why I was next to the witness stand. That's where I saw this young lady with the cheongsam. It got more and more each day.

SL: Now, where did the accused sit? On the other side?

MO: They were facing the court.

SL: So, directly opposite the court?

MO: Yes. Behind the Prosecution and Defence.

SL: And was the Prosecution on your side or the Defence side?

MO: I was on the left and the Prosecution was diagonally opposite me.

SL: So, they were facing Captain Kaul?

MO: That's right and the Defence were towards me.

SL: And the court clerks were sitting [below] you?

MO: The stenographers were underneath us. The court orderly, he hovered.

SL: Were there ever any problems of order in the courtroom?

MO: We never had any disorder, no. The young national servicemen who were sitting in behind the Jap prisoners, they looked incongruous to me, these young soldiers. We never felt threatened by the Japs at all.

SL: Did any members of the public threaten the Japanese?

MO: No. We didn't get many onlookers quite honestly. The only time we did get quite a few was when Colonel Noma [was being tried] because he was well-known in Hong Kong and we did get quite a few spectators.

SL: And presumably the Lantau case would have had a lot of spectators as well?

MO: Well, that was held in the Supreme Court. There were a lot of spectators because it was the first time. It was a gesture, I think.

SL: Can you remember how many cases you were a panel member for?

MO: Can't remember. When I prosecuted I got details of every case, but not as a member of the court I didn't. I started to keep them, I thought I would, but unfortunately I didn't keep a record when I was a member, but I did as Prosecutor because the Prosecution was me organising it, so that's why I wanted to keep those.

SL: As panel members, how did you work? You had a senior officer there who was a lawyer but what were the dynamics of how you reached decisions? Without going into anything confidential, how did you deliberate for example? Were you taking notes every day?

MO: Well, yes. We took our own notes and the President took his own notes. After the witnesses gave their evidence, the Court was allowed to question everyone, through the President really. Didn't often happen.

We had the unpleasant task of questioning the nurses who had been raped. It was held in camera. They didn't have to describe what rape means. They were asked 'do you understand what rape is?' and [they would respond] 'yes', we didn't go into any details about it. That was sufficient because after all, they were qualified nurses.

SL: I understand that a lot of the evidence was through affidavit?

MO: Yes.

SL: So, you didn't have the opportunity to question people that often?

MO: That is true, yes. There was a chap called Edwards.

SL: Jack Edwards, who was a Prisoner of War in Formosa?

MO: That's right. He stayed on in Hong Kong and became a housing officer or something.

SL: He worked for the government in Hong Kong.

MO: That's right.

SL: Do you remember his testimony about the camps? You questioned him. Is that why you remember him?

MO: Yes, he seemed to crop up several times.

SL: So, you placed your questions through Colonel Stewart?

MO: That's right. If we wanted to ask a question we did it through [him]. Sometimes, he would say 'go ahead and ask yourself' but we never suddenly questioned them without his permission. I don't remember if that was ordered, it was just a natural thing, we felt it was polite.

SL: And at the end of the day, would you relax together and talk about the proceedings?

MO: Yes, when we didn't go swimming.

SL: Where did you go swimming?

MO: Repulse Bay. It was sheltered and not open to the ocean. To the left of that it was open to the sea; it was dreadful and very dangerous. The rocks and the Pacific, it was very dramatic. Repulse Bay was quite romantic at night. But that's another story.

SL: At the end of the day, having heard testimony, you would sometimes go for a swim or you'd have a drink or have supper together and talk about the case?

MO: Yes, true. The hours were 10–4 and you had to be careful of the midday gun, it was just out there.

SL: So, you had to stop for the midday gun? You heard the gun and you saluted and then you had a break for lunch?

MO: A break for lunch yes, after the midday gun.

SL: Then you came back and sat from 2–4 I suppose?

MO: Yes, till 4.

SL: When was the copy ready?

MO: It was very quick. About 5 o'clock. These stenographers, we used 3, we could only pay two on establishment but they divided that between the three of them. $600 each and they worked it out between themselves but we were only allowed 2 but we used 3, but as long as they took the oath it didn't matter. Using 3 made it much easier to provide the copy because they were very good, those chaps. The copy was ready at 5 o'clock. They delivered it to the mess. We were billeted in Kennedy Doa. In what was a bit like an officer's mess overlooking the harbour. A wonderful view. Above the mosquito level, I think.

[...]

SL: Who paid for the Japanese lawyers' housing? Were they given a salary?

MO: We didn't have any dealings with the accommodation for them.

SL: Did the British government pay for their accommodation?

MO: Oh yes. I don't know whether they got it back through compensation. I've no idea.

SL: What did you think of the Japanese lawyers? How did they cope?

MO: Too polite! When the War Crimes trials started we had British defending officers. [The accused] got a marvellous defence because the British defending officers were not particularly polite and they could deal with the Prosecutor. They got a much better defence, I think, when they had British officers defending them because the Japanese lawyers were too polite, too nice. But the Japanese wanted it that way.

SL: Did the Japanese lawyers understand British law? These were War Crimes trials before a British court. The procedure was a British procedure?

MO: Yes.

SL: When the people were talking about murder it was, for example, murder as they understood it in a British sense?

MO: Sorry?

SL: I'm trying to look at it from the Japanese lawyer's perspective. He knows Japanese law but he doesn't know International Law and this is about War Crimes. And he doesn't know British law which also permeates the entire process.

MO: [The Japanese lawyers] had a British officer with them and he was supposed to advise on procedure.

SL: Advising on procedure as you did in Singapore? So, in Hong Kong [the Japanese lawyers] had somebody sitting next to them advising them on procedure?

MO: Yes, the Defence did. I think it was a token thing, though. Some of the officers they had there wouldn't know a court from a . . . In Singapore I was procedure advisor and I sat with the Defence advising on procedure saying 'you can get up now', 'you can re-examine now', 'you can make your closing address now'.

SL: But didn't the Japanese also have a proper legal advisor, a British lawyer advising them. I know sometimes they referred to the help that was given to them by the British legal officers.

MO: I don't recall that. They had an officer sitting with them who was supposed to tell them the procedures.

SL: I think this was more than about procedure. They were supposed to have had somebody because they didn't know the law and the system; they were supposed to have been advised by somebody sitting there who was familiar with the British system.

MO: Yes, they were supposed to have but I doubt whether the young officers were able to. When the War Crimes trials started, they had British officers detailed to defend and the Japanese got a very good defence. The British Defence was able to offset the cruel Prosecutor. The Japanese lawyers were too polite, in my view.

SL: But they were used to a different system where it is not like a clash. That's part of the problem of having a process like this when it is not the way they worked.

MO: That's true.

SL: I'd like to go back to the question of how the dynamics worked between the panel members. When it came to making a decision, and the hearing was concluded and the Prosecutor had rested his case, the Defence had had their closing submissions, how would you then decide on the verdict? Would you all retire together for the weekend? Was it a long and drawn out process or pretty quick?

MO: It depended on the complications. Some cases are more cut and dried than others. During the Hockley case I had this American lawyer sitting next to me because I was prosecuting.

SL: We'll move on to that later. I'm thinking now about in terms of when you were a Judge and a panel member. Was it very hierarchical at that stage? Did you always defer to what Colonel Stewart said or were you quite rigorous with your own perspective?

MO: How do you mean exactly?

SL: When Judges retire, the dynamics of their discussions can vary. There can be one that takes the lead or some are more dominant than the others or some like to have their own separate opinions or some just don't like to discuss with the others. How did it work? You have a military panel here and there is one much more senior officer there who is the presiding Judge. Was it whatever he wanted he got? If you disagreed with him did you feel free to say so?

MO: Oh, yes. Niimori! The interpreter. Though I shouldn't really discuss this....

SL: I'm not talking about a specific case. Generally, how did the decision making process take place?

MO: We discussed it quite openly. We retired; we didn't talk about it in the courtroom. The President only has to get up and say 'we're retiring'. There was a case where we wanted to consult the lawyer in Hong Kong, there was a resident lawyer in Hong Kong. Not particularly for War Crimes.

SL: The Army Legal Officer?

MO: Yes.

SL: Can you remember his name?

MO: No.

SL: Sometimes you consulted the Army Legal Officer. You had no advice from the Judge Advocate because there was no Judge Advocate sitting in the court room?

MO: No, because the President was legally qualified. So, we didn't have someone who advised on legal procedure, as there was in the UK, who would advise on legal procedure and who had no vote when it came to coming to a decision, whether he was guilty or not guilty and also the sentencing, he was just there to discuss the legal aspects, he didn't sit in when the court was discussing.

SL: Do you think that would have been beneficial? Would it have been a good idea to have a Judge Advocate advising you?

MO: The President of the Court was there.

SL: But you don't think it would have been helpful to have an independent person? There was no need?

MO: I don't know. That's a difficult question. We were so used to having a President who was legally qualified. But you're right in a way, especially with courts martial, in my experience.

SL: If I understood correctly from our conversation yesterday, when the file was completed, when you reached a decision and say, for example, you said 'yes, he committed a War Crime' then the entire case would be sent to Singapore to be reviewed there by the legal team who would prepare a brief advising the Commander of the Land Forces in Hong Kong. Then it would come back to Hong Kong and he would review it. Would the Commander sometimes ask for advice when he got the papers back?

MO: Yes, he did. Unofficially, I was sometimes called in by the General and he would say 'I've got all this stuff back from Singapore, come on give me your opinion'. Shouldn't have done, should I?

SL: Were you a Judge or a Prosecutor then?

MO: I was a Prosecutor.

SL: That was a bit naughty.

MO: A bit. Very unofficial.

SL: Was there just one Commander of Land Forces, Hong Kong?

MO: Festing was one. Who was the other? Funnily enough they were the same two Generals I met in the Suez Canal zone when stationed there. Was it McNeil? Festing was a great big chap, heavy; you knew he was there, a great big fella. He had a knob, what you call a stick, very Irish and he had presence. He would come in to listen but he didn't stay more than about 3 minutes and it was just a gesture. I don't think he could care less about what he was hearing but he made the gesture of sitting there.

SL: What they call 'showing one's face'.

MO: When the cases came back from Singapore for him to confirm, I was sometimes summoned and asked to sort it all out.

SL: Do you remember Tokunaga, he was the Commandant of all of the Prisoner of War camps in Hong Kong. Colonel Tokunaga.

MO: Tokunaga, yes.

SL: The British Commander did something very controversial. He reduced Tokunaga's sentence from life to 20 years. When the panel tried him, it wasn't you but No. 5 that did it, they gave him life; they sentenced him to death but the Commander of the Land Forces Hong Kong reduced it to 20 years. Do you remember any discussions about that?

MO: I don't, no.

[...]

SL: Of course the Australians were there, too?

MO: Yes, but quite separate. They made a film. Not about the Australians there but about the Australian War Crimes court. [In the film] the Prosecutor would go out seeking and interviewing witnesses, using all sorts of tricks behind the scenes. We didn't go seeking witnesses outside the court.

SL: Well, how did you build up your cases?

MO: The War Crimes investigation teams headed by a Colonel did it.

SL: I thought the War Crimes investigation team were headed by a Major?

MO: No, it was a half-Colonel. A full Colonel is quite rare as they aren't usually operational. For instance, when I went to the Falklands the Commandant was a full Colonel and he ended up as garrison Commander of Antwerp or something. That's a full Colonel. They were not operational.

SL: So, you're saying that as a Prosecutor you didn't do any investigations and you had a team that did all the main work?

MO: Absolutely. It was like a summary of evidence that I was used to doing. The War Crimes investigation team produced a summary on the accused and that's all we had to go by. You asked and made the witnesses say all that in court, and more of course.

SL: When you were prosecuting, you said you didn't meet the witnesses until they turned up in court. That was the first time you saw the witnesses?

MO: That's true. That's quite true. But the Australians I think they went seeking the witnesses.

SL: Yes, they were much more engaged in the investigation as well. They were supervising the investigations. If you have a Colonel in charge of the investigation team then you can understand them having a lot of independence and operating as a unit on their own and to finish their work. They would give the file to you?

MO: Yes, we didn't get entangled with the Australians. Didn't have anything to do with them really.

SL: Was this a problem? Were there any issues?

MO: No, no. I don't know why. I don't know whose fault it was. I don't know why, yet they were in Hong Kong. It has always been a puzzle to me, why we didn't mix and liaise with them.

SL: Well, they were on the Kowloon side, that might have been why.

MO: Yes, I suppose so but there was a good ferry, wasn't there? Backwards and forwards.

[. . .]

SL: Did you like being on the panel? Did you enjoy it? Did you have a sense that what you were doing was something worthwhile?

MO: Oh, yes. I enjoyed it. I volunteered to be a Prosecutor as I wanted more action. Just sitting there as a Judge was very bad for my morale. I wanted to be involved, you see?

SL: Did you not feel involved as the decision maker?

MO: Yes, but it is not the same, is it? When you're directing the witness it is quite different. I wanted more action and more to do. I volunteered, you see? I was cheeky, cheeky! I've always been a bit cheeky that way if that's the right expression.

SL: So, you didn't feel entirely satisfied that you were contributing enough by being on the panel?

MO: What's the word? Hands-on.

SL: Did you have a sense, like when you were in the Falklands, that you weren't doing enough? You wanted to be in the thick of things?

MO: Yes, but slightly different sort of reasons. I could have sat there right up until the time I retired but I thought 'I can't sit here on my backside not directing'. I wanted to be more involved and that's why I volunteered. I had to as I wasn't qualified, legally qualified, to do it. I was lucky to have been taken on, I suppose. It didn't cost a penny to send somebody from Singapore because Singapore was the headquarters and they had spare capacity.

SL: How closely was Singapore monitoring what you were doing?

MO: I don't recall there being any trouble or any difficulty.

SL: As a panel member, did you ever have a sense that you were being bullied into anything or anybody was impeding your independence? Did you feel happy with all the decisions that you took when you were a panel member? Did you ever have a sense that somebody was interfering?

MO: No. Only the Niimori Case again. I saved his life on that charge. It was just a voice. Some people are so good at copying voices and that's why with Niimori I saved his life. Literally, and one of your legal people wrote a book and he criticised the court, meaning me! I stood out you see. If I'd said yes, then he would have been hanged. But I stood out, as I didn't think a voice was good enough. What's the legal position on this?

SL: At the end of the day, the Judges must be satisfied beyond reasonable doubt. There wasn't sufficient evidence to convince you. There wasn't enough to satisfy you and you required unanimity, all three had to agree?

MO: That's right.

SL: Was this a rule that was set out in the Manual of Military Law or did you devise your own rule on this? Where did the rule on unanimity come from?

MO: I don't know. I can't remember.

SL: It sounds to me like the Niimori case was the one you remembered the most?

MO: Yes. People are so clever at imitating voices.

SL: I think also, with the kind of evidence you had, there was a lot of activity going on aboard the boat at that time, there were a lot of voices and there was the battening of the hatches going on as well. It would have been hard to distinguish whether Niimori was saying 'batten the hatches'.

MO: My innermost thoughts are that he was guilty as hell but on the evidence. I didn't think it was sufficient. I was criticised for it. One of your legal people wrote a book and commented on the court's decision.

SL: In the *Lisbon Maru* case, there was also the problem that the Prosecutor charged for the deaths of certain men in the hold. But actually there were 2 men who died over night and they had beriberi. They were sick men so there is this problem of causation. Did the men die from beriberi or did they die from the lack of air and the overheating of the holds.

MO: Yes, but it was this voice. There was this Canadian voice because he had been in Canada and had picked up this accent. But I didn't think a voice was sufficient. I felt that he may have been imitated. Sometimes you can't tell the difference and that's what I felt with this chap, Niimori. Part of me thought he was as guilty as hell.

SL: But you convicted him on the other charges, so he went down in the end. There were about 4 other charges including what he did in the Prisoner of War camps in Hong Kong. There were 4 or 5 incidents charged against him. The first charge was the *Lisbon Maru* what you were talking about, there was another boat and there was what he was doing in the Prisoner of War camps. He was an interpreter there. He was Tokunaga's interpreter. You also mentioned Colonel Noma, which was a powerful case for you as well because that was the number one case in Hong Kong.

MO: Yes, I was a member of the court then. That was the only time we got any spectators. He was such a character, with his white horse and all the rest of it.

SL: Why do you think so few people came to the hearings?

MO: We thought we'd be inundated but I don't know. Maybe time was an issue?

SL: People were perhaps getting on with life and rebuilding? But it is not as if these trials happen every day. They had never happened in Hong Kong up to that point. They were very rare in the scale of things. What you were involved in was something extremely rare so it really does surprise me that people weren't going to watch them on a more regular basis.

MO: Yes. I suppose he [Colonel Noma] was a figure of almost a joke, a nasty joke. But that was the only one where we got any spectators. He was known by everybody, you see. 'Only doing his job.'

SL: They were all 'only doing their job', all 'following orders'.

MO: Yes, this business of a lawful order, for instance. The Japanese don't know about such things. Ridiculous. How the hell does a Japanese know what that means? The Japanese peasant class, how do they know the difference between a lawful order and an unlawful order?

SL: Do you think they would have known that it was unlawful to kill women and children?

MO: They're so disciplined. If the Commander says 'you do this' then you do it. How the hell do they know what a lawful order is?

SL: The argument that is used is that something like killing women and children is so obviously illegal. You can't go round killing women and children, even in a wartime situation. If it is an enemy soldier then that's one thing, but women and children, no. It should be something that every human being knows is unlawful.

MO: Yes, I take that point.

SL: But not all situations were as blatant as that. If you take the Prisoner of War camp situation, and you tried some of those Prisoner of War camp cases, the abuse there was a system of abuse that they were part of. The individual guard was behaving the same way everybody else was behaving. He was part of a system that had a certain attitude about Prisoners of War. It is hard for him to distinguish in that situation. Some may ask, what is lawful and unlawful?

MO: Well, yes. How does a Japanese know, a working Japanese know, about lawful and unlawful. The ordinary rank Japanese not the higher ranks. What does he know about lawful or unlawful? He's told to do it.

SL: Do you think they could have said no? Was it possible for the lower ranking Japanese to say no?

MO: You mean if they were told to do something? No, they obeyed orders. Even punching someone is a War Crime. Water boarding, don't you love it? Water boarding.

SL: You did plenty of those cases, didn't you?

MO: It was water torture wasn't it? It wasn't water boarding!

SL: Well, it is an early form of it.

MO: They did sometimes tie them to a ladder and jump on their stomachs. Can you imagine going through that? Dreadful.

SL: Superior orders again. Somebody tells you to do that and you do it. Back to the situation on the ground. Could the soldier or the officer in the police station have said no? Do you think they were actually told to do that or did they just do it because that's the way they did things?

MO: They used to tell us that 'it was the Chinese that taught us to be cruel. We're not naturally that way but the Chinese, some years ago, forced us to be aggressive in that way.'

SL: And where did the Chinese teach them to be cruel? Was that during the war with China?

MO: Well, I don't know when. The Sino-Japanese war? Started in 1926, didn't it?

SL: 1937, the war started earlier with China, yes. Who do you mean by 'they' when you say 'they told us that they learned how to be cruel from the Chinese'?

MO: Oh, they? The Japanese. The Japanese accused. They didn't state it in court but unofficially. Sometimes, we used to meet the lawyers, unofficially of course, in their quarters. Everybody let their hair down.

SL: And this was when you were prosecuting? The Prosecution and Defence used to work together?

MO: Yes, not when I was a member of the court. As a Prosecutor I would see the lawyers in their own dingy quarters.

SL: These were the Japanese lawyers?

MO: Yes.

SL: And you brought interpreters with you?

MO: Yes, quite enlightening. Just interested to know what their views were. But they would have got a much better defence if they had kept their British defending officers. They argued with the British, they could argue with the British Prosecutor. The Japanese lawyers were too polite. But they insisted on having their own lawyers.

[...]

SL: How was it that you became a Prosecutor when you started off as a Judge?

MO: Mr McGregor was the Prosecutor. He went back to Australia. I then went and said 'There's obviously going to be a vacancy for the Prosecutor so I'll save the government money not importing from Singapore' because that was the Headquarters for South East Asia and that's where the personnel were. So, I said 'I believe I can do it. I've listened for a whole year to various cases and I honestly think I can do it.' 'Right, you're on' he said.

SL: That took a lot of confidence for a young man. McGregor was good and he was a lawyer so you had been watching somebody very skilled.

MO: Yes, I'd listened to all sorts of cases and I just picked up knowledge really and I thought I could do it which I hope I did. Out of all the cases I prosecuted, I only got one not-guilty and that was a 'no case to answer' which should never have come to court.

SL: That was an invasion case?

MO: No, it wasn't. It wasn't what we call an important case. It should never have got through. The War Crimes investigation team slightly boobed on it.

SL: How did the War Crimes investigation team work with the Prosecutors? Who told them which cases to investigate?

MO: We were just given the finished article.

SL: Okay, so you don't know anything about how it was that they got involved in looking at a case. There are some gaps. The sexual violence, for example, you mentioned the nurses, but there was a lot more that went on in Hong Kong that wasn't prosecuted.

MO: Sure, as you say.

SL: Would Singapore have told them what to do? Singapore did preliminary investigations and then they directed them to your team?

MO: Well, the preliminary investigations were the War Crimes investigation team in Hong Kong. Singapore only accepted the evidence of the War Crimes investigation team based in Hong Kong.

SL: It wasn't the other way round? You're telling me that the investigation team gave you a ready-made case and you had no control over it as a Prosecutor?

MO: No, unlike the Australian team, so I understand from the film, they used to go digging out and the Prosecutor would himself go digging out evidence but we didn't have to do any of that.

SL: So in the case like the one where you had a 'no case to answer' you could have gone back and asked them to strengthen the case?

MO: Yes, it sort of slipped through the net that one. The only one really. I encouraged the Defence to say 'no case' because they knew but they didn't know how to word it. So, I helped them I said 'there is no case to answer', say that.

SL: How did you know about this concept of 'no case to answer' when you hadn't had legal training?

MO: In the past there have been similar cases and I put 2 and 2 together and so it was based on previous experience. If I hadn't said that we'd have gone on trying to manufacture evidence and cross-examine and I knew that it'd never get any further. You see, lawyers don't like to be defeated, do they? I said there was no case to answer, simple as that. But they tried to make a case out of it. I don't blame the investigation team. Every other case was very good as they did produce evidence but this particular one I think they admitted it in the end—it shouldn't have gone further.

SL: I see. Now tell me, once they accepted you as a Prosecutor did you remain in Court No. 7? Did you not move to Court No. 5?

MO: I don't remember it all that well. I just remember when we were just the one court.

SL: So, you'd moved from being a panellist with Colonel Stewart to being a Prosecutor arguing before Stewart? Who took your place when you stepped down from being a panel member? Was it Loranger?

MO: I can't [really] remember. I think we imported somebody from Singapore, because you didn't have to be a lawyer, just an Army officer of Major rank or similar.

SL: Can you remember the first case that you argued as a Prosecutor?

MO: I don't recall it but I have evidence in the red book [newspaper clippings collection]. I was pretty green. The American lawyer sat in court for Hockley's case. He had organised the whole thing, it must've been awful for him but he couldn't address the court but he sat next to me always asking this and that, it was awful! I felt like asking him to be quiet but of course I couldn't. I could understand his feelings having organised it.

SL: So, he had built up the case in Japan? Why had the American done the case? Was it because he was investigating it in Japan?

MO: Yes, because part took place in Japan.

SL: And all the accused would have been in Japan because it was after the 15th of August so the fighting was over and those guys were in Japan when it happened. It was investigated by American investigators, the British must have asked the Americans to do it and they transferred it over when it was ready?

MO: Well, yes. That particular day was the 15th of August.

SL: In the evening?

MO: Right. They were all waiting for it [the Emperor's capitulation] to happen, so he [Hockley] was an embarrassment. They [the Allies] dropped the bomb.

SL: In any of the other cases did somebody assist you?

MO: No. All by myself but, of course, he was there, the American Prosecutor.

SL: But he was only there for the Hockley case?

MO: Yes.

SL: The rest of them you were by yourself with nobody giving you advice?

MO: Well, no, because I reckoned I knew it. I'd listened to many cases but nobody advised me, no.

SL: Did you not feel apprehensive about not knowing the law?

MO: Not really, because there was the President of the court [who was a lawyer].

SL: When I look at the transcripts, I don't see the President of the court talking much about law. He didn't actually discuss much law at all. In fact, the law seems to have been quite invisible in these cases.

MO: Yes, well, don't you think that was partly due to the ignorance of the Japanese lawyers?

SL: No, I think it is in the nature of military proceedings.

MO: They had a young officer sitting with them who was supposed to inform them of the procedure but, quite honestly, half the time they didn't know anything about procedure. They were young officers and I felt sorry for the Japanese lawyers because I did that in Singapore. I was asked to do that in that case so I sat in with them. But the only thing I could do was read out his opening address and his closing address but I couldn't do any cross-examining. I had to help him out and say 'you can cross-examine now' 'you can re-examine' 'you can ask questions'—that was my role there but I had no voice except for the closing address and opening address which I read out. He got it translated which was quite awkward sometimes because I didn't have time to study it but we got through anyway.

SL: I was wondering if it is just the nature of military courts martial proceedings that it is not very legalistic. They're designed to be straightforward so you don't have this extensive lawyering in a military proceeding. Court martials are designed to be straightforward summary proceedings and not tied up in all kinds of legal wranglings. The process is designed that way so then you have the parties that are also thinking in straightforward terms.

MO: In England if you had a Judge Advocate sitting in court purely to advise on legal points, he didn't cross-examine which you can do, as a court member. We could step in, if there was something we weren't quite clear about we were allowed to ask the witnesses to say things again. We did it through the President; we didn't just out of the blue say something. For politeness we asked the President 'can I come in here?' We didn't blurt out, we did it through the President and he always said 'yes, ask a question'.

SL: When you got a case, was it a ready-made file, the investigation team would say 'it is ready, here you go, Major Ormsby, take it to court'?

MO: Yes, it was like that. It was a folder with the summary of evidence. It came in the form of the summary of evidence. So you examined on that evidence which the investigation team had gone through and that was the basis of your prosecution.

SL: How long did you have to prepare the case? From the moment that you got the file to when you turned up in court.

MO: You probably had a day to review it, it was very quick.

SL: You often had prepared opening statements which were nicely typed up so you would have had to write the whole thing and then get somebody to type it up for you?

MO: Yes, well obviously we'd read it through or otherwise you wouldn't have any material for your opening address.

SL: The opening statements are all very neatly typed out for all the cases so you had enough time to go through the case quite thoroughly to put it all together and [write] up the very important Prosecutor's opening statement.

MO: We didn't have much time to prepare, really. It was all a big rush.

SL: It doesn't look rushed when I look at the files. It's quite extraordinary that this was done all that time ago after the war and everything is meticulously recorded, the files are very tidy. It seems so organised. When I look back, I think 'how did they do it?'!

MO: I see, I think 5 copies were made when the stenographers had finished. I kept 2 as an example thinking that maybe in the future I'd be able to show it and, of course, you are the future and there they are!

SL: Was there anyone older or more experienced? Did you ever consult the other Prosecutors? Did you ever discuss something if you weren't sure about something?

MO: Yes, sometimes. When I took over, Mac (McGregor) was away, he wasn't there so I didn't have him.

SL: But there were others there?

MO: Pudddicombe, yes. So I did sometimes consult him but not often because I wanted to work it out myself, so to speak.

SL: What did you feel about the people you were prosecuting? What did you feel about the Japanese at this stage?

MO: As a Prosecutor, I felt that they've been accused of this and I'm here to prove that they did it.

SL: You weren't clouded in any way by the emotions of the time? You were able to be objective?

MO: Yes, I think so because I had been sitting as a member, don't forget, so all those extraneous goings-on I had got rid of.

SL: Did you agree with all the cases that you had to argue? For example, some of the cases that you argued involved low-level guards and low-level police at the bottom of the hierarchical chain and you were bringing very serious military charges against them. Did you feel that all those cases were correctly brought against these people? How did you feel?

MO: Well, mostly except this 'no case to answer' which came up and I could see that I'm not going to get a prosecution out of this. The Defence didn't realise this, I was the one that said 'no case to answer', they didn't. If it had been a British officer he would have made a meal out of it.

SL: In all of the cases, you hear it over and over again, 'I was ordered to do it', 'I had to do it', 'my Commander told me', 'this was the Japanese law at the time and I was required to do it'. What did you feel about that?

MO: It became an illegal order or unlawful.

SL: It is the doctrine of Superior Orders. Before the Second World War, it [Superior Orders] had been a defence. If you were required to carry out an order then you could raise a defence of Superior Orders but they changed the law during the War, so you couldn't escape responsibility by saying 'oh, my Commander told me to do it so I had to do it' but you could get a mitigation of a sentence. Do you recall this? What were your thoughts about this?

MO: You had to sort of ask 'do you think this is an illegal order?' That's what we had to consider and play it that way. The bit I used to query was 'how could these Japanese know what an illegal order was?' Because a lot of them were tried. How are these people supposed to know what an illegal order is? It rather worried me.

SL: You had to argue those cases, as a Prosecutor, you had to bring a case against these people and their defence was 'I had to, I was ordered to, there was no way I could say no'. As an officer in the military, as a professional soldier, how did you feel about that?

MO: It's difficult. You can't equate the Japanese mind, the soldier, the coolie, with say a British soldier.

SL: Do you think they really were that different? Do you think they operated differently from the British soldier?

MO: Oh, yes. They were entirely under what the Emperor felt. What he says goes. You can imagine the difference between a private soldier and Japanese soldier.

SL: Now, this discussion was raised even at senior levels. Colonel Noma was saying the same thing and so were the Formosan camp Commanders that you helped prosecute. Do you feel that at that level where you had the Colonels or Majors that they could have also raised this defence of 'following orders'? Let's say for example that Colonel Noma or the camp Commander says 'we couldn't control the food because it was set out by Japanese regulations that came out of Tokyo that said that Prisoners of War get this amount of carbohydrates and this amount of protein and that's that'. The instructions out of Tokyo said Prisoners of War provide their own clothing and the Governor decides certain things. So when you're trying to prosecute the guy, he says 'I had no control, it was all regulated by law' and he's a Colonel, he's saying he was required by the law to do something. Do you have any sympathy with that view?

MO: Well, yes. It comes back to this awful business of an unlawful order.

SL: Do you remember ever having any big discussions in any court proceedings about this concept of orders?

MO: No. But this business of an illegal order, I could never get round that. I thought 'how could this poor little coolie know what an illegal order is?' To them it all came down from His Highness [the Emperor]. No such thing as an illegal order for them.

SL: Let's look at it from the Commanders' perspective and the concept of Command Responsibility. Do you understand what I mean when I talk about Command Responsibility?

MO: Yes.

SL: As a Prosecutor, how was it proved that a Commander, say for example one of those that you prosecuted for the invasion, how did you prove that he was responsible for the killings and the rape at the hospital? What's the link?

MO: You had to prove [who the people who committed the acts were and they could be way down the line; you had to show that that chain came back to the General].

SL: So your case was built on proving that the General was in charge of the guys who did it.

MO: Yes, of that unit who perpetrated the atrocity. We knew that the Commander would not admit that he knew about it but if you could prove that that unit was under his command then that was enough.

SL: So, as a Prosecutor, you were trying to prove: firstly, that a certain unit did that particular thing and, secondly, that that certain unit was under the command of the Commander?

MO: Yes.

SL: That he had control over them, that you could link him to them?

MO: Yes.

SL: As a military Prosecutor, what would you call the link? On a battlefield, you'd have your subordinates all over the place.

MO: It's trying to prove that that unit, that particular unit, was under the command, albeit in a distant fashion, but that somehow he [the Commander] was responsible.

SL: If he was just responsible on paper, for example, but he actually had nothing to do with them and did not exercise control over them, he never even encountered them and never ordered them to do anything, would he still be responsible?

MO: If it was proved that they were under his command then fair enough.

SL: When we lawyers look at it, there are things on paper that say 'you're the Commander' but the reality on the ground may be that he did not control his troops and they were out of control and went berserk. If they went berserk, is that going to be the Commander's fault simply because he was their Commander?

MO: Yes, it is all very well saying it wasn't his fault but the fact that they were under his command . . .

SL: In law we have a concept called 'strict liability'. It is rather like, if you jump a red traffic light, then you will get a ticket. You can have any excuse under the sun but they'll give you a ticket. Is this a similar thing? If your boys did it then you're done as a Commander.

MO: Yes, you had to prove that that unit was under his command. I don't mean just under his command because command goes down in a series of steps.

SL: Did you ever look at what the Commanders did, for example, if they tried to discipline their troops or if the Commanders ever issued orders to troops not to do anything?

What happens if the troops disobey orders? For example, they are told not to touch the women and the children and they go off and they kill the women and the children contrary to orders. Would you be able to prosecute the Commander in such a situation?

MO: Well, I think I would. My impression is that I would prosecute. I mean we had this difficulty all the time. St Stephen's Hospital for instance with the bayoneting in their beds. We had to just prove that those who carried it out were under his command. Maybe down the line. The General, everything that happens under his command, he can be liable for anything that happens like that.

SL: Would you have done that in a British court martial with British officers?

MO: Well, I've never been involved in that sort of situation but I can't see why not. I've never experienced that.

SL: I'm just trying to see if it is an unusual standard, if you would use that standard on a British person? If I had told the troops not to touch the women and the children and they had done it all the same and I was British? It's not a special rule that was developed for the Japanese?

MO: You knew that they were never going to admit to being responsible. What you had to prove was that the people who did it were under his command so far down the line. Even though he may have been too distant to do anything about it as long as it could be proved that it was under his command even if it was done down there and even if it was impractical for him to know about it.

[...]

SL: Those were technical questions and harder to remember as they involve legal issues. There's a technical side that I'm trying to trace and it is always harder trying to remember those things. It's extraordinary how you put these entire proceedings together.

MO: I'm not legally trained. I was a simple soldier.

SL: And you managed to do it and do it so well. This is really the lesson that my generation can take out of this, that things can be left simple and straightforward and you can let the facts speak to you using common sense and logic and not over-legalise things.

MO: That's it, that's me.

SL: It is amazing what all of you did. This is 1946 after the Second World War. The investigation teams managed to compile these cases and the Prosecutors managed to put them together and the Defence managed to at least put on some kind of a show, okay they didn't seem to have been that strong but the evidence seems quite overwhelming and there wasn't much you could say beyond 'I was ordered to do it' or 'they forced me to do it' or 'somebody else did it'. General Ito, he got off light. He was the superior of Tanaka Ryosaburo. Some people expected him to get death but he got [12] years.

MO: In respect of what? Because some minions down the line had done something wrong, you had to prove that they were under his command.

SL: But on the basis of what you were saying that wouldn't have been a problem. His minions did do it. Subordinates did do most of the atrocities. This chap, General Ito, he got 12 years...

MO: This is all very difficult to remember, I hope you appreciate that?

SL: I do! The facts are he got several years instead of being hanged. Perhaps there was some sympathy on the panel for him?

MO: There was another General with overall command of Hong Kong.

SL: Your classes in map-reading from Sandhurst came in useful with those cases?

MO: Captain King, yes! The ghost of Captain King! His teaching saved us getting out of Malaya.

SL: Can you remember when you had a group of people like here [referring to a file] there are 7 of them. You charged them together. Can you remember how you tried to connect them to things? Did you, for example, say they were 'together concerned in a crime'?

MO: In the first place, what I call the summary of evidence would be there for me to go on, for the Prosecutor to go on. The War Crimes investigation team, they produced the summaries of evidence.

SL: Who prepared the charge sheet? Each of the cases has a charge sheet.

MO: I think the investigation team had contact with Singapore, as far as I remember.

SL: You think it was drafted in Singapore? So Singapore probably checked the War Crimes investigation team's file before they gave it to you?

MO: Yes, it is a bit I can't remember really. It must have gone to Singapore first, surely. Investigation teams provided the summary of evidence. Going before a court martial, you have a summary of evidence, which I've taken quite a few times, witnesses on oath and all that sort of stuff. That was the basis for the trial, the subsequent trial. There's so much I forget. Does the summary go to Singapore first? I can't remember. I think it should have done.

SL: Do you remember ever preparing charges?

MO: No. It must have been done in Singapore, mustn't it? The Judge Advocates... My grade was DAJAG Deputy Assistant Judge Advocate and that was a grade that I was given.

SL: When I look at the documents here in front of me now, I see Major-General Erskine assembles a court. He assembles the court and the President is Lieutenant-Colonel Warwick. Attached to his form of assembly of the court, there was a schedule and in the schedule is where you have the charges. So somebody has prepared that. Not you?

MO: Well, I'm sure it was Singapore, wasn't it? Must've been, yes. The War Crimes investigation team evidence must've gone to Singapore, surely for them to prepare a case.

SL: So there was lots of to-ing and fro-ing of the file, at the beginning and then at the end for them to review it all again.

MO: Yes, a lot of to and fro, yes.

SL: Take an example. You have 6 accused in one case. One of the Prisoner of War camps on Formosa. The charges would contain something where they said 'everybody was together concerned in War Crimes'. Do you remember this concept of being 'together concerned in War Crimes'?

MO: No, I don't recall that. I haven't looked at these for years.

SL: But this was something that was in all of the cases. Every single one of the 46 cases in Hong Kong said that the accused was 'concerned in' some form of War Crime. Here you have 6 of them and all the court said was they were 'together concerned in'. Do you have any recollection about that?

MO: No. I haven't even looked at these cases.

SL: The President of the court never raised these issues? These kinds of cases were very complicated. For example, this case with 6 people. It was 6 people doing different types of things. Some were more senior than the others. One was maybe the camp Commander, one maybe the commandant, one maybe the guard, one maybe the interpreter so they're all doing different things but they are all somehow connected. When you tried to argue cases, how did you do the connections?

MO: Weren't they serving in the same unit? I'm sure they weren't separate.

SL: These were in relation to, for example, Daichoku camp in Formosa. They were all involved in different types of abusing the Prisoners of War. Sometimes, it is the guys at the bottom and they're beating the prisoners of war and then you have a little bit further up the Commander saying 'no food today' because they didn't salute and what have you. It's incredibly complex to link it all together but you managed to do that. For a lawyer, it is amazing for me to see this being done because we're so hung up on our legal principles as the glue that sticks things together. You managed to stick it all together and I'm trying to understand what the glue you used was.

MO: I don't remember.

SL: Did you like being Prosecutor?

MO: Yes, because, to use an awful expression, it was 'hands-on' and better than just sitting there like a zombie. It was hands-on and you controlled producing the evidence, it was up to you how long you took to pontificate and that's what I wanted, to not sit on my backside for a year as a member of the court! Talk about cushy time. 10–4 every day and an hour for lunch, midday gun firing at 12 o'clock just outside the door in Causeway Bay. They fired the gun as a signal to traders down the harbour that the goods were coming in because they could see it from Causeway Bay.

SL: After many years the reasons why things are done get forgotten. They are done and nobody can remember why.

MO: The thing with you, as a lawyer, I'm thinking 'these questions, what are they leading up to?' Do you understand that? I've got to be careful what I'm saying.

[...]

SL: Could you describe the office? You described to me how the Judges worked, now where were your offices as Prosecutors?

MO: We didn't really have one, did we? There were some offices at the end of the godown; the godown is the name for where we had the court. Normally, it was just storing dry goods but it was cleared out and chairs were put in, it was quite clean, to form a court room. There was a passage outside, a sort of glassed-in passage, and of course the witnesses were kept on the other side of the court. There was a court-orderly who was responsible for handling the witnesses. He'd be sitting in court by that fence, wall.

SL: So, as a Prosecutor, you didn't have an office? There wasn't a Judge Advocate General's office in Hong Kong? Where did you keep all your papers and where did the investigators keep the papers and the evidence?

MO: I took them back to the mess with me. I didn't have an office.

SL: When I look at documents in the file, like your closing address, it has all been nicely typed up. Who typed it for you?

MO: Our stenographers.

SL: From what I see, you presented a typed document to the court and you read from something that had already been typed up. How did you get it typed if you had no office?

MO: We had a typist, mainly for admin. We still had to pay people and have that sort of backup at the office at the back.

SL: The office at the back of the courtroom?

MO: We had a lady typist and she sat there doing her stuff and sorting out the pay for the stenographers, for instance, because we had 3 stenographers but were only allowed to pay 2 so they divided the money between the 3 of them.

SL: But those were the court's stenographers and not the Prosecutor's typists. Your one lady was separate from these three ladies?

MO: I didn't have a separate typist.

SL: But these were 3 ladies for typing all day long in the court. When did they find the time to do your closing address?

MO: Well, they just found time.

SL: Every single one [of the opening and closing submissions] is very nicely typed out. Here is an exhibit that has been submitted to the court. The Defence and the Prosecutors are reading from these so it has not been done by the stenographer in the courtroom. It is not a transcript but a separate document that has been prepared in advance.

MO: Frankly, I cannot remember. I can't remember whether it was the lady who did the admin behind the scenes. I'm not used to all this talking! Carry on with the cross-examination! You can't help it!

SL: Do you think that the Japanese got a fair trial?

MO: Yes, I did. I can't think anything else, can I? Being a member of the establishment.

SL: Earlier you had said that there were problems with the defence lawyers . . .

MO: They insisted upon having their own lawyers. I'm of the opinion that they would have been better off with British defending officers, frankly, but they insisted on having it. We couldn't refuse then, could we? Otherwise, they would have said 'you're prejudiced, you're prejudiced, we didn't have our own defence'. You see they were too nice, the Japanese lawyers, not the accused people, they were naughty boys.

SL: That leads me to ask how did the accused behave in court?

MO: Very well, very well. They were no trouble. They sat there behind the desk with one national service soldier guarding them. He wouldn't know what to do as he was a young national serviceman out from England. He provided the guard for them, marvellous, isn't it?

SL: So, there was no trouble and they were cooperative?

MO: They never caused any trouble; a highly disciplined race.

SL: What did you think of the interpretation? You had interpreters from Japanese to English or from Chinese to English.

MO: Oh, yes. Any kind of cross-examination, where you slightly bully the accused, don't you, 'why did you do that?', 'I see', 'well if you did that, why was that then?' You couldn't have that sort of cross-examination, you couldn't do that, because of course it had to be translated from Japanese to English to Chinese, it was like a flat balloon. You couldn't cross-examine properly in the old fashioned way where you could slightly bully the accused. It took too long, English to Japanese, to Chinese, it had lost its, what's the word, incisiveness.

SL: You lose the precision of the language. In your own language you craft your words carefully, you choose them carefully and, as they say, things get lost in translation.

MO: Exactly. Going from English to Chinese with Chinese witnesses, God knows what it sounded like! Sometimes, when I heard him translating, I would wonder whether he's put that across how we want it. But you couldn't do this quick-fire cross-examination. It lost its power.

SL: There were some other things, when I look at the cases, I have concern about. For instance, you had 1 Japanese lawyer defending a whole bunch of them. For example, 10 or so if you take the Lantau case. One lawyer defending a whole bunch of them. And in other cases you have the same 1 guy defending 5 or 6 fellows. Today, you couldn't do that because it is too demanding of the lawyer and you have conflicts of interest.

MO: I can remember that first case because the Prosecutor was a Glaswegian. What is your legal bible? Archbold. That's it! He, at the end of the day, would open up Archbold at a relevant page and would say we hadn't done this or we hadn't done that and he would leave that article open with a tag in there as to what we were doing wrong or right.

SL: So, he was referring to Archbold and you were using the Red Book, the Manual of Military Law?

MO: Right.

SL: Your bible was not Archbold? Your bible was the MML? How did the President feel about that [the Prosecutor citing Archbold at the court]?

MO: He was too cushy was old Stewart.

SL: Were you ever worried when you saw one defence lawyer for 10 accused men or 5 accused men?

MO: No, because that's the way they wanted to do it [so] it was OK.

SL: If there were 6 men, one was usually the subordinate who would say 'number 1 ordered me' but number 1 says 'I never ordered'. So they've got conflicting accounts. The problem with having only one lawyer is one minute he's saying 'no, my client didn't issue any orders' and the next he's saying 'yes, he issued orders'. Did you notice this and were you disturbed by it?

MO: I see what you mean, from a defence point of view.

SL: Did it weaken the Defence?

MO: Probably so. But, they insisted upon having their own lawyer though, so that's it.

SL: Yesterday we talked a little about the executions. Why was it that you were attending the executions, the hangings at Stanley Prison?

MO: It was decreed that when they were hanged, there should be a representative who was in the court at the time that this chap was sentenced. Had to be present at the execution to identify that that's the man we sentenced to death on such a date.

SL: So, you had to go to the hangings?

MO: Oh, yes. It was decreed that a member who was in court at the time this man was sentenced should attend the hanging to identify him. That's how we got entangled in the execution. And, of course, it was easier, was it not, to have the good old Prosecutor present because he had seen all the accused, so he attended most of the hangings. Sometimes actually the Defence, not their lawyer, but the officer they were given [the British advisory officer] but they were only young officers.

SL: It was a very difficult thing to have watched. How many hangings did you watch?

MO: About 3, I think.

SL: Very difficult

MO: Yes, it is not very pleasant. The ones that I witnessed were very good. They made a nice little speech. They asked to say a few words and they thanked the court and said 'sorry to cause this trouble and now I'm going to the land of my forefathers'. These were the last words they spoke.

SL: Did they express remorse?

MO: No. They just thanked us for looking after them. I didn't notice any remorse.

SL: When you look back now, at the age of 91, at what you did as a young man all those years ago, when you reflect on that time, did you realise when you were doing it that you were doing something historic?

MO: I feel that we pioneers of the War Crimes trials, we started it and finished it and we should have got some kind of recognition. I'm admitting that to you. I wouldn't say that because it would be misunderstood, wouldn't it? I do feel that we deserved a mention, a thanks, because it was quite a difficult time. I was a bit disappointed, not that we wanted to get the Victoria Cross but just some kind of mention or a letter because it was making history and it was quite difficult and painful. We were asked to witness hangings and that sort of thing and we weren't recognised by higher authority. A bit disappointing.

SL: Did the experience affect you? You said the hangings were difficult but you were also exposed to a lot of evidence of atrocities.

MO: Did it upset me? No. I suppose, I knew what sort of things I was going to be involved in. It didn't upset me.

SL: When you look back and think about the atrocities, have you reflected on why those things happened? Why they behaved that way? Why there were such things in the Prisoner of War camps? Why people were illegally killed during the invasion? Why did these things happen? You're a soldier. There are rules, certain conduct is unacceptable.

MO: Yes, well there was this awful business of when they dropped the bomb. That was a difficult one to come to terms with. But, of course, the result was something else, but difficult to come to terms with that loss of life. If there hadn't have been the bomb would there have been the same loss of life? How could we have stormed Japan? Japan had to be occupied didn't it? There was no other way, militarily. How do you do that except by dropping the bomb?

SL: Do you know that many of the Japanese who got imprisonment sentences were released very early?

MO: I can imagine they were. I didn't think they'd carry on myself. Is that true?

SL: The last ones were out by the end of the 1950s, within 10 years the last ones were out.

MO: I can appreciate that because, of course, we'd made the gesture.

SL: Do you have any closing thoughts, some lessons for the younger generation and for the military about this experience that you had at the end of the war.

MO: No, I don't think it made any difference about whether we go to war or not, do you think? No.

SL: Has it made any difference as to how people behave during war?

MO: No.

SL: Did it make any difference to you as you continued to be a soldier? Did you learn certain lessons about human nature?

MO: No, not really. It still came down to the rifle with a bayonet on the end, didn't it? Make love and not war, I do agree with that. Do you remember the Yanks used to say that? That's the answer, isn't it? Yes.

SL: Make love and not war, we'll end on that, shall we? Thank you so incredibly much, it is absolutely priceless having spoken to you and shared your memories. Thank you for sharing them.

MO: It has been quite difficult to get back in the mood.

[...]

## Follow-up telephone interview on 4 August 2011

SL: I thought we'd start off by talking a little bit about the Hockley case because we didn't go into it very much in our previous interview. What can you remember about the case of Fred Hockley?

MO: That was my first case and I had this American sitting next to me.

SL: What was his name?

MO: Howard D. Porter. He wrote to me afterwards and apologised for interfering and said 'you did very well' in a flattering way, and also said 'I'm sorry I interfered'.

I've lost the letter! It's a shame because I was talking to the nephew of Fred Hockley about it and I couldn't find the letter, you see.

SL: You must have told him off or something for him to write you a letter. Why did he write you a letter?

MO: Because he felt he interfered too much. I must have shown my annoyance at some time, because he kept interfering saying 'ask him that!', 'ask him that!' It is not very pleasant, is it? You can imagine yourself if you were prosecuting and someone was saying 'ask him that' and 'ask him this'.

SL: What was this American doing in court with you?

MO: The American was in court but he wasn't allowed to stand up and say anything. He was the one who prepared the case. You can't blame him really but he wasn't allowed to address the court.

SL: Did he prepare the case in Japan?

MO: He prepared it in Japan, yes.

SL: How come they didn't try the case in Japan then?

MO: Because he [Hockley] was a British subject; the only one that they knew about. I haven't heard of any others with a British subject as the accused or the victim. That's why it [the case] came to Hong Kong, you see.

SL: What happened to Fred Hockley?

MO: He was put to death. He was shot.

SL: How did that happen? He was a fighter pilot, right? Did they shoot him down or did he have problems with his plane?

MO: He parachuted. The plane was a Seafire, which was a Spitfire that lands on the decks of carriers. He was shot down over Tokyo Bay and he parachuted down and landed in a school playground. He parachuted down on the day of the rescript, when the Emperor was going to make his big broadcast. They'd already dropped the two bombs and were waiting for the surrender [of Japan] so it was a state of flux as you can imagine and this British flyer comes floating down into the playground and they were all rather embarrassed, they didn't know what to do as they were all waiting for this broadcast and so they got in touch with the local military and the local military got in touch with the staff and this is the way it went. For the trial we had the staff officer, the soldier who actually did the killing and the other officer; there were three accused.

SL: One of the officers was from the headquarters? There was senior then mid-level then lower ranking?

MO: This wonderful word 'sochi seyo' came out. He was a staff officer, you see. The CO and the staff officer got together, that's what was happening and the staff officer said 'oh look, dispose of the case we're waiting for the Emperor, this is embarrassing'. The Emperor did give his rescript. Then, it was 'you deal with it, old boy'. They were both very conniving. In the end, they had him shot as it was the easiest way out.

SL: What did 'sochi seyo' mean?

MO: Dispose of. You can imagine how they made a thing about that 'dispose of'. Of course, the staff officer said 'dispose of' and then the local people said 'dispose of, you mean dispose of the body' and he said 'oh, no, I meant dispose of the case'. Dispose of the case, not dispose of him. There was a lot of argument about that.

SL: Did you have any linguists or experts in the Japanese language helping you on that case?

MO: No. They said 'sochi seyo' means 'dispose of' and that's what the dictionary said; it meant 'dispose of'.

SL: Did you do it on the basis of what the dictionary said? You relied on the dictionary and perhaps witnesses?

MO: Yes, well I seem to remember the dictionary came into it because obviously, it was quite a substantial thing to say, and there's always doubt when you get the word 'dispose of'. What do you mean 'dispose of'? Oh, dispose of the case as you think fit and that's how we argued it—'sochi seyo'.

SL: So poor Fred Hockley got killed on the day of the capitulation?

MO: It was on the 15th of August.

SL: When did you start putting notices in the Daily Telegraph? [Major Ormsby had for some years put short notices remembering Fred Hockley every 15th of August in the Daily Telegraph.]

MO: I can't remember. I just cannot remember.

SL: And why did you do that? Had you been thinking of the case a lot?

MO: Quite a lot, yes, I was. I felt that he's a wonderful young man to stand that sort of bullying. In the end they came round to him because he was gasping for a cigarette and in the end they were very friendly to him because he hadn't sort of shown any aggression when he landed and they really came round to him.

SL: How old was Fred Hockley when he died?

MO: Twenties. I can't remember now. It'll be in the newspaper.

SL: So a young man, like yourself?

MO: Yes, you're right.

SL: You were about 28 at this time.

MO: Yes, that's right.

SL: Are you still putting notices about him in the Daily Telegraph?

MO: No, I thought of doing it again but I thought it is up to the nephew if he wants to. I've been to see the nephew, some time ago, in East Anglia and I left it with him. I handed over all the evidence I had. It is up to him if he wants to do it but I don't think he has done it.

SL: But, he [Fred Hockley] hasn't been forgotten.

MO: I hope not. In a way I'd thought about putting it back into a newspaper.

SL: Well, today is the 5th of August so we're remembering Fred Hockley on the 5th of August. 10 days early but it is symbolic.

MO: Yes, you and I are thinking about it. I really don't think it is up to me now, do you?

SL: No, I think you've done your bit.

MO: The nephew is still here, if he want to do it of course. I just thought it was a pity that people didn't know, and it is only because I put that in that the Daily Telegraph military correspondent got in touch with me and said 'what's this about?' I'd put in a note that he was executed and that's how it got into the newspaper. You've seen the cutting?

SL: Yes, I have. I've seen your wonderful book of cuttings.

Now, can you remember any of the *Kempeitai* cases that you did? Colonel Noma, perhaps?

MO: He rode on a white horse.

SL: You were a Judge on Colonel Noma's case and also in the case of the two interpreters?

MO: Niimori, you mean?

SL: Yes, the other interpreter was called Kanao. Niimori was on the boat *Lisbon Maru*.

MO: That's right and all you got was the voice, wasn't it? Yes. Well Niimori, of course, had been in Canada, hadn't he?

SL: I'm not sure about that but he'd obviously learned English somewhere.

MO: Yes, well I can't remember how. We were told but he spent time in Canada and acquired this Canadian accent, you see, which was relevant.

SL: Of course, yes. We talked about that the last time.

MO: I didn't think that the voice was sufficient to warrant the death penalty. What is the feeling in law about the voice?

SL: That was a weak case and I wouldn't have thought it met the burden of proof 'beyond reasonable doubt'. I would have gone with your instinct on that.

MO: But I was criticised, you know, by a well known lawyer who wrote a book and actually mentioned this case.

SL: If you can remember the book, then let me know because I can't find any record of this but I'd like to find out about that.

MO: Well, he criticised me without saying so.

SL: He wouldn't have known it was you.

MO: Well, he did know, he knew jolly well who it was.

SL: Do you remember anything about the case in Taiwan of the Kinkaseki mine?

MO: Kinkaseki mine, yes. Warrant Officer Edwards. Jack Edwards. He was one of the only live witnesses we had.

SL: That's one thing I was going to ask you. Pretty much the whole case was built on affidavits.

MO: Yes.

SL: That would have been problematic.

MO: It was incredible. It was new to us. We'd never had to rely on affidavits as Prosecutors, it was the first time ever, I think.

SL: It puts the Defence very much at a disadvantage because they can't cross-examine.

MO: Quite right.

SL: So when you were on the bench and you had all these affidavits, how did you deal with them in terms of weight of evidence?

MO: It depended on the sequencing, and how it was arranged. Some of the evidence we thought was a bit rocky, a bit awkward, but it just depended on how it was done.

SL: I can see that there was a huge effort to try and be fair about things. I was wondering how can you be fair when you have people in an affidavit accusing someone who has got no chance of challenging them?

MO: Absolutely.

SL: It is a hard one.

MO: Yes, it is, but you know, we had to carry on, you see.

[...]

SL: Yes. Can you remember the Generals?

MO: Yes, and you've got one of them.

SL: I have, his name is Ito.

MO: Yes.

SL: And he only got 12 years.

MO: He only got 12 years, you're right.

SL: Why do you think that was?

MO: I don't know. Can they blame the Prosecutor? It's very difficult to know and to prove that a senior officer like that [was guilty]. The best thing you can do is to prove that the unit that carried out the atrocity, or whatever it was, was under his command, even though it was a pretty long way down the thing, you know? Like a platoon Commander and a General having divisions. That's the best we could do with these Generals and these atrocities because not one of them admitted it, of course, they wouldn't would they?

SL: No, but what's interesting is there were three Generals tried in relation to the invasion.

MO: I don't remember three. I did two, didn't I?

SL: You did two of them; you did Tanaka and Ito. I think Puddicombe did the other one. [Shoji Toshishige]

MO: Did he? Yes. Puddicombe. Did he? I can't remember that.

SL: When I look at this I see all of them got off relatively lightly. One got acquitted which I think was your case. One got 20 years and your other guy got 12 years. So the way I look at this, it was the building of the case. You didn't do the building of the case, was the War Crimes investigation team . . . .

MO: It was a War Crimes investigation team, you're right.

SL: There were problems in showing which troops committed the crimes because these were three Generals with three separate areas of control.

MO: Yes.

SL: So, the challenge was identifying which of the Japanese troops [carried out these crimes].

MO: Well, it was trying to prove that the units which these Japanese came from were under the command of the General. Maybe in the hierarchy right up to the General is quite a list but that's the only way we could get the General in order to win the case, because they had no knowledge of it, of course they didn't.

SL: Do you remember if the Japanese had identifying marks on their uniforms that show what regiment they were with or what unit?

MO: Do you mean at the time they perpetrated [the crimes]?

SL: Yes, exactly. So that people could know. Everybody seems to say 'yes, they were Japanese troops that did this' but people can't identify which unit or which regiment they were with.

MO: No. I just can't remember the details.

SL: And the British Army, of course, can be identified by the markings on the uniform.

MO: Yes.

SL: And I think there was a problem in this case in that they couldn't say which units these Japanese came from.

MO: Yes, during the actual action even with the British Army they do not wear such identification in action. You do not wear these funny signs and numbers and things. As officers, we did not wear our badges of rank. Of course, we were presumably known by our other ranks, right? So we did not wear our badges of rank for obvious reasons.

SL: Yes, I see.

MO: A target, you see.

SL: I'm mentally going back to Hong Kong island and trying to think about the difficulties in proving the case, because there was a lot of very serious criminality that took place and the sentences are pretty light considering you've got these guys [from the *Kempeitai* who got the death penalty] and here we have the Army Commanders sitting on top of some very brutal actions that took place and they get 20 years, 12 years and acquittal. So definitely something was wrong, in the investigation and building of that case?

MO: Yes, I can't sort of remember details here.

SL: That's alright. Can you remember much about the witnesses who testified in these cases? For example, the rape victims. It must have been very difficult for them to come in and testify about all these things.

MO: Yes, I do remember this business of rape of the nurses; being raped in the Jockey Club and that sort of thing. That was very awful. We held it in camera. It took a lot of guts from these nurses to come back into court to talk about it; amazing. As witnesses, you know. A lot of it was held in camera.

SL: Did you speak to these ladies beforehand?

MO: They said 'we were qualified'—they gave their qualifications. 'What does the word rape mean to you? Are you aware of what rape means?' 'Yes, I do'. That was sufficient. They didn't have to go into detail.

SL: Over exactly what was done?

MO: Was done. They were aware of what rape consisted of.

SL: Before you called these witnesses, did you speak to them beforehand?

MO: Oh, yes. You had to as a Prosecutor.

SL: You had to brief them.

MO: Oh, yes.

SL: How was it dealing with these women? Did you have, for example, other nurses there, because it would have been very traumatic for them to be testifying. Were there other nurses in case they collapsed or anything like that?

MO: It was very awkward for them, a terrible thing. We were very aware of it and that it took a lot of courage for them to speak out. Mind you, the court was cleared when they were giving evidence, it was held in camera.

SL: Right. Now, you cleared the court for these [British] ladies, did you clear the court for the other ladies, the local ladies, the Chinese ladies?

MO: I don't remember.

SL: There was Blue Pool Road. There was another charge in Ito concerning killings and some sexual violence on Blue Pool Road towards Repulse Bay area.

MO: Oh, I see. I don't remember that.

SL: When you tried Ito, the General, I looked at what you wrote in your closing submissions, and they were quite legal. You were arguing on quite technical issues of command responsibility. Did somebody help you with those?

MO: This is what I found difficult to do as a non-legal man, right, in arguing some of these cases [it was] very difficult.

SL: I wondered, in that case you had somebody called Major Cross doing it with you and he was from the Army Legal Section. Does that mean he was a lawyer, from the War Crimes legal section?

MO: Cross wasn't. Cross was like me. He was graded. Like me, I was graded as a DAJAG, a Deputy Assistant Judge Advocate General, that was the grading for what we were doing.

SL: When I look at it, and having talked to you, I just wonder if you can remember if there were any lawyers who did help you with some of the submissions.

MO: I don't recall, no. Because, you see, the President himself was a lawyer always, or supposed to be! There was a man called Wait, Colonel Wait. He became manager of the Gloucester Hotel. I can't recall him being legally qualified—extraordinary!

SL: You mean he presided over one of the panels and he wasn't even a lawyer?

MO: No. [he was not a lawyer]

SL: How interesting.

MO: Interesting, isn't it? Yes.

SL: All these years later I'm finding things out—just like being a detective!

MO: He was not legally qualified. Should have been! But I don't remember him being legally qualified, no. Stewart and Laming... Laming was himself a prisoner, I think. You may wonder why he was having anything to do with the panel when he had been a prisoner, albeit for a short time. I don't know whether that was picked up.

[...]

SL: I imagine the shortage of manpower had a lot to do with it.

MO: I was surprised to be connected with various people who were allegedly tortured and yet became members of the court, I'm surprised... Laming, himself!

SL: Yes. Laming was British, he wasn't Canadian, was he?

MO: No, I don't think so, no.

SL: Let me look at my computer and see what I can find out. He turns up in 17 cases but not as much as you. You've got the record at 27. The first case that Laming turns up is when he's a barrister and he's with the Department of the Judge Advocate from India.

MO: Yes. They gave him a rank didn't they, half-Colonel?

SL: Yes, he was a Lieutenant Colonel, RC Laming, Barrister, Department of the Judge Advocate General, India.

MO: Ah, yes. That figures, right. Indian Army, wasn't he?

SL: Yes, and do you know what's also very interesting about the record on this case? It shows that you were also working with DG McGregor. The Prosecutor was Major DG McGregor from the Worcesters and then there was Assistant Prosecutor Major MI Ormsby.

MO: Assistant Prosecutor, did you say?

SL: Yes, and this was March 1947 so this was even before Kinkaseki. So can you remember working together with Mac?

MO: I don't remember. Was I supposed to have been with Mac?

SL: This record shows you were both working on this case. It was a *Kempeitai* case in Hong Kong.

MO: Oh, was it? Yes.

SL: It looks like a small case.

MO: It'll be in my red book, all this.

SL: One possibility, and it is utterly speculative, was that this was like a training run for you. Before Mac left you deputised with him, did one case together with him so you learned the ropes from an experienced Prosecutor?

MO: Yes, was that with Mac? McGregor? Yes. I must have done. I can't remember doing that. You see, I've listened to all these cases but I don't remember being attached. Was I attached to him or under him?

SL: You were under him. He was the Prosecutor and you were the assistant.

MO: I could have been, yes. I don't remember that, frankly.

SL: Yes, well you've remembered so much already! You've been remembering for 42 minutes, so now I have going on 5 hours of your remembering!
It is interesting that we've come across some new things over here now. It is quite fascinating.

MO: Yes, well it is trying to get the old memory back which I find difficult.

SL: It is amazing what you can remember; it really is. Now, did they teach you about War Crimes at Sandhurst?

MO: No.

SL: So, when you were in the Falklands and when you were in Normandy and when you were in Burma when people talked about War Crimes did you know what that meant?

MO: Not before it actually happened. The War Crimes Courts were all . . .

SL: Yes. But if they didn't teach you about [War Crimes] at Sandhurst, and you're an officer, how did you get to understand what War Crimes are about?

MO: It was never discussed. I don't remember War Crimes being discussed at Sandhurst. I do not recall that.

SL: There is a chapter in the Manual of Military Law that discusses War Crimes.

MO: I just don't recall. It is interesting that you mention that. I'm wondering myself if War Crimes were in the Manual of Military Law. I can't recall.

SL: That's alright. You told me when we spoke earlier that you relied very heavily on the MML—the Red Book.

MO: It was written by one of the finest lawyers ever, apparently. A fellow lawyer said it was the best chapter, talking about evidence, that existed and that's very important, isn't it?

SL: It is very important, absolutely. Evidence is critical. Particularly in the English system.

MO: Somebody like me, who is non-legally brought up, relied on that chapter! I was just a simple soldier, don't forget that.

SL: So, you used that Red Book. Did you use the Instructions that they sent out of Singapore—the ALFSEA Instructions on War Crimes trials? Do you remember any of those, there were a lot of rules?

MO: Yes, the way I was introduced to this, it was just a question of the Commanding Officer being asked to provide a Major and sometimes a Captain to fill in these Courts. That's how I got into that. It wasn't due to my experience or anything else. The Commanding Officers were ordered to name a Major and a Captain to form these courts.

[...]

SL: ... Now, you had some civilians involved in those cases, it was not just military but there were some civilians that were tried. Like the Kinkaseki Case, those were civilians. Most of them certainly were Japanese Military Police, which is the *Kempeitai*, and then there were a couple of Army and then a number of civilians that were tried for War Crimes.

MO: Would you call *Kempeitai* civilians?

SL: No, they came under the Army, they were *Kempeitai* so they wouldn't be civilians. But there were a few like the ones in Kinkaseki who were staff of the mining company. People like the Director of the mining company and the mining company guards who weren't part of the Japanese military. It is interesting that at that time you were already prosecuting civilians for involvement in War Crimes.

MO: This was the first time, wasn't it, in history?

SL: One of the very, very early cases, yes. It could well be the first time civilians were tried for War Crimes.

MO: Yes, apparently. So we were told.

SL: You were told at the time that this was the first time?

MO: Yes. I was in Singapore at the transit hotel taken over by the Army, and I used to walk to the Supreme Court in Singapore and listen in on the War Crimes Trials which was a very useful experience for me and actually, because I used to go to court every day, I was made the Defence Advisory Procedure Officer on the case where the General was accused of making the troops dig their latrines in the barracks square etc and making them sign a certificate of no-escape. Of course, the officers got together and said 'Look, this means absolutely nothing! It means nothing signing a piece of paper that you won't escape, sign it, otherwise you're going to suffer here digging drains in concrete.'

SL: Well, that was a big issue [the forced oath-taking] which factored in the case from Hong Kong and the ones from Formosa as well. The decision came out of Tokyo to make the prisoners sign an oath that they would not try to escape.

MO: That's right, but it didn't mean anything.

SL: And they mistreated and sometimes killed those who refused to sign.

MO: That's right, yeah.

SL: In the British Army, were you really legally obliged to try and escape?

MO: Yes, you were. In fact, in Burma you were issued with cloth maps, I've still got one. Would you like it?

SL: Really?

MO: It's a cloth map of Burma. Very detailed. And you could fold it into a small shape and I've still got one.

[...]

SL: Well, lucky thing you never got captured.

MO: I never got captured, no. I didn't get there until just before the end of hostilities. I didn't see much fighting in Burma. I was lucky. I was in a forward outpost then. This was August. Highly dangerous place. There was a track leading through the jungle and one of the officers who preceded me had been killed going down that track to far and that was one thing I was not going to do was go down the track. It wasn't a very pleasant duty being on the edge of this village with that track leading right down into the Japanese camp. I didn't sleep for a fortnight. Thank heavens the bomb was dropped. The villagers came saying 'War finished!'

SL: What do you think about the dropping of the bomb?

MO: Imagine what would have happened had we carried on the war. Imagine the casualties. I don't know though, it is difficult to argue the case, isn't it? We certainly would have lost more men. There's no doubt about it.

SL: When you look back at your life and the things you've done, looking at the Hong Kong years, looking at the War years, what kind of lessons do you think people can learn from that?

MO: From what?

SL: From the whole experience that you had of a young man going to war.

MO: Well, I was commissioned as an officer in the beginning of 1939.

SL: When you look back, what do you think about war? At the age of 91, when you look back and you think about what you did as a young man at the age of 18 going into the business of war?

MO: Well I agree with the Americans—'Make love and not war'.

SL: Do you think that sometimes you can't avoid war?

MO: Well, no. Of course you can't. But I like to think that we've got the facility to make love and not war.

SL: When you think about those Hong Kong years and what you did there in those trials, it must have been a very powerful experience, seeing that you can remember so clearly. Did you not think of perhaps becoming a lawyer afterwards?

MO: Not really, no.

SL: You were so put off by the experience, were you?

MO: Well, not really. But, as a lawyer you have to sort of defend people who you know are guilty and that sort of thing. I couldn't do that.

SL: That is not always the case. You've certainly shown that you could be a Prosecutor.

MO: I could be a Prosecutor but I certainly couldn't defend people who I considered to be guilty and a lawyer mustn't think like that.

SL: But you certainly showed that you could do it and do it very well. They must have used you for a lot of courts martial after that.

MO: Funny you should say that [but] yes, I did. When I got back home I was made courts martial officer in the unit I went to because there were lots of courts martial going on and they were principally arresting men who had avoided the call-up.

SL: Did they now?

MO: A lot of that went on. As you know, they called up men in '39 '40 and a lot of them ignored the call-up and became deserters and at the end of the War they were rounded up and I remember lots of courts martial of these chaps but although they were tried for desertion, it was terribly difficult to prove desertion, i.e they didn't intend ever to come back. That was awfully difficult to prove. Most of them it was just Absence Without Leave. Avoid the call-up paper and just stayed away. It was difficult to prove intention and that they were going to stay away forever. Very difficult. When I got back from doing this War Crimes thing, they said 'Ormsby, you're just the man to take charge of the courts martial'.

SL: Just like it was, 'Ormsby, they need a Major down in Singapore!'

MO: Yes!

SL: When you came back it was, 'Ormsby, you're doing these desertion cases!'

MO: Yes, well you can imagine, can't you. They were all rounded up and the Police had a busy time, you know. These chaps just disappeared and took on jobs at fairgrounds, that was a well known... [ploy]. A lot of them joined things like fairgrounds where they would take on casual labour. I had a lot of that to deal with when I got back to England.

SL: So when did you leave the Army?

MO: I came out early. I didn't stay for a pension, which is one of the biggest regrets of my life. I went out before pension because I just couldn't stand peace-time soldiering. After being through the War as I had done. Having been to Burma and Normandy and all that sort of thing, I couldn't fancy doing regular or routine stuff. That's why I came out. I resigned the commission.

[...]

# *Bibliography*

## BOOKS AND MONOGRAPHS


Archbold J F, Ross R E and Butler F T R (eds), *Archbold's Pleading, Evidence and Practice in Criminal Cases* (29th edn, Sweet & Maxwell 1934)

Banham T, *The Sinking of the Lisbon Maru: Britain's Forgotten Wartime Tragedy* (Hong Kong University Press 2006)

—— *We Shall Suffer There: Hong Kong's Defenders Imprisoned, 1942–45* (Hong Kong University Press 2009)

Barman C, *Resist to the End: Hong Kong, 1941–1945* (Hong Kong University Press 2009)

Best, W M, *The Principles of the Laws of Evidence: With Elementary Rules for Conducting the Examination and Cross-Examination of Witnesses* (11th edn, Sweet & Maxwell 1911)

Chaen Y (ed), *Furyo ni kansuru shohōki ruishū* (Collection of Laws Concerning Prisoners of War) (Fuji shuppan 1988)

Clayton J D (ed), *South to Bataan, North to Mukden: The Prison Diary of Brigadier General W E Brougher* (University of Georgia Press 1971)

Deacon R, *Kempei Tai: The Japanese Secret Service Then and Now* (Tuttle Publishing 1998)

Dinstein Y, *The Defence of Obedience to Superior Orders in International Law* (Sijthoff 1965)

Donnison F S V, *British Military Administration in the Far East, 1943–46* (HMSO 1956)

Dower J W, *War without Mercy: Race & Power in The Pacific War* (Pantheon Books 1986)

Durand A, *History of the International Committee of the Red Cross: From Sarajevo to Hiroshima* (Henry Dunant Institute 1984)

Emerson, G C, *Hong Kong Internment, 1942 to 1945: Life in the Japanese Civilian Camp at Stanley* (Hong Kong University Press 2008)

Fan S C, *The Population of Hong Kong* (The Committee for International Coordination of National Research in Demography Series, 1974)

Felton M, *Japan's Gestapo: Murder, Mayhem and Torture in Wartime Asia* (Pen & Sword Military 2012)

Friedman L (ed), *The Law of War: A Documentary History*, Vol 1 (Random House 1972)

Gittins J, *Stanley: Behind Barbed Wire* (Hong Kong University Press 1982)

Green L C, *Superior Orders in National and International Law* (Sijthoff 1976)

Greenspan M, *The Modern Law of Land Warfare* (University of California Press 1959)

Harries M and Harries S, *Soldiers of the Sun: The Rise and Fall of the Imperial Japanese Army* (Random House 1994)

Heller K J, *The Nuremberg Military Tribunals and the Origin of International Criminal Law* (Oxford University Press 2011)

Ikegami E, *The Taming of the Samurai: Honorific Individualism and the Making of Modern Japan* (Harvard University Press 1995)

Jervis, Sir J, *Archbold's Summary of the Law Relating to Pleading and Evidence in Criminal Cases* (11th edn, W N Welsby 1849)

Kalshoven F and Zegveld L, *Constraints On The Waging Of War* (3rd edn, ICRC 2001)

Lauterpacht H (ed), *Oppenheim's International Law* (5th edn, Longmans, Green and Co 1937)

Lauterpacht H (ed), *Oppenheim's International Law* (6th edn. Longmans, Green and Co 1944)

Levie H S (ed), *Documents on Prisoners of War, International Law Studies* (US Naval War College 1979), Vol 60

Lewis B, *Prisoner of the Rising Sun the Lost Diary of Brg. Gen Lewis Beebe* (University of Oklahoma Press 1993)

Lord Russell E F L, *The Knights of Bushido* (Cassell 1958)

McNair, A (ed), *Lassa Oppenheim's International Law* (4th edn, Longmans, Green and Company 1926 and 1928), Vol II

Newell W (ed), *Japan in Asia: 1942–1945* (Singapore University Press 1981)

Nitta M (ed), *Kyokutō kokusai gunji saiban sokkiroku* (Transcripts of the International Military Tribunal for the Far East) (Yūshōdō 1968)

Picigallo P R, *The Japanese On Trial: Allied War Crimes Operation In The East, 1945–1949* (University of Texas Press 1979)

Pritchard R J and Zaide S M (annot, comp and eds) *The Tokyo War Crimes Trial* (Garland 1981)

Reed A and Fitzpatrick B, *Criminal Law* (4th edn, Sweet & Maxwell 2009)

Ride E, *British Army Aid Group-BAAG: Hong Kong resistance 1942–1945* (Oxford University Press 1981)

Roland C G, *Long Night's Journey into Day: Prisoners of War in Hong Kong and Japan, 1941–1945* (Wilfried Laurier University Press 2001)

Schabas W A, *The International Criminal Court: A Commentary on the Rome Statute* (Oxford University Press 2010)

Schwarzenberger G, *International Law as Applied by International Courts and Tribunals: the Law of Armed Conflict* (Stevens & Sons 1968) vol ii

Smith F E, *International Law* (1st edn, J M Dent 1900)

Smith F E, *International Law* (2nd edn, Edinburgh University Press 1903)

Snow P, *The Fall of Hong Kong: Britain, China and the Japanese Occupation* (Yale University Press 2003)

Stephen, Sir J F, *A History of the Criminal Law of England: Volume II* (Macmillan 1883)

Taiwan sōtokufu (Government-General of Taiwan), *Taiwan tōchi gaiyō* (Summary of Taiwan Governance) (Government-General of Taiwan 1945)

Tōkyō saiban handobukku henshū iinkai (Tokyo Trial Handbook Compilation Committee) (ed) *Tōkyō saiban handobukku* (The Tokyo Trial Handbook) (Aoki shoten 1989)

Toland J, *The Rising Sun: The Decline and Fall of the Japanese Empire 1936–45* (Random House 1970)

Tsang S Y S, *A Modern History of Hong Kong* (I B Tauris 2004)

United Nations War Crimes Commission, *History of the United Nations War Crimes Commission and the Development of the Laws of War* (HMSO 1948)

Utsumi A, *Nihon-gun no horyo seisaku* (Prisoner-of-War Policies of the Japanese Military) (Aoki shoten 2005)

Van Der Post L, *A Bar of Shadow* (William Morrow & Company 1956)

Wainwright J M, *General Wainwright's Story: The Account of Four Years of Humiliating Defeat, Surrender, and Captivity* (Doubleday & Co 1946)

Whiteman M, *Digest of International Law,* Vol XI (US Government Printing Office 1968)

Wright-Nooth G, *Prisoner of the Turnip Heads: Horror, Hunger and Humour in Hong Kong, 1941–1945* (Leo Cooper 1994)

*Australia's Post World War II War Crimes Trials: A Systematic and Comprehensive Law Reports Series* (Martinus Nijhoff, forthcoming)

## BOOK CHAPTERS


Ambos K, 'Defences in International Criminal Law', in B Brown (ed), *Research Handbook on International Criminal Law* (Edward Elgar 2011)

Friedlander H, 'Nazi Crimes and the German Law', in N Stoltfus and H Friedlander (eds), *Nazi Crimes and the Law* (Cambridge University Press 2008)

Han W T, 'Bureaucracy and the Japanese Occupation of Hong Kong', in W Newell (ed), *Japan in Asia: 1942–1945* (Singapore University Press 1981)

Kita Y, 'The Japanese Military's Attitude towards International Law and the Treatment of Prisoners of War', in I Gow, Y Hirama, and J Chapman (eds), *The History of Anglo-Japanese Relations, 1600–2000: The Military Dimension* (Palgrave Macmillan 2003), Vol 3

Knoops G-J A, 'The Diverging Position of Criminal Law Defences before the ICTY and the ICC: Contemporary Developments', in J Doria, H-P Gasser, and M C Bassiouni (eds), *The Legal Regime of the International Criminal Court* (Martinus Nijhoff Publishers 2009)

Kondō M, 'Taiwan no rōmu dōin' (Mobilization of Labour Forces in Taiwan), in *Kindai Nihon no rekishiteki isō: kokka, minzoku, bunka* (Historical Topology of Modern Japan: Nation, Ethnicity, Culture) (Tōsui shobō 1999)

Russell, Sir W M O, 'Russell on Crimes and Misdemeanors', in W F Craies and L W Kershaw, *A Treatise on Crimes and Misdemeanors: Volume 1* (7th edn, Stevens and Sons 1910)

Saland P, 'International Criminal Law Principles', in R Lee (ed), *The International Criminal Court: The Making of the Rome Statute* (Kluwer Law International 1999)

Shahabuddeen M, 'Judicial Creativity and Joint Criminal Enterprise', in S Darcy and P Powderly (eds), *Judicial Creativity at the International Criminal Tribunals* (Oxford University Press 2010)

Zahar A, 'The Problem of False Testimony at the International Criminal Tribunal for Rwanda', in A Klip and G Sluiter (eds), *Annotated Leading Cases of International Criminal Tribunals, Vol 25: International Criminal Tribunal for Rwanda, 2006–2007* (Intersentia 2010)


## JOURNAL ARTICLES


Arsanjani M, 'The Rome Statute of the International Criminal Court' (1999) 93 *Journal of International Law* 22

Baxter R R, 'The Municipal and International Law Basis of Jurisdiction over War Crimes' (1951) 28 *British Yearbook of International Law* 382

Bloxham D, 'British War Crimes Trial Policy in Germany, 1945–1957: Implementation and Collapse' (2003) 42(1) *Journal of British Studies* 91

Cheah W L, 'Post-WWII British Hell-ship Trials in Singapore: Omissions and the Attribution of Responsibility' (2010) 8(4) *Journal of International Criminal Justice* 1035

Clarke R C, 'Return to Borkum Island, Extended Joint Criminal Enterprise Responsibility in the Wake of World War II' (2011) 9 *Journal of International Criminal Justice* 839

Dicks A, 'Treaty, Grant, Usage or Sufferance? Some Legal Aspects of the Status of Hong Kong' (1983) 95 *The China Quarterly* 427

Draper G I A D, 'The Place of the Laws of War in Military Instruction' (1966) 111(643) *Royal United Services Institute Journal* 189

Gaeta P, 'The Defence of Superior Orders: The Statute of the International Criminal Court versus Customary International Law' (1999) 10 *European Journal of International Law* 172

Green L C, 'Superior Orders and Command Responsibility' (1989) 27 *Canadian Yearbook of International Law* 167

Kalshoven F, 'The Undertaking to Respect and Ensure Respect in All Circumstances: From Tiny Seed to Ripening Fruit' (1999) 2 *Yearbook of International Humanitarian Law* 3

Lauterpacht H, 'The Law of Nations and the Punishment of War Crimes' (1944) 21 *British Yearbook of International Law* 58

Linton S, 'Rediscovering the War Crimes Trials in Hong Kong, 1946–48' (2012) 13(1) *Melbourne Journal of International Law* 284

McAuliffe deGuzman M, 'The Road from Rome: The Developing Law of Crimes against Humanity' (2000) 22(2) *Human Rights Quarterly* 335

Narayanan A, 'Japanese Atrocities and British Minor War Crimes Trials after World War II in the East' (2006) 33 *Jebat: Malaysian Journal of History, Politics and Strategic Studies* 1

Prévost A M, 'Race and War Crimes: The 1945 War Crimes Trial of General Tomoyuki Yamashita' (1992) 14(3) *Human Rights Quarterly* 303

Pritchard R J, 'The Historical Experience of British War Crimes Courts in the Far East, 1946–1948' (1978) 6 *International Relations* 311

——'The Gift of Clemency Following British War Crimes Trials in the Far East, 1946–1948' (1996) 7(1) *Criminal Law Forum* 15

Rogers A P V, 'War Crimes Trials under the Royal Warrant: British Practice 1945–1949' (1990) 39 *International and Comparative Law Quarterly* 780

Roland C G, 'Massacre and Rape in Hong Kong: Two Case Studies Involving Medical Personnel and Patients' (1997) 32(1) *Journal of Contemporary History* 43

——'Massacre and Rape in Hong Kong: Two Case Studies Involving Medical Personnel and Patients' (1997) 32 *Journal of Constitutional History* 43

Scaliotti M, 'Defences before the international criminal court: Substantive grounds for excluding criminal responsibility—Part 1' (2001) 1 *International Criminal Law Review* 111

Vine P, 'Experiences as a War Crimes Prosecutor in Hong Kong' (1995) 35 *Journal of the Hong Kong Branch of the Royal Asiatic Society* 205

## MILITARY MANUALS

Great Britain War Office, *Manual of Military Law 1929* (7th edition), as amended by Great Britain War Office, *Manual of Military Law 1929*, ch XIV (Amendment No 12 of 1936) and Great Britain War Office, *Manual of Military Law 1929*, ch XIV (Amendment No 34 of 1944)

Great Britain War Office, *Manual of Military Law 1929* (Reprinted December 1939, as amended 1936) (7th edn, HMSO 1949)

——*Manual of Military Law 1951* (8th edn, HMSO 1952)

War Department, *A Manual for Courts-Martial, Courts of Inquiry and of Other Procedure under Military Law* (Washington DC 1917)

War Department, *Field Manual 27–10, The Law Of Land Warfare* (Department Of The Army 1956)

## UK PARLIAMENTARY DEBATES

Hansard House of Lords Debates 14 May 1952, Vol 176

## ONLINE RESOURCES

Cambon K, *Guest of Hirohito* (P W Press 1990) app 1 at <http://fourthmarineband.com/cambon8.htm> accessed 20 August 2012

Schomburg W, 'Jurisprudence on JCE—Revisiting a Never Ending Story', *Cambodia Tribunal Monitor*, 3 June 2010, at <http://www.cambodiatribunal.org/blog/2010/06/jurisprudence-jce%E2%80%94revisiting-never-ending-story> accessed 16 January 2013

ICRC, International Humanitarian Law—Treaties & Documents Database, at <http://www.icrc.org/ihl> accessed 20 August 2012

## ONLINE RESOURCES (HONG KONG WAR CRIMES TRIALS DATABASE)

Linton S, *Record of Two Interviews with Major Murray I. Ormsby, on 21 July 2011 and 4 August 2011*, online at <http://hkwctc.lib.hku.hk/exhibits/show/hkwctc/accountsoftrials/oral>

——*Interview with Mr Stephen Tsui, on 17 September 2010*, online at <http://hkwctc.lib.hku.hk/exhibits/show/hkwctc/accountsoftrials/oral> accessed 20 December 2012

## PRESS RELEASES AND NEWS ITEMS

Cheung S, 'Sad tale of unsung hero's war death uncovered', *South China Morning Post*, 13 September 2010

China News, 13 September 2010, <http://www.chinanews.com/ga/2010/09–13/2528249.shtml> 港大推二战日本战犯数据库 档案揭日军酷刑 (Hong Kong University Established a Database on Japanese Felons/Criminals of World War II, Revealing the Crucial Torture Used by Japanese Armies), by Xiang Ji (editor)

*Ming Pao Daily*, 13 September 2010, <http://life.mingpao.com/cfm/dailynews3b.cfm?File=20100913/nalgo/goh1.txt> 港大推日戰犯資料庨 記述淪陷史無名英雄 (Hong Kong University Established a Database on Japanese Criminals of World War II, illuminating the history and nameless heroes during the occupied periods) (author not stated)

*Sina News*, 13 September 2010, <http://news.sina.com.hk/news/3/1/1/1852154/1.html> 港大推日戰犯資料庨 (Hong Kong University Established a Database on Japanese Felons of World War II), by Mansi Lu

*South China Morning Post*, 13 September 2010, <http://chinaoutlook.scmp.com/zh-cn/article.php?ArticleID=1000014072&OtherID=1000014073&Section=topstory> 被遗忘的二战英雄事迹重见天日 (Uncovering the forgotten story of a hero in World War II) (author not stated)

Wong Y, 'Lessons from Our Darkest Era', *Young Persons South China Morning Post*, 14 October 2010

## OTHERS

Hong Kong Annual Report 1946

Hong Kong Annual Report 1947

# Index of Names

Adams, Priv. J. H. 76
Ambos, K. 170, 179
Ando, Maj. T. 56
Archbold, J. F. 105, 142, 143, 203, 235–6
*see also* Jervis, Sir J.
Arisue, Maj. Gen. 81
Arsanjani, M. 197
Awa, Sgt. I. 27, 34, 46, 49, 52, 60, 61, 126, 182

Ball, Lt. Col. C. F. 26–7
Banham, T. 26, 59, 72
Barman, C. 72
Barnett, Capt. K. M. A. 79
Bassiouni, M. C. 4, 197
*see also* Doria, J., Gasser, H.-P.
Baxter, R. R. 105, 211
Beebe, L. 72
Berry, Col. K. L. 85–6
Berzenski, Lt. Corp. G. 76
Best, W. M. 203
Blackburn, Brig. A. S. 72, 85
Blackstone, W. 202
Bloxham, D. 14, 65, 68, 202
Brougher, Brig. Gen. W. E. 72, 86, 87
Brown, B. 170
Busfield, Capt. K. R. 76

Cassese, A. 4
Chan, B. 120
Chapman, J. 104
*see also* Gow, I; Hirama, Y.
Cheah, W. L. 5
Cheung, S. 3
Choy, Capt. R. 123
Choy, L.-C. 125
Clark, R. S. 7, 101, 165, 199–213
Cork and Orrery, Earl of 175
Craies, W. F. 142
*see also* Kershaw Crawford, Lt. Col. J. N. B. 75, 78–9
Cross, Maj. J. T. N 242

Darcy, S. 167
de Guzman, M. M. 22
Deacon, R. 10
Dicks, A. 107–8
Dinstein, Y. 176, 178, 186, 198
Dixon, R. 203
Doria, J. 197
*see also* Bassiouni, M. C.; Gasser, H.-P.
Doucett, Rifl. P. 126

Dower, J. W. 104
Duque, J. Brig. Gen. C. 71–2
Durand, A. 105

Edwards, J. 84, 220, 240
Ellis, Priv. P. J. 76
Emerson, G. C. 133
Erskine, Maj. Gen. G. V. E. J. 77, 233

Fan, S. C. 107
Faure, C. M. 120
Felton, M. 10
Fitzpatrick, B. 144
Fitzwalter Butler, T. R. 105, 203
Friedlander, H. 162
*see also* Stoltfus, N.
Friedman, L. 177
Fujino, Capt. N. 155–6, 184–5
Fulford, Judge A. 209

Gaeta, P. 196–7
Gardner, A. G. 125
Gasser, H.-P. 197
*see also* Bassiouni, M. C.; Doria, J.
Gittins, J. 133
Gow, I. 104
*see also* Chapman, J.; Hirama, Y.
Green, L. C. 170, 198
Greenspan, M. 179–80

Haggan, Lt. J. R. 66
Han, W. T. 108
Hanada, Sgt. Z. 27, 33, 34, 49, 52, 53, 61, 148
Hankey, Lord 175
Hara, Vice-Ad. T. 115–17
Harnes, M. 104
Heller, K. J. 179–80, 200
*see also* Simpson, G.
Hioki, S. 84
Hirama, Y. 104
*see also* Chapman, J.; Gow, I.
Hirano, Maj. N. 48, 61, 63, 155–6, 184
Hirao, Maj. Y. 21, 27, 44–5, 49, 53, 63, 118, 120, 122, 183–4
Hockley, F. 25, 48, 55, 63, 155, 184, 215, 222, 228, 238–9
Hui, S. P. 122

Ikegami, E. 104
Inouye, K. 21, 27, 46, 49, 52, 69, 147, 148, 187, 239
Isogai, Lt. Gen. R. 114–15, 118

Ito, Lt. Gen. T. 53, 97, 99, 106, 128, 133, 214–15, 232, 240–2
Ito, Sgt. Maj. J. (Trial No 1) 21, 23, 27, 33, 50, 52, 53, 57, 63, 64, 183, 213
Ito, Sgt. Maj. J. (Trial No 2) 27, 44, 50, 52, 57, 63

Jackson, Judge R. 212
James, D. C. 72
Jervis, Sir J. 142
*see also* Archbold, J. F.
Jia, B. B. 7, 54, 100, 169–98, 202, 210
Jo, S. K. 84
Jones, Maj. Gen. A. M. 87–8
Jørgensen, N. 6, 9, 100, 120, 123, 137–67, 206, 207
Jowitt, Earl 175, 176

Kahn, K. A. A. 203
Kamada, Sgt. Maj. Y. 27, 28, 39, 50, 51, 53
Kameda, K. 84
Kaname, A. 56
Kanazawa, Lt. Col. A. 6, 27, 50, 53, 61, 64, 66, 109, 113–14, 118, 120, 124–5, 133, 186, 208
Kalshoven, F. 103, 129
*see also* Zegveld, L.
Kaul, Capt. B. N. 218
Kawai, Sgt. H. 27, 44, 49, 52, 55, 189–90
*see also* Ogasawara, Sgt. Maj. H.
Kawaida, Lt. S. 192–3
Kawamoto, Sgt. K. 21, 27, 34, 46, 49, 52, 61, 62, 146
Keith, A. B. 202
Kerr, Lt. Col. S. R. 27
Kershaw, L. W. 142
Kinoshita, Lt. Gen. E. 27, 30, 49, 53, 67, 68 149–51
*see also* Yoshida, H.
Kishi, Lt. Y. 23, 26, 27, 29, 33, 36, 48, 49, 52, 55, 56, 57, 66, 67, 128–9, 132, 134, 138, 147, 148, 191–2
Klip, A. 45
Knoops, G. J. A. 197
Kondō, M. 83
Kotewall, Sir R. 109, 110
Kuroda, Lt. Gen. S. 71
Kuruta, Lt. I. 192–3
Kuwaki, Sgt. Maj. K. 27, 49, 53, 59, 63
*see also* Nakajima, Sgt. T.
Kuwano, Sgt. N. 27, 50, 53, 59, 63
Kyoda, S. 13, 25, 26, 27, 33, 38, 40, 43, 46, 50, 51, 52, 55, 56, 59, 60, 61, 69, 193
Kyte, Maj. A. E. 44, 58

Lai, K.-S. 111
Lam, C.-S. 119, 125, 126, 129
Lam, K.-W. 126
Laming, Lt. Col. R. C. 27, 51, 76, 242–3
Lavalle, R. M. 133
Law, J. E. 119, 120
Lauterpacht, H. 102, 105, 174–5
Lee, R. 196
Levie, H. S. 105
Li, C. C. 110
Li, K. C. 109
Linton, S. 1, 6–7, 14, 16, 19, 20, 22–4, 26, 28–30, 35, 38, 44, 46–7, 54–5, 63–4, 67–8, 95–135, 152, 186, 200–2
Liu, M. 100
Loranger, Maj. J. T. 76, 228
Lowry, D. 214

Maltby, Air Vice. M. P. C. 75, 87
Maltby, Maj. Gen. C. M. 73, 75
Massie, Lt. Col. L. A. 27
Matsuda, Sgt. K. 27, 33, 40, 49, 50, 52, 60, 66, 106, 126, 127
Matsunobu, S. 21, 27, 34, 36, 38, 43, 45, 50, 52, 54, 60, 61
Matsumoto, Lt. C. 191
Maugham, Viscount 176
May, Judge R. 203
Mayazumi, Capt. H. 25, 27, 46, 48, 50, 53, 54, 55, 155, 188–9, 208
*see also* Sakonju, R. Adm. N.
McGregor, D. G. 219, 227, 229
McNair, A. 202
*see also* Oppenheim, L.
Mitchell, Lt. Col. E. J. R. 79
Miyasue, Sgt. S. 27, 50, 52, 60, 63

Nakajima, M. 182
Nakajima, Sgt. T. 27, 49, 53, 59, 63
Nakano, Col. J. 27, 52, 43, 44, 49, 50, 72, 82
Narayanan, A. 4–5, 95
Newell, W. 108
Niimori, G. 27, 50, 51, 52, 61, 126, 153, 154, 193–4, 222, 225, 239
Nitta, M. 90
Noma, I. 125
Noma, Col. K. 6, 8–10, 26–7, 29, 47, 49, 50, 52, 55, 61, 66, 105–15, 118–26, 133, 149, 152, 156, 184, 186, 208, 214, 220, 225, 230, 239

Oba, Sgt. Maj. T. 21, 22, 27, 49, 52, 151–2
Ogasawara, Sgt. Maj. H. 27, 44, 49, 52, 55, 189–90
*see also* Kawai, Sgt. H.
Ogmore, Lord 176
Oldnall Russell, Sir W. M. 142
Omar, A. K. 125
Omura, W. O. K. 16, 27, 37, 39, 41, 42, 45, 49, 51, 52, 53, 61, 63, 120, 122, 135
Oppenheim, L. 129, 131, 174–5, 202

Ormsby, Maj. M. I. 2, 7, 19, 23, 26, 28–9, 32–3, 38, 43–4, 46, 47, 49, 54, 58, 63, 64, 66–8, 91, 215–46

Pal, Judge R. 4, 204
Pang, Y.-S. 111
Pang, T.-K. 125
Payne, Sgt. J. O. 76
Percival, Lt. Gen. A. F. 72
Picigallo, P. R. 95
Porter, H. D. 237
Powderly, J. 167
Prévost, A. M. 4
Pritchard, R. J. 13–14, 16, 20–2, 24, 34, 41–2, 54–5, 58, 64–5, 67–9, 95, 211
Puddicombe, Maj. G. B. 75–6, 239, 241

Ramler, D. S. 119
Reed, A. 144, 165
*see also* Fitzpatrick, B.
Reid, Capt. J. A. G. 79
Reilly, Capt. J. F. 33
Ride, Col. L. 120
Ride, E. 120
Rikichi, Gen. A. 83
Rogers, A. P. V. 13–14, 20, 41, 172–3, 200, 203, 207
Rohde, W. 159
Roland, C. G. 38, 72, 74–5, 133
Röling, B. V. A. 95
Ross, R. E. 105, 203
Russell of Liverpool, Lord 10, 104, 142, 143, 144
Rüter, C. F. 95

Saitō, Capt. S. 75
Sakai, Lt. Gen. T. 10, 107, 108, 114, 133
Sakonju, R. Adm. N. 25, 27, 46, 48, 50, 53, 54, 55, 155, 188–9, 208
*see also* Mayazumi, Capt. H.
Saland, P. 196
Sannomiya, T. 84
Sato, Lt. C. 27, 37, 49, 50, 52, 61, 147
Sazawa, Col. H. 27, 36, 49, 52, 73, 82, 84, 86, 87, 88, 89, 152–3
Scaliotti, M. 170
Schabas, W. 197, 212
Schomburg, W. 163, 167
Schonfeld, F. 140, 158, 162
Schwarzenberger, G. 170
Selwyn-Clarke, Dr. P. 61, 77, 185–6
Shahabuddeen, Judge M. 167
Shibata, Capt. S. 21, 22, 27, 49, 52, 151–2
*see also* Oba, Sgt. Maj. T.
Shigenori, K. 71
Shih, Judge M. 101
Shoji, Maj. Gen. T. 27, 39, 50, 52, 99, 106
Simon, Viscount 176
Simpson, G. 200
*see also* Heller, K. J.
Sitwell, Maj. Gen. H. D. W. 72, 85
Sling, W. H. 125
Sluiter, G. 45
Smith, F. E. 202
Snow, P. 107, 133
Sowerby, Capt. E. W. 88–9
Stephen, Sir J. F. 167
Stewart, Lt. Col. J. C. 27, 28, 29, 51, 67, 217, 218, 219, 220, 222, 228, 236, 242
Stoltfus, N. 162
*see also* Friedlander, H.
Suzuki, Lt. N. 182–3
Sykes, E. D. 124

Tamaki, Lt. K. 27, 43, 49, 50, 52
Tamura, T. 25, 27, 32, 48, 49, 52, 55, 61, 63, 155–6, 157
Tanaka, Lt. H. 77, 185
Tanaka, Maj. Gen. R. 27, 37, 38, 49, 50, 52, 56, 97, 99, 104, 106, 214, 232, 241
Tanaka, Y. 153
Tamura Col. T. 25, 27, 32, 48, 49, 52, 55, 61, 63, 184–5, 208
Tashiro, Sgt. T. 27, 39, 43, 49, 50, 52, 56, 61
Toda, M. 20, 21, 27, 28, 32, 33, 35, 44, 45, 49, 52, 55, 74, 82, 83, 84, 90, 91–3, 94, 153–4
Togo, S. 105
Tokunaga, Col. I. 27, 36, 49, 52, 55, 56, 61, 64, 73–82, 93, 98, 104, 152, 185–6, 223
Toland, J. 104
Totani, Y. 6, 9, 71–94, 98–9, 152, 200
Touvier, P. 4
Triffterer, O. 3
Tsang, M.-T. 111
Tsang, S. Y. S. 107, 120
Tse, Y. F. 125
Tsui, S. 135

Uete, Maj. T. 27, 49, 53, 61, 73, 82, 192–3, 208
Ushiyama, Capt. Y. 27, 38, 47, 49, 50, 53, 149
Utsumi, A. 75, 82, 83, 84, 88, 90

Van den Wyngaert, C. Judge 209
Van der Post, L. 137, 167
Victor, D. 119
Vine, P. 19, 21, 22, 26, 32–3, 35, 40, 42–3, 54, 69

Wainwright, J. M. 71–3, 86
Wait, Lt. Col. N. G. 26, 27, 28, 242
Wan, T.-C. 125
Wang, J. 101
Warwick, Lt. Col. P. 26–7, 51
Wavell, Earl of 176
Wheaton, H. 202
Whiteman, M. 181
Wilson, Lord 175
Winster, Lord 176

Wong, Y. H. 3
Wright of Durley, Lord 5
Wright-Nooth, G. 72
Wu, Dr. T. P. 125

Yabuki, W. O. R. 27, 43, 46, 49, 50, 52, 54
Yamada, Sgt. Maj. K. 27, 34, 46, 49, 52, 60, 61, 126, 182
*see also* Awa, Sgt. I.
Yamaguchi, Corp. K. 190–1
Yokohata, Sgt. Maj. T. 21, 27, 31, 43, 44, 50, 53, 56, 58, 194–5
Yokota, Col. H. 83
Yoshida, Sgt. B. 27, 30, 49, 53, 67, 68, 149–51
Yoshida, H. 89, 150–1
Yoshimi, Capt. T. 25, 27, 49, 53, 190–1
Young, Sir M. 72

Zahar, A. 5, 6, 9, 13–69, 45, 127, 135, 204, 205, 212, 213
Zegveld, L. 129
*see also* Kalshoven, F.
Zeng, Gen. S. 120
Zindel, R. 79–80

# General Index


**abuse** 1, 6, 72, 96, 99, 101, 103, 110, 113, 119, 121–3, 126–8, 132–4, 186, 202, 208, 210, 226
 beating(s) 21, 38, 72, 77, 79, 84, 119, 121, 123, 126–8, 138, 147–8, 153, 189, 191–2, 234
 cruel xi, 72, 95, 96, 111, 113, 124, 134, 147–8, 150, 154, 202, 210, 222, 226
 cruel inhumane or degrading treatment or punishment 96, 113, 202
 degrading 68, 87, 96, 202
 forced labour 71, 72, 74, 82–5, 88, 91, 93, 96, 98–9, 105, 112, 114, 201–2, 246
 inhumane v, vi, xi, 44, 46, 95, 96, 98, 111, 113, 118, 122–3, 134, 138, 150, 152, 202
 internment, during 81, 133
 interrogation, during 21, 36, 76, 102, 118–19, 121, 124–7, 134, 155, 182
 by *Kempeitai* (includes Gendarmes/ Gendarme) vi, 6, 10, 12, 21, 34, 38, 44, 48, 66, 64, 108, 109–13, 117, 119, 120–7, 134, 144, 146, 149, 150–1, 164, 182, 183–4, 186, 189, 194–5, 208, 215, 239, 241, 243
 maltreatment 6, 77, 110, 118, 123–4, 126–8, 133, 138, 146–9, 191–2
 power of 208, 210
 Red Cross flag and badge/emblem of 101
 shipwrecked captives, of 97, 99
 sustained cruelty 124, 154
 torture *see* torture
 *see also* forced displacement
 *see also* POWs
 *see also* war crimes
**airman**
 captured airman (Fred Hockley) 25, 48, 55, 63, 155, 184, 215, 222, 228, 237–9
**Allied Land Forces South East Asia (ALFSEA)** vi, 3, 15, 16, 20–6, 28, 30, 32–6, 40–1, 44, 46, 48, 51, 53–4, 60, 96, 101–2, 105, 124, 135, 145, 171, 173, 201–2, 204, 244
 ALFSEA headquarters in Singapore 3, 5, 26, 29, 30, 34, 60, 63, 101, 105, 173, 201, 216, 217, 221, 223–4, 227–9, 233, 244
 ALFSEA Instruction (2nd ed) *see* international and domestic law applicable at the time of the Hong Kong Military Courts (1946–1948)
 ALFSEA procedures *see* procedure at the Hong Kong Military Courts (1946–1948)
 *see also* Department of the Judge Advocate General (DJAG)
**amnesia about the past** 3
**Andaman Islands** 6, 112, 115–17, 134
**arbitrary (unlawful)** v, vi, xi, 95, 110, 112–13, 134
 arbitrary (unlawful) arrest 10, 76, 96, 109–10, 113–14, 119, 121, 125, 127, 132, 138, 145, 148, 162, 182, 186, 189, 192, 202
 arbitrary (unlawful) detention v, vi, 1, 95–6, 110, 117, 119, 122–7, 132, 151, 202
 arbitrary (unlawful) punishment 35, 68, 120, 130, 131, 137, 173, 212–13
 summary (unlawful) execution vi, 21, 48, 55, 81, 123–5, 130–1, 147, 183–5, 188, 192, 215
**Australia** 5, 85, 102, 103, 212, 227
 Australian 72, 93, 134, 165, 200, 212, 223, 224, 227
 Australian trials 93

***Behar*** 99, 155, 188
 *see also Tone*, High Seas

**Canada** 21, 74–5, 79, 102–3, 170, 197, 212, 225, 239
 attempted escape from North Point camp 76, 81, 93
 Canadian 21, 46, 49, 74–9, 81, 93, 126, 134, 147, 184, 187, 194, 225, 239, 243
 Doucett, Peter 126
 Royal Rifles 74–5, 79, 126
 Winnipeg Grenadiers 74, 76
**China** v, vi, viii, xi, 1, 3, 6, 23, 67, 72, 75, 77, 82, 94, 95, 100, 102–4, 107–8, 112, 114, 117–18, 127, 199, 200–1, 219, 226
 Chinese viii, 3, 4, 6, 10, 44, 64, 77, 89, 94, 103, 107–10, 115, 119–22, 125, 127–8, 138, 147, 183, 192, 199, 200, 226, 235, 242
 Nanking viii, 11, 99, 107, 114–15, 119, 133, 200
 Chinese refugees/displaced in Hong Kong 107, 108–15
 Shanghai 1, 23, 43–4, 93, 95, 149–50, 194–5
 treaty/treaties 102–4, 108, 200
  1842 Nanking Treaty (supplemented in 1843, renewed in 1858) 107
  1906 Wounded and Sick Convention 102
  1907 Hague Regulations 103
  1929 POW Convention 103

**China** (*cont.*)
1929 Red Cross Convention 103
trials at the Chinese Military Tribunal, Nanking
Isogai Rensuke *see* Table of Cases and Legal Materials
Sakai Takashi *see* Table of Cases and Legal Materials
Wai On Hospital, Waichow 127
Waichow 23, 95, 127
*see also* Taiwan, China
**civilian(s)** v, vi, 1, 6, 7, 10, 20–2, 36, 44, 46, 55, 60, 63, 71–4, 77, 80, 84, 88, 91, 95–7, 99–102, 105, 107, 111–19, 121–5, 127–9, 131–4, 146–51, 153, 170, 182–4, 185–6, 189–90, 192–6, 201, 203, 208, 244
*see also* abuse
*see also* arbitrary (unlawful)
*see also* resistance
*see also* war crimes
**Communist activities** 119–20, 126
**court martial procedure**
*see* international and domestic law applicable at the time of the Hong Kong Military Courts (1946–1948)
*see* procedure at the Hong Kong Military Courts (1946–1948)

**dangerous or hazardous work** 72, 96, 98, 102, 202
**Defence Advisory Officer** 29, 33, 38, 41, 45, 54, 216
**Defence Counsel** vii, xii, 7, 33, 37, 38, 41, 43, 46, 47, 48, 49, 51, 54, 55, 56, 78, 105, 122, 130, 131, 134, 153, 177, 201
**defences/justification/exclusion of responsibility**
alibi 48, 148
diminished responsibility 210–11
duress 7, 55, 85, 108, 134, 170–1, 180–1, 186–8, 191–2, 197, 210
insanity 41–2, 211
mistaken identity 42, 48, 211
necessity 95, 121, 132, 134, 175–6, 180, 201, 211
provocation 211
reprisal 87, 176
self-defence 132
*see also* superior orders
**Department of the Judge Advocate General (DJAG)** 26–7, 29–30, 32, 33, 60, 76, 243
**disappearance** 95, 121, 246
**disease** *see* sickness and disease
**dog** 22, 119, 123

**escape**
Indians, of 121
pledge of no-escape *see* oath
POWs, of 76–81, 85, 90, 93, 116, 120, 185, 244

**evidence** vii, viii, 2, 13, 15, 17–18, 21–2, 25, 26, 28, 32, 34–45, 47–8, 51, 53, 56, 57, 60, 62–4, 66, 71, 74, 78, 80–1, 89–90, 98, 105–6, 108, 111–12, 113, 115, 117–18, 120, 122–5, 133, 135, 139–40, 142, 145, 136, 147, 150, 152–3, 157, 159–62, 166, 172, 180–1, 195, 197, 198, 203, 205–6, 209, 220, 224–5, 227–9, 232–4, 237, 239–40, 242, 244
**Extraordinary Chambers in the Courts of Cambodia (ECCC)** 137, 140, 142–3, 145, 163, 165–7

**food** vi, 3, 21, 71, 73, 77, 96, 102, 105, 107, 110, 115–17, 119, 123, 153, 186, 202, 230, 234
failure to provide adequate food and nutrition 72–3, 75, 85–6, 108, 116, 123, 147, 153
famine vi, 107–8
rice 85, 109–11, 219
**Formosa** *see* Taiwan, China

**1949 Geneva Conventions** *see* international and domestic law applicable at the time of the Hong Kong Military Courts (1946–1948)

**hanchō** 9, 91–2
**High Seas** 1, 15, 23, 25, 95, 154–5, 188, 193–4, 199
*see also Tone*
*see also Behar*
*see also Lisbon Maru*
**history/historical** v, vi, viii, ix, 3–6, 13–16, 20–2, 24, 41, 64–8, 82–3, 95, 104–5, 107, 137–8, 160, 167, 173–4, 177, 196, 200, 202, 215, 236, 244
**Hong Kong**
battle for Hong Kong/fall of Hong Kong v, 96, 99, 107, 133, 200, 216
Blue Pool Road 128, 133, 242
China Command Headquarters 77
civilian authorities in 21, 52, 74, 105, 109, 115, 117, 128
Director of Medical Services 61, 77
Governor of British vi, 72
Governor-General of occupied 78, 80–1, 98, 107, 110, 113–14, 118, 133, 186
Happy Valley (Jockey Club) 128, 133, 194, 241
hospitals v, 61, 71–2, 77, 79, 101–2, 127, 147, 231–2
beating at 79
bombardment of 101–2
Bowen Road Hospital 77
Hong Kong Red Cross Hospital *see* St Stephen's Hospital (College)
Indian Military Hospital 77

killing at v, 231–2
maltreatment at v, 77, 79, 147
rape at v, 231
St Stephen's Hospital (College) v, 99, 133, 232
Stanley Gaol (Prison) Hospital 147
Japanese POWs in 1, 35
Kowloon vi, 1, 23, 82, 107–8, 120–3, 133, 183, 199, 217, 224
Lantau Island (Silver Mine Bay/Mui Wo) 1, 120, 124, 128–9, 131, 138, 147–8, 191, 215, 218, 220, 235
media and public interest 3
military administration of 24, 78, 107–9
New Territories 1, 23, 95, 107, 119–21, 123–4, 182, 199, 219
places of detention (POW and civilian)
Argyle Street Camp 77
Central police station 38, 123
Kowloon Magistracy 121, 125
North Point Camp 75–8, 81, 111
Sham Shui Po Camp vi, 77, 79, 152, 187
Stanley Gaol (Prison) 38, 61, 90, 111, 133, 147, 236
Stanley Internment (Civilian) Camp 133
Supreme Court 49, 123, 147, 218, 220
population of vi, 10, 74, 107–10, 112–13, 117, 122, 134
return of British to 105, 128
Stanley 38, 61, 90, 111, 133, 147, 236
Tai Po 119, 121, 125, 182
Tsun Wan 125, 183
**Hong Kong Volunteer Defence Corps (HKVDC)** 74, 79
**Hong Kong War Crimes Trials Collection Database** *see* List of Names and Table of Cases and Legal Materials for case references
**hospital ship** 102

**ill-treatment**
*see* abuse
*see* involuntary displacement
*see* POWs
*see* war crimes
**Indian** 4, 77, 82, 99, 119, 121, 143, 155, 184, 188, 217, 219, 243
escape of Indians 121
guards 119
Indian Military Hospital *see* Hong Kong, Indian Military Hospital
Indian Ocean 99, 155, 188
**International Military Tribunal at Nuremberg (IMT Nuremberg)** v, xi, 2, 4, 7, 13, 16, 22, 59, 65, 101, 103, 112–14, 129, 145, 170, 177–9, 186, 195–7, 199–201, 204–6, 210, 212
Charter xii, 22, 103, 112–13, 145, 170, 177–9, 195, 197, 200–1, 205–6, 210, 212
Judgment 101, 103, 170, 177–9, 186, 195–7
**International Military Tribunal at Tokyo (IMT Tokyo)** *see* International Military Tribunal for the Far East (IMTFE)
**International Military Tribunal for the Far East (IMTFE)** 10, 13, 90, 95, 103–5, 200–1, 207
Charter 200–1
Judgment 95, 103–5, 200, 207
**International Committee of the Red Cross (ICRC)** *see* Red Cross
**International Criminal Court (ICC)** ix, xii, 57, 163–5, 169–70, 196–7, 199–201, 203–5, 209–11
Statute (Rome Statute) xii, 7, 164, 169, 195–9, 201–4, 206–12
**International Criminal Tribunal for Rwanda (ICTR)** 45, 140, 166, 197, 201, 205, 212
Statute (ICTR) 197, 201, 212
**International Criminal Tribunal for the former Yugoslavia (ICTY)** 137, 138, 140, 164, 166, 167, 197, 201, 205, 212
Statute (ICTY) 139, 197, 201
**international and domestic law applicable at the time of the Hong Kong Military Courts (1946–1948)**
ALFSEA Instruction (2nd ed) 3, 15–16, 20–3, 25– 6, 28, 30–6, 40–2, 44, 46, 48, 51, 53–4, 60, 96, 101–2, 124, 135, 201–2, 204, 244
Army Act, Rules of Procedure (1939) 14–15, 16–18, 22–5, 28–32, 36, 38–42, 44–5, 47, 50, 51, 53, 57–8, 62, 65, 89, 200
British Manual of Military Law 1929 (7th ed and 7th ed with amendments) 14–15, 18–19, 22–4, 30, 36, 38, 41, 45, 50, 57–60, 62, 66, 96, 100–2, 105–6, 116, 129–31, 145–6, 158, 170, 172–7, 181, 195, 202–4, 206–7, 209–11, 225, 236, 243
Control Council Law No 10 114, 140, 145, 163, 177, 179–80, 191, 197, 200
customary international law vii, 2, 15–16, 57, 93, 97, 101, 103–5, 123, 129, 138–43, 164–6, 169–70, 176–7, 180–1, 196–201, 204
general sources of law vii, 14–16, 100–6, 129, 171–81, 202–4, 207
Hague Regulations (1907) vii, xii, 15, 97–8, 102–3, 115, 117–18, 128–30, 177, 199–200
humanitarian law v, xii, 15, 67, 80, 87, 96–7, 102–5, 129, 195, 201, 203, 207
Martens Clause 118, 121, 129, 199
Protocols additional to the 1949 Geneva Conventions 129, 195, 201, 207

**international and domestic law** (*cont.*)
Regulations annexed to Royal Warrant (1945) 14–16, 22–6, 30, 35, 38, 41, 42, 46, 48, 57–60, 62, 100, 145, 172, 200
Royal Warrant (1945) vi, vii, xi, 7, 13, 14, 20, 22–3, 30, 41, 65, 68, 97, 100, 105, 135, 145, 171–3, 176–7, 181, 195, 200–9, 211
1906 Wounded and Sick Convention 97, 102
1929 POW Convention 96, 98, 103–6
1929 Red Cross Convention 97, 103, 105
1949 Geneva Conventions xii, 129, 201, 203, 207
*see also* IMTFE
*see also* IMT Nuremberg
*see also* List of Names and Table of Cases and Legal Materials for case references
*see also* procedure at the Hong Kong Military Courts (1946–1948)
*see also* superior orders
*see also* war crimes
**interpreter** vii, 38, 51, 53, 74, 77–9, 89, 92, 117, 119, 121–2, 125–6, 146, 187, 193, 222, 225, 227, 233, 235, 239
**interrogation**
*see* abuse
*see Kempeitai*
**involuntary displacement/banishment/deportation/evacuation/expulsion/repatriation**
abuse, during 107–18, 186
banishment 107, 114–15
Co-operative Council (Advisory Council) 109
deportation vi, 64, 100, 107–14, 116, 118, 123, 186, 201
displacement v, 6, 100, 107, 108, 111–15, 117, 118, 133–4
evacuation 107–10, 112–13, 182, 186, 192
expulsion 111
repatriation vi, 1, 68, 107–9

**Japan**
Air Force 25
Army v, 10, 20, 25, 56, 61, 79, 80, 83, 90–1, 104, 128, 138, 153, 182–5, 187, 189, 190–3
Constitution of 68
cultural approaches to capture 103–4
*Bushido* 10, 104
Emperor of 68, 97, 197, 128, 134, 155, 184, 215, 228, 230–1, 238
government of vii, 73, 82, 83, 99, 105
Japanese law 38, 56, 61, 78, 81, 87, 92, 98, 104, 221, 230
Japanese lawyers vii, 135, 221, 222, 227–9, 235
Japan Mining Company/Kinkaseki Nippon Mining Company *see* Taiwan, China
Navy 25, 26, 38, 46, 104, 105, 115, 184, 188, 189
surrender v, vi, 1, 23, 34, 35, 128, 129, 155, 184, 238
Emperor's capitulation 97, 128, 129, 134, 215, 228, 239
surrendered personnel 1, 34, 35
treaties
1906 Wounded and Sick Convention 102
1907 Hague Regulations vii, 15, 98, 103, 117, 199–200
1929 POW Convention 98, 103, 104, 105, 106
1929 Red Cross Convention 103
United States, nuclear attacks on 67, 215
War Ministry 6, 10, 78, 80, 81, 82, 89, 93, 183
wartime Empire of viii, 71, 82, 83, 84, 93, 98
**Judge Advocate(s)** xii, 2, 8–9, 17–21, 26–34, 37, 39, 43, 44–5, 51, 55, 57, 59–64, 66–8, 76–7, 105, 112–17, 125–7, 132–4, 138, 146, 148, 150–2, 156–9, 161, 165, 172–3, 177, 181–95, 202, 204–5, 207, 222, 229, 233–4, 242–3
**jurisdiction** vi, xi, 3, 16, 20–3, 28, 45–6, 95, 100, 103, 105, 112, 124, 171–2, 187, 196, 199, 200–1, 203–4, 206, 210
challenges to 20–1
personal jurisdiction 20, 23
subject-matter jurisdiction 22, 95–100, 200
temporal jurisdiction 21, 23

***kantoku*** 9, 91–2
***Kempeitai*** vi, 6, 10, 21, 38, 44, 66, 108, 111–13, 117–25, 127, 134, 149–51, 182–4, 186, 189, 194–5, 208, 215, 239, 241–4
abuse of civilians *see* abuse
anti-espionage measures 10, 121–2, 195
function of 10, 119–22
Gendarme/Gendarmes/Gendarmerie 10, 64, 66, 109–11, 119, 121, 125, 146, 148–9, 186
interrogation 21, 36, 58, 111, 118–19, 121, 123–4, 125–7, 134, 182
*see also* abuse
*see also* war crimes
*see also* high seas

***Lisbon Maru*** 25, 26, 59, 69, 154, 193, 225, 239
**looting** vi, 95, 133, 138, 192

**murder** *see* taking life
**manslaughter** *see* taking life
**medical** v, 3, 21, 38–9, 40, 61, 71–5, 77–9, 85, 95–7, 99, 102, 116, 118, 123, 125, 127, 133, 147, 153, 180, 185, 186, 190
doctors v, 38–9, 125, 190

failure to provide adequate medical care or treatment 3, 21, 71, 85, 116, 123, 125, 147
formations and establishments 96
medicine 71, 77, 125
nurse v, 99, 127, 133, 220, 227, 241–2
personnel v, 38, 95, 97, 99, 127, 133

**mitigation** xii, 7, 31, 55, 56–9, 62, 66, 78, 115, 127, 131–2, 156, 169–71, 170–1, 175, 177–8, 182–3, 185, 191, 193–5, 197, 209–11, 230
plea in vii, xii, 7, 54–7, 78, 80–1, 90, 93, 120, 132, 169–98, 211
*see also* procedure at the Hong Kong Military Courts (1946–1948)
*see also* superior orders

**name(s)** 10–11
**nature of abuses, maltreatment and killings, etc**
organized 3, 21, 117
sustained 124, 152, 154, 191
systematic 6, 93, 94, 124, 151, 153, 161
widespread 6, 73, 85 93, 124
*see also* policy

**Nuremberg (Nürnberg)** v, xi, 2, 4, 7, 13, 16, 22, 59, 65, 101, 103, 112–14, 129–30, 140, 145, 166, 170, 177–80, 186, 195–7, 199–201, 204–6, 210, 212

**oath(s)** 41–2, 57, 79–80, 96, 123, 178, 202, 221, 233, 244
**occupied territory/military occupation** v, vi, vii, viii, ix, xi, 3, 6, 10, 20, 23, 35, 71, 72, 73, 78, 93–7, 100–1, 107–35, 145, 184, 201, 237
*see also* Hong Kong
*see also* China
*see also* international and domestic law applicable at the time of the Hong Kong Military Courts (1946–1948)
*see also* war crimes
**Opium War** 107
**orders** *see* superior orders

**participation in crime/'committing' a crime/ modes of responsibility** 137–67
acquiescence 149–51, 191
collective criminality xii, 47, 65, 137–9, 145, 165
command responsibility 7, 120, 123, 150–3, 156, 170, 198, 207, 231, 242
condoning 77, 153, 156
contribution to 126, 139, 149, 152, 164, 165, 210
criminal responsibility 15, 65, 139–41, 145, 160, 169–70, 184, 196, 199, 210
instigation of crime 2, 145, 206–7, 209
joint criminal enterprise (JCE) 6–7, 137–67
'being concerned' or 'together concerned' xii, 6–7, 9, 64, 90, 111, 120–3, 126–8, 137–167, 189–92, 207, 210, 233
as embryonic JCE 137–67
contextual backdrop 137–8
Hong Kong cases 146–57
origins of phrase 142–4
modern international criminal law 138–42
modes of participation 205–9
modes of responsibility/liability vii, 100, 137–8, 153, 166–7, 206, 209
neglect 53, 61, 64, 72, 147, 152, 156
negligence, ill-treatment through 147
negligence or neglect, death by 116, 147, 152
neglect, wilful 116
negligence 116, 147, 160
negligence, culpable/criminal 156, 174
scope of responsibility 82–3, 142

**persecution** 151
**petition** *see* procedure at the Hong Kong Military Courts (1946–1948)
**plunder** v, 95, 133, 201
**policy** vi, 7, 10, 14, 68, 80–6, 90, 93, 104, 108, 124, 151–3, 186
early release 67–9
forced displacement/repatriation vi, 108, 186
Governor-General 80, 86
ill-treatment 104, 124, 151–3
in international criminal law 7, 14, 166, 211
preventing/punishing POW escapes 79–81, 90, 93, 185
starvation 153
Japanese POW, administration of 73, 80, 82–6, 153
POW labour, use of 82–6, 90
senior officer, abuse of POWs 85–6
sustained cruelty 124
War Ministry 10, 80–1, 93
**politics** 14, 67–9, 103
political viii, 20, 44, 65, 67–8, 103, 209, 210–11
*see also* ALFSEA
*see also* procedure at the Hong Kong Military Courts (1946–1948)
*see also* sentencing
**poor conditions of detention** 73, 79, 85–6, 88, 96, 119, 122, 125–7, 151, 202
*see also* abuse
*see also* Hong Kong (places of detention)
*see also* POWs
*see also* war crime
**poor conditions of work** 20, 72, 84, 86–7, 91, 96, 98–9, 102, 116, 153, 182–3, 202
*see also* abuse; POWs
**prisoners of war (POWs)** v, vi, viii, xi, 4, 6, 15, 20, 25–6, 33–6, 38, 44–5, 59, 61, 68–9, 71–94, 96–9, 101–6, 120, 126, 129, 146, 152–4, 157,

**prisoners of war (POWs)** (*cont.*)
159–61, 170, 182–3, 185, 187, 190, 192–4, 202, 208
abuse of v, vi, 4, 6, 15, 20, 25, 33, 61, 69, 71–94, 96–9, 101–5, 126, 146, 152–4, 154, 157, 159–61, 170, 182–3, 185, 187, 190, 192–4, 202
Barnett Incident 79–80
discipline of 79, 85, 87–88, 182, 104
POW camp trials vi, 36, 56, 64, 73, 71–94, 98, 104, 152–3, 156, 160, 182–3, 185–6, 190, 192–3, 204, 208, 223, 225
POW camp regulations 78, 81, 87, 92, 98
targeting of senior officers 85–7
*see also* abuse
*see also* Hong Kong
*see also* Japan
*see also* medical
*see also* oaths
*see also* Taiwan, China
*see also* taking of life

**procedure at the Hong Kong Military Courts** (1946–1948)
British court-martial procedure (c. 1946) 5, 16, 17–20, 22–4, 28–30, 32, 36, 38, 40–2, 46, 50–1, 57–9, 62, 204–5
British military court structure 17, 20–36, 43–4, 76, 86, 109–10, 115–16, 223–4, 227–9, 232–4, 241
commutation of sentence 60–4, 77, 152, 185, 208
concurrent representation of multiple accused 47–50
conflict of interests 47
confirmation of decision 1–2, 17–18, 21, 31, 43, 45, 52, 60–4, 67, 77, 113–14, 117, 171–2, 182–6, 189–94, 204–5, 223
Confirming Officer 2, 18, 21, 57, 60–4, 67, 77, 172, 192, 204–5, 211
*see also* Judge Advocate
Contextual background 13–20
Convening Officer/Convening Authority 17, 21–7, 30–1, 33–4, 35–7, 39–1, 45–7, 59–60
Defence concerns vii, 16–17, 24, 29, 31–2, 37, 40–54, 55–65
defence experience 65–7
guilty plea 57–8, 213, 194
justice or politics? 67–9
length of proceedings 13, 24, 42, 47, 61, 63, 52–3, 204–5
mitigation *see* mitigation
petition 20, 21, 31, 43, 51, 58, 60–4, 67–8, 77, 116, 120, 172, 183–5, 187–93, 205
proceedings, review of vii, xi, xii, 2, 20, 30–1, 33, 63, 68, 77, 112–13, 125, 127, 132, 134–5, 171–2, 182–6, 189–95, 204–5, 223, 229, 233
*see also* Judge Advocate
proof (evidence) vii, viii, 2, 13, 15, 17–18, 21–2, 25–6, 28, 32, 34–45, 47–8, 51, 53, 56–7, 60, 62–4, 66, 71, 78, 80–1, 89–90, 98, 105–6, 108, 111–13, 115, 117–18, 120, 122–5, 133, 135, 139–40, 142, 145–7, 150, 152, 153, 157, 159–62, 166, 172, 180–1, 197–8, 203, 205–6, 209, 220, 224–5, 227–9, 232–4, 237, 239–40, 242, 244
hearsay 36, 41–5
written witness statements 2, 9, 28, 34, 36–7, 39, 41–5, 58, 61, 72–3, 75, 84–7, 89, 122–3, 133, 220, 240
identification of accused 131, 241
parades 34
witness evidence (oral) xii, 8, 17, 18, 36, 37, 39, 41–3, 89, 123, 224
defence witnesses 39–41, 78
superior orders *see* superior orders
verdict vii, 1, 2, 9, 13, 31, 58–9, 60, 71, 77–8, 81, 92, 104, 113, 122, 123, 127–8, 132, 134–5, 171, 182–4, 186, 189–91, 193–5, 205, 222
proceedings, summary nature of 6, 24, 31–2, 40, 48, 50–1, 130–1, 135, 204–5, 229
punish/punishment vi, vii, viii, 10, 14, 31, 35, 45, 55–9, 62, 68, 78, 92, 101, 104–5, 112, 120, 130–1, 137, 141, 166, 170, 173, 174, 177–8, 183, 188, 190–1, 200, 208–13
*see also* commutation of sentence (procedure at the Hong Kong Military Courts)
death penalty 7, 14, 24, 30, 49, 57, 59, 61, 63, 99, 114, 122, 134, 143, 182–3, 185, 189, 192, 202, 208, 212, 225, 232, 236, 240–1
life sentence 77, 115, 117, 151–2, 185, 208, 212
release, early 20, 68, 237
review *see* review of proceedings
term of years viii, 13, 14, 23, 31, 43, 47, 59, 60, 64, 68–9, 76–7, 89, 92, 117, 122, 125, 148–9, 151–3, 155–6, 159, 183–5, 189–95, 208, 212, 237

**protected groups** 97
civilians v, vi, 1, 6–7, 10, 20–2, 36, 44, 46, 55, 60, 63, 71–4, 77, 80, 84, 88, 91, 95–7, 99–102, 105, 107–35, 146–51, 153, 170, 182–7, 189, 190–6, 201–3, 208, 244
*hors de combat* 95–7, 99, 202
medical personnel v, 38–9, 95, 97, 99, 125, 127, 133, 190, 220, 227, 241–2
POWs v, vi, 4, 6, 15, 20, 25–6, 33–6, 59, 61, 68–9, 71–94, 96–9, 101–6, 120, 126, 146, 152–4, 157, 159–61, 170, 182–3, 185, 187, 190, 192–4, 202, 208
sick and wounded v, vi, 72, 96–7, 99, 101–3, 202, 225

**rape** v, vi, 38, 99, 114, 133, 203, 220, 231, 241–2
*see also* sexual violence
**ration card** 109, 111, 115
**Red Cross, International Committee of the (ICRC)**
flag and badge/emblem 101
Red Cross 79, 80, 87–8, 102–3, 129
representatives 79, 80, 87–8
supplies/parcels 77, 79–80, 96, 194, 202
**rescue** 73, 111, 188
**research and methodology** 8–11
**resistance to Japanese occupation** 6, 72, 119–21, 126, 129–30, 134
British Aid Assistance Group (BAAG) 108, 120–1
Communist activities 119, 126
East River Column 120
espionage 10, 101, 121–2, 195
guerrilla activity 119, 128, 132, 134
anti-espionage measure 121
anti-guerrilla operations 132, 134
anti-Japanese activity 6, 121
*see also* abuse
*see also* war crimes
**review of proceedings** *see* procedure at the Hong Kong Military Courts (1946–1948)
**Royal Warrant 1945** vii, xi, 7, 13–14, 20–3, 30, 41, 65, 68, 97, 100, 105, 135, 145, 171–3, 176–7, 181, 195, 200–9, 211
**Russo-Japanese War** 73

**sexual violence** 133, 227, 242
*see also* rape
**shipwreck** 26, 59, 154–5, 193
*see also Behar*
*see also* High Seas
*see also Lisbon Maru*
*see also Tone*
**sickness and disease** v, vi, 72, 75, 84, 96 7, 99, 102–3, 125, 147, 202, 225
**slavery** 143–4
slave labour 112, 201
slave-like conditions 98
*see also* war crimes
**sources of law** *see* international and domestic law applicable at the time of the Hong Kong Military Courts (1946–1948)
**Special Court for Sierra Leone (SCSL)** 140
**starvation** vi, 75, 85–7, 96, 108, 111, 115–17, 119, 123–4, 153, 202, 211
death by vi, 75, 85, 96, 108, 111, 115–16, 124, 202
policy of 124, 151–3
*see also* abuse
*see also* food
*see also* war crimes
**stealing** 96, 110, 116, 144, 182, 202, 211
**suicide** 127, 187
**summary justice** 24, 131
**superior orders, plea of** vi, vii, xii, 7, 48, 54–7, 78, 81, 93, 100, 106, 132, 134, 155, 156, 169–98, 210–11, 226, 230
contextual backdrop 169–71, 195–8
customary international law 177–81
Manual of Military Law (7th ed as amended) 173–7
para 433, Ch. XIV 15, 96, 101, 106, 146
mitigating factor, as a 194–5
by civilian officials 193–4
containing an element of duress 132, 186–91
raised as a defence 181–94
raised in conjunction with other factors 132, 191–3
without an element of duress 181–6

**Taiwan, China** v, vi, 1, 6, 11, 23, 72–5, 82–90, 95, 100, 104, 152–3, 182–3, 190, 192–3, 199, 208, 240,
order for execution of all POWs in the event of the arrival of American forces in Taiwan 89
camp commanders 230
Japan Mining Company/Kinkaseki Mining Company 6, 20, 74, 82–4, 90–1, 98–9, 153, 182, 240, 244
POW camps/centres
Daichōku 88–9, 190, 234
Heitō 88
Karenkō 85, 88
Kinkaseki 82, 88–9, 90, 99, 153, 182
Kōkutsu 88, 182
Matsuyama 88
Shirakawa 75, 84–5, 87–8
Taichū 88
Tamasato 88
Toroku 88
Yūboku 88–9
forced oath-taking *see* oath
Formosa 11, 83–4, 89, 220, 230, 233, 234, 244
Kinkaseki Nippon Mining Company/Japan Mining Company *see* Japan
mine, copper 83–4, 153
mine, gold 83
POW labour
*see* Japan Mining Company/Kinkaseki Mining Company
*see* POW
*see* Taiwan, China (POW camps/centres)
non-escape oaths *see* oath

**taking life**
killing v, vi, viii, 3, 21, 48, 63, 76–7, 81, 90, 96–7, 99–103, 111–12, 115–17, 121–5, 127–8, 131–2, 134, 137–9, 142, 144–5, 147–8, 155, 157–63, 170, 183–4, 188–9, 192, 201–2, 208, 226, 231–2, 237–9, 242, 244–5
manslaughter 102, 105, 160
murder v, vi, 16, 61, 95, 99, 102, 105, 121, 127, 133, 139, 142–3, 144, 147, 158–9, 160, 162, 166, 201, 203, 211, 221
**terminology** 9–10
commonly used terms 9–10
names 10–11
*Tone* 25, 155, 188–9, 208
*see also* abuse
*see also* Behars
*see also* High Seas
*see also* POWs
*see also* war crimes
**torture** v, vi, 3, 10, 21, 22, 33, 38, 44–5, 63, 79, 95–6, 100, 102, 114, 118–19, 120–6, 128, 132, 134–5, 138, 146–8, 150–1, 170, 189, 191, 202, 226, 242
aeroplane 119, 121
beating 21, 38, 45, 77, 79, 119, 121, 123–8, 138, 147–8, 153, 189, 191, 192, 234
burning 21, 119, 121
electrocution 21, 119
water 21, 38, 45, 119, 121, 125–6, 126, 146, 189, 226
**translator/translation** 51, 54, 98–100, 107, 114–15, 229, 235
**treason** 101, 142–4, 147, 187

**United Nations** 178, 212
General Assembly (UNGA) 178–9
Security Council (UNSC) 212
**United Nations War Crimes Commission** 1–2, 5, 99, 106, 130, 139–40, 145, 156–7, 158, 159, 160, 169, 173–4, 196, 202

**war crime** v, vi, viii, ix, xi, xii, xiii, 1–8, 13–16, 19–24, 26, 28–30, 32, 33–5, 40–2, 48, 54–5, 57–8, 64, 67–9, 71, 73, 76, 82, 85, 89–90, 93–135, 137–40, 145–7, 150–2, 154–62, 169–75, 177, 179, 181–94, 196, 199–203, 205–8, 210–2, 215–18, 221–4, 226–7, 233, 236, 241–6
abuse (beating, torture, starvation, neglect, cruelty etc) *see* abuse
against civilians vi, 1, 6, 21–2, 38, 44–5, 63, 96–7, 100, 102, 104, 107–33, 135, 138, 146–51, 182, 186, 189, 191, 201–2, 226
against POWs v, vi, 4, 6, 15, 20, 25, 59, 68–9, 71–94, 96–9, 101–5, 146, 152–4, 157, 159–61, 170, 182–3, 185, 187, 190, 192–4, 202, 208
against sick and wounded (*hors de combat*) v, 61, 71, 79, 96–7, 99, 101–2, 126, 127, 133, 147, 202, 232
forcible displacement or deportation see involuntary displacement
law *see* international and domestic law applicable at the time of the Hong Kong Military Courts (1946–1948)
starvation *see* starvation
taking life (murder, manslaughter, killing) *see* taking life
violation of laws and customs/usages of war vii, 1, 2, 6, 14–16, 20, 38, 57, 76, 82, 88, 90, 93, 96–7, 100–5, 111, 118, 123, 128–43, 147, 151, 153, 164–6, 169–70, 172, 174, 176–81, 196–202, 204

**water** 3, 21, 38, 45, 85, 87, 102, 116, 119, 121, 123, 125–6, 146, 189, 202, 226
**witnesses** *see* procedure at the Hong Kong Military Courts (1946–1948)
**War Crimes Sentences Review Board** 68
**World War II/Second World War** v, vi, viii, ix, 2–5, 8, 10, 67, 95, 129, 137, 139–40, 142, 156–7, 163, 165, 169–72, 179, 181, 196–7, 216, 230, 232
Pacific War 3, 72–5, 82–4, 90, 93, 104